THE *SIGNS* READER

THE *SIGNS* READER
Women, Gender
&
Scholarship

EDITED BY
ELIZABETH ABEL
AND
EMILY K. ABEL

The University of Chicago Press
Chicago and London

The articles in this volume appeared in past issues of *SIGNS: JOURNAL OF WOMEN IN CULTURE AND SOCIETY,*

The University of Chicago Press, Chicago 60637
The University of Chicago Press, Ltd., London
90 89 88 87 86 85 84   5 4 3 2 1

Library of Congress Cataloging in Publication Data
Main entry under title:

The Signs reader.

"The articles . . . were previously published in past
issues of Signs, journal of women in culture and
society"—T.p. verso.
   1. Women—Addresses, essays, lectures, 2. Women's
studies—Addresses, essays, lectures. 3. Feminism—
Addresses, essays, lectures. I. Abel, Elizabeth.
II. Abel, Emily K.
HQ1206.S52 1983   305.4   83-5781
ISBN 0-226-00074-5
ISBN 0-226-00075-3 (pbk.)

Contents

Introduction

The opening editorial of *Signs: Journal of Women in Culture and Society* declares the journal's "animating purpose": to publish the "new scholarship about women" generated by the new consciousness about the "social, political, economic, cultural, and psychological arrangements that have governed relations between females and males."[1] To accomplish this goal, the journal adopted an interdisciplinary structure that offers a comprehensive picture of new research about women, sex, and gender in the social sciences, the humanities, and the natural sciences. This selection of representative articles from the first thirty issues of *Signs* thus indicates salient trends in the scholarship created since the journal's inception in 1975.

The mid-1970s were a period of exuberance and enthusiasm for pursuing and disseminating research about women. The number of women's studies teachers more than tripled between 1974 and 1976, and an increasing proportion of faculty in traditional departments made women the central focus of their scholarship.[2] This was also a time of institution building: women's studies programs proliferated, and the founding of *Signs* was followed two years later by the establishment of the National Women's Studies Association. Although many women's studies programs are currently under attack, research about women continues to flourish. In the present era of conservatism and financial stringency, it is essential to document the breakthroughs achieved by this scholarship, which has permanently altered accustomed patterns of thought.

Despite the current political climate, certain tenets of the scholarship on women are gaining wider currency throughout the academy. This progress is revealed, in part, by a shift in terminology. The original editors of *Signs* used the phrase "new scholarship about women" to designate a multidiscipline that included work both by scholars who attached the label "feminist" to their research and by those who refrained from adopting such an explicitly political term. Recently, however, the

1. "Editorial," *Signs: Journal of Women in Culture and Society* 1, no. 1 (Autumn 1975): v. This selection from *Signs* spans the editorships of Catharine R. Stimpson (1974–80) and Barbara C. Gelpi (1980–). We are grateful to both, and to Elsa Dixler, former managing editor of *Signs,* for their assistance with this project.

2. Florence Howe, *Seven Years Later: Women's Studies Programs in 1976* (Washington, D.C.: National Advisory Council on Women's Educational Programs, 1977), p. 15n.

phrase "feminist scholarship" has appeared more often on the pages of *Signs,* suggesting that the phrase—and its significance—have won greater acceptance in the academy at large. Although we value the inclusive stance of the founding editors, we believe the term "feminist scholarship" best characterizes the essays in this volume. Eight years after the establishment of *Signs,* we celebrate a scholarly tradition that incorporates the study of women as a group and the critique of the established gender system.

Because most feminist scholars pay tribute to this growing tradition and acknowledge the collective nature of their enterprise, the task of choosing specific articles is inevitably difficult. To accentuate the revisionary force of feminist scholarship, we looked for essays that raise theoretical issues and expand traditional disciplinary boundaries. We also sought articles that criticize feminist scholarship itself by calling attention to biases about race, class, and sexual identity. By selecting essays diverse in methodology, subject matter, and political perspective, we tried to indicate the range of voices that have contributed to *Signs.* Limitations of space compelled us to exclude some of *Signs'* distinctive features: the review essays, the "reports/revisions," the book reviews, and the edited archival material.

Placing women's experience at the center of inquiry challenges basic theoretical frameworks in most academic disciplines. Yet success in redefining critical questions has been uneven. Whereas certain fields provide methodologies that can be adapted to feminist purposes, others are committed to orientations more thoroughly alien to feminist inquiry. The development of social history, for example, which focuses on powerless, nonelite groups and on the private lives of individuals, coincided with the emergence of the contemporary women's movement. Although feminist historians posed new questions and developed distinctive methodologies, they were able to draw on some of the categories of analysis developed by social historians. This fortuitous conjunction accelerated the pace of feminist scholarship. By the mid-1970s feminist historians could point with justifiable pride to their achievements.

In the opening essay of this volume, "The Social Relation of the Sexes: Methodological Implications of Women's History," originally published in 1976, Joan Kelly-Gadol argues that feminist historiography has revitalized theory by forcing a reassessment of accepted notions about periodization, social categories, and historical change. Traditional concepts of historical periods, she observes, ignore the experience of women, who have often lost status during eras celebrated for progressive change: "There was no 'renaissance' for women—at least not during the Renaissance." The study of women, Kelly-Gadol asserts, necessarily leads to the study of the relation between the sexes, a social phenomenon which varies with changes in social organization; thus, women's history has revised the practice of history by making sex a category as fundamental as class or race. To integrate changes in the sexual order with those in class relations, Kelly-Gadol proposes that historians focus on the property relations which determine the connection between the public and domestic spheres. Citing anthropological studies that correlate women's status with the relation between these spheres, Kelly-Gadol identifies society's mode of production as the central variable determining the relation of the sexes.[3]

Although feminist historians agree that social factors determine our conceptions of the sexes, scholars emphasize different aspects of the social context. Whereas Kelly-Gadol stresses economic factors, Carroll Smith-Rosenberg calls attention to cultural influences. In "The Female World of Love and Ritual: Relations between Women in Nineteenth-Century America," the essay that opened the first issue of *Signs*, Smith-Rosenberg challenges twentieth-century models of psychopathology by analyzing female bonding in nineteenth-century America, a topic considered trivial by traditional historians. In a society marked by rigid gender-role divisions, which ensured that girls grew to womanhood in a "closed and intimate female world," the development of powerful, enduring, and often sensual female friendships provide no evidence of "abnormality," but rather argue for psychosexual models adapted to cultural norms and arrangements. Drawing from letters and diaries written between the 1760s and the 1880s, Smith-Rosenberg evokes the ceremonies and passions that linked women in networks which often spanned generations and which offered love and sympathy through "marriage and pregnancy, childbirth and weaning, sickness and death." In this rich and vibrant homosocial culture, women found the emotional and physical intimacy that marriage, typically the first extended contact with a "member of an alien group," failed to provide.

Smith-Rosenberg's article sparked a tradition of writing about a distinctive female culture revealed through women's own perceptions of their most significant experiences. This tradition provoked a wide-ranging debate about the political consequences of the separate female sphere. Some historians caution against glorifying an enclave that fostered adaptation rather than change; nurtured and sustained by their broad networks of friends, they argue, women failed to demand admission to the public sphere. Other scholars, however, contend that female bonds provided an understanding of the potential power of collective

---

3. Kelly-Gadol draws most extensively from the studies collected by Michelle Zimbalist Rosaldo and Louise Lamphere in *Women, Culture and Society* (Stanford, Calif.: Stanford University Press, 1974), and especially from the opening essay by Rosaldo, "Woman, Culture, and Society: A Theoretical Overview," pp. 17–42. In a later essay, "The Use and Abuse of Anthropology: Reflections on Feminism and Cross-Cultural Understanding," *Signs* 5, no. 3 (Spring 1980): 389–417, Rosaldo revises her position. For other critiques of Rosaldo's thesis, see the review essays on anthropology by Rayna Rapp, *Signs*, vol. 4, no. 3 (Spring 1979), esp. pp. 508–10, and by Jane Monnig Atkinson, *Signs*, vol. 8, no. 2 (Winter 1982), esp. p. 238.

action and thereby facilitated the emergence of feminism.[4] The complex social functions of a separate female world are described by Fatima Mernissi in "Women, Saints, and Sanctuaries," a study of the relationships Moroccan women established in religious sanctuaries. Mernissi claims that Moroccan women took advantage of the space provided by saints' tombs to create "an intrinsically female community of soothers, supporters, and advisors" that they found more congenial than patriarchal institutions, such as hospitals. These sanctuaries, however, served to defuse discontent. Despite the similarity between the activities of Moroccan women in saints' tombs and the prototypical feminist consciousness-raising session, Mernissi argues that the sanctuaries had the same consequence as traditional psychotherapy in capitalist society: "Saints . . . help women to adjust to the oppression of the system. The waves of resentment die at the sanctuary's threshold."

A similar controversy about the status of the female sphere has animated feminist literary criticism. In contrast to the affinity between social history and feminist scholarship, the friction between the formalist orientation of the New Criticism, only now waning in literary studies, and the ideological cast of feminist criticism exacerbated tensions between feminist readers and the prevailing critical schools. As feminist critics shifted from documenting stereotypes of women in texts by men to establishing connections among recognized and neglected texts by women, moreover, the focus on a separate female tradition threatened to isolate both women writers and feminist readers from the mainstream of literary study. Recently, however, many feminist critics have turned to examining the intersections between women's writing and the dominant literary tradition. In her controversial essay, "Archimedes and the Paradox of Feminist Criticism," Myra Jehlen argues for a "radical comparativism" that would stress "the relations between situations rather than . . . the situations themselves" and that would interpret women's writing, not in isolation, but "as an external ground for seeing the dominant literature whole."[5] By exploiting, not evading, the contradictions inherent in applying ethical as well as aesthetic standards to literary texts, the feminist critic can disclose the vital junctures between "a definition of women and a definition of the world," between the sexual roles accorded literary characters and the social roles performed by fiction, between the requirements of a genre and its limited rendition of female

4. For the outlines of this debate, see Ellen DuBois, Mari Jo Buhle, Temma Kaplan, Gerda Lerner, and Carroll Smith-Rosenberg, "Politics and Culture in Women's History: A Symposium," *Feminist Studies* 6, no. 1 (Spring 1980): 26–64. See also Estelle Freedman, "Separatism as Strategy: Female Institution Building and American Feminism, 1870–1930," *Feminist Studies* 5, no. 3 (Fall 1979): 512–29.

5. See the responses to Jehlen's essay in *Signs* 8, no. 1 (Autumn 1982): 160–76, and the related exchange between Peggy Kamuf and Nancy K. Miller in *Diacritics* 12, no. 2 (Summer 1982): 42–53.

personality. Like Kelly-Gadol, Jehlen proposes that feminist scholars examine, not a separate female sphere, but the questions about traditional criteria of evaluation and periodization raised by the existence of that sphere.

The question of a female tradition is posed somewhat differently in feminist theology. Feminism has influenced religious studies in various ways: by revealing the exclusion of women from significant religious experiences and roles; by identifying the gendered features of religious rhetoric; by documenting the relationship of sexism to dualistic patterns of religious thought; by proposing new religious rituals and symbols that reflect female experience; and by reinterpreting religious history in the light of documents recording unorthodox religious traditions. Elaine Pagel's essay, "What Became of God the Mother? Conflicting Images of God in Early Christianity," now a chapter of her book, *The Gnostic Gospels,* demonstrates that the feminist study of religious history raises issues analogous to those addressed by literary criticism: How are canonical texts established? What alternative traditions were suppressed in the establishment of orthodoxy? What challenge did heterodox texts present to the accepted relation of the sexes? By examining Jewish and Christian gnostic texts condemned as heretical by A.D. 200, Pagels discovers a pervasive feminine symbolism applied to God, in contrast to the exclusively masculine character of the orthodox Jewish and Christian deity; she also detects hints of the belief that human nature is androgynous. The explosive social implications of these attitudes contributed to the rejection of these gnostic texts and to the consolidation of a patriarchal orthodox tradition. Like Jehlen, Pagels concentrates on the interaction between dominant and subordinate textual traditions that diverge in the status they accord the feminine.

The natural sciences might appear the discipline most resistant to a feminist perspective. Yet, as Evelyn Fox Keller argues in "Feminism and Science," recent developments in the history and philosophy of science have facilitated a feminist critique by calling attention to the social and political contexts that shape the evolution of scientific knowledge. Keller distinguishes between the readily accommodated liberal feminist critique of science—which focuses on sexual discrimination in employment, on the definition of "significant" scientific problems, and on experimental methods that equate the species with the male—and the more radical feminist critique, directed at fundamental scientific assumptions about objectivity. Cautioning against the dismissal of objectivity as an exclusively masculine ideal, Keller argues instead that we should reject the opposition between (traditionally male) objectivity and (traditionally female) subjectivity. Objectivity should be reconceptualized as a dialectical process that discriminates between the "objectivist illusion," which denies all intrusions of the self, and the "objective effort," which admits and accounts for these intrusions. Relying on the psychoanalytic theory of object relations, Keller examines the association of objectivity with autonomy and masculinity, and concludes that "in the access of domination to the goals of scientific knowledge one finds the intrusion of a self we begin to recognize as partaking in the cultural construct of masculinity." The radical feminist critique of science, Keller proposes, should begin as a historical analysis of the processes through which the scientific community selects its theoretical orientations. Disclosing the role of masculinist ideology in these processes creates the springboard for feminist change.

Donna Haraway's essay, "Animal Sociology and a Natural Economy of the Body Politic, Part I: A Political Physiology of Dominance," exemplifies the mode of historical analysis Keller recommends and shares the commitment to altering the "logic of domination" that connects the body politic to scientific inquiry. Focusing on animal sociology, which has been used repeatedly to legitimate social theories, Haraway examines the interplay between ideologies of dominance prevalent in the 1920s and 1930s and Clarence Ray Carpenter's contemporaneous experiments with primate populations. She finds that assumptions about dominance pervasively colored Carpenter's experimental methods, and that the supposedly "natural" prototype of social organization had already been conceptualized in terms of human social patterns. Consequently, Haraway challenges "all forms of the ideological claims for pure objectivity rooted in the subject-object split that has legitimated our logic of domination of nature and ourselves." Haraway's argument works two ways: feminism needs to overcome its aversion to the natural sciences, and these sciences need a socialist-feminist critique which would transform hierarchical divisions, such as culture/nature, subject/object, into a dialectic that would recreate both terms.

By presenting new perspectives in the social sciences, the humanities, and the natural sciences, feminist scholarship has challenged preconceptions that structure academic disciplines. Yet feminist scholars themselves have not been free of biases. Two essays in this volume castigate feminists for insensitivity to issues of sexual identity, race, and class. Adrienne Rich begins her essay, "Compulsory Heterosexuality and Lesbian Experience," with a critique of the classic feminist works by Barbara Ehrenreich and Deirdre English, Jean Baker Miller, Dorothy Dinnerstein, and Nancy Chodorow.[6] The neglect of lesbian existence in these and many other feminist studies, Rich claims, not only misrepresents women's experience but also precludes questioning the assumption that heterosexuality is freely chosen. To demonstrate the power of heterosexuality as a political institution, Rich carefully de-

6. See the responses to Rich's essay by Ann Ferguson, Jacqueline N. Zita, and Kathryn Pyne Addelson in *Signs* 7, no. 1 (Autumn 1981): 158–99, reprinted in *Feminist Theory: A Critique of Ideology*, ed. Nannerl O. Keohane, Michelle Z. Rosaldo, and Barbara C. Gelpi (Chicago: University of Chicago Press, 1982), pp. 147–88.

lineates the set of forces that compel women to regard this sexual identity as normal and inevitable. Rich also reveals a wide range of woman-identified experience she considers a "lesbian continuum" that includes diverse forms of "primary intensity between and among women." Investigating this experience, Rich contends, will enable us to recover the erased history of women's resistance to male authority.

Assumptions about race and class also have restricted feminist analysis. Diane K. Lewis's essay, "A Response to Inequality: Black Women, Racism, and Sexism," presents one example of this limitation by highlighting divisions between black and white women.[7] Like Kelly-Gadol, Lewis discusses Michelle Rosaldo's influential analysis of the inequality created by the split between the (male) economic and political sphere and the (female) private, domestic domain. According to Rosaldo, women's inferior status is related directly to the gap between these two spheres. Because black men traditionally have been excluded from public life, Lewis argues, Rosaldo's model does not account for gender inequalities among blacks. Black women, moreover, have felt greater allegiance to black men, who share their racial oppression, than to white women, who often obtain the privileges of the dominant group. What did impel black women to embrace feminism was their realization that the gains wrested by the civil rights movement were distributed inequitably: more men than women reaped the benefits of expanded opportunities in education, employment, and politics. Because disproportionate numbers of black women head households, moreover, such feminist issues as child care and discrimination in the work force have attracted blacks from divergent class backgrounds. Thus, Lewis claims, black feminists have been more successful than whites in transcending barriers of class and working together for common goals.

By examining interconnections among race, class, and gender, Lewis points to a thorny issue in feminist scholarship: the relation between feminist and Marxist analysis. Feminist scholars have challenged, not only particular academic disciplines, but also overarching theoretical perspectives. Two essays in this collection explore what has been called the "unhappy marriage of Marxism and feminism."[8] In an early and influential article, "Capitalism, Patriarchy, and Job Segregation by Sex," Heidi Hartmann contends that orthodox Marxists have failed to explain the sexual division of the labor force because they have focused exclusively on the structure of capitalism. Drawing on a range of an-

7. See Alison Bernstein's response to Lewis, and Lewis's reply, in *Signs* 3, no. 3 (Spring 1978): 733–37.

8. We borrow this phrase from Heidi Hartmann's influential essay, "The Unhappy Marriage of Marxism and Feminism: Towards a More Progressive Union," in *Women and Revolution: A Discussion of the Unhappy Marriage of Marxism and Feminism*, ed. Lydia Sargent (Boston: South End Press, 1981), pp. 1–41. Hartmann provides the governing metaphor for the collection.

thropological writings, Hartmann points out that the hierarchical division of labor by sex antedated capitalism, which changed the form, but
not the force, of these gender inequalities. Marxist analysis, moreover,
stresses the advantages employers gain from a segmented work force
and ignores the actions of working men, who also have a vested interest
in relegating women to distinct job categories. Hartmann concludes by
arguing that feminists must fight simultaneously against capitalism and
the sexual division of labor.

Catherine A. MacKinnon's essay, "Feminism, Marxism, Method,
and the State: An Agenda for Theory," explores both the parallels between Marxist and feminist analyses and the failure of attempts to syn-
thesize them. The incompatibility of these frameworks, MacKinnon
claims, is a function of the methods that define class and sex as each
system's governing categories. The basic feminist concept, "the personal
is political," implies that the politics of gender can be discovered through
women's collective analysis of their experience of sexual objectification.
In contrast to the scientific claims of dialectical materialism, the feminist
method rejects "the distinction between the knowing subject and the
known   object—the   division   between   subjective   and   objective
postures—as the means to comprehend social life. . . . Through consciousness raising, women grasp the collective reality of women's condition from within the perspective of that experience, not from outside it."
Like both Keller and Haraway, MacKinnon sees the feminist perspective—even the distinctively feminist method—as a critique of the
claim to objectivity: "Feminism stands in relation to marxism as marxism
does to classical political economy: its final conclusion and ultimate
critique . . . a seizure of power that penetrates subject with object and
theory with practice. In a dual motion, feminism turns marxism inside
out and on its head."

Feminist method thus demonstrates the political character of personal relationships and the dominant place of sexuality in women's
exploitation and alienation. The concluding two essays in this collection
explore, from very different perspectives, the politics of sexuality. Incest
is the form of sexual exploitation that Judith Herman and Lisa
Hirschman examine in "Father-Daughter Incest," recently expanded
into a book-length study. They begin by noting both the prevalence of
parent-child incest, dismissed by Freud as a (female) fantasy, and the
predominance of father-daughter incest in particular. This asymmetry,
they contend, can be explained by the structure of patriarchy: in a
male-dominated society, the incest taboo exerts less force on men than
on women. Father-daughter incest thus presents an extreme case of
women's sexual vulnerability. In their clinical study of female incest
victims, Herman and Hirschman describe the emotional damage in-
flicted on daughters, who cannot afford to hate their seducers and who
feel intense shame about any pleasure they may have derived from the

relationship. Conventional psychotherapy has been ineffective in alleviating the suffering of incest victims, since male therapists generally identify with the father and attempt to excuse or deny his behavior, and female therapists typically identify with the daughter and avoid confronting the powerful emotions this identification evokes. Like MacKinnon, Herman and Hirschman see consciousness raising as the feminist practice designed to redress, through the discovery of shared experience, the effects of male power over female sexuality.

The volume concludes with the celebrated manifesto of French feminism, Hélène Cixous's "The Laugh of the Medusa." The contrasts between the last two essays epitomize differences between American and French feminism: between the empirical investigation of sexual abuse healed through the collectively spoken word, and the poetic exhortation to sexual discovery inscribed through "female-sexed texts" (or "sexts").[9] Like other feminist theorists in France, Cixous considers female writing (*écriture féminine*) both the means and the product of releasing the libido repressed by a masculine economy that represents woman only as lack, as the castrated, deficient mirror of man. By inscribing women's desire, female writing becomes a subversive, explosive "antilogos weapon" which will create "an impregnable language that will wreck partitions, classes, and rhetorics, regulations and codes." Representing the silenced female body is thus *the* feminist political act, for "writing is precisely *the very possibility of change,* the space that can serve as a springboard for subversive thought, the precursory movement of a transformation of social and cultural structures."

Cixous's exhortation articulates a pervasive impulse in feminist scholarship: to transform as well as to elucidate gender relations in society. The essays in this volume strive not only to redefine the questions that structure academic disciplines, but also to recommend the political strategies suggested by studying women's oppression. However diverse these strategies—which range from the advocacy of lesbian separatism, to the call for an autonomous women's movement within socialist struggles, to the endorsement of consciousness raising, to the plea for a new form of female writing—their presence in these essays testifies to the distinctive stance of feminist scholars, who often hold themselves accountable to the women's movement as well as to the academy, and who typically make their politics explicit in their scholarship.

By eschewing the disinterested stance, feminists challenge a basic

9. French feminist theory, of course, is not monolithic. For an introduction to the varieties of this theory, see Elaine Marks, "Women and Literature in France" and Carolyn Greenstein Burke, "Report from Paris: Women's Writing and the Women's Movement" in *Signs* 3, no. 4 (Summer 1978): 832–55; the special section on "French Feminist Theory" in *Signs* 7, no. 1 (Autumn 1981): 5–86; *Yale French Studies,* vol. 62 (1981), "Feminist Readings: French Texts/American Contexts"; and *The Future of Difference,* ed. Hester Eisenstein and Alice Jardine (Boston: G. K. Hall & Co., 1980).

convention of scholarly discourse and suggest an emerging convention of feminist scholarship: a commitment to undoing polarities—between conceptions of the sexes, between academic disciplines, between the academic and political communities, between theory and experience, and between the postures of objectivity and subjectivity. Through its goals and procedures, as well as through its subject, feminist scholarship challenges and stimulates the larger enterprise of scholarship itself. In so doing, it holds out the prospect of change beyond as well as within the academy—for, as Cixous reminds us, writing is *the very possibility of change*.

ELIZABETH ABEL
EMILY K. ABEL

The Social Relation of the Sexes: Methodological Implications of Women's History

Joan Kelly-Gadol

Women's history has a dual goal: to restore women to history and to restore our history to women. In the past few years, it has stimulated a remarkable amount of research as well as a number of conferences and courses on the activities, status, and views of and about women. The interdisciplinary character of our concern with women has also newly enriched this vital historical work. But there is another aspect of women's history that needs to be considered: its theoretical significance, its implications for historical study in general.[1] In seeking to add women to the fund of historical knowledge, women's history has revitalized theory, for it has shaken the conceptual foundations of historical study. It has done this by making problematical three of the basic concerns of historical thought: (1) periodization, (2) the categories of social analysis, and (3) theories of social change.

Since all three issues are presently in ferment, I can at best suggest how they may be fruitfully posed. But in so doing, I should also like to show how the conception of these problems expresses a notion which is basic to feminist consciousness, namely, that the relation between the

1. The central theme of this paper emerged from regular group discussions, from which I have benefited so much, with Marilyn Arthur, Blanche Cook, Pamela Farley, Mary Feldblum, Alice Kessler-Harris, Amy Swerdlow, and Carole Turbin. Many of the ideas were sharpened in talks with Gerda Lerner, Renate Bridenthal, Dick Vann, and Marilyn Arthur, with whom I served on several panels on women's history and its theoretical implications. My City College students in Marxism/feminism and in fear of women, witchcraft, and the family have stimulated my interests and enriched my understanding of many of the issues presented here. To Martin Fleisher and Nancy Miller I am indebted for valuable suggestions for improving an earlier version of this paper, which I delivered at the Barnard College Conference on the Scholar and the Feminist II: Toward New Criteria of Relevance, April 12, 1975.

sexes is a social and not a natural one. This perception forms the core idea that upsets traditional thinking in all three cases.

Periodization

Once we look to history for an understanding of woman's situation, we are, of course, already assuming that woman's situation is a social matter. But history, as we first came to it, did not seem to confirm this awareness. Throughout historical time, women have been largely excluded from making war, wealth, laws, governments, art, and science. Men, functioning in their capacity as historians, considered exactly those activities constitutive of civilization: hence, diplomatic history, economic history, constitutional history, and political and cultural history. Women figured chiefly as exceptions, those who were said to be as ruthless as, or wrote like, or had the brains of men. In redressing this neglect, women's history recognized from the start that what we call compensatory history is not enough. This was not to be a history of exceptional women, although they too need to be restored to their rightful places. Nor could it be another subgroup of historical thought, a history of women to place alongside the list of diplomatic history, economic history, and so forth, for all these developments impinged upon the history of women. Hence feminist scholarship in history, as in anthropology, came to focus primarily on the issue of women's status. I use "status" here and throughout in an expanded sense, to refer to woman's place and power—that is, the roles and positions women hold in society by comparison with those of men.

In historical terms, this means to look at ages or movements of great social change in terms of their liberation or repression of woman's potential, their import for the advancement of her humanity as well as "his." The moment this is done—the moment one assumes that women are a part of humanity in the fullest sense—the period or set of events with which we deal takes on a wholly different character or meaning from the normally accepted one. Indeed, what emerges is a fairly regular pattern of relative loss of status for women precisely in those periods of so-called progressive change. Since the dramatic new perspectives that unfold from this shift of vantage point have already been discussed at several conferences, I shall be brief here.[2] Let me merely point out

2. Conference of New England Association of Women Historians, Yale University (October 1973): Marilyn Arthur, Renate Bridenthal, Joan Kelly-Gadol; Second Berkshire Conference on the History of Women, Radcliffe (October 1974): panel on "The Effects of Women's History upon Traditional Historiography," Renate Bridenthal, Joan Kelly-Gadol, Gerda Lerner, Richard Vann (papers deposited at Schlesinger Library); Sarah Lawrence symposium (March 1975): Marilyn Arthur, Renate Bridenthal, Gerda Lerner, Joan Kelly-Gadol (papers available as *Conceptual Frameworks in Women's History* [Bronxville, N.Y.: Sarah Lawrence Publications, 1976]). For some recent comments along some of these same lines, see Carl N. Degler, *Is There a History of Women?* (Oxford: Clarendon Press, 1975). As I

that if we apply Fourier's famous dictum—that the emancipation of women is an index of the general emancipation of an age—our notions of so-called progressive developments, such as classical Athenian civilization, the Renaissance, and the French Revolution, undergo a startling re-evaluation. For women, "progress" in Athens meant concubinage and confinement of citizen wives in the gynecaeum. In Renaissance Europe it meant domestication of the bourgeois wife and escalation of witchcraft persecution which crossed class lines. And the Revolution expressly excluded women from its liberty, equality, and "fraternity." Suddenly we see these ages with a new, double vision—and each eye sees a different picture.

Only one of these views has been represented by history up to now. Regardless of how these periods have been assessed, they have been assessed from the vantage point of men. Liberal historiography in particular, which considers all three periods as stages in the progressive realization of an individualistic social and cultural order, expressly maintains—albeit without considering the evidence—that women shared these advances with men. In Renaissance scholarship, for example, almost all historians have been content to situate women exactly where Jacob Burckhardt placed them in 1890: "on a footing of perfect equality with men." For a period that rejected the hierarchy of social class and the hierarchy of religious values in its restoration of a classical, secular culture, there was also, they claim, "no question of 'woman's rights' or female emancipation, simply because the thing itself was a matter of course."[3] Now while it is true that a couple of dozen women can be assimilated to the humanistic standard of culture which the Renaissance imposed upon itself, what is remarkable is that *only* a couple of dozen women can. To pursue this problem is to become aware of the fact that there was no "renaissance" for women—at least not during the Renaissance. There was, on the contrary, a marked restriction of the scope and powers of women. Moreover, this restriction is a consequence of the very developments for which the age is noted.[4]

---

edit this paper for printing, the present economic crisis is threatening the advances of feminist scholarship once again by forcing the recently arrived women educators out of their teaching positions and severing thereby the professional connections necessary to research and theory, such as the conferences mentioned above.

3. *The Civilization of the Renaissance in Italy* (London: Phaidon Press, 1950), p. 241. With the exception of Ruth Kelso, *Doctrine for the Lady of the Renaissance* (Urbana: University of Illinois Press, 1956), this view is shared by every work I know of on Renaissance women except for contemporary feminist historians. Even Simone de Beauvoir, and of course Mary Beard, regard the Renaissance as advancing the condition of women, although Burckhardt himself pointed out that the women of whom he wrote "had no thought of the public; their function was to influence distinguished men, and to moderate male impulse and caprice."

4. See the several contemporary studies recently or soon to be published on Renaissance women: Susan Bell, "Christine de Pizan," *Feminist Studies* (Winter 1975/76); Joan

What feminist historiography has done is to unsettle such accepted evaluations of historical periods. It has disabused us of the notion that the history of women is the same as the history of men, and that significant turning points in history have the same impact for one sex as for the other. Indeed, some historians now go so far as to maintain that, because of woman's particular connection with the function of reproduction, history could, and women's history should, be rewritten and periodized from this point of view, according to major turning points affecting childbirth, sexuality, family structure, and so forth.[5] In this regard, Juliet Mitchell refers to modern contraception as a "world-historic event"—although the logic of her thought, and my own, protests against a periodization that is primarily geared to changes in reproduction. Such criteria threaten to detach psychosexual development and family patterns from changes in the general social order, or to utterly reverse the causal sequence. Hence I see in them a potential isolation of women's history from what has hitherto been considered the mainstream of social change.

To my mind, what is more promising about the way periodization has begun to function in women's history is that it has become *relational*. It relates the history of women to that of men, as Engels did in *The Origin of the Family, Private Property and the State*, by seeing in common social developments institutional reasons for the advance of one sex and oppression of the other. Handled this way, traditional periodizing concepts may well be retained—and ought to be insofar as they refer to major structural changes in society. But in the evaluation of such changes we need to consider their effects upon women as distinct from men. We expect by now that those effects may be so different as to be opposed and that such opposition will be socially explicable. When women are excluded from the benefits of the economic, political, and cultural advances made in certain periods, a situation which gives women a different historical experience from men, it is to those "advances" we must look to find the reasons for that separation of the sexes.

Sex as a Social Category

Two convictions are implicit in this more complete and more complex sense of periodization: one, that women do form a distinctive social

---

Kelly-Gadol, "Notes on Women in the Renaissance and Renaissance Historiography," in *Conceptual Frameworks in Women's History* (n. 2 above); Margaret Leah King, "The Religious Retreat of Isotta Nogarola, 1418–66," *Signs* (in press); an article on women in the Renaissance by Kathleen Casey in *Liberating Women's History*, Berenice Carroll, ed. (Urbana: University of Illinois Press, 1976); Joan Kelly-Gadol, "Did Women Have a Renaissance?" in *Becoming Visible*, ed. R. Bridenthal and C. Koonz (Boston: Houghton Mifflin Co., 1976).

    5. Vann (n. 2 above).

group and, second, that the invisibility of this group in traditional history is not to be ascribed to female nature. These notions, which clearly arise out of feminist consciousness, effect another, related change in the conceptual foundations of history by introducing sex as a category of social thought.

Feminism has made it evident that the mere fact of being a woman meant having a particular kind of social and hence historical experience, but the exact meaning of "woman" in this historical or social sense has not been so clear. What accounts for woman's situation as "other," and what perpetuates it historically? The "Redstockings Manifesto" of 1969 maintained that "women are an oppressed class" and suggested that the relations between men and women are class relations, that "sexual politics" are the politics of class domination. The most fruitful consequence of this conception of women as a social class has been the extension of class analysis to women by Marxist feminists such as Margaret Benston and Sheila Rowbotham.[6] They have traced the roots of woman's secondary status in history to economics inasmuch as women as a group have had a distinctive relation to production and property in almost all societies. The personal and psychological consequences of secondary status can be seen to flow from this special relation to work. As Rowbotham and Benston themselves make clear, however, it is one thing to extend the tools of class analysis to women and quite another to maintain that women *are* a class. Women belong to social classes, and the new women's history and histories of feminism have borne this out, demonstrating, for example, how class divisions disrupted and shattered the first wave of the feminist movement in nonsocialist countries, and how feminism has been expressly subordinated to the class struggle in socialist feminism.[7]

On the other hand, although women may adopt the interests and ideology of men of their class, women as a group cut through male class systems. Although I would quarrel with the notion that women of all classes, in all cultures, and at all times are accorded secondary status, there is certainly sufficient evidence that this is generally, if not univer-

6. "Redstockings Manifesto," in *Sisterhood Is Powerful*, ed. Robin Morgan (New York: Random House, 1970), pp. 533–36. Margaret Benston, *The Political Economy of Women's Liberation* (New York: Monthly Review reprint, 1970). Sheila Rowbotham, *Woman's Consciousness, Man's World* (Middlesex: Pelican Books, 1973), with bibliography of the periodical literature. A number of significant articles applying Marxist analysis to the oppression of women have been appearing in issues of *Radical America* and *New Left Review*.

7. Eleanor Flexner, *Century of Struggle* (New York: Atheneum Publishers, 1970); Sheila Rowbotham, *Women, Resistance and Revolution* (New York: Random House, 1974); panel at the Second Berkshire Conference on the History of Women, Radcliffe (n. 2 above), on "Clara Zetkin and Adelheid Popp: The Development of Feminist Awareness in the Socialist Women's Movement—Germany and Austria, 1890–1914," with Karen Honeycutt, Ingurn LaFleur, and Jean Quataert. Karen Honeycutt's paper on Clara Zetkin is in *Feminist Studies* (Winter 1975/76).

sally, the case. From the advent of civilization, and hence of history proper as distinct from prehistorical societies, the social order has been patriarchal. Does that then make women a caste, a hereditary inferior order? This notion has its uses, too, as does the related one drawn chiefly from American black experience, which regards women as a minority group.[8] The sense of "otherness" which both these ideas convey is essential to our historical awareness of women as an oppressed social group. They help us appreciate the social formation of "femininity" as an internalization of ascribed inferiority which serves, at the same time, to manipulate those who have the authority women lack. As explanatory concepts, however, notions of caste and minority group are not productive when applied to women. *Why* should this majority be a minority? And why is it that the members of this particular caste, unlike all other castes, are not of the same rank throughout society? Clearly the minority psychology of women, like their caste status and quasi-class oppression, has to be traced to the universally distinguishing feature of all women, namely their sex. Any effort to understand women in terms of social categories that obscure this fundamental fact has to fail, only to make more appropriate concepts available. As Gerda Lerner put it, laying all such attempts to rest: "All analogies—class, minority group, caste —approximate the position of women, but fail to define it adequately. Women are a category unto themselves: an adequate analysis of their position in society demands new conceptual tools."[9] In short, women have to be defined as women. We are the social opposite, not of a class, a caste, or of a majority, since we are a majority, but of a sex: men. We are a sex, and categorization by gender no longer implies a mothering role and subordination to men, except as social role and relation recognized as such, as socially constructed and socially imposed.

A good part of the initial excitement in women's studies consisted of this discovery, that what had been taken as "natural" was in fact man-made, both as social order and as description of that order as natural and physically determined. Examples of such ideological reasoning go back to the story of Eve, but the social sciences have been functioning the same way, as myth reinforcing patriarchy. A feminist psychologist argues: "It is scientifically unacceptable to advocate the natural superiority of women as child-rearers and socializers of children when there have been so few studies of the effects of male-infant or father-infant interaction on the subsequent development of the child."[10] An anthropologist

8. Helen Mayer Hacker did interesting work along these lines in the 1950s, "Women as a Minority Group," *Social Forces* 30 (October 1951–May 1952): 60–69, and subsequently, "Women as a Minority Group: Twenty Years Later" (Pittsburgh: Know, Inc., 1972). Degler has recently taken up these classifications and also finds he must reject them (see n. 2 above).

9. "The Feminists: A Second Look," *Columbia Forum* 13 (Fall 1970): 24–30.

10. Rochelle Paul Wortis, "The Acceptance of the Concept of Maternal Role by Be-

finds herself constrained to reject, and suspect, so-called scientific contentions that the monogamous family and male dominance belong to primates in general. In fact, she points out, "these features are *not* universal among non-human primates, including some of those most closely related to humans." And when male domination and male hierarchies do appear, they "seem to be adaptations to particular environments."[11]

Historians could not lay claim to special knowledge about the "natural" roles and relation of the sexes, but they knew what that order was, or ought to be. History simply tended to confirm it. *Bryan's Dictionary of Painters and Engravers* of 1904 says of the Renaissance artist, Propertia Rossi: "a lady of Bologna, best known as a sculptor and carver, but who also engraved upon copper, and learnt drawing and design from Marc Antonio. She is said to have been remarkable for her beauty, virtues, and talents, and to have died at an early age in 1530, in consequence of unrequited love. Her last work was a bas-relief of Joseph and Potiphar's wife!"[12] An exclamation mark ends the entry like a poke in the ribs, signifying that the "lady" (which is not a class designation here), who was beautiful and unhappy in love, was naturally absorbed by just that. Historians really *knew* why there were no great women artists. That is why it was not a historical problem until the feminist art historian, Linda Nochlin, posed it as such—by inquiring into the institutional factors, rather than the native gifts, that sustain artistic activity.[13]

When the issue of woman's place did appear openly, and male historians such as H. D. Kitto rose to defend "their" society, the Greek in his case, the natural order of things again came to the rescue.[14] If Athenian wives were not permitted to go about at will, weren't they too delicate for the strain that travel imposed in those days? If they played no role in political life—the activity that was the source of human dignity to the Greek—was it not because government covered "matters which, inescapably, only men could judge from their own experience and execute by their own exertions"? If girls were not being schooled, weren't they being instructed by mother in the arts of the female citizen? ("If we say 'housework,' " Kitto admits, "it sounds degrading, but if we say Domestic Science it sounds eminently respectable; and we have seen how varied and responsible it was.") But Kitto's major argument was reserved for the family: its religious and social importance in Athenian society. His

havioral Scientists: Its Effects on Women," *American Journal of Orthopsychiatry* 41 (October 1971): 733–46.

11. Kathleen Gough, "The Origin of the Family," *Journal of Marriage and the Family* 33 (November 1971): 760–71.

12. London: Geo. Bell, 1904, 4:285.

13. "Why Have There Been No Great Women Artists?" *Art News* 69, no. 9 (January 1971): 22–39, 67–71.

14. *The Greeks* (Baltimore: Penguin Books, 1962), pp. 219–36.

reasoning on this point sounds to us like an incomplete sentence. He rightly points out that extinction of a family or dissipation of its property was regarded as a disaster. But for him, this fact is an argument, for his position is that it *is* woman's "natural" place to serve that family and continue it by raising legitimate heirs through whom to pass on its property and its rites. If under the conditions of Greek society that task should require confinement to the household and its rounds, that justifies the legal disabilities of wives. As for the other orders of women Athenian society demanded and regulated by law, concubines are not mentioned and hetaerae are "adventuresses who had said No to the serious business of life. Of course they amused men—'But, my dear fellow, one doesn't *marry* a woman like that.'"

Kitto wrote his history in 1951.

If our understanding of the Greek contribution to social life and consciousness now demands an adequate representation of the life experience of women, so too the sexual order, as shaped by the institutions of family and state, is a matter we now regard as not merely worthy of historical inquiry but central to it. This, I think, is a second major contribution women's history has made to the theory and practice of history in general. We have made of sex a category as fundamental to our analysis of the social order as other classifications, such as class and race. And we consider the relation of the sexes, as those of class and race, to be socially rather than naturally constituted, to have its own development, varying with changes in social organization. Embedded in and shaped by the social order, the relation of the sexes must be integral to any study of it. Our new sense of periodization reflects an assessment of historical change from the vantage point of women as well as men. Our use of sex as a social category means that our conception of historical change itself, as change in the social order, is broadened to include changes in the relation of the sexes.

I find the idea of the social relation of the sexes, which is at the core of this conceptual development, to be both novel and central in feminist scholarship and in works stimulated by it. An art historian, Carol Duncan, asks with respect to modern erotic art, "what are the male-female relations it implies," and finds those relations of domination and victimization becoming more pronounced precisely as women's claims for equality were winning recognition.[15] Michelle Zimbalist Rosaldo, coeditor of a collection of studies by feminist anthropologists, speaks of the need for anthropology to develop a theoretical context "within which the social relation of the sexes can be investigated and understood."[16]

15. Unpublished paper on "The Esthetics of Power" to appear in *The New Eros*, ed. Joan Semmel (New York: Hacker Art Books, 1975). See also Carol Duncan, "Virility and Domination in Early 20th Century Vanguard Painting," *Artforum* 12 (December 1973): 30–39.

16. *Women, Culture and Society*, ed. Michelle Zimbalist Rosaldo and Louise Lamphere (Stanford, Calif.: Stanford University Press, 1974), p. 17.

Indeed almost all the essays in this collective work are concerned with the structure of the sexual order—patriarchal, matrifocal, and otherwise—of the societies they treat. In art history, anthropology, sociology, and history, studies of the status of women necessarily tend to strengthen the social and relational character of the idea of sex. The activity, power, and cultural evaluation of women simply cannot be assessed except in relational terms: by comparison and contrast with the activity, power, and cultural evaluation of men, and in relation to the institutions and social developments that shape the sexual order. To conclude this point, let me quote Natalie Zemon Davis's address to the Second Berkshire Conference on the History of Women in October 1975:

> It seems to me that we should be interested in the history of both women and men, that we should not be working only on the subjected sex any more than an historian of class can focus exclusively on peasants. Our goal is to understand the significance of the *sexes,* of gender groups in the historical past. Our goal is to discover the range in sex roles and in sexual symbolism in different societies and periods, to find out what meaning they had and how they functioned to maintain the social order or to promote its change.[17]

Theories of Social Change

If the relationship of the sexes is as necesssary to an understanding of human history as the social relationship of classes, what now needs to be worked out are the connections between changes in class and sex relations.[18] For this task, I suggest that we consider significant changes in the respective roles of men and women in the light of fundamental changes in the mode of production. I am not here proposing a simple socioeconomic scheme. A theory of social change that incorporates the relation of the sexes has to consider how general changes in production affect and shape production in the family and, thereby, the respective roles of men and women. And it has to consider, as well, the flow in the other direction: the impact of family life and the relation of the sexes upon psychic and social formations.

The study of changes in the social relation of the sexes is new, even if we trace it as far back as Bachhofen, Morgan, and Engels. Engels in particular solidly established the social character of woman's relation to man, although it was only one change in that relation—albeit the major one—that concerned him: the transition to patriarchy with the advance from kin society to civilization, and the overthrow of patriarchy with the advent of socialism. His analysis of the subordination of women in terms

---

17. To be published in *Feminist Studies* (Winter 1975/76).
18. See panel papers, *Conceptual Frameworks in Women's History* (n. 2 above).

of the emergence of private property and class inequality is basic to much of feminist scholarship today. Engels had almost no effect upon historical scholarship, except for socialist theorists such as August Bebel, and historians of women such as Emily James Putnam and Simone de Beauvoir, but contemporary efforts to understand the social causes of patriarchy, and the reasons for the various forms it takes, tend to confirm his ideas on the social relation of the sexes. Certain conclusions, which in turn open new directions for historical and anthropological research, can already be drawn from this recent work. One is that "woman's social position has not always, everywhere, or in most respects been subordinate to that of men."[19] I am quoting here from an anthropologist because the historical case for anything other than a patriarchal sexual order is considerably weaker. The dominant causal feature that emerges from anthropological studies of the sexual order (in the Rosaldo and Lamphere collection I have mentioned) is whether, and to what extent, the domestic and the public spheres of activity are separated from each other. Although what constitutes "domestic" and what "public" varies from culture to culture, and the lines of demarcation are differently drawn, a consistent pattern emerges when societies are placed on a scale where, at one end, familial and public activities are fairly merged, and, at the other, domestic and public activities are sharply differentiated.

Where familial activities coincide with public or social ones, the status of women is comparable or even superior to that of men. This pattern is very much in agreement with Engels's ideas, because in such situations the means of subsistence and production are commonly held and a communal household is the focal point of both domestic and social life. Hence it is in societies where production for exchange is slight and where private property and class inequality are not developed that sex inequalities are least evident. Women's roles are as varied as men's, although there are sex-role differences; authority and power are shared by women and men rather than vested in a hierarchy of males; women are highly evaluated by the culture; and women and men have comparable sexual rights.

The most one can say about the sexual division of labor in societies at this end of the scale is that there is a tendency toward mother/child or women/children grouping and toward male hunting and warfare. This "natural" division of labor, if such it is, is not yet socially determined. That is, men as well as women care for children and perform household tasks, and women as well as men hunt. The social organization of work, and the rituals and values that grow out of it, do not serve to separate out

19. Karen Sacks, "Engels Revisited," in Rosaldo and Lamphere, p. 207. See also Eleanor Leacock's introduction to Engels, *The Origin of the Family, Private Property and the State* (New York: International Publishers, 1972); also Leacock's paper delivered at Columbia University Seminar on Women in Society, April 1975.

the sexes and place one under the authority of the other. They do just
that at the opposite end of the scale where the domestic and public
orders are clearly distinguished from each other. Women continue to be
active producers all the way up the scale (and must continue to be so
until there is considerable wealth and class inequality), but they steadily
lose control over property, products, and themselves as surplus increases, private property develops, and the communal household becomes a private economic unit, a family (extended or nuclear) represented by a man. The family itself, the sphere of women's activities, is
in turn subordinated to a broader social or public order—governed by a
state—which tends to be the domain of men. This is the general pattern
presented by historical or civilized societies.[20]

As we move in this direction on the scale, it becomes evident that
sexual inequalities are bound to the control of property. It is interesting
to note in this regard that in several societies class inequalities are expressed in sexual terms. Women who have property, in livestock, for
example, may use it for bridewealth to purchase "wives" who serve
them.[21] This example, which seems to confound sex and class, actually
indicates how sex and class relations differ. Although property estab-
lishes a class inequality among such women, it is nevertheless "wives,"
that is, women as a group, who constitute a propertyless serving order
attached to a domestic kind of work, including horticulture.

How does this attachment of women to domestic work develop, and
what forms does it take? This process is one of the central problems
confronting feminist anthropology and history. By definition, this query
rejects the traditional, simple biological "reasons" for the definition of
woman-as-domestic. The privatizing of child rearing and domestic work
and the sex typing of that work are social, not natural, matters. I suggest,
therefore, that in treating this problem, we continue to look at *property
relations* as the basic determinant of the sexual division of labor and of
the sexual order. The more the domestic and the public domains are
differentiated, the more work, and hence property, are of two clearly
distinguishable kinds. There is production for subsistence and production for exchange. However the productive system of a society is organized, it operates, as Marx pointed out, as a continuous process which
reproduces itself: that is, its material means and instruments, its people,
and the social relations among them. Looked at as a continuous process

20. On this point, one would like to see many more specific studies, as in n. 19 above,
which trace in detail the process of social change that fosters male control of the new means
of production for exchange, and with the new wealth, control of the broader social or
public order and of the family as well. Historical studies of civilized societies would be
useful for examples of extended processes of social change, including those of our own
society.
21. E.g., among the Ibo, Mbuti, and Lovedu (see Rosaldo and Lamphere, pp. 149,
216).

(what Marx meant by reproduction), the productive work of society thus includes procreation and the socialization of children who must find their places within the social order.[22] I suggest that what shapes the relation of the sexes is the way this work of procreation and socialization is organized in relation to the organization of work that results in articles for subsistence and/or exchange. In sum, what patriarchy means as a general social order is that women function as the property of men in the maintenance and production of new members of the social order; that these relations of production are worked out in the organization of kin and family; and that other forms of work, such as production of goods and services for immediate use, are generally, although not always, attached to these procreative and socializing functions.[23]

Inequalities of sex as well as class are traced to property relations and forms of work in this scheme, but there are certain evident differences between the two. In the public domain, by which I mean the social order that springs from the organization of the general wealth and labor of society, class inequalities are paramount. For the relation of the sexes, control or lack of control of the property that separates people into owners and workers is not significant. What *is* significant is whether women *of either class* have equal relations to work or property with men of their class.

In the household or family, on the other hand, where ownership of all property resides in historic societies characterized by private property, sex inequalities are paramount and they cut through class lines.

22. In *Woman's Estate* (New York: Random House, 1973), Juliet Mitchell (developing an earlier essay) offered the categories of reproduction/production within which to consider the history of women. This is roughly equivalent to the domestic/public categorization, except that she added sexuality and socialization as two further socially ordered functions which need not be attached to reproduction universally, although they have been under capitalism. I believe we must consider sexuality and socialization in any study of the sexual order: what are the relations among love, sex, and marriage in any society, for women and for men, heterosexual and homosexual, and who socializes which groups of children, by sex and by age, so that they find their places in the social order —including their sexual places. I also believe, as Juliet Mitchell does, that the evidence clearly warrants working out relations between the dominant mode of production in a society and the forms of reproduction, sexuality, and socialization. However, certain difficulties emerge, not in using this scheme so much as in using its terms—especially when we deal with precapitalist societies. Neither cultural nor political activities have a clearly definable place under the heading of production, as they do, e.g., when we use the terms domestic/public or, more simply, family and society. Another reason I prefer family/society or domestic/public, is that the terms production/reproduction tend to confound biological reproduction with social reproduction, and this obscures the essentially *productive* work of the family and the property relation between husband and wife. See my review of Rowbotham in *Science and Society* 39, no. 4 (Winter 1975/76): 471–74, and Lise Vogel's review essay on Juliet Mitchell, "The Earthly Family," *Radical America* 7 (Fall 1973): 9–50.

23. Ideas along these lines have been developed by Rowbotham, *Woman's Consciousness, Man's World;* Bridget O'Laughlin, "Mediation of Contradiction: Why Mbum Women Do Not Eat Chicken," in Rosaldo and Lamphere, pp. 301–20.

What is significant for the domestic relation is that women in the family, like serfs in feudal Europe, can both have and *be* property. To quote from an ancient description of early Roman law,

> a woman joined to her husband by a holy marriage, should share in all his possessions and sacred rites. . . . This law obliged both the married women, as having no other refuge, to conform themselves entirely to the temper of their husbands and the husbands to rule their wives as necessary and inseparable possessions. Accordingly, if a wife was virtuous and in all things obedient to her husband, she was mistress of the house to the same degree as her husband was master of it, and after the death of her husband she was heir to his property in the same manner as a daughter. . . . But if she did any wrong, the injured party was her judge, and determined the degree of her punishment. . . .[24]

Regardless of class, and regardless of ownership (although these modify the situation in interesting ways), women have generally functioned as the property of men in the procreative and socializing aspect of the productive work of their society. Women constitute part of the means of production of the private family's mode of work.

Patriarchy, in short, is at home at home. The private family is its proper domain. But the historic forms that patriarchy takes, like its very origin, are to be traced to the society's mode of production. The sexual order varies with the general organization of property and work because this shapes both family and public domains and determines how they approach or recede from each other.

These relations between the domestic and the public orders, in turn, account for many of the unexpected oppositions and juxtapositions expressed by our new sense of historical periods.[25] Blurring the lines between family and society diminished a number of sexual inequalities, including the double standard, for feudal noblewomen, for example, as well as for women in advanced capitalistic societies. The status of the feudal noblewoman was high before the rise of the state when the family order *was* the public order of her class; and the scope that familial political power gave women included the Church where aristocratic women also commanded a sphere of their own. Again today, the two domains approach each other as private household functions—child

24. Dionysius of Halicarnassus, *The Roman Antiquities*, trans. E. Cary (Cambridge, Mass.: Harvard University Press), 1:381–82. Milton extended the property relationship between husband and wife to the Garden of Eden where Adam's possession of Eve constitutes the first example of private property: "Hail, wedded Love, mysterious law, true source / Of human offspring, sole propriety / In Paradise of all things common else!" *(Paradise Lost*, pt. 4, lines 750–51). Needless to say, where Eve serves Adam while he serves God, the "propriety" is not a mutual relation.

25. For the examples given here, see the articles on the periods in question in Bridenthal and Koonz (n. 4 above).

rearing, production of food and clothing, nursing, and so forth
—become socially organized. Women can again work and associate with
each other outside the household, and the sexual division of labor, although far from overcome, appears increasingly irrational.

Where domestic and public realms pulled apart, however, sexual
inequalities became pronounced as did the simultaneous demand for
female chastity and prostitution. This was the case with Athens of the
classical period, where the private household economy was the basic
form of production and the social or public order of the polis consisted
of many such households which were subordinate to and governed by it.
Wives of the citizenry were confined to the order of the household: to
production of legitimate heirs and supervision of indoor slave production of goods and services for use. Although necessary to the public
order, wives did not directly belong to or participate in it, and free
women who fell outside the domestic order and its property arrangements fell outside the public order as well. The situation of women was
much the same in the middle classes of modern Europe, although here
capitalist commodity production moved out of the home and became
socially organized. What capitalist production did was to turn the
working-class family, too, after an initial, almost disastrous onslaught
upon it, into a complement of social production. The family in modern
society has served as the domain for the production and training of the
working class. It has been the alleged reason for women having to function as underpaid, irregular laborers whose wages generally had to be
supplemented by sexual attachment to a man, inside or outside family
arrangements. And it has served to compensate the worker whose means
of subsistence were alienated from him but who could have private
property in his wife.

Such has been the institutionally determined role of the family
under capitalism, and women of both the owning and the working classes, women both in and outside the family, have had their outer and
inner lives shaped by the structure of its social relations.

Surely a dominant reason for studying the social relation of the
sexes is political. To understand the interests, aside from the personal
interests of individual men, that are served by the retention of an unequal sexual order is in itself liberating. It detaches an age-old injustice
from the blind operation of social forces and places it in the realm of
choice. This is why we look to the organization of the productive forces
of society to understand the shape and structure of the domestic order
to which women have been primarily attached.

But women's history also opens up the other half of history, viewing
women as agents and the family as a productive and social force. The
most novel and exciting task of the study of the social relation of the
sexes is still before us: to appreciate how we are all, women and men,
initially humanized, turned into social creatures by the work of that

domestic order to which women have been primarily attached. Its character and the structure of its relations order our consciousness, and it is through this consciousness that we first view and construe our world.[26] To understand the historical impact of women, family, and the relation of the sexes upon society serves a less evident political end, but perhaps a more strictly feminist one. For if the historical conception of civilization can be shown to include the psychosocial functions of the family, then with that understanding we can insist that any reconstruction of society along just lines incorporate reconstruction of the family—all kinds of collective and private families, and all of them functioning, not as property relations, but as personal relations among freely associating people.

City College, City University of New York
Institute for Research in History

26. This is one of Rowbotham's points in *Woman's Consciousness, Man's World*. I believe it should lead to development of the genre of psychohistorical studies and studies in family history exemplified by Philippe Ariès, *Centuries of Childhood: A Social History of Family Life* (New York: Alfred A. Knopf, 1965); Nancy Chodorow, "Family Structure and Feminine Personality," in Rosaldo and Lamphere (n. 16), pp. 43–67; David Hunt, *Parents and Children in History* (New York: Harper & Row, 1972); the Frankfort school in *Autorität und Familie,* ed. Max Horkheimer (Paris: Alcan, 1936); Wilhelm Reich, *The Mass Psychology of Fascism* (New York: Farrar, Straus & Giroux, 1970); and Eli Zaretsky, "Capitalism, the Family and Personal Life," *Socialist Revolution* nos. 13, 14, 16 (1973). See the excellent article on this mode of historical inquiry by Lawrence Stone, in the *New York Review of Books* 21 (November 14, 1974): 25.

The Female World of Love and Ritual: Relations between Women in Nineteenth-Century America

Carroll Smith-Rosenberg

The female friendship of the nineteenth century, the long-lived, intimate, loving friendship between two women, is an excellent example of the type of historical phenomena which most historians know something about, which few have thought much about, and which virtually no one has written about.[1] It is one aspect of the female experience which consciously or unconsciously we have chosen to ignore. Yet an abundance of manuscript evidence suggests that eighteenth- and nineteenth-century women routinely formed emotional ties with other women. Such deeply felt, same-sex friendships were casually accepted in American society. Indeed, from at least the late eighteenth through the mid-nineteenth century, a female world of varied and yet highly structured relationships

Research for this paper was supported in part by a grant from the Grant Foundation, New York, and by National Institutes of Health trainee grant 5 FO3 HD48800-03. I would like to thank several scholars for their assistance and criticism in preparing this paper: Erving Goffman, Roy Schafer, Charles E. Rosenberg, Cynthia Secor, Anthony Wallace. Judy Breault, who has just completed a biography of an important and introspective nineteenth-century feminist, Emily Howland, served as a research assistant for this paper and her knowledge of nineteenth-century family structure and religious history proved invaluable.

1. The most notable exception to this rule is now eleven years old: William R. Taylor and Christopher Lasch, "Two 'Kindred Spirits': Sorority and Family in New England, 1839–1846," *New England Quarterly* 36 (1963): 25–41. Taylor has made a valuable contribution to the history of women and the history of the family with his concept of "sororial" relations. I do not, however, accept the Taylor-Lasch thesis that female friendships developed in the mid-nineteenth century because of geographic mobility and the breakup of the colonial family. I have found these friendships as frequently in the eighteenth century as in the nineteenth and would hypothesize that the geographic mobility of the mid-nineteenth century eroded them as it did so many other traditional social institutions. Helen Vendler (*Review of Notable American Women, 1607–1950,* ed. Edward James and Janet James, *New York Times*) [November 5, 1972]: sec. 7) points out the significance of these friendships.

appears to have been an essential aspect of American society. These relationships ranged from the supportive love of sisters, through the enthusiasms of adolescent girls, to sensual avowals of love by mature women. It was a world in which men made but a shadowy appearance.[2]

Defining and analyzing same-sex relationships involves the historian in deeply problematical questions of method and interpretation. This is especially true since historians, influenced by Freud's libidinal theory, have discussed these relationships almost exclusively within the context of individual psychosexual developments or, to be more explicit, psychopathology.[3] Seeing same-sex relationships in terms of a dichotomy between normal and abnormal, they have sought the origins of such apparent deviance in childhood or adolescent trauma and detected the symptoms of "latent" homosexuality in the lives of both those who later became "overtly" homosexual and those who did not. Yet theories concerning the nature and origins of same-sex relationships are frequently contradictory or based on questionable or arbitrary data. In recent years such hypotheses have been subjected to criticism both from within and without the psychological professions. Historians who seek to work within a psychological framework, therefore, are faced with two hard questions: Do sound psychodynamic theories concerning the nature and origins of same-sex relationships exist? If so, does the historical datum exist which would permit the use of such dynamic models?

I would like to suggest an alternative approach to female friendships—one which would view them within a cultural and social setting rather than from an exclusively individual psychosexual perspective. Only by thus altering our approach will we be in the position to evaluate the appropriateness of particular dynamic interpretations. Intimate friendships between men and men and women and women ex-

2. I do not wish to deny the importance of women's relations with particular men. Obviously, women were close to brothers, husbands, fathers, and sons. However, there is evidence that despite such closeness relationships between men and women differed in both emotional texture and frequency from those between women. Women's relations with each other, although they played a central role in the American family and American society, have been so seldom examined either by general social historians or by historians of the family that I wish in this article simply to examine their nature and analyze their implications for our understanding of social relations and social structure. I have discussed some aspects of male-female relationships in two articles: "Puberty to Menopause: The Cycle of Femininity in Nineteenth-Century America," *Feminist Studies* 1 (1973): 58–72, and, with Charles Rosenberg, "The Female Animal: Medical and Biological Views of Women in 19th Century America," *Journal of American History* 59 (1973): 331–56.

3. See Freud's classic paper on homosexuality, "Three Essays on the Theory of Sexuality," in *The Standard Edition of the Complete Psychological Works of Sigmund Freud*, trans. James Strachey (London: Hogarth Press, 1953), 7:135–72. The essays originally appeared in 1905. Prof. Roy Shafer, Department of Psychiatry, Yale University, has pointed out that Freud's view of sexual behavior was strongly influenced by nineteenth-century evolutionary thought. Within Freud's schema, genital heterosexuality marked the height of human development (Schafer, "Problems in Freud's Psychology of Women," *Journal of the American Psychoanalytic Association* 22 [1974]: 459–85).

isted in a larger world of social relations and social values. To interpret such friendships more fully they must be related to the structure of the American family and to the nature of sex-role divisions and of male-female relations both within the family and in society generally. The female friendship must not be seen in isolation; it must be analyzed as one aspect of women's overall relations with one another. The ties between mothers and daughters, sisters, female cousins and friends, at all stages of the female life cycle constitute the most suggestive framework for the historian to begin an analysis of intimacy and affection between women. Such an analysis would not only emphasize general cultural patterns rather than the internal dynamics of a particular family or childhood; it would shift the focus of the study from a concern with deviance to that of defining configurations of legitimate behavioral norms and options.[4]

This analysis will be based upon the correspondence and diaries of women and men in thirty-five families between the 1760s and the 1880s. These families, though limited in number, represented a broad range of the American middle class, from hard-pressed pioneer families and orphaned girls to daughters of the intellectual and social elite. It includes families from most geographic regions, rural and urban, and a spectrum of Protestant denominations ranging from Mormon to orthodox Quaker. Although scarcely a comprehensive sample of America's increasingly heterogeneous population, it does, I believe, reflect accurately the literate middle class to which the historian working with letters and diaries is necessarily bound. It has involved an analysis of many thousands of letters written to women friends, kin, husbands, brothers, and children at every period of life from adolescence to old age. Some collections encompass virtually entire life spans; one contains over 100,000 letters as well as diaries and account books. It is my contention that an analysis of women's private letters and diaries which were never intended to be published permits the historian to explore a very private world of emotional realities central both to women's lives and to the middle-class family in nineteenth-century America.[5]

The question of female friendships is peculiarly elusive; we know so little or perhaps have forgotten so much. An intriguing and almost alien form of human relationship, they flourished in a different social structure and amidst different sexual norms. Before attempting to reconstruct their social setting, therefore, it might be best first to describe two not atypical friendships. These two friendships, intense, loving, and

4. For a novel and most important exposition of one theory of behavioral norms and options and its application to the study of human sexuality, see Charles Rosenberg, "Sexuality, Class and Role," *American Quarterly* 25 (1973): 131–53.

5. See, e.g., the letters of Peggy Emlen to Sally Logan, 1768–72, Wells Morris Collection, Box 1, Historical Society of Pennsylvania; and the Eleanor Parke Custis Lewis Letters, Historical Society of Pennsylvania, Philadelphia.

openly avowed, began during the women's adolescence and, despite
subsequent marriages and geographic separation, continued throughout their lives. For nearly half a century these women played a central
emotional role in each other's lives, writing time and again of their love
and of the pain of separation. Paradoxically to twentieth-century minds,
their love appears to have been both sensual and platonic.

Sarah Butler Wister first met Jeannie Field Musgrove while vaca-
tioning with her family at Stockbridge, Massachusetts, in the summer of
1849.[6] Jeannie was then sixteen, Sarah fourteen. During two subsequent years spent together in boarding school, they formed a deep and
intimate friendship. Sarah began to keep a bouquet of flowers before
Jeannie's portrait and wrote complaining of the intensity and anguish of
her affection.[7] Both young women assumed nom de plumes, Jeannie a
female name, Sarah a male one; they would use these secret names into
old age.[8] They frequently commented on the nature of their affection:
"If the day should come," Sarah wrote Jeannie in the spring of 1861,
"when you failed me either through your fault or my own, I would
forswear all human friendship, thenceforth." A few months later Jeannie commented: "Gratitude is a word I should never use toward you. It is
perhaps a misfortune of such intimacy and love that it makes one regard
all kindness as a matter of course, as one has always found it, as natural
as the embrace in meeting."[9]

Sarah's marriage altered neither the frequency of their correspondence nor their desire to be together. In 1864, when twenty-nine, married, and a mother, Sarah wrote to Jeannie: "I shall be entirely alone
[this coming week]. I can give you no idea how desperately I shall want
you. . . ." After one such visit Jeannie, then a spinster in New York,
echoed Sarah's longing: "Dear darling Sarah! How I love you & how
happy I have been! You are the joy of my life. . . . I cannot tell you how
much happiness you gave me, nor how constantly it is all in my thoughts.
. . . My darling how I long for the time when I shall see you. . . ." After
another visit Jeannie wrote: "I want you to tell me in your next letter, to
assure me, that I am your dearest. . . . I do not doubt you, & I am not
jealous but I long to hear you say it once more & it seems already a long

6. Sarah Butler Wister was the daughter of Fanny Kemble and Pierce Butler. In 1859
she married a Philadelphia physician, Owen Wister. The novelist Owen Wister is her son.
Jeannie Field Musgrove was the half-orphaned daughter of constitutional lawyer and New
York Republican politician David Dudley Field. Their correspondence (1855–98) is in the
Sarah Butler Wister Papers, Wister Family Papers, Historical Society of Pennsylvania.

7. Sarah Butler, Butler Place, S.C., to Jeannie Field, New York, September 14, 1855.

8. See, e.g., Sarah Butler Wister, Germantown, Pa., to Jeannie Field, New York,
September 25, 1862, October 21, 1863; or Jeannie Field, New York, to Sarah Butler
Wister, Germantown, July 3, 1861, January 23 and July 12, 1863.

9. Sarah Butler Wister, Germantown, to Jeannie Field, New York, June 5, 1861,
February 29, 1864; Jeannie Field to Sarah Butler Wister November 22, 1861, January 4
and June 14, 1863.

time since your voice fell on my ear. So just fill a quarter page with caresses & expressions of endearment. Your silly Angelina." Jeannie ended one letter: "Goodbye my dearest, dearest lover—ever your own Angelina." And another, "I will go to bed . . . [though] I could write all night—A thousand kisses—I love you with my whole soul—your Angelina."

When Jeannie finally married in 1870 at the age of thirty-seven, Sarah underwent a period of extreme anxiety. Two days before Jeannie's marriage Sarah, then in London, wrote desperately: "Dearest darling—How incessantly have I thought of you these eight days—all today—the entire uncertainty, the distance, the long silence—are all new features in my separation from you, grievous to be borne. . . . Oh Jeannie. I have thought & thought & yearned over you these two days. Are you married I wonder? My dearest love to you wherever and *who*ever you are."[10] Like many other women in this collection of thirty-five families, marriage brought Sarah and Jeannie physical separation; it did not cause emotional distance. Although at first they may have wondered how marriage would affect their relationship, their affection remained unabated throughout their lives, underscored by their loneliness and their desire to be together.[11]

During the same years that Jeannie and Sarah wrote of their love and need for each other, two slightly younger women began a similar odyssey of love, dependence and—ultimately—physical, though not emotional, separation. Molly and Helena met in 1868 while both attended the Cooper Institute School of Design for Women in New York City. For several years these young women studied and explored the city together, visited each other's families, and formed part of a social network of other artistic young women. Gradually, over the years, their initial friendship deepened into a close intimate bond which continued throughout their lives. The tone in the letters which Molly wrote to Helena changed over these years from "My dear Helena," and signed "your attached friend," to "My dearest Helena," "My Dearest," "My Beloved," and signed "Thine always" or "thine Molly."[12]

10. Sarah Butler Wister, London, to Jeannie Field Musgrove, New York, June 18 and August 3, 1870.

11. See, e.g., two of Sarah's letters to Jeannie: December 21, 1873, July 16, 1878.

12. This is the 1868–1920 correspondence between Mary Hallock Foote and Helena, a New York friend (the Mary Hallock Foote Papers are in the Manuscript Division, Stanford University). Wallace E. Stegner has written a fictionalized biography of Mary Hallock Foote (*Angle of Repose* [Garden City, N.Y.: Doubleday & Co., 1971]). See, as well, her autobiography: Mary Hallock Foote, *A Victorian Gentlewoman in the Far West: The Reminiscences of Mary Hallock Foote*, ed. Rodman W. Paul (San Marino, Calif.: Huntington Library, 1972). In many ways these letters are typical of those women wrote to other women. Women frequently began letters to each other with salutations such as "Dearest," "My Most Beloved," "You Darling Girl," and signed them "tenderly" or "to my dear dear sweet friend, good-bye." Without the least self-consciousness, one woman in her frequent letters to a female friend referred to her husband as "my other love." She was by no means

The letters they wrote to each other during these first five years permit us to reconstruct something of their relationship together. As Molly wrote in one early letter:

> I have not said to you in so many or so few words that I was happy with you during those few so incredibly short weeks but surely you do not need words to tell you what you must know. Those two or three days so dark without, so bright with firelight and contentment within I shall always remember as proof that, for a time, at least—I fancy for quite a long time—we might be sufficient for each other. We know that we can amuse each other for many idle hours together and now we know that we can also work together. And that means much, don't you think so?

She ended: "I shall return in a few days. Imagine yourself kissed many times by one who loved you so dearly."

The intensity and even physical nature of Molly's love was echoed in many of the letters she wrote during the next few years, as, for instance in this short thank-you note for a small present: "Imagine yourself kissed a dozen times my darling. Perhaps it is well for you that we are far

---

unique. See, e.g., Annie to Charlene Van Vleck Anderson, Appleton, Wis., June 10, 1871, Anderson Family Papers, Manuscript Division, Stanford University; Maggie to Emily Howland, Philadelphia, July 12, 1851, Howland Family Papers, Phoebe King Collection, Friends Historical Library, Swarthmore College; Mary Jane Burleigh to Emily Howland, Sherwood, N.Y., March 27, 1872, Howland Family Papers, Sophia Smith Collection, Smith College; Mary Black Couper to Sophia Madeleine DuPont, Wilmington, Del.: n.d. [1834] (two letters), Samuel Francis DuPont Papers, Eleutherian Mills Foundation, Wilmington, Del.; Phoebe Middleton, Concordiville, Pa., to Martha Jefferis, Chester County, Pa., February 22, 1848; and see in general the correspondence (1838–49) between Rebecca Biddle of Philadelphia and Martha Jefferis, Chester County, Pa., Jefferis Family Correspondence, Chester County Historical Society, West Chester, Pa.; Phoebe Bradford Diary, June 7 and July 13, 1832, Historical Society of Pennsylvania; Sarah Alden Ripley, to Abba Allyn, Boston, n.d. [1818–20], and Sarah Alden Ripley to Sophia Bradford, November 30, 1854, in the Sarah Alden Ripley Correspondence, Schlesinger Library, Radcliffe College; Fanny Canby Ferris to Anne Biddle, Philadelphia, October 11 and November 19, 1811, December 26, 1813, Fanny Canby to Mary Canby, May 27, 1801, Mary R. Garrigues to Mary Canby, five letters n.d., [1802–8], Anne Biddle to Mary Canby, two letters n.d., May 16, July 13, and November 24, 1806, June 14, 1807, June 5, 1808, Anne Sterling Biddle Family Papers, Friends Historical Society, Swarthmore College; Harriet Manigault Wilcox Diary, August 7, 1814, Historical Society of Pennsylvania. See as well the correspondence between Harriet Manigault Wilcox's mother, Mrs. Gabriel Manigault, Philadelphia, and Mrs. Henry Middleton, Charleston, S.C., between 1810 and 1830, Cadwalader Collection, J. Francis Fisher Section, Historical Society of Pennsylvania. The basis and nature of such friendships can be seen in the comments of Sarah Alden Ripley to her sister-in-law and long-time friend, Sophia Bradford: "Hearing that you are not well reminds me of what it would be to lose your loving society. We have kept step together through a long piece of road in the weary journey of life. We have loved the same beings and wept together over their graves" (Mrs. O. J. Wister and Miss Agnes Irwin, eds., *Worthy Women of Our First Century* [Philadelphia: J. B. Lippincott & Co., 1877] p. 195).

apart. You might find my thanks so expressed rather overpowering. I have that delightful feeling that it doesn't matter much what I say or how I say it, since we shall meet so soon and forget in that moment that we were ever separated. . . . I shall see you soon and be content."[13]

At the end of the fifth year, however, several crises occurred. The relationship, at least in its intense form, ended, though Molly and Helena continued an intimate and complex relationship for the next half-century. The exact nature of these crises is not completely clear, but it seems to have involved Molly's decision not to live with Helena, as they had originally planned, but to remain at home because of parental insistence. Molly was now in her late twenties. Helena responded with anger and Molly became frantic at the thought that Helena would break off their relationship. Though she wrote distraught letters and made despairing attempts to see Helena, the relationship never regained its former ardor—possibly because Molly had a male suitor.[14] Within six months Helena had decided to marry a man who was, coincidentally, Molly's friend and publisher. Two years later Molly herself finally married. The letters toward the end of this period discuss the transition both women made to having male lovers—Molly spending much time reassuring Helena, who seemed depressed about the end of their relationship and with her forthcoming marriage.[15]

It is clearly difficult from a distance of 100 years and from a post-Freudian cultural perspective to decipher the complexities of Molly and Helena's relationship. Certainly Molly and Helena were lovers —emotionally if not physically. The emotional intensity and pathos of their love becomes apparent in several letters Molly wrote Helena during their crisis: "I wanted so to put my arms round my girl of all the girls in the world and tell her . . . I love her as wives do love their husbands, as *friends* who have taken each other for life—and believe in her as I believe in my God. . . . If I didn't love you do you suppose I'd care about anything or have ridiculous notions and panics and behave like an old fool who ought to know better. I'm going to hang on to your skirts. . . . You can't get away from [my] love." Or as she wrote after Helena's decision to marry: "You know dear Helena, I really was in love with you. It was a passion such as I had never known until I saw you. I don't think it was the noblest way to love you." The theme of intense female love was one Molly again expressed in a letter she wrote to the man Helena was to marry: "Do you know sir, that until you came along I believe that she loved me almost as girls love their lovers. *I know I loved her so.* Don't you

13. Mary Hallock [Foote] to Helena, n.d. [1869–70], n.d. [1871–72], Folder 1, Mary Hallock Foote Letters, Manuscript Division, Stanford University.

14. Mary Hallock [Foote] to Helena, September 15 and 23, 1873, n.d. [October 1873], October 12, 1873.

15. Mary Hallock [Foote] to Helena, n.d. [January 1874], n.d. [Spring 1874].

wonder that I can stand the sight of you." This was in a letter con-
gratulating them on their forthcoming marriage.[16]

The essential question is not whether these women had genital contact and can therefore be defined as heterosexual or homosexual. The
twentieth-century tendency to view human love and sexuality within a
dichotomized universe of deviance and normality, genitality and
platonic love, is alien to the emotions and attitudes of the nineteenth
century and fundamentally distorts the nature of these women's emotional interaction. These letters are significant because they force us to
place such female love in a particular historical context. There is every
indication that these four women, their husbands and families—all eminently respectable and socially conservative—considered such love both
socially acceptable and fully compatible with heterosexual marriage.
Emotionally and cognitively, their heterosocial and their homosocial
worlds were complementary.

One could argue, on the other hand, that these letters were but an
example of the romantic rhetoric with which the nineteenth century
surrounded the concept of friendship. Yet they possess an emotional
intensity and a sensual and physical explicitness that is difficult to dismiss. Jeannie longed to hold Sarah in her arms; Molly mourned her
physical isolation from Helena. Molly's love and devotion to Helena, the
emotions that bound Jeannie and Sarah together, while perhaps a
phenomenon of nineteenth-century society were not the less real for
their Victorian origins. A survey of the correspondence and diaries of
eighteenth- and nineteenth-century women indicates that Molly, Jeannie, and Sarah represented one very real behavioral and emotional option socially available to nineteenth-century women.

This is not to argue that individual needs, personalities, and family
dynamics did not have a significant role in determining the nature of
particular relationships. But the scholar must ask if it is historically possible and, if possible, important, to study the intensely individual aspects
of psychosexual dynamics. Is it not the historian's first task to explore the
social structure and the world view which made intense and sometimes
sensual female love both a possible and an acceptable emotional option?
From such a social perspective a new and quite different series of questions suggests itself. What emotional function did such female love
serve? What was its place within the hetero- and homosocial worlds
which women jointly inhabited? Did a spectrum of love-object choices

16. Mary Hallock [Foote] to Helena, September 23, 1873; Mary Hallock [Foote] to
Richard, December 13, 1873. Molly's and Helena's relationship continued for the rest of
their lives. Molly's letters are filled with tender and intimate references, as when she wrote,
twenty years later and from 2,000 miles away: "It isn't because you are good that I love
you—but for the essence of you which is like perfume" (n.d. [1890s?]).

exist in the nineteenth century across which some individuals, at least, were capable of moving? Without attempting to answer these questions it will be difficult to understand either nineteenth-century sexuality or the nineteenth-century family.

Several factors in American society between the mid-eighteenth and the mid-nineteenth centuries may well have permitted women to form a variety of close emotional relationships with other women. American society was characterized in large part by rigid gender-role differentiation within the family and within society as a whole, leading to the emotional segregation of women and men. The roles of daughter and mother shaded imperceptibly and ineluctably into each other, while the biological realities of frequent pregnancies, childbirth, nursing, and menopause bound women together in physical and emotional intimacy. It was within just such a social framework, I would argue, that a specifically female world did indeed develop, a world built around a generic and unself-conscious pattern of single-sex or homosocial networks. These supportive networks were institutionalized in social conventions or rituals which accompanied virtually every important event in a woman's life, from birth to death. Such female relationships were frequently supported and paralleled by severe social restrictions on intimacy between young men and women. Within such a world of emotional richness and complexity devotion to and love of other women became a plausible and socially accepted form of human interaction.

An abundance of printed and manuscript sources exists to support such a hypothesis. Etiquette books, advice books on child rearing, religious sermons, guides to young men and young women, medical texts, and school curricula all suggest that late eighteenth- and most nineteenth-century Americans assumed the existence of a world composed of distinctly male and female spheres, spheres determined by the immutable laws of God and nature.[17] The unpublished letters and diaries of Americans during this same period concur, detailing the existence of sexually segregated worlds inhabited by human beings with different values, expectations, and personalities. Contacts between men and women frequently partook of a formality and stiffness quite alien to twentieth-century America and which today we tend to define as "Victorian." Women, however, did not form an isolated and oppressed subcategory in male society. Their letters and diaries indicate that women's sphere had an essential integrity and dignity that grew out of women's

17. I am in the midst of a larger study of adult gender-roles and gender-role socialization in America, 1785–1895. For a discussion of social attitudes toward appropriate male and female roles, see Barbara Welter, "The Cult of True Womanhood: 1820–1860," *American Quarterly* 18 (Summer 1966): 151–74; Ann Firor Scott, *The Southern Lady: From Pedestal to Politics, 1830–1930* (Chicago: University of Chicago Press, 1970), chaps. 1–2; Smith-Rosenberg and Rosenberg.

shared experiences and mutual affection and that, despite the profound changes which affected American social structure and institutions between the 1760s and the 1870s, retained a constancy and predictability. The ways in which women thought of and interacted with each other remained unchanged. Continuity, not discontinuity, characterized this female world. Molly Hallock's and Jeannie Fields's words, emotions, and experiences have direct parallels in the 1760s and the 1790s.[18] There are indications in contemporary sociological and psychological literature that female closeness and support networks have continued into the twentieth century—not only among ethnic and working-class groups but even among the middle class.[19]

Most eighteenth- and nineteenth-century women lived within a world bounded by home, church, and the institution of visiting—that endless trooping of women to each others' homes for social purposes. It was a world inhabited by children and by other women.[20] Women helped each other with domestic chores and in times of sickness, sorrow, or trouble. Entire days, even weeks, might be spent almost exclusively with other women.[21] Urban and town women could devote virtually every day to visits, teas, or shopping trips with other women. Rural women developed a pattern of more extended visits that lasted weeks and sometimes months, at times even dislodging husbands from their beds and bedrooms so that dear friends might spend every hour of every day together.[22] When husbands traveled, wives routinely moved in with other women, invited women friends to teas and suppers, sat together sharing and comparing the letters they had received from other close

18. See, e.g., the letters of Peggy Emlen to Sally Logan, 1768–72, Wells Morris Collection, Box 1, Historical Society of Pennsylvania; and the Eleanor Parke Custis Lewis Letters, Historical Society of Pennsylvania.

19. See esp. Elizabeth Botts, *Family and Social Network* (London: Tavistock Publications, 1957); Michael Young and Peter Willmott, *Family and Kinship in East London*, rev. ed. (Baltimore: Penguin Books, 1964).

20. This pattern seemed to cross class barriers. A letter that an Irish domestic wrote in the 1830s contains seventeen separate references to women and but only seven to men, most of whom were relatives and two of whom were infant brothers living with her mother and mentioned in relation to her mother (Ann McGrann, Philadelphia, to Sophie M. DuPont, Philadelphia, July 3, 1834, Sophie Madeleine DuPont Letters, Eleutherian Mills Foundation).

21. Harriett Manigault Diary, June 28, 1814, and passim; Jeannie Field, New York, to Sarah Butler Wister, Germantown, April 19, 1863; Phoebe Bradford Diary, Janurary 30, February 19, March 4, August 11, and October 14, 1832, Historical Society of Pennsylvania; Sophie M. DuPont, Brandywine, to Henry DuPont, Germantown, July 9, 1827, Eleutherian Mills Foundation.

22. Martha Jefferis to Anne Jefferis Sheppard, July 9, 1843; Anne Jefferis Sheppard to Martha Jefferis, June 28, 1846; Anne Sterling Biddle Papers, passim, Biddle Family Papers, Friends Historical Society, Swarthmore College; Eleanor Parke Custis Lewis, Virginia, to Elizabeth Bordley Gibson, Philadelphia, November 24 and December 4, 1820, November 6, 1821.

women friends. Secrets were exchanged and cherished, and the husband's return at times viewed with some ambivalence.[23]

Summer vacations were frequently organized to permit old friends to meet at water spas or share a country home. In 1848, for example, a young matron wrote cheerfully to her husband about the delightful time she was having with five close women friends whom she had invited to spend the summer with her; he remained at home alone to face the heat of Philadelphia and a cholera epidemic.[24] Some ninety years earlier, two young Quaker girls commented upon the vacation their aunt had taken alone with another woman; their remarks were openly envious and tell us something of the emotional quality of these friendships: "I hear Aunt is gone with the Friend and wont be back for two weeks, fine times indeed I think the old friends had, taking their pleasure about the country . . . and have the advantage of that fine woman's conversation and instruction, while we poor young girls must spend all spring at home. . . . What a disappointment that we are not together. . . ."[25]

Friends did not form isolated dyads but were normally part of highly integrated networks. Knowing each other, perhaps related to each other, they played a central role in holding communities and kin systems together. Especially when families became geographically mobile women's long visits to each other and their frequent letters filled with discussions of marriages and births, illness and deaths, descriptions of growing children, and reminiscences of times and people past provided an important sense of continuity in a rapidly changing society.[26] Central to this female world was an inner core of kin. The ties between sisters, first cousins, aunts, and nieces provided the underlying structure upon which groups of friends and their network of female relatives clustered. Although most of the women within this sample would appear to be living within isolated nuclear families, the emotional ties between nonresidential kin were deep and binding and provided one of the fundamental existential realities of women's lives.[27] Twenty years after

23. Phoebe Bradford Diary, January 13, November 16–19, 1832, April 26 and May 7, 1833; Abigail Brackett Lyman to Mrs. Catling, Litchfield, Conn., May 3, 1801, collection in private hands; Martha Jefferis to Anne Jefferis Sheppard, August 28, 1845.

24. Lisa Mitchell Diary, 1860s, passim, Manuscript Division, Tulane University; Eleanor Parke Custis Lewis to Elizabeth Bordley [Gibson] February 5, 1822; Jeannie McCall, Cedar Park, to Peter McCall, Philadelphia, June 30, 1849, McCall Section, Cadwalader Collection, Historical Society of Pennsylvania.

25. Peggy Emlen to Sally Logan, May 3, 1769.

26. For a prime example of this type of letter, see Eleanor Parke Custis Lewis to Elizabeth Bordley Gibson, passim, or Fanny Canby to Mary Canby, Philadelphia, May 27, 1801; or Sophie M. DuPont, Brandywine, to Henry DuPont, Germantown, February 4, 1832.

27. Place of residence is not the only variable significant in characterizing family structure. Strong emotional ties and frequent visiting and correspondence can unite

Parke Lewis Butler moved with her husband to Louisiana, she sent her two daughters back to Virginia to attend school, live with their grand-mother and aunt, and be integrated back into Virginia society.[28] The constant letters between Maria Inskeep and Fanny Hampton, sisters separated in their early twenties when Maria moved with her husband from New Jersey to Louisiana, held their families together, making it possible for their daughters to feel a part of their cousins' network of friends and interests.[29] The Ripley daughters, growing up in western Massachusetts in the early 1800s, spent months each year with their mother's sister and her family in distant Boston; these female cousins and their network of friends exchanged gossip-filled letters and gradu-ally formed deeply loving and dependent ties.[30]

Women frequently spent their days within the social confines of such extended families. Sisters-in-law visited each other and, in some families, seemed to spend more time with each other than with their husbands. First cousins cared for each other's babies—for weeks or even months in times of sickness or childbirth. Sisters helped each other with housework, shopped and sewed for each other. Geographic separation was borne with difficulty. A sister's absence for even a week or two could cause loneliness and depression and would be bridged by frequent let-ters. Sibling rivalry was hardly unknown, but with separation or illness the theme of deep affection and dependency reemerged.[31]

---

families that do not live under one roof. Demographic studies based on household struc-ture alone fail to reflect such emotional and even economic ties between families.

28. Eleanor Parke Custis Lewis to Elizabeth Bordley Gibson, April 20 and September 25, 1848.

29. Maria Inskeep to Fanny Hampton Correspondence, 1823–60, Inskeep Collection, Tulane University Library.

30. Eunice Callender, Boston, to Sarah Ripley [Stearns], September 24 and October 29, 1803, February 16, 1805, April 29 and October 9, 1806, May 26, 1810.

31. Sophie DuPont filled her letters to her younger brother Henry (with whom she had been assigned to correspond while he was at boarding school) with accounts of family visiting (see, e.g., December 13, 1827, January 10 and March 9, 1828, February 4 and March 10, 1832; also Sophie M. DuPont to Victorine DuPont Bauday, September 26 and December 4, 1827, February 22, 1828; Sophie M. DuPont, Brandywine, to Clementina B. Smith, Philadelphia, January 15, 1830; Eleuthera DuPont, Brandywine, to Victorine Du-Pont Bauday, Philadelphia, April 17, 1821, October 20, 1826; Evelina DuPont [Biderman] to Victorine DuPont Bauday, October 18, 1816). Other examples, from the Historical Society of Pennsylvania, are Harriet Manigault [Wilcox] Diary, August 17, September 8, October 19 and 22, December 22, 1814; Jane Zook, Westtown School, Chester County, Pa., to Mary Zook, November 13, December 7 and 11, 1870, February 26, 1871; Eleanor Parke Custis [Lewis] to Elizabeth Bordley [Gibson], March 30, 1796, February 7 and March 20, 1798; Jeannie McCall to Peter McCall, Philadelphia, November 12, 1847; Mary B. Ashew Diary, July 11 and 13, August 17, Summer and October 1858, and, from a private collection, Edith Jefferis to Anne Jefferis Sheppard, November 1841, April 5, 1842; Abigail Brackett Lyman, Northampton, Mass., to Mrs. Catling, Litchfield, Conn., May 13, 1801; Abigail Brackett Lyman, Northampton, to Mary Lord, August 11, 1800. Mary Hallock Foote vacationed with her sister, her sister's children, her aunt, and a female cousin in the

Sisterly bonds continued across a lifetime. In her old age a rural Quaker matron, Martha Jefferis, wrote to her daughter Anne concerning her own half-sister, Phoebe: "In sister Phoebe I have a real friend—she studies my comfort and waits on me like a child. . . . She is exceedingly kind and this to all other homes (set aside yours) I would prefer—it is next to being with a daughter." Phoebe's own letters confirmed Martha's evaluation of her feelings. "Thou knowest my dear sister," Phoebe wrote, "there is no one . . . that exactly feels [for] thee as I do, for I think without boasting I can truly say that my desire is for thee."[32]

Such women, whether friends or relatives, assumed an emotional centrality in each others' lives. In their diaries and letters they wrote of the joy and contentment they felt in each others' company, their sense of isolation and despair when apart. The regularity of their correspondence underlines the sincerity of their words. Women named their daughters after one another and sought to integrate dear friends into their lives after marriage.[33] As one young bride wrote to an old friend shortly after her marriage: "I want to see you and talk with you and feel that we are united by the same bonds of sympathy and congeniality as ever."[34] After years of friendship one aging woman wrote of another: "Time cannot destroy the fascination of her manner . . . her voice is music to the ear. . . ."[35] Women made elaborate presents for each other, ranging from the Quakers' frugal pies and breads to painted velvet bags and phantom bouquets.[36] When a friend died, their grief was deeply felt. Martha Jefferis was unable to write to her daughter for three weeks because of the sorrow she felt at the death of a dear friend. Such distress was not unusual. A generation earlier a young Massachusetts farm woman filled pages of her diary with her grief at the death of her "dearest friend" and transcribed the letters of condolence other women

---

summer of 1874; cousins frequently visited the Hallock farm in Milton, N.Y. In later years Molly and her sister Bessie set up a joint household in Boise, Idaho (Mary Hallock Foote to Helena, July [1874?] and passim). Jeannie Field, after initially disliking her sister-in-law, Laura, became very close to her, calling her "my little sister" and at times spending virtually every day with her (Jeannie Field [Musgrove] New York, to Sarah Butler Wister, Germantown, March 1, 8, and 15, and May 9, 1863).

32. Martha Jefferis to Anne Jefferis Sheppard, January 12, 1845; Phoebe Middleton to Martha Jefferis, February 22, 1848. A number of other women remained close to sisters and sisters-in-law across a long lifetime (Phoebe Bradford Diary, June 7, 1832, and Sarah Alden Ripley to Sophia Bradford, cited in Wister and Irwin, p. 195).

33. Rebecca Biddle to Martha Jefferis, 1838–49, passim; Martha Jefferis to Anne Jefferis Sheppard, July 6, 1846; Anne Jefferis Sheppard to Rachael Jefferis, January 16, 1865; Sarah Foulke Farquhar [Emlen] Diary, September 22, 1813, Friends Historical Library, Swarthmore College; Mary Garrigues to Mary Canby [Biddle], 1802–8, passim; Anne Biddle to Mary Canby [Biddle], May 16, July 13, and November 24, 1806, June 14, 1807, June 5, 1808.

34. Sarah Alden Ripley to Abba Allyn, n.d., Schlesinger Library.

35. Phoebe Bradford Diary, July 13, 1832.

36. Mary Hallock [Foote] to Helena, December 23 [1868 or 1869]; Phoebe Bradford Diary, December 8, 1832; Martha Jefferis and Anne Jefferis Sheppard letters, passim.

sent her. She marked the anniversary of Rachel's death each year in her diary, contrasting her faithfulness with that of Rachel's husband who had soon remarried.[37]

These female friendships served a number of emotional functions. Within this secure and empathetic world women could share sorrows, anxieties, and joys, confident that other women had experienced similar emotions. One mid-nineteenth-century rural matron in a letter to her daughter discussed this particular aspect of women's friendships: "To have such a friend as thyself to look to and sympathize with her—and enter into all her little needs and in whose bosom she could with freedom pour forth her joys and sorrows—such a friend would very much relieve the tedium of many a wearisome hour. . . ." A generation later Molly more informally underscored the importance of this same function in a letter to Helena: "Suppose I come down . . . [and] spend Sunday with you quietly," she wrote Helena ". . . that means talking all the time until you are relieved of all your latest troubles, and I of mine. . . ."[38] These were frequently troubles that apparently no man could understand. When Anne Jefferis Sheppard was first married, she and her older sister Edith (who then lived with Anne) wrote in detail to their mother of the severe depression and anxiety which they experienced. Moses Sheppard, Anne's husband, added cheerful postscripts to the sisters' letters—which he had clearly not read—remarking on Anne's and Edith's contentment. Theirs was an emotional world to which he had little access.[39]

This was, as well, a female world in which hostility and criticism of other women were discouraged, and thus a milieu in which women could develop a sense of inner security and self-esteem. As one young woman wrote to her mother's longtime friend: "I cannot sufficiently thank you for the kind unvaried affection & indulgence you have ever shown and expressed both by words and actions for me. . . . Happy would it be did all the world view me as you do, through the medium of kindness and forbearance."[40] They valued each other. Women, who had little status or power in the larger world of male concerns, possessed status and power in the lives and worlds of other women.[41]

37. Martha Jefferis to Anne Jefferis Sheppard, August 3, 1849; Sarah Ripley [Stearns] Diary, November 12, 1808, January 8, 1811. An interesting note of hostility or rivalry is present in Sarah Ripley's diary entry. Sarah evidently deeply resented the husband's rapid remarriage.

38. Martha Jefferis to Edith Jefferis, March 15, 1841; Mary Hallock Foote to Helena, n.d. [1874–75?]; see also Jeannie Field, New York, to Sarah Butler Wister, Germantown, May 5, 1863, Emily Howland Diary, December 1879, Howland Family Papers.

39. Anne Jefferis Sheppard to Martha Jefferis, September 29, 1841.

40. Frances Parke Lewis to Elizabeth Bordley Gibson, April 29, 1821.

41. Mary Jane Burleigh, Mount Pleasant, S.C., to Emily Howland, Sherwood N.Y., March 27, 1872, Howland Family Papers; Emily Howland Diary, September 16, 1879, January 21 and 23, 1880; Mary Black Couper, New Castle, Del., to Sophie M. DuPont, Brandywine, April 7, 1834.

An intimate mother-daughter relationship lay at the heart of this female world. The diaries and letters of both mothers and daughters attest to their closeness and mutual emotional dependency. Daughters routinely discussed their mother's health and activities with their own friends, expressed anxiety in cases of their mother's ill health and concern for her cares.[42] Expressions of hostility which we would today consider routine on the part of both mothers and daughters seem to have been uncommon indeed. On the contrary, this sample of families indicates that the normal relationship between mother and daughter was one of sympathy and understanding.[43] Only sickness or great geographic distance was allowed to cause extended separation. When marriage did result in such separation, both viewed the distance between them with distress.[44] Something of this sympathy and love between

42. Harriet Manigault Diary, August 15, 21, and 23, 1814 Historical Society of Pennsylvania; Polly [Simmons] to Sophie Madeleine DuPont, February 1822; Sophie Madeleine DuPont to Victorine Bauday, December 4, 1827; Sophie Madeleine DuPont to Clementina Beach Smith, July 24, 1828, August 19, 1829; Clementina Beach Smith to Sophie Madeleine DuPont, April 29, 1831; Mary Black Couper to Sophie Madeleine DuPont, December 24, 1828, July 21, 1834. This pattern appears to have crossed class lines. When a former Sunday school student of Sophie DuPont's (and the daughter of a worker in her father's factory) wrote to Sophie she discussed her mother's health and activities quite naturally (Ann McGrann to Sophie Madeleine DuPont, August 25, 1832; see also Elizabeth Bordley to Martha, n.d. [1797], Eleanor Parke Custis [Lewis] to Elizabeth Bordley [Gibson], May 13, 1796, July 1, 1798; Peggy Emlen to Sally Logan, January 8, 1786. All but the Emlen/Logan letters are in the Eleanor Parke Custis Lewis Correspondence, Historical Society of Pennsylvania).

43. Mrs. S. S. Dalton, "Autobiography," (Circle Valley, Utah, 1876), pp. 21–22, Bancroft Library, University of California, Berkeley; Sarah Foulke Emlen Diary, April 1809; Louisa G. Van Vleck, Appleton, Wis., to Charlena Van Vleck Anderson, Göttingen, n.d. [1875], Harriet Manigault Diary, August 16, 1814, July 14, 1815; Sarah Alden Ripley to Sophy Fisher [early 1860s], quoted in Wister and Irwin (n. 12 above), p. 212. The Jefferis family papers are filled with empathetic letters between Martha and her daughters, Anne and Edith. See, e.g., Martha Jefferis to Edith Jefferis, December 26, 1836, March 11, 1837, March 15, 1841; Anne Jefferis Sheppard to Martha Jefferis, March 17, 1841, January 17, 1847; Martha Jefferis to Anne Jefferis Sheppard, April 17, 1848, April 30, 1849. A representative letter is this of March 9, 1837 from Edith to Martha: "My heart can fully respond to the language of my own precious Mother, that absence has not diminished our affection for each other, but has, if possible, strengthened the bonds that have united us together & I have had to remark how we had been permitted to mingle in sweet fellowship and have been strengthened to bear one another's burdens. . . ."

44. Abigail Brackett Lyman, Boston, to Mrs. Abigail Brackett (daughter to mother), n.d. [1797], June 3, 1800; Sarah Alden Ripley wrote weekly to her daughter, Sophy Ripley Fisher, after the latter's marriage (Sarah Alden Ripley Correspondence, passim); Phoebe Bradford Diary, February 25, 1833, passim, 1832–33; Louisa G. Van Vleck to Charlena Van Vleck Anderson, December 15, 1873, July 4, August 15 and 29, September 19, and November 9, 1875. Eleanor Parke Custis Lewis's long correspondence with Elizabeth Bordley Gibson contains evidence of her anxiety at leaving her foster mother's home at various times during her adolescence and at her marriage, and her own longing for her daughters, both of whom had married and moved to Louisiana (Eleanor Parke Custis [Lewis] to Elizabeth Bordley [Gibson], October 13, 1795, November 4, 1799, passim, 1820s and 1830s). Anne Jefferis Sheppard experienced a great deal of anxiety on moving two

mothers and daughters is evident in a letter Sarah Alden Ripley, at age sixty-nine, wrote her youngest and recently married daughter: "You do not know how much I miss you, not only when I struggle in and out of my mortal envelop and pump my nightly potation and no longer pour into your sympathizing ear my senile gossip, but all the day I muse away, since the sound of your voice no longer rouses me to sympathy with your joys or sorrows. . . . You cannot know how much I miss your affectionate demonstrations."[45] A dozen aging mothers in this sample of over thirty families echoed her sentiments.

Central to these mother-daughter relations is what might be described as an apprenticeship system. In those families where the daughter followed the mother into a life of traditional domesticity, mothers and other older women carefully trained daughters in the arts of housewifery and motherhood. Such training undoubtedly occurred throughout a girl's childhood but became more systematized, almost ritualistic, in the years following the end of her formal education and before her marriage. At this time a girl either returned home from boarding school or no longer divided her time between home and school. Rather, she devoted her energies on two tasks: mastering new domestic skills and participating in the visiting and social activities necessary to finding a husband. Under the careful supervision of their mothers and of older female relatives, such late-adolescent girls temporarily took over the household management from their mothers, tended their young nieces and nephews, and helped in childbirth, nursing, and weaning. Such experiences tied the generations together in shared skills and emotional interaction.[46]

---

days' journey from her mother at the time of her marriage. This loneliness and sense of isolation persisted through her marriage until, finally a widow, she returned to live with her mother (Anne Jefferis Sheppard to Martha Jefferis, April 1841, October 16, 1842, April 2, May 22, and October 12, 1844, September 3, 1845, January 17, 1847, May 16, June 3, and October 31, 1849; Anne Jefferis Sheppard to Susanna Lightfoot, March 23, 1845, and to Joshua Jefferis, May 14, 1854). Daughters evidently frequently slept with their mothers—into adulthood (Harriet Manigault [Wilcox] Diary, February 19, 1815; Eleanor Parke Custis Lewis to Elizabeth Bordley Gibson, October 10, 1832). Daughters also frequently asked mothers to live with them and professed delight when they did so. See, e.g., Sarah Alden Ripley's comments to George Simmons, October 6, 1844, in Wister and Irwin, p. 185: "It is no longer 'Mother and Charles came out one day and returned the next,' for mother is one of us: she has entered the penetratice, been initiated into the mystery of the household gods, . . . Her divertissement is to mend the stockings . . . whiten sheets and napkins, . . . and take a stroll at evening with me to talk of our children, to compare our experiences, what we have learned and what we have suffered, and, last of all, to complete with pears and melons the cheerful circle about the solar lamp. . . ." We did find a few exceptions to this mother-daughter felicity (M.B. Ashew Diary, November 19, 1857, April 10 and May 17, 1858). Sarah Foulke Emlen was at first very hostile to her stepmother (Sarah Foulke Emlen Diary, August 9, 1807), but they later developed a warm supportive relationship.

45. Sarah Alden Ripley to Sophy Thayer, n.d. [1861].

46. Mary Hallock Foote to Helena [winter 1873] (no. 52); Jossie, Stevens Point, Wis., to Charlena Van Vleck [Anderson], Appleton, Wis., October 24, 1870; Pollie Chandler,

Daughters were born into a female world. Their mother's life expectations and sympathetic network of friends and relations were among the first realities in the life of the developing child. As long as the mother's domestic role remained relatively stable and few viable alternatives competed with it, daughters tended to accept their mother's world and to turn automatically to other women for support and intimacy. It was within this closed and intimate female world that the young girl grew toward womanhood.

One could speculate at length concerning the absence of that mother-daughter hostility today considered almost inevitable to an adolescent's struggle for autonomy and self-identity. It is possible that taboos against female aggression and hostility were sufficiently strong to repress even that between mothers and their adolescent daughters. Yet these letters seem so alive and the interest of daughters in their mothers' affairs so vital and genuine that it is difficult to interpret their closeness exclusively in terms of repression and denial. The functional bonds that held mothers and daughters together in a world that permitted few alternatives to domesticity might well have created a source of mutuality and trust absent in societies where greater options were available for daughters than for mothers. Furthermore, the extended female network—a daughter's close ties with her own older sisters, cousins, and aunts—may well have permitted a diffusion and a relaxation of mother-daughter identification and so have aided a daughter in her struggle for identity and autonomy. None of these explanations are mutually exclusive; all may well have interacted to produce the degree of empathy evident in those letters and diaries.

At some point in adolescence, the young girl began to move outside the matrix of her mother's support group to develop a network of her own. Among the middle class, at least, this transition toward what was at the same time both a limited autonomy and a repetition of her mother's life seemed to have most frequently coincided with a girl's going to school. Indeed education appears to have played a crucial role in the lives of most of the families in this study. Attending school for a few months, for a year, or longer, was common even among daughters of relatively poor families, while middle-class girls routinely spent at least a

---

Green Bay, Wis., to Charlena Van Vleck [Anderson], Appleton, n.d. [1870]; Eleuthera DuPont to Sophie DuPont, September 5, 1829; Sophie DuPont to Eleuthera DuPont, December 1827; Sophie DuPont to Victorine Bauday, December 4, 1827; Mary Gilpin to Sophie DuPont, September 26, 1827; Sarah Ripley Stearns Diary, April 2, 1809; Jeannie McCall to Peter McCall, October 27 [late 1840s]. Eleanor Parke Custis Lewis's correspondence with Elizabeth Bordley Gibson describes such an apprenticeship system over two generations—that of her childhood and that of her daughters. Indeed Eleanor Lewis's own apprenticeship was quite formal. She was deliberately separated from her foster mother in order to spend a winter of domesticity with her married sisters and her remarried mother. It was clearly felt that her foster mother's (Martha Washington) home at the nation's capital was not an appropriate place to develop domestic talents (October 13, 1795, March 30, May 13, and [summer] 1796, March 18 and April 27, 1797, October 1827).

year in boarding school.[47] These school years ordinarily marked a girl's first separation from home. They served to wean the daughter from her home, to train her in the essential social graces, and, ultimately, to help introduce her into the marriage market. It was not infrequently a trying emotional experience for both mother and daughter.[48]

In this process of leaving one home and adjusting to another, the mother's friends and relatives played a key transitional role. Such older women routinely accepted the role of foster mother; they supervised the young girl's deportment, monitored her health and introduced her to their own network of female friends and kin.[49] Not infrequently women, friends from their own school years, arranged to send their daughters to the same school so that the girls might form bonds paralleling those their mothers had made. For years Molly and Helena wrote of their daughters' meeting and worried over each others' children. When Molly finally brought her daughter east to school, their first act on reaching New York was to meet Helena and her daughters. Elizabeth Bordley Gibson virtually adopted the daughters of her school chum, Eleanor Custis Lewis. The Lewis daughters soon began to write Elizabeth Gibson letters

47. Education was not limited to the daughters of the well-to-do. Sarah Foulke Emlen, the daughter of an Ohio Valley frontier farmer, for instance, attended day school for several years during the early 1800s. Sarah Ripley Stearns, the daughter of a shopkeeper in Greenfield, Mass., attended a boarding school for but three months, yet the experience seemed very important to her. Mrs. S. S. Dalton, a Mormon woman from Utah, attended a series of poor country schools and greatly valued her opportunity, though she also expressed a great deal of guilt for the sacrifices her mother made to make her education possible (Sarah Foulke Emlen Journal, Sarah Ripley Stearns Diary, Mrs. S. S. Dalton, "Autobiography").

48. Maria Revere to her mother [Mrs. Paul Revere], June 13, 1801, Paul Revere Papers, Massachusetts Historical Society. In a letter to Elizabeth Bordley Gibson, March 28, 1847, Eleanor Parke Custis Lewis from Virginia discussed the anxiety her daughter felt when her granddaughters left home to go to boarding school. Eleuthera DuPont was very homesick when away at school in Philadelphia in the early 1820s (Eleuthera DuPont, Philadelphia, to Victorine Bauday, Wilmington, Del., April 7, 1821; Eleuthera DuPont to Sophie Madeleine DuPont, Wilmington Del., February and April 3, 1821).

49. Elizabeth Bordley Gibson, a Philadelphia matron, played such a role for the daughters and nieces of her lifelong friend, Eleanor Parke Custis Lewis, a Virginia planter's wife (Eleanor Parke Custis Lewis to Elizabeth Bordley Gibson, January 29, 1833, March 19, 1826, and passim through the collection). The wife of Thomas Gurney Smith played a similar role for Sophie and Eleuthera DuPont (see, e.g., Eleuthera DuPont to Sophie Madeleine DuPont, May 22, 1825; Rest Cope to Philema P. Swayne [niece] West Town School, Chester County, Pa., April 8, 1829, Friends Historical Library, Swarthmore College). For a view of such a social pattern over three generations, see the letters and diaries of three generations of Manigault women in Philadelphia: Mrs. Gabrielle Manigault, her daughter, Harriet Manigault Wilcox, and granddaughter, Charlotte Wilcox McCall. Unfortunately the papers of the three women are not in one family collection (Mrs. Henry Middleton, Charleston, S.C., to Mrs. Gabrielle Manigault, n.d. [mid 1800s]; Harriet Manigault Diary, vol. 1; December 1, 1813, June 28, 1814; Charlotte Wilcox McCall Diary, vol. 1, 1842, passim. All in Historical Society of Philadelphia).

with the salutation "Dearest Mama." Eleuthera DuPont, attending boarding school in Philadelphia at roughly the same time as the Lewis girls, developed a parallel relationship with her mother's friend, Elizabeth McKie Smith. Eleuthera went to the same school and became a close friend of the Smith girls and eventually married their first cousin. During this period she routinely called Mrs. Smith "Mother." Indeed Eleuthera so internalized the sense of having two mothers that she casually wrote her sisters of her "Mamma's" visits at her "mother's" house —that is at Mrs. Smith's.[50]

Even more important to this process of maturation than their mother's friends were the female friends young women made at school. Young girls helped each other overcome homesickness and endure the crises of adolescence. They gossiped about beaux, incorporated each other into their own kinship systems, and attended and gave teas and balls together. Older girls in boarding school "adopted" younger ones, who called them "Mother."[51] Dear friends might indeed continue this pattern of adoption and mothering throughout their lives; one woman might routinely assume the nurturing role of pseudomother, the other the dependency role of daughter. The pseudomother performed for the other woman all the services which we normally associate with mothers; she went to absurd lengths to purchase items her "daughter" could have obtained from other sources, gave advice and functioned as an idealized figure in her "daughter's" imagination. Helena played such a role for Molly, as did Sarah for Jeannie. Elizabeth Bordley Gibson bought almost all Eleanor Parke Custis Lewis's necessities—from shoes and corset covers to bedding and harp strings—and sent them from Philadelphia to Virginia, a procedure that sometimes took months. Eleanor frequently asked Elizabeth to take back her purchases, have them redone, and argue with shopkeepers about prices. These were favors automatically asked and complied with. Anne Jefferis Sheppard made the analogy very explicitly in a letter to her own mother written shortly after Anne's marriage, when she was feeling depressed about their separation: "Mary

50. Frances Parke Lewis, Woodlawn, Va., to Elizabeth Bordley Gibson, Philadelphia, April 11, 1821, Lewis Correspondence; Eleuthera DuPont, Philadelphia, to Victorine DuPont Bauday, Brandywine, December 8, 1821, January 31, 1822; Eleuthera DuPont, Brandywine, to Margaretta Lammont [DuPont], Philadelphia, May 1823.

51. Sarah Ripley Stearns Diary, March 9 and 25, 1810; Peggy Emlen to Sally Logan, March and July 4, 1769; Harriet Manigault [Wilcox] Diary, vol. 1, December 1, 1813, June 28 and September 18, 1814, August 10, 1815; Charlotte Wilcox McCall Diary, 1842, passim; Fanny Canby to Mary Canby, May 27, 1801, March 17, 1804; Deborah Cope, West Town School, to Rest Cope, Philadelphia, July 9, 1828, Chester County Historical Society, West Chester, Pa.; Anne Zook, West Town School, to Mary Zook, Philadelphia, January 30, 1866, Chester County Historical Society, West Chester, Pa.; Mary Gilpin to Sophie Madeleine DuPont, February 25, 1829; Eleanor Parke Custis [Lewis] to Elizabeth Bordley [Gibson], April 27, July 2, and September 8, 1797, June 30, 1799, December 29, 1820; Frances Parke Lewis to Elizabeth Bordley Gibson, December 20, 1820.

Paulen is truly kind, almost acts the part of a mother and trys to aid and *comfort me,* and also to *lighten my new cares.*"[52]

A comparison of the references to men and women in these young women's letters is striking. Boys were obviously indispensable to the elaborate courtship ritual girls engaged in. In these teenage letters and diaries, however, boys appear distant and warded off—an effect produced both by the girl's sense of bonding and by a highly developed and deprecatory whimsy. Girls joked among themselves about the conceit, poor looks or affectations of suitors. Rarely, especially in the eighteenth and early nineteenth centuries, were favorable remarks exchanged. Indeed, while hostility and criticism of other women were so rare as to seem almost tabooed, young women permitted themselves to express a great deal of hostility toward peer-group men.[53] When unacceptable suitors appeared, girls might even band together to harass them. When one such unfortunate came to court Sophie DuPont she hid in her room, first sending her sister Eleuthera to entertain him and then dispatching a number of urgent notes to her neighboring sister-in-law, cousins, and a visiting friend who all came to Sophie's support. A wild female romp ensued, ending only when Sophie banged into a door, lacerated her nose, and retired, with her female cohorts, to bed. Her brother and the presumably disconcerted suitor were left alone. These were not the antics of teenagers but of women in their early and mid-twenties.[54]

Even if young men were acceptable suitors, girls referred to them formally and obliquely: "The last week I received the unexpected intelligence of the arrival of a friend in Boston," Sarah Ripley wrote in her diary of the young man to whom she had been engaged for years and whom she would shortly marry. Harriet **Manigault** assiduously kept a lively and gossipy diary during the three years preceding her marriage, yet did not once comment upon her own engagement nor indeed make any personal references to her fiance—who was never identified as such but always referred to as Mr. Wilcox.[55] The point is not that these young women were hostile to young men. Far from it; they sought marriage and domesticity. Yet in these letters and diaries men appear as an other or out group, segregated into different schools, supported by their own male network of friends and kin, socialized to different be-

52. Anne Jefferis Sheppard to Martha Jefferis, March 17, 1841.

53. Peggy Emlen to Sally Logan, March 1769, Mount Vernon, Va.; Eleanor Parke Custis [Lewis] to Elizabeth Bordley [Gibson], Philadelphia, April 27, 1797, June 30, 1799; Jeannie Field, New York, to Sarah Butler Wister, Germantown, July 3, 1861, January 16, 1863, Harriet Manigault Diary, August 3 and 11–13, 1814; Eunice Callender, Boston, to Sarah Ripley [Stearns], Greenfield, May 4, 1809. I found one exception to this inhibition of female hostility. This was the diary of Charlotte Wilcox McCall, Philadelphia (see, e.g., her March 23, 1842 entry).

54. Sophie M. DuPont and Eleuthera DuPont, Brandywine, to Victorine DuPont Bauday, Philadelphia, January 25, 1832.

55. Sarah Ripley [Stearns] Diary and Harriet Manigault Diary, passim.

havior, and coached to a proper formality in courtship behavior. As a consequence, relations between young women and men frequently lacked the spontaneity and emotional intimacy that characterized the young girls' ties to each other.

Indeed, in sharp contrast to their distant relations with boys, young women's relations with each other were close, often frolicsome, and surprisingly long lasting and devoted. They wrote secret missives to each other, spent long solitary days with each other, curled up together in bed at night to whisper fantasies and secrets.[56] In 1862 one young woman in her early twenties described one such scene to an absent friend: "I have sat up to midnight listening to the confidences of Constance Kinney, whose heart was opened by that most charming of all situations, a seat on a bedside late at night, when all the household are asleep & only oneself & one's confidante survive in wakefulness. So she has told me all her loves and tried to get some confidences in return but being five or six years older than she, I know better. . . ."[57] Elizabeth Bordley and Nelly Parke Custis, teenagers in Philadelphia in the 1790s, routinely secreted themselves until late each night in Nelly's attic, where they each wrote a novel about the other.[58] Quite a few young women kept diaries, and it was a sign of special friendship to show their diaries to each other. The emotional quality of such exchanges emerges from the comments of one young girl who grew up along the Ohio frontier:

> Sisters CW and RT keep diaries & allow me the inestimable plea-sure of reading them and in turn they see mine—but O shame covers my face when I think of it; theirs is so much better than mine, that every time. Then I think well now I *will* burn mine but upon second thought it would deprive me the pleasure of reading theirs, for I esteem it a very great privilege indeed, as well as very improving, as we lay our hearts open to each other, it heightens our love & helps to cherish & keep alive that sweet soothing friendship and endears us to each other by that soft attraction.[59]

56. Sophie Madeleine DuPont to Eleuthera DuPont, December 1827; Clementina Beach Smith to Sophie Madeleine DuPont, December 26, 1828; Sarah Faulke Emlen Diary, July 21, 1808, March 30, 1809; Annie Hethroe, Ellington, Wis., to Charlena Van Vleck [Anderson], Appleton, Wis., April 23, 1865; Frances Parke Lewis, Woodlawn, Va., to Elizabeth Bordley [Gibson], Philadelphia, December 20, 1820; Fanny Ferris to Debby Ferris, West Town School, Chester County, Pa., May 29, 1826. An excellent example of the warmth of women's comments about each other and the reserved nature of their refer-ences to men are seen in two entries in Sarah Ripley Stearn's diary. On January 8, 1811 she commented about a young woman friend: "The amiable Mrs. White of Princeton . . . one of the loveliest most interesting creatures I ever knew, young fair and blooming . . . beloved by everyone . . . formed to please & to charm. . . ." She referred to the man she ultimately married always as "my friend" or "a friend" (February 2 or April 23, 1810).

57. Jeannie Field, New York, to Sarah Butler Wister, Germantown, April 6, 1862.

58. Elizabeth Bordley Gibson, introductory statement to the Eleanor Parke Custis Lewis Letters [1850s], Historical Society of Pennsylvania.

59. Sarah Foulke [Emlen] Diary, March 30, 1809.

Girls routinely slept together, kissed and hugged each other. Indeed, while waltzing with young men scandalized the otherwise flighty and highly fashionable Harriet Manigault, she considered waltzing with other young women not only acceptable but pleasant.[60]

Marriage followed adolescence. With increasing frequency in the nineteenth century, marriage involved a girl's traumatic removal from her mother and her mother's network. It involved, as well, adjustment to a husband, who, because he was male came to marriage with both a different world view and vastly different experiences. Not surprisingly, marriage was an event surrounded with supportive, almost ritualistic, practices. (Weddings are one of the last female rituals remaining in twentieth-century America.) Young women routinely spent the months preceding their marriage almost exclusively with other women—at neighborhood sewing bees and quilting parties or in a round of visits to geographically distant friends and relatives. Ostensibly they went to receive assistance in the practical preparations for their new home —sewing and quilting a trousseau and linen—but of equal importance, they appear to have gained emotional support and reassurance. Sarah Ripley spent over a month with friends and relatives in Boston and Hingham before her wedding; Parke Custis Lewis exchanged visits with her aunts and first cousins throughout Virginia.[61] Anne Jefferis, who married with some hesitation, spent virtually half a year in endless visiting with cousins, aunts, and friends. Despite their reassurance and support, however, she would not marry Moses Sheppard until her sister Edith and her cousin Rebecca moved into the groom's home, met his friends, and explored his personality.[62] The wedding did not take place until Edith wrote to Anne: "I can say in truth I am entirely willing thou shouldst follow him even away in the Jersey sands believing if thou art not happy in thy future home it will not be any fault on his part. . . ."[63]

Sisters, cousins, and friends frequently accompanied newlyweds on their wedding night and wedding trip, which often involved additional family visiting. Such extensive visits presumably served to wean the daughter from her family of origin. As such they often contained a note of ambivalence. Nelly Custis, for example, reported homesickness and loneliness on her wedding trip. "I left my Beloved and revered Grandmamma with sincere regret," she wrote Elizabeth Bordley. "It was sometime before I could feel reconciled to traveling without her." Perhaps

60. Harriet Manigault Diary, May 26, 1815.

61. Sarah Ripley [Stearns] Diary, May 17 and October 2, 1812; Eleanor Parke Custis Lewis to Elizabeth Bordley Gibson, April 23, 1826; Rebecca Ralston, Philadelphia, to Victorine DuPont [Bauday], Brandywine, September 27, 1813.

62. Anne Jefferis to Martha Jefferis, November 22 and 27, 1840, January 13 and March 17, 1841; Edith Jefferis, Greenwich, N.J., to Anne Jefferis, Philadelphia, January 31, February 6 and February 1841.

63. Edith Jefferis to Anne Jefferis, January 31, 1841.

they also functioned to reassure the young woman herself, and her friends and kin, that though marriage might alter it would not destroy old bonds of intimacy and familiarity.[64]

Married life, too, was structured about a host of female rituals. Childbirth, especially the birth of the first child, became virtually a *rite de passage*, with a lengthy seclusion of the woman before and after delivery, severe restrictions on her activities, and finally a dramatic reemergence.[65] This seclusion was supervised by mothers, sisters, and loving friends. Nursing and weaning involved the advice and assistance of female friends and relatives. So did miscarriage.[66] Death, like birth, was structured around elaborate unisexed rituals. When Nelly Parke Custis Lewis rushed to nurse her daughter who was critically ill while away at school, Nelly received support, not from her husband, who remained on their plantation, but from her old school friend, Elizabeth Bordley. Elizabeth aided Nelly in caring for her dying daughter, cared for Nelly's other children, played a major role in the elaborate funeral arrangements (which the father did not attend), and frequently visited the girl's grave at the mother's request. For years Elizabeth continued to be the confidante of Nelly's anguished recollections of her lost daughter.

64. Eleanor Parke Custis Lewis to Elizabeth Bordley, November 4, 1799. Eleanor and her daughter Parke experienced similar sorrow and anxiety when Parke married and moved to Cincinnati (Eleanor Parke Custis Lewis to Elizabeth Bordley Gibson, April 23, 1826). Helena DeKay visited Mary Hallock the month before her marriage; Mary Hallock was an attendant at the wedding; Helena again visited Molly about three weeks after her marriage; and then Molly went with Helena and spent a week with Helena and Richard in their new apartment (Mary Hallock [Foote] to Helena DeKay Gilder [Spring 1874] (no. 61), May 10, 1874 [May 1874], June 14, 1874 [Summer 1874]. See also Anne Biddle, Philadelphia, to Clement Biddle (brother), Wilmington, March 12 and May 27, 1827; Eunice Callender, Boston, to Sarah Ripley [Stearns], Greenfield, Mass., August 3, 1807, January 26, 1808; Victorine DuPont Bauday, Philadelphia, to Evelina DuPont [Biderman], Brandywine, November 25 and 26, December 1, 1813; Peggy Emlen to Sally Logan, n.d. [1769–70?]; Jeannie Field, New York, to Sarah Butler Wister, Germantown, July 3, 1861).

65. Mary Hallock to Helena DeKay Gilder [1876] (no. 81); n.d. (no. 83), March 3, 1884; Mary Ashew Diary, vol. 2, September–January, 1860; Louisa Van Vleck to Charlena Van Vleck Anderson, n.d. [1875]; Sophie DuPont to Henry DuPont, July 24, 1827; Benjamin Ferris to William Canby, February 13, 1805; Benjamin Ferris to Mary Canby Biddle, December 20, 1825; Anne Jefferis Sheppard to Martha Jefferis, September 15, 1884; Martha Jefferis to Anne Jefferis Sheppard, July 4, 1843, May 5, 1844, May 3, 1847, July 17, 1849; Jeannie McCall to Peter McCall, November 26, 1847, n.d. [late 1840s]. A graphic description of the ritual surrounding a first birth is found in Abigail Lyman's letter to her husband Erastus Lyman, October 18, 1810.

66. Fanny Ferris to Anne Biddle, November 19, 1811; Eleanor Parke Custis Lewis to Elizabeth Bordley Gibson, November 4, 1799, April 27, 1827; Martha Jefferis to Anne Jefferis Sheppard, January 31, 1843, April 4, 1844; Martha Jefferis to Phoebe Sharpless Middleton, June 4, 1846; Anne Jefferis Sheppard to Martha Jefferis, August 20, 1843, February 12, 1844; Maria Inskeep, New Orleans, to Mrs. Fanny G. Hampton, Bridgeton, N.J., September 22, 1848; Benjamin Ferris to Mary Canby, February 14, 1805; Fanny Ferris to Mary Canby [Biddle], December 2, 1816.

These memories, Nelly's letters make clear, were for Elizabeth alone.
"Mr. L. knows nothing of this," was a frequent comment.[67] Virtually
every collection of letters and diaries in my sample contained evidence of
women turning to each other for comfort when facing the frequent and
unavoidable deaths of the eighteenth and nineteenth centuries.[68] While
mourning for her father's death, Sophie DuPont received elaborate letters and visits of condolence—all from women. No man wrote or visited
Sophie to offer sympathy at her father's death.[69] Among rural Pennsylvania Quakers, death and mourning rituals assumed an even more extreme same-sex form, with men or women largely barred from the
deathbeds of the other sex. Women relatives and friends slept with the
dying woman, nursed her, and prepared her body for burial.[70]

Eighteenth- and nineteenth-century women thus lived in emotional
proximity to each other. Friendships and intimacies followed the biological ebb and flow of women's lives. Marriage and pregnancy, childbirth
and weaning, sickness and death involved physical and psychic trauma
which comfort and sympathy made easier to bear. Intense bonds of love
and intimacy bound together those women who, offering each other aid
and sympathy, shared such stressful moments.

These bonds were often physical as well as emotional. An undeniably romantic and even sensual note frequently marked female relationships. This theme, significant throughout the stages of a woman's life,
surfaced first during adolescence. As one teenager from a struggling
pioneer family in the Ohio Valley wrote in her diary in 1808: "I laid with

67. Eleanor Parke Custis Lewis to Elizabeth Bordley Gibson, October–November
1820, passim.

68. Emily Howland to Hannah, September 30, 1866; Emily Howland Diary, February
8, 11, and 27, 1880; Phoebe Brandford Diary, April 12 and 13, and August 4, 1833;
Eunice Callender, Boston, to Sarah Ripley [Stearns], Greenwich, Mass., September 11,
1802, August 26, 1810; Mrs. H. Middleton, Charleston, to Mrs. Gabrielle Manigault,
Philadelphia, n.d. [mid 1800s]; Mrs. H. C. Paul to Mrs. Jeannie McCall, Philadelphia, n.d.
[1840s]; Sarah Butler Wister, Germantown, to Jeannie Field [Musgrove], New York, April
22, 1864; Jeannie Field [Musgrove] to Sarah Butler Wister, August 25, 1861, July 6, 1862;
S. B. Raudolph to Elizabeth Bordley [Gibson], n.d. [1790s]. For an example of similar
letters between men, see Henry Wright to Peter McCall, December 10, 1852; Charles
McCall to Peter McCall, January 4, 1860, March 22, 1864; R. Mercer to Peter McCall,
November 29, 1872.

69. Mary Black [Couper] to Sophie Madeleine DuPont, February 1827, [November 1,
1834], November 12, 1834, two letters [late November 1834]; Eliza Schlatter to Sophie
Madeleine DuPont, November 2, 1834.

70. For a few of the references to death rituals in the Jefferis papers see: Martha
Jefferis to Anne Jefferis Sheppard, September 28, 1843, August 21 and September 25,
1844, January 11, 1846, summer 1848, passim; Anne Jefferis Sheppard to Martha Jefferis,
August 20, 1843; Anne Jefferis Sheppard to Rachel Jefferis, March 17, 1863, February 9,
1868. For other Quaker families, see Rachel Biddle to Anne Biddle, July 23, 1854; Sarah
Foulke Farquhar [Emlen] Diary, April 30, 1811, February 14, 1812; Fanny Ferris to Mary
Canby, August 31, 1810. This is not to argue that men and women did not mourn together. Yet in many families women aided and comforted women and men, men. The
same-sex death ritual was one emotional option available to nineteenth-century Americans.

my dear R[ebecca] and a glorious good talk we had until about 4[A.M.]—O how hard I do *love* her. . . ."[71] Only a few years later Bostonian Eunice Callender carved her initials and Sarah Ripley's into a favorite tree, along with a pledge of eternal love, and then waited breathlessly for Sarah to discover and respond to her declaration of affection. The response appears to have been affirmative.[72] A half-century later urbane and sophisticated Katherine Wharton commented upon meeting an old school chum: "She was a great pet of mine at school & I thought as I watched her light figure how often I had held her in my arms—how dear she had once been to me." Katie maintained a long intimate friendship with another girl. When a young man began to court this friend seriously, Katie commented in her diary that she had never realized "how deeply I loved Eng and how fully." She wrote over and over again in that entry: "Indeed I love her!" and only with great reluctance left the city that summer since it meant also leaving Eng with Eng's new suitor.[73]

Peggy Emlen, a Quaker adolescent in Philadelphia in the 1760s, expressed similar feelings about her first cousin, Sally Logan. The girls sent love poems to each other (not unlike the ones Elizabeth Bordley wrote to Nellie Custis a generation later), took long solitary walks together, and even haunted the empty house of the other when one was out of town. Indeed Sally's absences from Philadelphia caused Peggy acute unhappiness. So strong were Peggy's feelings that her brothers began to tease her about her affection for Sally and threatened to steal Sally's letters, much to both girls' alarm. In one letter that Peggy wrote the absent Sally she elaborately described the depth and nature of her feelings: "I have not words to express my impatience to see My Dear Cousin, what would I not give just now for an hours sweet conversation with her, it seems as if I had a thousand things to say to thee, yet when I see thee, everything will be forgot thro' joy. . . . I have a very great friendship for several Girls yet it dont give me so much uneasiness at being absent from them as from thee. . . . [Let us] go and spend a day down at our place together and there unmolested enjoy each others company."[74]

Sarah Alden Ripley, a young, highly educated women, formed a similar intense relationship, in this instance with a woman somewhat older than herself. The immediate bond of friendship rested on their atypically intense scholarly interests, but it soon involved strong emotions, at least on Sarah's part. "Friendship," she wrote Mary Emerson, "is fast twining about her willing captive the silken hands of dependence, a

71. Sarah Foulke [Emlen] Diary, December 29, 1808.

72. Eunice Callender, Boston, to Sarah Ripley [Stearns] Greenfield, Mass., May 24, 1803.

73. Katherine Johnstone Brinley [Wharton] Journal, April 26, May 30, and May 29, 1856, Historical Society of Pennsylvania.

74. A series of roughly fourteen letters written by Peggy Emlen to Sally Logan (1768–71) has been preserved in the Wells Morris Collection, Box 1, Historical Society of Pennsylvania (see esp. May 3 and July 4, 1769, January 8, 1768).

dependence so sweet who would renounce it for the apathy of self-sufficiency?" Subsequent letters became far more emotional, almost conspiratorial. Mary visited Sarah secretly in her room, or the two women crept away from family and friends to meet in a nearby woods. Sarah became jealous of Mary's other young woman friends. Mary's trips away from Boston also thrust Sarah into periods of anguished depression. Interestingly, the letters detailing their love were not destroyed but were preserved and even reprinted in a eulogistic biography of Sarah Alden Ripley.[75]

Tender letters between adolescent women, confessions of loneliness and emotional dependency, were not peculiar to Sarah Alden, Peggy Emlen, or Katie Wharton. They are found throughout the letters of the thirty-five families studied. They have, of course, their parallel today in the musings of many female adolescents. Yet these eighteenth- and nineteenth-century friendships lasted with undiminished, indeed often increased, intensity throughout the women's lives. Sarah Alden Ripley's first child was named after Mary Emerson. Nelly Custis Lewis's love for and dependence on Elizabeth Bordley Gibson only increased after her marriage. Eunice Callender remained enamored of her cousin Sarah Ripley for years and rejected as impossible the suggestion by another woman that their love might some day fade away.[76] Sophie DuPont and her childhood friend, Clementina Smith, exchanged letters filled with love and dependency for forty years while another dear friend, Mary Black Couper, wrote of dreaming that she, Sophie, and her husband were all united in one marriage. Mary's letters to Sophie are filled with avowals of love and indications of ambivalence toward her own husband. Eliza Schlatter, another of Sophie's intimate friends, wrote to her at a time of crisis: "I wish I could be with you present in the body as well as the mind & heart—I would turn your *good husband out of bed*—and snuggle into you and we would have a long talk like old times in Pine St.—I want to tell you so many things that are not *writable*. . . ."[77]

75. The Sarah Alden Ripley Collection, the Arthur M. Schlesinger, Sr., Library, Radcliffe College, contains a number of Sarah Alden Ripley's letters to Mary Emerson. Most of these are undated, but they extend over a number of years and contain letters written both before and after Sarah's marriage. The eulogistic biographical sketch appeared in Wister and Irwin (n. 12 above). It should be noted that Sarah Butler Wister was one of the editors who sensitively selected Sarah's letters.

76. See Sarah Alden Ripley to Mary Emerson, November 19, 1823. Sarah Alden Ripley routinely, and one must assume ritualistically, read Mary Emerson's letters to her infant daughter, Mary. Eleanor Parke Custis Lewis reported doing the same with Elizabeth Bordley Gibson's letters, passim. Eunice Callender, Boston, to Sarah Ripley [Stearns], October 19, 1808.

77. Mary Black Couper to Sophie M. DuPont, March 5, 1832. The Clementina Smith–Sophie DuPont correspondence of 1,678 letters is in the Sophie DuPont Correspondence. The quotation is from Eliza Schlatter, Mount Holly, N.J., to Sophie DuPont, Brandywine, August 24, 1834. I am indebted to Anthony Wallace for informing me about this collection.

Such mutual dependency and deep affection is a central existential reality coloring the world of supportive networks and rituals. In the case of Katie, Sophie, or Eunice—as with Molly, Jeannie, and Sarah—their need for closeness and support merged with more intense demands for a love which was at the same time both emotional and sensual. Perhaps the most explicit statement concerning women's lifelong friendships appeared in the letter abolitionist and reformer Mary Grew wrote about the same time, referring to her own love for her dear friend and lifelong companion, Margaret Burleigh. Grew wrote, in response to a letter of condolence from another women on Burleigh's death: "Your words respecting my beloved friend touch me deeply. Evidently . . . you comprehend and appreciate, as few persons do . . . the nature of the relation which existed, which exists, between her and myself. Her only surviving niece . . . also does. To me it seems to have been a closer union than that of most marriages. We know there have been other such between two men and also between two women. And why should there not be. Love is spiritual, only passion is sexual."[78]

How then can we ultimately interpret these long-lived intimate female relationships and integrate them into our understanding of Victorian sexuality? Their ambivalent and romantic rhetoric presents us with an ultimate puzzle: the relationship along the spectrum of human emotions between love, sensuality, and sexuality.

One is tempted, as I have remarked, to compare Molly, Peggy, or Sophie's relationships with the friendships adolescent girls in the twentieth century routinely form—close friendships of great emotional intensity. Helena Deutsch and Clara Thompson have both described these friendships as emotionally necessary to a girl's psychosexual development. But, they warn, such friendships might shade into adolescent and postadolescent homosexuality.[79]

It is possible to speculate that in the twentieth century a number of cultural taboos evolved to cut short the homosocial ties of girlhood and to impel the emerging women of thirteen or fourteen toward heterosexual relationships. In contrast, nineteenth-century American society did not taboo close female relationships but rather recognized them as a socially viable form of human contact—and, as such, acceptable throughout a woman's life. Indeed it was not these homosocial ties that were inhibited but rather heterosexual leanings. While closeness, freedom of emotional expression, and uninhibited physical contact charac-

78. Mary Grew, Providence, R.I., to Isabel Howland, Sherwood, N.Y., April 27, 1892, Howland Correspondence, Sophia Smith Collection, Smith College.
79. Helena Deutsch, *Psychology of Women* (New York: Grune & Stratton, 1944), vol. 1, chaps. 1–3; Clara Thompson, *On Women*, ed. Maurice Green (New York: New American Library, 1971).

terized women's relationships with each other, the opposite was frequently true of male-female relationships. One could thus argue that
within such a world of female support, intimacy, and ritual it was only to
be expected that adult women would turn trustingly and lovingly to each
other. It was a behavior they had observed and learned since childhood.
A different type of emotional landscape existed in the nineteenth century, one in which Molly and Helena's love became a natural development.

Of perhaps equal significance are the implications we can garner
from this framework for the understanding of heterosexual marriages
in the nineteenth century. If men and women grew up as they did in
relatively homogeneous and segregated sexual groups, then marriage
represented a major problem in adjustment. From this perspective we
could interpret much of the emotional stiffness and distance that we
associate with Victorian marriage as a structural consequence of contemporary sex-role differentiation and gender-role socialization. With
marriage both women and men had to adjust to life with a person who
was, in essence, a member of an alien group.

I have thus far substituted a cultural or psychosocial for a
psychosexual interpretation of women's emotional bonding. But there
are psychosexual implications in this model which I think it only fair to
make more explicit. Despite Sigmund Freud's insistence on the bisexuality of us all or the recent American Psychiatric Association decision on
homosexuality, many psychiatrists today tend explicitly or implicitly to
view homosexuality as a totally alien or pathological behavior—as totally
unlike heterosexuality. I suspect that in essence they may have adopted
an explanatory model similar to the one used in discussing schizophrenia. As a psychiatrist can speak of schizophrenia and of a borderline
schizophrenic personality as both ultimately and fundamentally different from a normal or neurotic personality, so they also think of both
homosexuality and latent homosexuality as states totally different from
heterosexuality. With this rapidly dichotomous model of assumption,
"latent homosexuality" becomes the indication of a disease in
progress—seeds of a pathology which belie the reality of an individual's
heterosexuality.

Yet at the same time we are well aware that cultural values can effect
choices in the gender of a person's sexual partner. We, for instance, do
not necessarily consider homosexual-object choice among men in prison,
on shipboard or in boarding schools a necessary indication of pathology.
I would urge that we expand this relativistic model and hypothesize that
a number of cultures might well tolerate or even encourage diversity in
sexual and nonsexual relations. Based on my research into this
nineteenth-century world of female intimacy, I would further suggest
that rather than seeing a gulf between the normal and the abnormal we
view sexual and emotional impulses as part of a continuum or spectrum

of affect gradations strongly effected by cultural norms and arrangements, a continuum influenced in part by observed and thus learned behavior. At one end of the continuum lies committed heterosexuality, at the other uncompromising homosexuality; between, a wide latitude of emotions and sexual feelings. Certain cultures and environments permit individuals a great deal of freedom in moving across this spectrum. I would like to suggest that the nineteenth century was such a cultural environment. That is, the supposedly repressive and destructive Victorian sexual ethos, may have been more flexible and responsive to the needs of particular individuals than those of mid-twentieth century.

University of Pennsylvania

Women, Saints, and Sanctuaries

Fatima Mernissi

... The next morning I went to see my mother. I had a snack with her and the children and then I went to spend the day at the Marabout [a sanctuary]. I lay down there and slept for a very long time.

Q: Do you go to the Marabout often?

A: Yes, quite often. For example I prefer to go there on the days of *Aïd* [religious festivals]. When one has a family as desperate as mine, the shrine is a haven of peace and quiet. I like to go there.

Q: What do you like about the shrine? Can you be more precise?

A: Yes. The silence, the rugs, and the clean mats which are nicely arranged ... the sound of the fountain in the silence. An enormous silence where the sound of water is as fragile as thread. I stay there hours, sometimes whole days.

Q: The day of *Aïd* it must be full of people.

A: Yes, there are people, but they are lost in their own problems. So they leave you alone. Mostly it's women who cry without speaking, each in her own world.

Q: Aren't there any men at the shrine?

A: Yes, but men have their side, women theirs. Men come to visit the shrine and leave very quickly; the women, especially those with problems, stay much longer.

Q: What do they do and what do they say?

A: That depends. Some are happy just to cry. Others take hold of the saint's garments and say, "Give me this, oh saint, give me that.

Gathering of historical data on saints, mainly female saints, was done with the collaboration and critical supervision of the Moroccan historian, Halima Ferhat, a Maître de Conférence at the University Mohammed V.

. . ." "I want my daughter to pass her exam . . ." [she laughs]. You
know the saints are men, human beings. But sometimes, imagine,
the woman gets what she asks for! Then she brings a sacrifice . . .
she kills an animal and prepares a meal of the meat and then offers
it to the visitors. Do you know Sid El Gomri?

Q: No.

A: [laughs] Salé is full of shrines . . . full, full. You know, there is a
proverb, "If you want to make a pilgrimage, just go around Salé
barefooted . . ." [laughs]. They do say that. . . . All of Salé is a
shrine. There are so many that some don't have names [laughs].
My father is a native of Salé. He knows the shrines and talks a lot
about them. When you are separated from someone or when you
have a very bad fight, the saint helps you overcome your problem.
When I go I listen to the women. You see them tell everything to
the tomb and mimicking all that took place. Then they ask Sid El
Gomri to help them get out of the mess. They cry, they scream.
Then they get hold of themselves and come back, join us, and sit in
silence. I like the shrine.

Q: Are you ever afraid?

A: Afraid of what? In a shrine, what a question? I love shrines.

Q: And when do you go?

A: They are shut in the evenings except for those that have rooms,
like Sidi Ben Achir, for example. You can rent a room there and
you can stay a long time.

Q: Rent a room for how much?

A: Oh, fifteen dirhams.[1]

Q: Fifteen dirhams a night?!

A: No, for ten dirhams you can stay as long as you like, even a
month. You know, they call Sidi Ben Achir a doctor. Sick people
come with their family; they rent a room and stay until they are
well. You know, it's not Sidi Ben Achir that cures them, it's God,
but they think it's Sidi Ben Achir.

Q: Can anybody rent a room?

A: Not any more. Now you have to have the authorization of the
Mokkadem [local officials]. They want to know where you live and be
sure that you are really sick. Once a woman rented a room and told
them she had a sick person, but it was her lover. Since then they've
made renting rooms more difficult.

Q: Are there young people your own age at the shrine?

A: Yes, but they don't come for the shrine, only for the view. A lot
of young men from the neighborhood come to the shrine for pic-
nics during the spring and summer. You should see the shrine
then: the Hondas, the motors roaring, the boys all dressed up, the
girls with short skirts, all made up and suntanned. It's beautiful. It's
relaxing . . . the silence inside of the shrine, and life outside . . . it's
crawling with young people. You know they have even made a slide
in the wall that goes down to the beach. I will show it to you when

---

1. A dirham is roughly equivalent to $0.20 (U.S. dollars).

we go. It's faster. You jump off the rampart, go down the slide and you're on the beach. You know some people come to the shrine during the summer for their vacations instead of going to a hotel where you pay ten or fifteen dirhams a day. In the shrine a whole family pays fifteen or twenty dirhams a week or month. It's especially the people who live outside of the city and come from far away, the north, the south, all corners of Morocco. For them the shrine is ideal for vacations. The old people can pray and the young can go to the beach. In the summer I meet people from all over Morocco. It's as if I were in Mecca, but I'm in Salé! You must come and see it. We can go in the summer if you want, it's more pleasant. You don't have to come to pray, you can just come and look. I told you, when I go to the shrine it's not to pray. I never ask for anything. When I want something I'll ask God directly, but not the saint . . . he's a human being like I am.

This excerpt from an interview with a twenty-year-old maid, who works in a luxurious, modern part of Salé and lives in its *bidonville* section, suggests the great variety of experiences which take place in the sanctuary according to individual needs. Although they vary throughout the *Maghreb* (North Africa) from a humble pyramid of stones to a pretentious palace-like building,[2] all sanctuaries have one element in common: the saint's presence is supposed to be hosted there, because it is his tomb, a place he inhabited, or the site of an event in his life. The sanctuary testifies to the saint's welcomed presence in the community, but as an institution in a dynamic developing society it also reflects the society's economic and ideological contradictions.

Sanctuaries as Therapy

For women, the sanctuary offers a dramatic contrast to their subordinate position in a bureaucratic, patriarchal society where decision-making positions are held by men. In the courts and hospitals, women hold a classically powerless position, condemned to be subjects, receptacles of impersonal decisions, executors of orders given by males. In a public hospital, the doctor is the expert, the representative of the bureaucratic order, empowered by the written law to tell her what to do; the illiterate woman can only execute his orders. In the diagnosis process, she expresses her discomfort in awkward colloquial Arabic and realizes, because of the doctor's impatience and irritation, that she cannot provide him with the precise, technical information he needs. Moreover, the hospital is a strange, alien setting, a modern building full of enigmatic written signs on doors and corridors, white-robed, clean,

2. Emile Derminghem, "Les Edifices," in *Le Culte des saints dans l'Islam maghrébin* (Paris: Gallimard, 1954), p. 113.

and arrogant civil servants who speak French for all important communications and only use Arabic to issue elementary orders (come here,
go there, take off your dress, etc.).

In comparison to the guardians who stand at the hospital's gates and
in its offices, the saint's tomb is directly accessible to troubled persons.
Holding the saint's symbolical drape or another object like a stone or a
tree, the woman describes what ails her, and it is she who makes the
diagnosis, suggests the solution or solutions which might suit her, and
explains to the saint the one she prefers. Saints know no French and
often no literate Arabic; the language of this supernatural world is colloquial dialects, Berber or Arabic, the only ones women master. The task
of the saint is to help her reach her goal. She will give him a gift or a
sacrifice only if he realizes her wishes, not before. With a doctor, she has
to buy the prescription first and has no way of retaliating if the medicine
does not have the proper effect. It is no wonder, then, that in spite of
modern health services, women still go to the sanctuaries in swarms,
before they go to the hospital, or simultaneously, or after. Saints give
women vital help that modern public health services cannot give. They
embody the refusal to accept arrogant expertise, to submit blindly to
authority, to be treated as subordinate. This insistence on going to saints'
tombs exemplifies the North African woman's traditional claim that she
is active, can decide her needs for herself and do something about them,
a claim that the Muslim patriarchal system denies her. Visits to and
involvement with saints and sanctuaries are two of the rare options left
to women to *be,* to shape their world and their lives. And this attempt at
self-determination takes the form of an exclusively female collective endeavor.

In the sanctuaries, there are always more women than men. They
speak and shout with loud voices as if they are the secure owners of the
premises. Men, although allowed in, often have to shorten their *Ziara*
(visit) because they are overwhelmed by the inquisitive and curious looks
of ubiquitous female visitors. Women gather around each other at the
saint's supposed tomb and feel directly in contact with a sacred source of
power that reflects their own energies. Distressed and suffering, these
women have a very important bond: the will to find a solution, to find a
happier balance between themselves and their surroundings, their fate,
the system that thwarts them. They know they are *wronged (Madluma)* by
the system. Their desire to find an answer to their urgent needs is a
desire to regain their rights. That other women are in exactly the same
situation creates a therapeutic network of communication among them.

When a woman enters the sanctuary, she goes directly to the tomb,
walking over the stretched feet of sitting women, the stretched bodies of
sleeping women. If women have already cried and screamed, they often
lie in a fetal position with their heads on the floor. The newly arrived
woman will put her hand on the tomb, or on the drape over it, and will

explain her problem either in a loud voice or silently. She might go into great detail about her son who failed his examination or was driven away from her by his bride. When describing an intimate fight with her husband, the woman will mimic what happened, name the actors, explain their gestures and attitudes. After she has expressed her needs, she will come to sit among the other women. Eventually, they will gather around her, ask her more details, and offer her the only expertise these women have: experience in suffering. Outraged by her situation and encouraged by this female community, the woman may fall on the floor and scream, twisting her body violently. Some women will rush to her, hold her, hug her, soothe her by talking to her about their own cases and problems. They will massage her forehead, cool her off with a drink of water, and replace on her head her displaced headgear or scarf. She recovers quickly, regains her composure, and leaves the scene to the next newcomer. Undeniably therapeutic, the sanctuary stimulates the energies of women against their discontent and allows them to bathe in an intrinsically female community of soothers, supporters, and advisors.

Sanctuaries as Antiestablishment Arenas

It is primarily as an informal women's association that the sanctuary must be viewed. It is not a religious space, a mistake which is often made. Most saint's sanctuaries are not mosques. With very few exceptions, they are not places where official orthodox Muslim prayer takes place. As Derminghem remarks, "En principe, la cubba n'est pas une mosquée, Mesjid, où l'on fait le soujoùd, la prosternation de la prière rituelle, çala, encore moins, la Jam', la mosquée cathédrale où se fait l'office du vendredi. On peut faire la dou'a, prière de demande et d'invocation facultative, mais non la sala, prière sacrementale devant un tombeau."[3] The institution of saints that is enacted in the sanctuary has an evident antiorthodox, antiestablishment component which has been the object of a prolific literature. But studies of the woman-saint relation have placed excessive emphasis on its magical aspect. Western scholars who investigated the institution were fascinated by the "paralogical" component of the "Moroccan personality structure" and the importance of magical thinking patterns in the still heavily agrarian Moroccan economy and paid little attention to what I would call the phenomenological aspect, namely, what the practitioners themselves derive from their involvement with the saint and the sanctuary.

Such practices have also been interpreted as evidence of the mystical

3. Ibid. "In principal, the *cubba* is not a mosque (*Mesjid*) where one does *soujoùd*, the prostration of ritual prayer (*çala*), even less so, the *Jam'*, the cathedral mosque where Friday service is held. One can do the *dou'a*, prayer of supplication and optional invocation, but not the *sala*, sacramental prayer before a grave."

thinking of primitives as opposed to the secularity of the modern mind. As Mary Douglas points out,

> Secularization is often treated as a modern trend attributable to the growth of cities or to the prestige of science, or just to the breakdown of social forms. But we shall see that it is an age-old cosmological type, a product of a definable social experience, which need have nothing to do with urban life or modern science. Here it would seem that anthropology has failed to hold up the right reflecting mirror to contemporary man. The contrast of secular with religious has nothing whatever to do with the contrast of modern with traditional or primitive. The idea that primitive man is by nature deeply religious is nonsense. . . . The illusion that all primitives are pious, credulous and subject to the teaching of priests or magicians has probably done even more to impede our understanding of our civilization.[4]

Women, in particular, who are always the ones to be kept illiterate (and 97 percent of rural Moroccan women still are),[5] are described as simple-minded, superstitious creatures, incapable of sophisticated thinking, who indulge in esoteric mysticism. This view of women has gained even greater support with the advent of the development and nascent industrialization in Third World economies. If women in industrialized societies are granted some capacity for rational thinking, women in Third World societies are still described as enthralled in magical thinking, despite the fact that their societies are leaping into a modernity enraptured with rationality, technology, and environmental mastery.

Sainthood as an Alternative to Male-defined Femininity

Far from magical, a visit to a saint's tomb, an ongoing relation with a supernatural creature, can be a genuine attempt to mediate one's place in the material world. Interaction with the saint can represent an effort to experience reality fully: "Le sacré c'est le réel par excellence, à la fois puissance, efficience, source de vie et de fécondité. Le désir de l'homme religieux de vivre dans le sacré équivaut en fait à son désir de se situer dans la réalité objective, de ne pas se laisser paralyser par la réalité sans

---

4. Mary Douglas, *Natural Symbols: Exploration in Cosmology* (New York: Random House, Vintage Books, 1973), p. 36.

5. *Recensement général de la population et de l'habitat, 1971* (Rabat: Direction de la statistique, Ministère de Planification, 1971), 3:5. The illiteracy rate is evaluated to be 75 percent for rural women between the ages of ten and twenty-four and between 93 percent and 97 percent for older women.

fin des expériences purement subjectives, de vivre dans un monde réel et efficient, et non pas dans une illusion."[6]

At bottom, women in an unflinchingly patriarchal society seek through the saint's mediation a bigger share of power, of control. One area in which they seek almost total control is reproduction and sexuality, the central notions of any patriarchal system's definition of women, classical orthodox Islam included.[7] Women who are desperate to find husbands, women whose husbands have sexual problems, women who have lost their husband's love or their own reproductive capacities go to the saint to get help and find solutions. One of the important functions of sanctuaries is precisely their involvement with sexuality and fertility. Indeed, if power can be defined as "the chance of a person or a number of persons to realize their own will in a communal action, even against the resistance of others, who are participating in the action,"[8] then women's collaboration with saints is definitely a power operation. Excluded from ritualistic orthodox religion, women walking in processions around saints' tombs express their quest for power in the vast horizons of the sacred space, untouched, unspoiled by human authority and its hierarchies:

> Des jeunes filles pâles jettent dans la source des fleurs rouges, d'autres du sucre, des rayons de miel, pourque leur parole devienne douce, spirituelle, persuasive. Les femmes qui y lancent du musc rêvent de se faire aimer . . . nul ne s'y rend sans henné, sans benjoin. En brûlant son cierge vert ou rose, la vierge dit, "Maître de la source, allumes-moi mon cierge" ce qui veut dire "mariez-moi," ou encore "donnez-moi une santé brillante." La puissance à laquelle on s'adresses est capable de donner tous les biens de ce monde: vie, force, fortune, amour, enfants.[9]

Now this quest for power that underlies the woman-saint relation is

6. Mircea Eliade, *Le Sacré et le profane* (Paris: Gallimard, 1965), p. 27. "The sacred is the real *par excellence,* at one and the same time power, efficiency, source of life and fertility. The religious desire to live within the sacred is in fact equivalent to the desire to be in objective reality, not to be paralyzed by endless and purely subjective experience, but to live in a world which is real and efficient, and not illusory."

7. Fatima Mernissi, *Beyond the Veil* (Cambridge, Mass.: Schenkman Publishing Co., 1975), esp. the chapter entitled, "The Traditional Muslim View of Women and Their Place in the Social Order."

8. Max Weber, *From Max Weber, Essays in Sociology,* trans. and ed. with an introduction by H. Gerth and C. Wright Mills (New York: Oxford University Press, 1958), p. 180.

9. Desparmet, "Le Mal magique," in Derminghem, p. 44. "Pale young girls throw red flowers into the spring, others sugar or honeycombs, so that their voice may become sweet, spiritual, persuasive. The women who throw musk dream of being loved. . . . None goes to the spring without henna, without benjamin. While burning her green or red candle, the virgin says, 'Master of the spring, light my candle' which means 'marry me,' or else 'give me splendid health.' The power to which they speak is capable of granting them all the goods of the world: life, strength, fortune, love, children."

further confirmed by the fact that there are women saints who occupy a
preeminent place and who specialize in solving problems of sexuality
and reproduction.[10] They assume what Freud would certainly have
called a phallic role and function. Some female saints go beyond the
stage of penis envy and reverse traditional patriarchal relations: they are
the ones who give penises to men suffering from sexual disturbances;
such is the case of the Algerian female saint, Lalla Nfissa.[11] But this is not
their only function. Unlike the emphasized passivity of women in the
material, real world, supernatural women lead intensively active lives,
perform all kinds of acts, from benign motherly protection to
straightforward aggression, such as rape of men.[12] These women in the
supernatural realm do not respect the traditional Muslim sexual division
of labor which excludes women from power in religion and politics. In
the supernatural realm, women may refuse to assume domestic roles
and play active roles in both religion and politics.

In one of the most respected saint's biographies, the thirteenth-
century *At-Tasawwuf Ila Rijal At-Tasawwuf*,[13] the biographer, Abu Yaqub
At Tadili, makes no specific reference to the fact that some saints were
women: they enjoy exactly the same rights and privileges and assume the
same characteristics as male saints. At one point, a woman saint, Munia
Bent Maymoun Ad-Dukali, says, "This year, hundreds of women saints
visited this sanctuary." At another, a male insists that, "In Al Masamida
[a region], there were twenty-seven saints who have the power to fly in
the air, among whom fourteen are women."[14]

Female saints seem to fall into two categories, those who are saints
because they were the sisters, wives, or daughters of a saint[15] and those
who were saints in their own right.[16] Many of these saints have strikingly
"unfeminine" personalities and interests. Imma Tiffelent, for example,
literally fled her domestic condition: "Ne voulant pas se marier, Imma
Tiffelent s'échappa sous forme de colombe et se fit prostituée dans la
montagne. . . . Vingt-sept jeunes gens disparurent après l'avoir aimée.

10. Léon L'Africain, *Description de l'Afrique,* trans. from Italian by A. Epaulard Adrien
(Paris: Maison Neuve, 1956), p. 216; and E. Doutté, *Magie et religion dans l'Afrique du Nord*
(Alger: Typographia Adolphe Jourdan, 1908), chap. 1, p. 31.

11. Derminghem, p. 43.

12. Vincent Crapanzano, "The Transformation of the Eumenides: A Moroccan
Example" (unpublished manuscript, Princeton University, 1974), and "Saints, Jinns and
Dreams: An Essay on Moroccan Ethnopsychology" (unpublished manuscript, Princeton
University, Department of Anthropology).

13. Abu Yaqub Yusuf Ibn Yahya At-Tadili, *At-Tasawwuf Ila Rijal At-Tasawwuf; vie de
saints du sud Morocain des V, VI, VIIIème siècles de l'Hégire. Contribution à l'étude de l'histoire
religieuse du Maroc,* ed. A. Faure (Rabat: Editions Techniques Nord Africaines, 1958). I will
refer to this work as *Tasawaf* and cite the number of each saint's biography.

14. *Tasawaf,* no. 160, p. 312; no. 209, p. 397.

15. See *Tasawaf,* no. 240, p. 431; no. 7, p. 70; no. 25, p. 111; and Derminghem, Lalla
Mimouna, p. 68; Lalla Aicha, p. 125, Mana Aicha, p. 107.

16. See *Tasawaf,* no. 160, p. 312; no. 209, p. 397; no. 207, p. 394; no. 210, p. 398; no.
167, p. 331.

Puis elle devint ascète, dans une hutte, au sommet de la montagne . . .
déguenillée, hiruste, elle prêche la religion dans la vallée, revint à sa
hutte, quitte même ses haillons, vit nue, prophétise. Il est interdit de
toucher aux arbres autour de sa tombe, de tuer les oiseaux, de dénicher
les oeufs de perdrix."[17] The same identical flight from patriarchal
"womanhood" can be seen in Sida Zohra El Kouch, "qui fut aussi savante
que belle, resista à Moulay Zidane, mourut vierge, et n'est visitée que par
les femmes."[18] No less important, a prolific body of literature shows a
number of female saints played important roles in the political arena.[19]
One of the most famous is certainly the Berber saint Lalla Tagurrami,
who played a strategic role in her region's history as a referee in conflicts
between tribes and between tribes and the central authority.[20] Politically,
she was so influential and successful that the king imprisoned her:

> Comme elle était parmi les plus belles jeunes filles du village, elle
> fut recherchée pour le mariage, mais refusa tous les prétendants.
> La réputation de sainte de la jeune fille en grandit et s'étendit au
> loin. Le sultan voulut connaître Lalla Aziza et la fit demander à
> Marrakech. Elle s'y rendit et continua dans la ville à se faire remar-
> quer par sa piété et par le bien qu'elle faisait autour d'elle. Elle fut
> très honorée, mais son influence devint tellement grande que le
> sultan en prit ombrage et Lalla Aziza fut jetée en prison. Elle
> mourut empoisonnée.[21]

It is of course possible that her fate was devised by myth tellers to
discourage other women from taking such paths.

Male Saints as Antiheroes

Male saints, on the other hand, were profoundly concerned with
what we would call a housework issue: how to eat without exploiting

17. Trumelet, "Blida," and "Saints de l'Islam," as quoted in Derminghem, p. 53: "Not
wanting to marry, Imma Tiffelant took the shape of a dove, escaped, and became a
prostitute. . . .Twenty-seven young men disappeared after having loved her. Then she
became an ascetic, in a hut, at the top of the mountain. . . . Ragged, unkempt, she preached
religion in the valley, returned to her hut, shed even her rags, lived nude, and prophesied.
It is forbidden to touch the trees around her grave, to kill the birds, to take the partridge
eggs from the nest."

18. Derminghem, p. 49.

19. Jacques Berque, *Structures sociales du Haut Atlas* (Paris: Presses Universitaires de
France, 1955), p. 296.

20. Ibid., pp. 281, 286.

21. Ibid., p. 290. "As she was among the most beautiful girls of the village, she was
sought after for marriage, but refused all suitors. . . . Her reputation as a saint grew and
extended far. The sultan wanted to meet Lalla Aziza and asked her to come to Marrakesh.
Once there, she continued to distinguish herself by her piety and the good she did. She was
very honored, but her influence became so great that the sultan took offense and had Lalla
Aziza thrown into prison. She was poisoned and died."

somebody else's work. Most analyses of the saint's lives fail to emphasize their constant preoccupation with food and its preparation; that they walk on water, fly in the skies, are given more weight than their efforts not to exploit the traditional domestic labor force available—women. Around this question clustered all other issues, such as the repudiation of possessions, privileges, political power, and the condemnation of wars and violence, the very characteristics of a phallocratic system. Most saints fled urban centers and their sophisticated exploitative lives, tried hunting, fishing, gathering, and cooking for themselves.[22] Some fasted as often as they could[23] and trained themselves to eat very little; one went as far as to feed himself on one mouthful.[24] Still others had supernatural help which ground their own wheat or simply which gave them food.[25] They all tried to do without housework and to avoid food cooked by others,[26] and they also tried, to the community's dismay, to perform daily domestic chores themselves, such as taking the bread to the neighborhood oven.[27] One of the most famous of saints, Bou Yazza, went so far as to assume the appearance of a female domestic and to serve a woman for months.[28]

Some saints have families and children, some abstain and live in celibacy. But those who marry are unsuccessful fathers and husbands and live like embarrassed heads of families who can't provide properly for their dependents.[29] Others, especially elderly saints, did not hesitate to renounce their marital rights when these appeared to be totally opposed to the woman's happiness.[30] They definitely did not play the patriarchal role well. Among those who did not marry, one saint explained he was afraid to be unjust to his wife;[31] for him, apparently, marriage was an unjust institution to women. Another said he saw a beautiful woman walking down the street and thought he was in paradise; she was exactly like a *houri,* females provided to good Muslim believers in paradise.[32] Although he secluded himself because he was afraid females would turn him away from God,[33] he did not identify them with the devil, as classical Muslim ideology does, but with paradise, the most positive aspect of Muslim cosmogony.[34] Another saint fainted when he found himself

22. *Tasawaf,* no. 73, p. 186; no. 67, p. 170; no. 13, p. 88; no. 87, p. 217; no. 12, p. 86; no. 59, p. 162.

23. *Tasawaf,* no. 68, p. 76; no. 96, p. 228; no. 33, p. 124.

24. *Tasawaf,* no. 25, p. 111.

25. *Tasawaf,* no. 93, p. 223; no. 63, p. 171; no. 54, p. 156.

26. *Tasawaf,* no. 62, p. 166; no. 132, p. 184.

27. *Tasawaf,* no. 93, p. 224; no. 77, p. 197; no. 162, p. 321.

28. *Tasawaf,* no. 77, p. 200.

29. *Tasawaf,* no. 92, p. 222; no. 51, p. 152; no. 48, p. 144; no. 34, pp. 125–26.

30. *Tasawaf,* no. 99, p. 233; no. 56, p. 158.

31. *Tasawaf,* no. 45, p. 141.

32. *Koran,* Sourate 44, verses 53–54.

33. *Tasawaf,* no. 84, p. 214.

34. Abu Hasan Muslim, *Al-Jami' As-Sahih* (Beirut: Al Maktaba at Tijaria, n.d.), 8:130.

alone with a woman in a room,[35] an unmasculine gesture to say the very least. Indeed, all these fears are not those of a self-confident, patriarchal male.

Like the women who come to visit their sanctuaries, a large number of saints were of humble origin and were involved in manual or physical activities as shepherds, butchers, or doughnut makers.[36] Others had no jobs and lived off nature, eating wild fruits, roots, or fish. Some saints were learned men, even judges, who refused to use their knowledge to obtain influential positions and accumulate wealth, or even to teach,[37] and encouraged illiterates to be proud of their illiteracy. Like the women in the sanctuaries, however, many of them were illiterates. They reminded their communities, which respected them, of their illiteracy,[38] perhaps in order to demystify knowledge as a prerequisite for decision-making positions. Moulay Bou Azza made a point of not speaking literate or even colloquial Arabic.[39] Moulay Abdallah Ou Said, for example, tried to practice a teaching method for the masses "without the intervention of written texts."[40] Although it shocked the learned mandarins, the illiterate female saint Lalla Mimouna constantly insisted she did not use the customary complicated Koranic verses in her prayers because she did not know them. "Mimouna knows God and God knows Mimouna"[41] was the prayer she invented. This resistance to hierarchical knowledge is a persistent characteristic of saints' lives and their battles, which finds sympathy with the oppressed of the new developing economies: the illiterates, who are predominantly women. It is, therefore, no wonder that in the disintegrating agrarian economies of the Maghreb, sanctuaries, among all institutions, are almost the only ones women go to spontaneously and feel at home in. The sanctuary offers a world where illiteracy does not prevent a human being from being a wholesome, thinking, and reasonable person.

* * *

The psychic and emotional value of women's experience in sanctuaries is uncontested and evident. Sanctuaries, which are the locus of antiestablishment, antipatriarchal mythical figures, provide women with a space where complaint and verbal vituperations against the system's injustices are allowed and encouraged. They give women the opportunity to develop critical views of their condition, to identify problems, and to try to find their solution. At the same time, women invest all of their

---

35. *Tasawaf,* no. 94, p. 224.

36. *Tasawaf,* no. 10, p. 79; no. 26, p. 115; no. 96, p. 228.

37. *Tasawaf,* no. 17, p. 95; no. 69, p. 178; no. 6, p. 69.

38. *Tasawaf,* no. 93, p. 223; no. 77, p. 197.

39. V. Loulignac, *Un Saint Berbère—Moulay Bou Azza; Histoire et légende* (Rabat: Hesperis, 1946), 31:29.

40. Jean Chaumel, *Histoire d'une tribu maraboutique de l'Anti-Atlas, le Aît Abdallah ou Said,* vol. 39, 1er et 2ème trimestre (Rabat: Hesperes, 1952), p. 206.

41. Derminghem, p. 69.

efforts and energies in trying to get a supernatural force to influence the oppressive structure on their behalf. This does not affect the formal power structure, the outside world. It has a collective therapeutic effect on the individual women visitors, but it does not enable them to carry their solidarity outside, to affect the system and shape it to suit their own needs. For these needs spring from their structural economic reliance on males and on the services they must give them in exchange: sex and reproduction. The saint in the sanctuary plays the role of the psychiatrist in the capitalist society, channeling discontent into the therapeutic processes and thus depriving it of its potential to combat the formal power structure. Saints, then, help women adjust to the oppression of the system. The waves of resentment die at the sanctuary's threshold. Nothing leaves with the woman except her belief that her contact with the saint triggered mechanisms which are going to affect the world, change it, and make it suit her conditions better. In this sense, sanctuaries are "happenings" where women's collective energies and combative forces are invested in alienating institutions which strive to absorb them, lower their explosive effect, neutralize them. Paradoxically, the arena where popular demonstrations against oppression, injustice, and inequality are most alive become, in developing economies, the best ally of unresponsive national bureaucracies. Encouragement of traditional saints' rituals by administrative authorities who oppose any trade unionist or political movement is a well-known tactic in Third World politics.

Department of Sociology
Mohammed V University
Rabat, Morocco

Archimedes and the Paradox of Feminist Criticism

Myra Jehlen

I

Feminist thinking is really *re*thinking, an examination of the way certain assumptions about women and the female character enter into the fundamental assumptions that organize all our thinking. For instance, assumptions such as the one that makes intuition and reason opposite terms parallel to female and male may have axiomatic force in our culture, but they are precisely what feminists need to question—or be reduced to checking the arithmetic, when the issue lies in the calculus.

Such radical skepticism is an ideal intellectual stance that can generate genuinely new understandings; that is, reconsideration of the relation between female and male can be a way to reconsider that between intuition and reason and ultimately between the whole set of such associated dichotomies: heart and head, nature and history. But it also creates unusual difficulties. Somewhat like Archimedes, who to lift the earth with his lever required someplace else on which to locate himself

For their numerous helpful suggestions and suggestive objections, I am grateful to Sacvan Bercovitch, Rachel Blau DuPlessis, Carolyn Heilbrun, Evelyn Keller, Helene Moglen, Sara Ruddick, Catharine Stimpson, and Marilyn Young.

and his fulcrum, feminists questioning the presumptive order of both nature and history—and thus proposing to remove the ground from under their own feet—would appear to need an alternative base. For as Archimedes had to stand somewhere, one has to assume something in order to reason at all. So if the very axioms of Western thought already incorporate the sexual teleology in question, it seems that, like the Greek philosopher, we have to find a standpoint off this world altogether.

Archimedes never did. However persuasively he established that the earth could be moved from its appointed place, he and the lever remained earthbound and the globe stayed where it was. His story may point another moral, however, just as it points to another science able to harness forces internally and apply energy from within. We could then conclude that what he really needed was a terrestrial fulcrum. My point here, similarly, will be that a terrestrial fulcrum, a standpoint from which we can see our conceptual universe whole but which nonetheless rests firmly on male ground, is what feminists really need. But perhaps because being at once on and off a world seems an improbable feat, the prevailing perspectives of feminist studies have located the scholar one place or the other.

Inside the world of orthodox and therefore male-oriented scholarship, a new category has appeared in the last decade, the category of women. Economics textbooks now draw us our own bell curves, histories of medieval Europe record the esoterica of convents and the stoning of adulterous wives, zoologists calibrate the orgasmic capacities of female chimpanzees. Indeed, whole books on "women in" and "women of" are fast filling in the erstwhile blanks of a questionnaire—one whose questions, however, remain unquestioned. They never asked before what the mother's occupation was, now they do. The meaning of "occupation," or for that matter of "mother," is generally not at issue.

It is precisely the issue, however, for the majority of feminist scholars who have taken what is essentially the opposite approach; rather than appending their findings to the existing literature, they generate a new one altogether in which women are not just another focus but the center of an investigation whose categories and terms are derived from the world of female experience. They respond to the Archimedean dilemma by creating an alternative context, a sort of female enclave apart from the universe of masculinist assumptions. Most "women's studies" have taken this approach and stressed the global, structural character of their separate issues. Women are no longer to be seen as floating in a man's world but as a coherent group, a context in themselves. The problem is that the issues and problems women define from the inside as global, men treat from the outside as insular. Thus, besides the exfoliation of reports on the state of women everywhere and a certain piety on the subject of pronouns, there is little indication of feminist impact on the universe of male discourse. The theoretical cores of the various disciplines remain essentially unchanged, their terms and methods are as always. As always, therefore, the intellectual arts bespeak a world dominated by men, a script that the occasional woman at a podium can hardly revise. Off in the enclaves of women's studies, our basic research lacks the contiguity to force a basic reconsideration of all research, and our encapsulated revisions appear inorganic (or can be made to appear inorganic) to the universal system they mean to address. Archimedes' problem was getting off the world, but ours might be getting back on.

For we have been, perhaps, too successful in constructing an alternative footing. Our world apart, our female intellectual community, becomes increasingly cut off even as it expands. If we have little control over being shunted aside, we may nonetheless render the isolation of women's scholarship more difficult. At least we ought not to accept it, as in a sense we do when we ourselves conflate feminist thought with thinking about women, when we remove ourselves and our lever off this man's world to study the history or the literature, the art or the anatomy of women alone. This essay is about devising a method for an alternative definition of women's studies as the investigation, from women's viewpoint, of everything, thereby finding a way to engage the dominant intellectual systems directly and organically: locating a feminist terrestrial fulcrum. Since feminist thinking is the thinking of an insurgent group that in the nature of things will never possess a world of its own, such engagement would appear a logical necessity.

Logical but also contradictory. To a degree, any analysis that rethinks the most basic assumptions of the thinking it examines is contradictory or at least contrary, for its aim is to question more than to explain and chart. From it we learn not so much the intricacies of how a particular mode of thinking works as the essential points to which it can be reduced. And nowhere is such an adversary rather than appreciative stance more problematical than it is in literary criticism. This is my specific subject here, the perils and uses of a feminist literary criticism that confronts the fundamental axioms of its parent discipline.

What makes feminist literary criticism especially contradictory is the peculiar nature of literature as distinct from the objects of either physical or social scientific study. Unlike these, literature is itself already an interpretation that it is the critic's task to decipher. It is certainly not news that the literary work is biased; indeed that is its value. Critical objectivity enters in only at a second level to provide a reliable reading, though even here many have argued that reading too is an exercise in creative interpretation. On the other hand, while biologists and historians will concede that certain a priori postulates affect their gathering of data, they always maintain that they have tried to correct for bias, attempting, insofar as this is ever possible, to discover the factual, undistorted truth. Therefore expositions of subjectivity are always both relevant and revelatory about the work of biologists and historians. But as a way of judging the literary work per se, exposing its bias is essentially beside the point. Not that literature, as the New Critics once persuaded us, transcends subjectivity or politics. Paradoxically, it is just because the fictional universe is wholly subjective and therefore ideological that the value of its ideology is almost irrelevant to its literary value. The latter instead depends on what might be thought of as the quality of the *apologia,* how successfully the work transforms ideology into ideal, into a myth that works to the extent precisely that it obscures its provenance. Disliking that provenance implies no literary judgment, for a work may be, from my standpoint, quite wrong and even wrongheaded about life and politics and still an extremely successful rendering of its contrary vision. Bad ideas, even ideas so bad that most of humanity rejects them, have been known to make very good literature.

I am not speaking here of what makes a work attractive or meaningful to its audience. The politics of a play, poem, or story may render it quite unreadable or, in the opposite case, enhance its value for particular people and situations. But this poses no critical issue, for what we like, we like and can justify that way; the problem, if we as feminists want to address our whole culture, is to deal with what we do not like but recognize as nonetheless valuable, serious, good. This is a crucial problem at the heart of feminism's wider relevance. No wonder we have tried to avoid it.

One way is to point out that "good" changes its definition according to time and place. This is true, but not true enough. Perhaps only because we participate in this culture even while criticizing it, we do (most of us) finally subscribe to a tradition of the good in art and philosophy that must sometimes be a political embarrassment—and what else could it be, given the entire history of both Western and Eastern civilizations and their often outright dependence on misogyny? Nor is it true enough, I believe, to argue that the really good writers and thinkers unconsciously and sometimes consciously rejected such misogyny. As couched in the analogous interpretation of Shylock as hero because Shakespeare could not really have been anti-Semitic, this argument amounts to second-guessing writers and their works in terms of a provincialism that seems especially hard to maintain in these linguistically and anthropologically conscious times. For such provincialism not only assumes that our view of things is universal and has always been the substance of reality but also that all other and prior representations were insubstantial. So when Shakespeare depicted bastards as scheming subversives, Jews as merchants of flesh, and women as hysterics, he meant none of it but was only using the local idiom. What he meant, thereby demonstrating his universality, was what we mean.

I want to suggest that we gain no benefit from either disclaiming the continuing value of the "great tradition" or reclaiming it as after all an expression of our own viewpoint. On the contrary, we lose by both. In the first instance, we isolate ourselves into irrelevance. In the second—

denying, for example, that Shakespeare shared in the conventional prejudices about women—we deny by implication that there is anything necessarily different about a feminist outlook. Thus, discovering that the character of Ophelia will support a feminist interpretation may appear to be a political reading of *Hamlet,* but, in fact, by its exegetical approach it reaffirms the notion that the great traditions are all-encompassing and all-normative, the notion that subsumes women under the heading "mankind."

It seems to me perfectly plausible, however, to see Shakespeare as working within his own ideology that defined bastards, Jews, and women as by nature deformed or inferior, and as understanding the contradictions of that ideology without rejecting its basic tenets—so that, from a feminist standpoint, he was a misogynist—and as being nonetheless a great poet. To be sure, greatness involves a critical penetration of conventions but not necessarily or even frequently a radical rejection of them. If, in his villains, Shakespeare revealed the human being beneath the type, his characterization may have been not a denial of the type but a recognition of the complexity of all identity. The kingly ambition of the bastard, the "white" conscience of the Moor, the father love of the Jew, the woman's manly heart: these complexities are expressed in the terms of the contemporary ideology, and in fact Shakespeare uses these terms the more tellingly for not challenging them at the root.

But the root is what feminists have to be concerned with: what it means not to be a good woman or a bad one but to be a woman at all. Moreover, if a great writer need not be radical, neither need a great radical writer be feminist—but so what? It was only recently that the great Romantic poets conned us into believing that to be a great poet was to tell *the* absolute truth, to be the One prophetic voice for all Mankind. As the philosophy of the Other, feminism has had to reject the very conception of such authority—which, by extension, should permit feminist critics to distinguish between appreciative and political readings.

We should begin, therefore, by acknowledging the separate wholeness of the literary subject, its distinct vision that need not be ours—what the formalists have told us and told us about: its integrity. We need to acknowledge, also, that to respect that integrity by not asking questions of the text that it does not ask itself, to ask the text what questions to ask, will produce the fullest, richest reading. To do justice to Shelley, you do not approach him as you do Swift. But doing justice can be a contrary business, and there are aspects of the text that, as Kate Millett demonstrated,[1] a formalist explication actively obscures. If her intentionally tangential approach violated the terms of Henry Miller's work, for example, it also revealed aspects of the work that the terms had masked.

1. Kate Millett, *Sexual Politics* (Garden City, N.Y.: Doubleday & Co., 1970).

But she would not claim, I think, that her excavation of Miller's under-lying assumptions had not done damage to his architecture.

The contradiction between appreciation and political analysis is not peculiar to feminist readings, but those who encountered it in the past did not resolve it either. In fact, they too denied it, or tried to. Sartre, for instance, argued in *What Is Literature?* that a good novel could not pro-pound fascism. But then he also recognized that "the appearance of the work of art is a new event which cannot *be explained* by anterior data."[2] More recently, the Marxist Pierre Macherey has hung on the horns of the same dilemma by maintaining that the literary work is tied in-extricably to the life that produces it, but, although not therefore "in-dependent," it is nonetheless "autonomous" in being defined and struc-tured by laws uniquely proper to it.[3] (I cite Sartre and Macherey more or less at random among more or less left-wing critics because theirs is a situation somewhat like that of feminists, though less difficult, many would argue, in that they already have a voice of their own. Perhaps for that reason, the position of black critics in a world dominated by whites would more closely resemble that of women. But at any rate, the large category to which all these belong is that of the literary critic who is also and importantly a critic of her/his society, its political system, and its culture.)

My point is simply that there is no reason to deny the limits of ideological criticism, its reduction of texts that, however, it also illumi-nates in unique ways. As feminists at odds with our culture, we are at odds also with its literary traditions and need often to talk about texts in terms that the author did not use, may not have been aware of, and might indeed abhor. The trouble is that this necessity goes counter not only to our personal and professional commitment to all serious litera-ture but also to our training as gentlemen and scholars, let alone as Americans, taught to value, above all, value-free scholarship.

Doubtless the possibility of maintaining thereby a sympathetic ap-preciative critical posture is one of the attractions of dealing only or mainly with women's writings. With such material, ironically, it is possi-ble to avoid political judgment altogether, so that the same approach that for some represents the integration into their work of a political com-mitment to women can serve Patricia Meyer Spacks to make the point that "criticism need not be political to be aware."[4] She means by this that she will be able to recognize and describe a distinct female culture with-out evaluating either it or its patriarchal context politically. Of course she

2. Jean-Paul Sartre, *What Is Literature?* (New York: Harper Colophon, 1965), p. 40; emphasis in original.
3. Pierre Macherey, *Pour une théorie de la production littéraire* (Paris: Librairie François Maspero, 1966), pp. 66–68.
4. Patricia Meyer Spacks, *The Female Imagination* (New York: Avon Books, 1976), pp. 5, 6.

understands that all vision is mediated, so that the very selection of texts in which to observe the female imagination is judgment of a kind. But it is not ideological or normative judgment; rather it is an "arbitrary decision" that "reflects the operations of [her] imagination," a personal point of view, a "particular sensibility" with no particular political outlook. The important thing is that her "perception of the problems in every case derived from her reading of the books; the books were not selected to depict preconceived problems."

Spacks seeks in this way to disavow any political bias; but even critics who have chosen a woman-centered approach precisely for its political implications reassure us about their analytical detachment. Ellen Moers stipulates in her preface to *Literary Women* that "the literary women themselves, their language, their concerns, have done the organizing of this book." At the same time she means the book to be "a celebration of the great women who have spoken for us all."[5] Her choice of subject has thus been inspired by feminist thinking, but her approach remains supposedly neutral for she has served only as an informed amanuensis. The uncharacteristic naiveté of this stance is enforced, I think, by Moers's critical ambivalence—her wish, on the one hand, to serve a feminist purpose, and her sense, on the other, that to do so will compromise the study as criticism. So she strikes a stance that should enable her to be, like Spacks, aware but not political. Since in posing a question one already circumscribes the answer, such analytical neutrality is a phantom, however; nor was it even Spacks's goal. Her method of dealing with women separately but traditionally, treating their work as she would the opus of any mainstream school, suits her purpose, which is to define a feminine aesthetic transcending sexual politics. She actively wants to exclude political answers. Moers, seeking to discover the feminist in the feminine, is not as well served by that method; and Elaine Showalter's explicitly feminist study, *A Literature of Their Own*,[6] suggests that a political criticism may require something like the methodological reverse.

Showalter wrote her book in the hope that it would inspire women to "take strength in their independence to act in the world" and begin to create an autonomous literary universe with a "female tradition" as its "center." Coming at the end of the book, these phrases provide a resonant conclusion, for she has shown women writing in search of a wholeness the world denies them and creating an art whose own wholeness seems a sure ground for future autonomy. But if, in an effort to flesh out this vision, one turns back to earlier discussions, one finds that there she has depicted not actual independence but action despite dependence—and not a self-defined female culture either, but a sub-

5. Ellen Moers, *Literary Women: The Great Writers* (Garden City, N.Y.: Doubleday & Co., 1976), p. xvi.

6. Elaine Showalter, *A Literature of Their Own: British Women Novelists from Brontë to Lessing* (Princeton, N. J.: Princeton University Press, 1977), pp. 319, 11–12.

culture born out of oppression and either stunted or victorious only at often-fatal cost. Women, she writes at the beginning of the book, form such a "subculture within the framework of a larger society," and "the female literary tradition comes from the still-evolving relationships between women writers and their society." In other words, the meaning of that tradition has been bound up in its dependence. Now, it seems to me that much of what Showalter wants to examine in her study, indeed much of what she does examine, resolves itself into the difference for writers between acting independently as men do and resisting dependence as women do. If her conclusion on the contrary conflates the two, it is because the approach she takes, essentially in common with Spacks and Moers, is not well suited to her more analytical goals.

Like theirs, her book is defined territorially as a description of the circumscribed world of women writers. *A Literature of Their Own* is thus "an attempt to fill in the terrain between [the Austen peaks, the Brontë cliffs, the Eliot range, and the Woolf hills] and to construct a more reliable map from which to explore the achievements of English women novelists." The trouble is that the map of an enclosed space describes only the territory inside the enclosure. Without knowing the surrounding geography, how are we to evaluate this woman's estate, whose bordering peaks we have measured anyway, not by any internal dimensions, but according to those of Mount Saint Dickens and craggy Hardy? Still less can one envision the circumscribed province as becoming independently global—hence probably the visionary vagueness of Showalter's ending. Instead of a territorial metaphor, her analysis of the world of women as a subculture suggests to me a more fluid imagery of interacting juxtapositions the point of which would be to represent not so much the territory as its defining borders. Indeed, the female territory might well be envisioned as one long border, and independence for women not as a separate country but as open access to the sea.

Women (and perhaps some men not of the universal kind) must deal with their situation as a *pre*condition for writing about it. They have to confront the assumptions that render them a kind of fiction in themselves in that they are defined by others, as components of the language and thought of others. It hardly matters at this prior stage what a woman wants to write; its political nature is implicit in the fact that it is she (a "she") who will do it. All women's writing would thus be congenitally defiant and universally characterized by the blasphemous argument it makes in coming into being. And this would mean that the autonomous individuality of a woman's story or poem is framed by engagement, the engagement of its denial of dependence. We might think of the form this necessary denial takes (however it is individually interpreted, whether conciliatory or assertive) as analogous to genre, in being an issue, not of content, but of the structural formulation of the work's relationship to the inherently formally patriarchal language which is the only language we have.

Heretofore, we have tended to treat the anterior act by which women writers create their creativity as part of their lives as purely psychological, whereas it is also a conceptual and linguistic act: the construction of an enabling relationship with a language that of itself would deny them the ability to use it creatively. This act is part of their work as well and organic to the literature that results. Since men (on the contrary) can assume a natural capacity for creation, they begin there, giving individual shape to an energy with which they are universally gifted. If it is possible, then, to analyze the writings of certain men independently—not those of all men, but only of those members of a society's ruling group whose identity in fact sets the universal norm—this is because their writings come into existence independent of prior individual acts. Women's literature begins to take its individual shape before it is properly literature, which suggests that we should analyze it inclusive of its *ur*-dependence.

In fact, the criticism of women writers has of late more and more focused on the preconditions of their writing as the inspiration not only of its content but also of its form. The writer's self-creation is the primary concern of Sandra Gilbert and Susan Gubar's *Madwoman in the Attic*,[7] whose very title identifies global (therefore mad) denial as the hot core of women's art. This impressive culmination of what I have called the territorial approach to feminist criticism does with it virtually everything that can be done. In the way of culminations, it delivers us then before a set of problems that cannot be entirely resolved in its terms but that Gilbert and Gubar have uncovered. My earlier questioning can thus become a question: What do we understand about the world, about the whole culture, from our new understanding of the woman's sphere within it? This question looks forward to a development of the study of women in a universal context, but it also has retrospective implications for what we have learned in the female context.

Gilbert and Gubar locate the female territory in its larger context and examine the borders along which the woman writer defined herself. Coming into being—an unnatural being, she must give birth to herself—the female artist commits a double murder. She kills "Milton's bogey" and the specter Virginia Woolf called the "angel in the house," the patriarch and his wife, returning then to an empty universe she will people in her own image. Blasphemy was not until the woman artist was, and the world of women writers is created in sin and extends to a horizon of eternal damnation. For all women must destroy in order to create.

Gilbert and Gubar argue with erudition and passion, and their projection of the woman writer has a definitive ring. It also has a familiar and perhaps a contradictory ring. The artist as mad defiant blasphemer

7. Sandra Gilbert and Susan Gubar, *The Madwoman in the Attic: The Woman Writer and the Nineteenth-Century Literary Imagination* (New Haven, Conn.: Yale University Press, 1979). The chapter referred to at some length in this discussion is chap. 7, "Horror's Twin: Mary Shelley's Monstrous Eve."

or claustrophobic deviant in a society that denies such a person soulroom
is a Romantic image that not only applies also to men but does so in a way
that is particularly invidious to women, even more stringently denying
them their own identities than earlier ideologies did. That there be contradiction is only right, for when Blake hailed Satan as the hero of
Paradise Lost, he cast heroism in a newly contradictory mold. Satan is
archfiend and Promethean man, individualistic tyrant and revolutionary, architect and supreme wrecker of worlds. It should not be surprising that he is also at once the ultimate, the proto-exploiter of women,
and a feminist model. But it does complicate things, as Gilbert and
Gubar recognize: Mary Shelley found, in Milton, cosmic misogyny to
forbid her creation—and also the model for her rebellion. But then, was
her situation not just another version of the general Romantic plight,
shared with her friends and relatives, poet-blasphemers all?

No, because she confronted a contradiction that superseded and
preceded theirs; she was additionally torn and divided, forbidden to be
Satan by Satan as well as by God, ambivalent about being ambivalent. If
Satan was both demon and hero to the male poets, he offered women a
third possibility, that of Byronic lover and master, therefore a prior
choice: feminist assertion or feminine abandon. Here again, women had
to act before they could act, choose before they could choose.

But it is just the prior choosing and acting that shape the difference
between women's writing and men's that no study of only women's writing can depict. So, for instance, Gilbert and Gubar suggest that the
monster in Mary Shelley's *Frankenstein* embodies in his peculiar horror a
peculiarly female conception of blasphemy. It may well be, but I do not
think we can tell by looking only at *Frankenstein.* At the least we need to
go back and look at Satan again, not as a gloss already tending toward
Frankenstein but as an independent term, an example of what sinful
creation is—for a man. Then we need to know what it was for Mary
Shelley's fellow Romantics. We might then see the extra dimension of
her travail, being able to recognize it because it was extra—outside the
requirements of her work and modifying that work in a special way. To
reverse the frame of reference, if male critics have consistently missed
the woman's aspect of *Frankenstein,* it may be only in part because they
are not interested. Another reason could be that in itself the work appears as just another individual treatment of a common Romantic
theme. Put simply, then, the issue for a feminist reading of *Frankenstein* is
to distinguish its female version of Romanticism: an issue of relatedness
and historicity. Women cannot write monologues; there must be two in
the world for one woman to exist, and one of them has to be a man.

So in *The Madwoman in the Attic,* building on *Literary Women* and *A
Literature of Their Own,* feminist criticism has established the historical
relativity of the gender definitions that organize this culture; the patriarchal universe that has always represented itself as absolute has been

revealed as man-tailored to a masculine purpose. It is not nature we are looking at in the sexual politics of literature, but history: we know that now because women have rejected the natural order of ying and yang and lived to tell a different tale. I have been arguing that, to read this tale, one needs ultimately to relate it to the myths of the culture it comments on. The converse is also true; in denying the normative universality of men's writing, feminist criticism historicizes it, rendering it precisely, as "men's writing." On the back cover of *The Madwoman in the Attic* Robert Scholes is quoted as having written that "in the future it will be embarrassing to teach Jane Austen, Mary Shelley, the Brontës, George Eliot, Emily Dickinson, and their sisters without consulting this book." Not so embarrassing, one would like to add, as it should be to teach Samuel Richardson, Percy Bysshe Shelley, Charles Dickens, William Makepeace Thackeray, Walt Whitman, and their brothers without consulting a feminist analysis.

Indeed, in suggesting here that women critics adopt a method of radical comparativism, I have in mind as one benefit the possibility of demonstrating thereby the contingency of the dominant male traditions as well. Comparison reverses the territorial image along with its contained methodology and projects instead, as the world of women, something like a long border. The confrontations along that border between, say, *Portrait of a Lady* and *House of Mirth*, two literary worlds created by two gods out of one thematic clay, can light up the outer and most encompassing parameters (perimeters) of both worlds, illuminating the philosophical grounds of the two cosmic models, "natures" that otherwise appear unimpeachably absolute. This border (this no-man's-land) might have provided Archimedes himself a standpoint. Through the disengagements, the distancings of comparative analyses, of focusing on the relations between situations rather than on the situations themselves, one might be able to generate the conceptual equivalent of getting off this world and seeing it from the outside. At the same time, comparison also involves engagement by requiring one to identify the specific qualities of each term. The overabstraction of future visions has often been the flip side of nonanalytical descriptions of the present viewed only in its own internal terms. To talk about then and now as focuses of relations may be a way of tempering both misty fantasies and myopic documentations.

Thus the work of a woman—whose proposal to be a writer in itself reveals that female identity is not naturally what it has been assumed to be—may be used comparatively as an external ground for seeing the dominant literature whole. Hers is so fundamental a denial that its outline outlines as well the assumption it confronts. And such comparison works in reverse, too, for juxtaposed with the masculinist assumption we can also see whole the feminist denial and trace its limits. Denial always runs the risk of merely shaping itself in the negative image of what it rejects. If there is any danger that feminism may become trapped, either in winning for women the right to be men or in taking the opposite sentimental tack and celebrating the feminine identity of an oppressed past as ideal womanhood, these extremes can be better avoided when women's assumptions too can be seen down to their structural roots— from the other ground provided by men's writing.

Lest it appear that I am advocating a sort of comparison mongering, let me cite as a model, early blazing a path we have not followed very far, a study that on the surface is not at all comparative. Millett's *Sexual Politics* was all about comparison, however, about the abysses between standpoints, between where men stood to look at women and where women stood to be looked at. Facing these two at the book's starting point was Millett's construction of yet another lookout where a feminist might stand. As criticism per se, *Sexual Politics* may be flawed by its simplifying insistence on a single issue. But as ideological analysis, as model illuminator and "deconstructor," it remains our most powerful work. It is somewhat puzzling that, since then, so little has been written about the dominant literary culture whose ideas and methods of dominance were Millett's major concerns.[8] It may be that the critical shortcomings of so tangential an approach have been too worrisome. Certainly it is in reading the dominant "universal" literature that the contradictions of an ideological criticism become most acute. There are many ways of dealing with contradictions, however, of which only one is to try to resolve them. Another way amounts to joining a contradiction—engaging it not so much for the purpose of overcoming it as to tap its energy. To return one last time to the fulcrum image, a fulcrum is a point at which force is transmitted—the feminist fulcrum is not just any point in the culture where misogyny is manifested but one where misogyny is pivotal or crucial to the whole. The thing to look for in our studies, I believe, is the connection, the meshing of a definition of women and a definition of the world. And insofar as the former is deleterious, the connection will be contradictory; indeed, as the literary examples that follow suggest, one may recognize a point of connection by its contradictions. It will turn out, or I will try to show, that contradictions just such as that between ethical and aesthetic that we have tried to resolve away lest they belie our argument frequently are our

8. I want to cite two works, one recently published and one in progress, that do deal with the traditions of male writing. Judith Fetterley in *The Resisting Reader: A Feminist Approach to American Fiction* (Bloomington: Indiana University Press, 1978) writes that women should "resist the view of themselves presented in literature by refusing to believe what they read, and by arguing with it, begin to exorcize the male ideas and attitudes they have absorbed." Lee Edwards in her forthcoming *Labors of Psyche: Female Heroism and Fictional Form* expresses the somewhat different but related purpose of reclaiming language and mythology for women. My objections to both these approaches will be clear from the essay. Let me add here only that I also find them nonetheless extremely suggestive and often persuasive.

firmest and most fruitful grounds. The second part of this essay will attempt to illustrate this use of contradiction through the example of the American sentimental novel, a kind of women's writing in which the contradiction between ideology and criticism would appear well-nigh overwhelming.

II

The problem is all too easily stated: the sentimental novels that were best-sellers in America from the 1820s to the 1870s were written and read mostly by women, constituting an oasis of women's writing in an American tradition otherwise unusually exclusively male. But this oasis holds scant nourishment; in plain words, most of the women's writing is awful. What is a feminist critic to do with it? It is not that as a feminist she must praise women unthinkingly, but there is little point either in her just contributing more witty summaries of improbable plots and descriptions of impossible heroines to enliven the literary histories. There hardly needs a feminist come to tell us that E. D. E. N. Southworth's cautionary tales are a caution; and as to whether Susan Warner's *Wide Wide World* does set "an all-time record for frequency of references to tears and weeping,"[9] there are others already counting. We might do best, with Elizabeth Hardwick, to simply let it alone. In her collection of more or less unknown women's writings,[10] Hardwick selected works that were commendable in their own rights and discarded most of what she read as "so bad I just had to laugh—I wasn't even disappointed. The tradition was just too awful in the nineteenth-century."

Still, there it is, the one area of American writing that women have dominated and defined ostensibly in their own image, and it turned out just as the fellows might have predicted. It is gallant but also a little ingenuous of Hardwick to point out that men's sentimental writing was just as bad. For Hawthorne, whose *cri de coeur* against the "damned mob of scribbling women" still resonates in the hearts of his countrymen, did not invent the association between sentimentality and women. The scribbling women themselves did, ascribing their powers to draw readers deep into murky plots and uplift them to heavenly visions to the special gifts of a feminine sensibility. If there is no question of celebrating in the sentimentalists "great women who have spoken for us all," it seems just as clear that they spoke as women to women, and that, if we are to criticize the place of women in this culture, we need to account for the very large place they occupied—and still do; the sentimental mode re-

9. Henry Nash Smith, "The Scribbling Women and the Cosmic Success Story," *Critical Inquiry* 1, no. 1 (September 1974): 49–70.

10. Elizabeth Hardwick, *Rediscovered Fiction by American Women* (New York: Arno Press, 1978).

mains a major aspect of literary commerce, still mostly written and read
by women.

Although at bottom either way presents the same contradiction between politics and criticism, the sentimental novel would seem, therefore, to flip the problems encountered in *A Literature of Their Own, Literary Women,* and *The Madwoman in the Attic.* The issue there was to uncover
new aspects of works and writers that had more or less transcended the
limitations of the patriarchal culture—or failed and found tragedy. Inspired by their example, one had nonetheless to temper admiration with
critical distance. Here the difficulty lies instead in tempering rejection
with a recognition of kinship, kinship one is somewhat hesitant to acknowledge in that it rests on a shared subordination in which the sentimental novel appears altogether complicitous. For the sentimentalists
were prophets of compliance, to God the patriarch as to his viceroys on
earth. Their stories are morality dramas featuring heroines prone at the
start to react to unjust treatment by stamping their feet and weeping
rebellious tears, but who learn better and in the end find happiness in
"unquestioning submission to authority, whether of God or an earthly
father figure or society in general." They also find some more substantial
rewards, Mammon rising like a fairy godmother to bestow rich husbands
and fine houses. Conformity is powerful, and Henry Nash Smith's explication of it all has a definitive clarity: "The surrender of inner freedom,
the discipline of deviant impulses into rapturous conformity, and the
consequent achievement of both worldly success and divine grace merge
into a single mythical process, a cosmic success story."[11] If that success is
ill-gotten by Smith's lights, it can only appear still more tainted to a
feminist critic whose focus makes her acutely aware that the sweet sellout
is a woman and the inner freedom of women her first sale. With over-
grown conscience and shrunken libido, the sentimental heroine
enumerating her blessings in the many rooms of her husband's mansion
is the prototype of that deformed angel Virginia Woolf urged us to kill.

To kill within ourselves, that is. Thus we return to the recognition of
kinship that makes it necessary to understand the sentimentalists not
only the way critics generally have explained them but also as writers
expressing a specifically female response to the patriarchal culture. This
is a controversial venture that has resulted thus far in (roughly defined)
two schools of thought. One of these starts from Hawthorne's charge
that the popular novels usurped the place of serious literature. The title
of Ann Douglas's *Feminization of American Culture*[12] announces her thesis
that the sentimentalists exploited a literary Gresham's law to debase the
cultural currency with their feminine coin. But gold is at least hoarded,
while this bad money devalued outright Hawthorne's and Melville's
good. A tough, iconoclastic, and individualistic masculine high culture,

11. Smith, p. 51.
12. Ann Douglas, *The Feminization of American Culture* (New York: Avon Books, 1978).

the potential worthy successor of the tough Puritan ethos, was thus routed from the national arena by a conservative femininity that chained the arts to the corners of hearths and to church pews. Henceforth, and still today, a stultifying mass culture has emasculated the American imagination. Douglas does not blame women for this, for she sees them as themselves defined by their society. Even in the exploitation of their destructive power, she thinks, they meant well; nor would she wish for an equivalently simpleminded macho replacement to the feminized culture. But the implied alternative is nonetheless definitely masculine—in a good way, of course: strong, serious, and generously accepting of women who have abjured their feminine sensibilities. Not a hard thing to do, for if the choice is between Susan Warner and Melville, why were we not all born men?

That choice, however, is just the problem, its traditional limits generated by the Archimedean bind of trying to think about new issues in the old terms, when those terms do not merely ignore the new issues but deny them actively and thus force one instead into the old ways, offering choices only among them. The terms here are masculine and feminine as they participate in clusters of value that interpret American history and culture. It has been generally understood among cultural and social historians that the creative force in America is individualistic, active . . . masculine. Perhaps to a fault: Quentin Anderson would have liked the American self less imperially antisocial,[13] and before him Leslie Fiedler worried that its exclusive masculinity excluded heterosexual erotic love.[14] These analysts of American individualism do not necessarily come to judge it the same way, but they define it alike and alike therefore project as its logical opposition conformity, passive compliance, familialism . . . femininity. Huck Finn and Aunt Polly. The critical literature has until now mostly concentrated on Huck Finn, and *The Feminization of American Culture* completes the picture by focusing on Aunt Polly.

In the sense that its features are composed from real facts, "Aunt Polly" may well be a true picture. But her position in the composite American portrait, opposed in her trite conventionality to "his" rugged individualism, is not a function of facts alone but also of an interpretive scheme secured by a set of parallel dichotomies that vouch for one another: Aunt Polly is to Huck as feminine is to masculine; feminine is to masculine as Aunt Polly is to Huck. Only if we pull these apart will we be able to question the separate validity of either.

Potentially even more radically, Nina Baym[15] sets out to reconsider the component terms of the generally accepted dichotomy in the nineteenth century between female conformity and manly individu-

---

13. Quentin Anderson, *The Imperial Self* (New York: Alfred A. Knopf, Inc., 1971).

14. Leslie Fiedler, *Love and Death in the American Novel* (New York: Delta Books, 1966).

15. Nina Baym, *Woman's Fiction: A Guide to Novels by and about Women, 1820–1870* (Ithaca, N.Y.: Cornell University Press, 1978). Page numbers indicated in text.

alism, between female social conservatism and masculine rebellion. Representing the other school of thought about sentimentalism, this one in line with recent historical reconsideration of such ridiculed women's movements as temperance and revivalism, she argues that the women novelists too had their reasons. She answers Smith's accusation that the novels' "cosmic success story" pointed an arch-conservative moral by suggesting that for disenfranchised and property-deprived women to acquire wealth, social status, and some measure of control over their domestic environment could be considered a radical achievement, as ruling a husband by virtue of virtue might amount to subversion. As she sees it, "The issue [for the women in the novels] is power and how to live without it." They do not run their society and never hope to, so, short of revolution, no direct action can be taken. Even from their state of total dependence, however, these women can rise to take practical charge of their lives and acquire a significant measure of power by implementing the conservative roles to which the patriarchal society has relegated them. In this light, what Smith terms their "ethos of conformity" takes on another aspect and almost becomes a force for change, all depending on how you look at it.

Which is precisely the problem of this essay, emerging here with unusual clarity because both Smith and Baym approach the material ideologically. Even their descriptions, let alone their interpretations, show the effects of divergent standpoints. Consider how each summarizes the typical sentimental plot. Smith reports that *Wide Wide World* is the tale of "an orphan exposed to poverty and psychological hardships who finally attains economic security and high social status through marriage."[16] Baym reads the same novel as "the story of a young girl who is deprived of the supports she had rightly or wrongly depended on to sustain her throughout life and is faced with the necessity of winning her own way in the world" (p. 19). The second account stresses the role of the girl herself in defining her situation, so that the crux of her story becomes her passage from passivity to active engagement. On the contrary, with an eye to her environment and its use of her, Smith posits her as passive throughout, "exposed" at first, in the end married. Clearly this is not a matter of right or wrong readings but of a politics of vision.

It is as a discussion of the politics of vision that *Woman's Fiction* is perhaps most valuable. Baym has set out to see the novels from a different perspective, and indeed they look different. The impossible piety of the heroine, for instance, Baym views as an assertion of her moral strength against those who consider her an empty vessel, lacking ego and understanding and in need of constant supervision. Typically the heroine starts out sharing this view, taking herself very lightly and looking to the world to coddle and protect her. With each pious stand she

16. Smith, p. 49.

takes over the course of the novel, she becomes more self-reliant, until by the end she has "developed a strong conviction of her own worth" (p. 19) and becomes a model for female self-respect. Thus, the heroine's culminating righteousness and its concomitant rewards, that from one viewpoint prove the opportunistic virtues of submission, indicate to Baym a new and quite rare emergence of female power manifested in the avalanche of good things with which the story ends. To Smith those cornucopia endings are the payoff for mindless acquiescence, sweets for the sweet ruining the nation's palate for stronger meat. For Douglas they are a banquet celebrating the women's takeover; a starving Melville is locked out. But for Baym the comfort in which the heroine rests at last is her hard-earned just reward, the sentimental cult of domesticity representing a pragmatic feminism aimed primarily at establishing a place for women under their own rule.

In that spirit, she sees a more grown-up kind of sense than do most critics in the novels' prudishness, pointing out that, when they were written, the Richardsonian model they otherwise followed had become a tale of seduction. The women novelists, she suggests, were "unwilling to accept . . . a concept of woman as inevitable sexual prey" (p. 26); in a world where sexual politics hardly offered women a democratic choice, they preferred to eschew sex altogether rather than be raped. Here again, point of view is all. One recalls that Fiedler had a more ominous reading. According to him, the middle-class ladies who wrote the sentimental fiction had "grown too genteel for sex" but, being female, they still yearned "to see women portrayed as abused and suffering, and the male as crushed and submissive in the end";[17] so they desexed their heroes by causing them to love exceptionally good girls with whom sex was unthinkable.

Without sharing Fiedler's alarm over the state of American manhood, one has to concede that the sentimental novel, with its ethereal heroines and staunchly buttoned heroes, was indeed of a rarefied spirituality. That its typical plot traced, instead of physical seduction, the moral regeneration and all-around strengthening of erstwhile helpless women would appear all to the good; it is surely an improvement for women to cease being portrayed as inevitable victims. But the fact is that the sentimental heroines, perhaps rich as models, are rather poor as characters. Those inner possibilities they discover in becoming selfsufficient seem paradoxically to quench any interior life, so that we nod in both senses of the word when such a heroine "looks to marry a man who is strong, stable and safe." For, "she is canny in her judgment of men, and generally immune to the appeal of a dissolute suitor. When she feels such attraction, she resists it" (p. 41). Quite right, except we actually wish she would not: do we then regret the fragile fair who fell instantly

17. Fiedler, pp. 259–60.

and irrevocably in an earlier literature, or the "graceful deaths that created remorse in all one's tormentors" (p. 25) and in the story some sparks of life?

Baym is well aware of the problem and offers two possible analyses. In the first place, she says, the women novelists never claimed to be writing great literature. They thought of "authorship as a profession rather than a calling, as work and not art. Often the women deliberately and even proudly disavowed membership in an artistic fraternity." So they intentionally traded art for ideology, a matter of political rather than critical significance. "Yet," she adds (and here she is worth quoting at length because she has articulated clearly and forcefully a view that is important in feminist criticism),

> I cannot avoid the belief that "purely" literary criteria, as they have been employed to identify the best American works, have inevitably had a bias in favor of things male—in favor, say of whaling ships rather than the sewing circle as a symbol of the human community; in favor of satires on domineering mothers, shrewish wives, or betraying mistresses rather than tyrannical fathers, abusive husbands, or philandering suitors; displaying an exquisite compassion for the crises of the adolescent male, but altogether impatient with the parallel crises of the female. While not claiming literary greatness for any of the novels introduced in this study, I would like at least to begin to correct such a bias by taking their content seriously. And it is time, perhaps—though this task lies outside my scope here—to reexamine the grounds upon which certain hallowed American classics have been called great. [Pp. 14–15]

On the surface this is an attractive position, and, indeed, much of it is unquestionably valid; but it will not bear a close analysis. She is having it both ways, admitting the artistic limitations of the women's fiction ("I have not unearthed a forgotten Jane Austen or George Eliot, or hit upon even one novel that I would propose to set alongside *The Scarlet Letter*" [p. 14]) and at the same time denying the validity of the criteria that measure those limitations; disclaiming any ambition to reorder the literary canon, and, on second thought, challenging the canon after all—or rather challenging not the canon itself but the grounds for its selection.

There is much reason to reconsider these grounds, and such reconsideration should be one aim of an aggressive feminist criticism. But it has little to do with the problem at hand—the low quality of the women's fiction—that no reconsideration will raise. True, whaling voyages are generally taken more seriously than sewing circles, but it is also true that Melville's treatment of the whale hunt is a more serious affair than the sentimentalists' treatment of sewing circles. And the latter, when treated in the larger terms of the former, do get recognized—for example, Penelope weaving the shroud for Ulysses surrounded by her suitors, or, for that matter, the opening scene of *Middlemarch* in which two young girls quibble over baubles, situations whose resonance not even the most misogynist reader misses.

The first part of the explanation, that the women did not take *themselves* seriously, seems more promising. Baym tells us that they "were expected to write specifically for their own sex and within the tradition of their woman's culture rather than within the Great Tradition"; certainly, "they never presented themselves as followers in the footsteps of Milton or Spenser, seekers after literary immortality, or competitors with the male authors of their own time who were aiming at greatness" (p. 178). With this we come closer to the writing itself and therefore to the sources of its intrinsic success or failure. I want to stress intrinsic here as a way of recalling the distinction between a work as politics—its external significance—and as art. So when seeking to explain the intrinsic failures of the sentimentalists, one needs to look beyond their politics, beyond their relationships with publishers, critics, or audiences, to their relationship to writing as such. Melville wrote without the support of publishers, critics, and audiences—indeed, despite their active discouragement—so those cannot be the crucial elements. He did, however, have himself, he took himself seriously; as Whitman might have said, he *assumed* himself.

Now, no woman can assume herself because she has yet to create herself, and this the sentimentalists, acceding to their society's definition, did not do. To the extent that they began by taking the basic order of things as given, they forswore any claim on the primary vision of art[18] and saw themselves instead as interpreters of the established ethos, its guardians, or even, where needed, its restorers. My point is that, for all their virtual monopoly of the literary marketplace, the women novelists, being themselves conceived by others, were conceptually totally dependent. This means dependent on Melville himself and on the dominant culture of which he, but not they, was a full, albeit an alienated or even a reviled, member. His novel in the sentimental mode could take on sentimentalism because he had an alternative world on which to stand: himself. And although no one would wish on a friendly author the travail that brought forth *Pierre,* there it is nonetheless, the perfect example of what no woman novelist conceiving of herself not as an artist or maker but as a "professional"—read practitioner, implementor, transmitter, follower of a craft—could ever have written. *Pierre* does not know how to be acquiescently sentimental, it can only be *about* sentimentalism. The issue is self-consciousness, and in self-consciousness, it

18. I am aware that this analysis assumes a modern psychology of art, that "creation" has not always been the artist's mission, or tacit acceptance of the established ethos considered fatal. But we are here speaking of the nineteenth century, not of all time; and writers who did not challenge their society's values would also not have questioned its fundamental construction of artistic identity as individualistic and as authentically creative.

is self. With the example of Melville, we might then reconsider the relationship of the rebel to conventions. The rebel has his conventional definition too—that is, his is one possible interpretation of the conventions—so that he stands fully formed within the culture, at a leading edge. On the other hand, in this society women stand outside any of the definitions of complete being; hence perhaps the appeal to them of a literature of conformity and inclusion—and the extraordinary difficulty, but for the extraordinary few, of serious writing.

Indeed, Baym's defense of the women novelists, like that generally of the lesser achievement of women in any art, seems to me finally unnecessary. If history has treated women badly, it is entirely to be expected that a reduced or distorted female culture, one that is variously discouraged, embittered, obsessively parochial, or self-abnegating, will show it. There is little point then in claiming more than exists or in looking to past achievement as evidence of future promise: at this stage of history, we have the right, I think, simply to assert the promise.

If there is no cause for defensiveness, moreover, it does have its cost. In the case of the sentimental novel, for instance, too much apologia can obscure the hard question Baym implies but does not quite articulate, to wit, why are the ways in which the sentimental novel asserts that women can succeed precisely the ways that it fails as literature? *Is its ideological success tied to its artistic failure?* Is its lack of persuasiveness as art in some way the result of the strong ideological argument it makes for female independence? The issue, it seems, is not merely neglecting art for the sake of politics but actively sacrificing it. Which brings the discussion back to the Douglas thesis that since the sentimentalists universalized (Americanized) a debased feminine culture, the more powerful the women (authors and heroines both), the worse the literature and thereby the consequences for the whole culture. The great appeal of this argument is that it confronts squarely the painful contradiction of women becoming powerful not by overcoming but by exploiting their impotence.

I would like to suggest another possible explanation. The contradiction between the art and the politics of the sentimental novel arises, not surprisingly, at the point where the novelists confronted the tradition in which they were working and, for political reasons, rejected it formally: when they refused to perpetuate the image of the seduced and abandoned heroine and substituted in her stead the good girl who holds out to the happy (bitter or boring) end. The parent tradition is that of the novel of sensibility as it was defined in *Clarissa.* But before *Clarissa,* Richardson wrote *Pamela,* probably the prototype of the female "cosmic success story." Pamela begins powerless and ends up in charge, rewarded for her tenacious virtue (or her virtuous tenacity) by a commodious house, a husband, and all those same comforts of upper middle-class life that crowned the goodness of America's sentimental heroines. Indeed, *Pamela* had helped set up their new world, being the first novel actually printed here—by Benjamin Franklin, who understood both romance and commerce and knew how well they could work together. So did Pamela, of course, a superb pragmatist who not only foils a seducer but also turns him into a very nice husband. She is perhaps not so finely tuned or morally nice as her sentimental descendants, but she is quite as careful and controlled, as certain of her values, as unwilling to be victimized—and ultimately as triumphant. In contrast, Clarissa is helplessly enamored, seduced, destroyed. She is also the more interesting character and *Clarissa* the more complex story—can it be that weak victimized women make for better novels?

In the first part of this discussion, I made the point that the madness into which women artists are characterized as driven by social constraints needs to be compared with the similar state often attributed to male artists. The same need arises here, for male protagonists too are generally defeated, and, of course, Clarissa's seducer Lovelace dies along with her. But he is neither weak (in the helpless sense that she is) nor victimized; nor (to name doomed heroes at random) is Stendhal's Julien Sorel or Melville's Pierre. There is certainly no surprise in the contrast as such; we expect male characters to be stronger than female. The juxtaposition, however, may be suggesting something not already so evident: that as the distinctive individual identity of a male character typically is generated by his defiance, so that of a female character seems to come from her vulnerability, which thus would be organic to the heroine as a novelistic construct.

It seems reasonable to suppose that the novel, envisioning the encounter of the individual with his world in the modern idiom, posits as one of its structuring assumptions (an assumption that transcends the merely thematic, to function formally) the special form that sexual hierarchy has taken in modern times. The novel, we know, is organically individualistic: even when it deals with several equally important individuals, or attacks individualism itself, it is always about the unitary self versus the others. Moreover, it is about the generation, the becoming, of that self. I want to suggest that this process may be so defined as to require a definition of female characters that effectively precludes their becoming autonomous, so that indeed they would do so at the risk of the novel's artistic life.

Pamela represents the advent of a new form to deal with such new problems of the modern era as the transformation of the family and the newly dynamic mode of social mobility. *Pamela* works these out very well for its heroine, but there is something wrong in the resolution. Pamela's triumph means the defeat of Mr. B., who in his chastened state can hardly be the enterprising, potent entrepreneur that the rising middle class needs him to be. Her individualism has evolved at the cost of his; later Freud would develop a special term for such misadventures, but

Richardson must already have known that this was not the way it should be.

At any rate, he resolved this difficulty in his next work simply by raising the social status of his heroine. Since she was a servant, Pamela's quest for independent selfhood necessarily took a public form. To affirm her value and remain in possession of her self, Pamela had to assert her equality publicly; to claim herself, she had, in effect, to claim power. But as an established member of the powerful class, Clarissa is in full possession of its perquisites, notably that of being taken as honorably marriageable by the lords of her world. Though it is true that her family's greed for yet more wealth and status precipitates her crisis, the problems she faces are really not those of upward mobility. Standing at the other end of that process, she is profoundly unhappy with its results and with the internal workings of her society. Her story is about the conflict within, the problems that arise inside the middle-class world; and its marvelously suited theater for exploring these is the self within.

In thus locating itself inside the life of its dominant class, the novel only followed suit after older genres. But what is peculiar to this genre is that it locates the internal problems of its society still deeper inside, inside the self. Richardson's earlier novel had retained an older conception more like that of Defoe, identifying the self externally—hence *Pamela*'s interpretation of romance as commerce. *Clarissa*, on the contrary, now treats commerce in the terms of romance. Pamela had projected her inner world outward and identified her growth as a character with the extension of her power. But this approach tends to vitiate the distinction between the private self and the world out there that is the powerful crux of middle-class identity. *Clarissa* takes that distinction as its theme, and the locale of the novel henceforth is the interior life. I want to propose the thesis that this interior life, *whether lived by man or woman, is female,* so that women characters define themselves and have power only in this realm. Androgyny, in the novel, is a male trait enabling men to act from their male side and feel from their female side.

One common feminist notion is that the patriarchal society suppresses the interior lives of women. In literature, at least, this does not seem altogether true, for indeed the interior lives of female characters are the novel's mainstay. Instead, it is women's ability to act in the public domain that novels suppress, and again Richardson may have shown the way. *Pamela* developed its heroine by reducing its hero (in conventional terms). This compensation was, in fact, inevitable as long as the characters defined themselves the same way, by using and expanding the individualistic potency of the self. Since by this scheme Pamela would be less of a person and a character if she were less active, she had to compete with Mr. B. to the detriment of one of them—to the detriment also of conjugal hierarchy and beyond that, of their society, whose resulting universal competitiveness must become dangerously atomizing and possibly centrifugal. In a middle-class society, however, the family unit is meant to generate coherence, in that the home provides both a base and a terminus for the competitive activity of the marketplace. The self-reliant man necessarily subsumes his family, chief among them his wife, to his own identity; it is in the middle-class society above all that a man's home is his castle. But how can this subsuming be accomplished without denying identity to women altogether and thus seriously undermining their potency as helpmates as well? The problem lies in retaining this potency, that can come only from individualism, without suffering the consequences of its realization in individualistic competition. Tocqueville particularly admired the way this problem had been resolved in America. Women in the New World were free, strong, and independent, but they *voluntarily* stayed home. In other words, their autonomy was realized by being freely abandoned, after which, of course, they ceased to exist as characters—witness their virtual absence from the American novel.

The European novelist, at least the English and the French, either less sanguine about the natural goodness of middle-class values or more embattled with older norms, saw that this voluntary subjugation could be problematical. If women too are people, and people are individualists, might they not rebel? If they succeeded in this, social order would crumble; indeed, they could not succeed because they did not have the power. But the possibility, arising from the most basic terms of middle-class thought and also doomed by the very prevalence of that thought, emerged as the central drama of the modern imagination. It is precisely the drama of the suppressed self, the self who assumes the universal duty of self-realization but finds its individual model in absolute conflict with society. Then as it becomes the more heroically individualistic, the more self-realized, the more it pushes toward inevitable doom. If there is a tragic dimension to the novel, it is here in the doomed encounter between the female self and the middle-class world. This is the encounter Gilbert and Gubar have observed and attributed, too exclusively I think, to women. The lack of a comparative dimension can tend to obscure the distinction between representation and reality, to fuse them so that the female self simply is woman, if woman maligned. But, as Flaubert might have pointed out, many a male novelist has represented at least part of himself as female.

Which is not to suggest that European novelists were champions of women's rights. Their interest lay rather in the metaphorical potential of the female situation to represent the great Problem of modern society, the reconciliation of the private and the public realms, once the cornerstone of the new social and economic order has been laid in their alienation. Such reconciliation is problematical in that the self, granted its freedom, may not willingly accept social control; it may insist on its separate and other privacy, on the integrity of its interior vision. Clarissa wants to be and do otherwise than her world permits, and with that impulse, her inner self comes into view. It grows as she becomes less and less able to project her will, or rather as the incursions against her private self become more ferocious. Who, and what, Clarissa is finally *is* that private world.

I want to stress that in championing her alienated private self, the novel is not taking the side of real women, or even of female characters as female. Recent praise of *Clarissa* as a feminist document, or vindications of its heroine's behavior against her patriarchal oppressors, have not dealt clearly enough with the fact that her creator was a patriarch. If nonetheless he envisioned his heroine in terms with which feminists may sympathize, it is, I believe, because he viewed her as representing not really woman but the interior self, the female interior self in all men—in all men, but especially developed perhaps in writers, whose external role in this society is particularly incommensurate with their vision, who create new worlds but earn sparse recognition or often outright scorn in this one.

It is in this sense, I think, that Emma Bovary was Flaubert, or Anna Karenina, Tolstoy, or Isabel Archer, James. But the way Dorothea Brooke was George Eliot reveals the edge of this common identification between author and heroine, for Eliot, though herself a successful woman, cannot envision Dorothea as equally so.[19] One might suppose that she at least could have imagined her heroine, if not triumphant like Julien Sorel, acting out her doom rather than accepting it. It is one thing for male novelists to assume that women are incapable of effective action, but that women do so as well is more disturbing. I am suggesting that George Eliot was compelled by the form of her story to tell it as she did, that the novel as a genre precludes androgynously heroic women while and indeed *because* it demands androgynous heroes. In other words, the novel demands that the hero have an interior life and that this interior life be metaphorically female. The exterior life, on the other hand, is just as ineluctably male (and the novel has its share of active, manly women). These identifications are not consciously made as being convenient or realistic, in which case they would be vulnerable to conscious change. They are assumed, built into the genre as organic and natural; for, if action were either male or female, we would be back with the potentially castrating Pamela. She, however, bent her considerable force to enter the middle class, endorsing its values wholeheartedly. A similarly active Clarissa, an effective and militant Dorothea, must threaten the entire order of things.

The novel is critical, it examines and even approves the rebellions of

19. For an illuminating discussion of this phenomenon—of women novelists being unable to imagine female characters as strong as themselves—see Carolyn Heilbrun, "Women Writers and Female Characters: The Failure of Imagination," in *Reinventing Womanhood* (New York: W. W. Norton & Co., 1979), pp. 71–92.

Clarissa and Dorothea, but only after signaling its more basic acceptance of an order it locates, beyond political attack, in nature itself. Julien Sorel's alienation, however Napoleonic his aspirations, is associated throughout with the female part of his character; his sensitivity, his inability to accept the life and values his father offers him, these are repeatedly described as feminine traits, and the final act that destroys him bespeaks his feminine nature, much to the dismay of his male friends. In the mirror world of this and other novels, femaleness is not conservative but potentially revolutionary. At the same time, it is by cultural definition incapable of active fulfillment. In taking woman as metaphor for the interior life, then, and—far from suppressing her—expanding hers almost to the exclusion of any other life, the novel both claimed its interior, individualistic, alienated territory and placed the limits of that territory within the structures of the middle-class world it serves. George Eliot could have made Dorothea strong only by challenging these structures or by accepting them and depicting her as manly, thereby telling another story, perhaps *The Bostonians*. And no more than this latter would that story have challenged the conventional notions of feminine and masculine.

There is a third possibility for the novel, which is to return to *Pamela* and close down the alienated interior realm by having Dorothea act not out of internal impulses but in response to social dictates. This is what the sentimental novel does, its heroines realizing themselves in society actively but in full accord with its values and imperatives. This solution to the subversive threat posed by female individualism amounts to reversing the Richardsonian development from *Pamela* to *Clarissa*. We have a precise representation of that reversal—wrought, one is tempted to think, in deference to the greater solidity of the middle-class ethic in this country—in the first American novel, *Charlotte Temple* (1791). Its author, Susanna Rowson, copies the contemporary fashion of *Clarissa*-like stories but then, apparently thinking the better of such downbeat endings, tacks on a *Pamela* conclusion. Charlotte Temple, the disastrously fragile English heroine of the story, is carried off by a soldier en route to America; no sooner carried off than pregnant, no sooner pregnant than abandoned, no sooner abandoned than wandering the icy roads in winter in slippers and a thin shawl. She is charitably taken in to a hospitable fireside only to pass away, leaving an innocent babe and much remorse all around. At this point, however, with one perfectly satisfactory ending in place, Susanna Rowson adds a second.

While neglecting Charlotte, her faithless lover Montraville has fallen in love with New York's most desirable belle, Julia Franklin, an orphaned heiress who is "the very reverse of Charlotte Temple." Julia is strong, healthy, and of independent means and spirit. Her guardian entertains "too high an opinion of her prudence to scrutinize her actions so much as would have been necessary with many young ladies who were not blest with her discretion." Though Montraville has behaved badly toward the hapless Charlotte, he seems to be capable of a New World redemption. Overcome by guilt at Charlotte's death, he fights a duel to avenge her honor and is dangerously wounded but, more fortunate than Lovelace, is nursed back to health by the discreet Julia. A representative of the new American womanhood, far too sensible to be tempted by rakes, far too clear about the uses of romantic love ever to separate it from marriage, Julia has accomplished the "Pamela" reform. She marries Montraville, and he becomes one of New York's most upright (and affluent) citizens, the fallen seducer risen a husband through the ministrations of a woman who is not merely good but also strong—strong, of course, in being all that she should be. Thus in Julia Franklin the private and the public selves are one, and the novel, with no relation between them to explore and therefore no way or need to envision the private, comes to a speedy end. About Charlotte a far better novel could have and has been written, but about Julia really nothing but exemplary tales for young girls and their spinster aunts. Pioneer mother of sentimental heroines, she deeds them an ability to take care of themselves (by taking care) that Baym rightly applauds from a feminist viewpoint but that effectively does them in as literature. This implies a possibility no less drastic than that the novel, evolved to deal with the psychological and emotional issues of a patriarchal society, may not permit a feminist interpretation.

The possibility that an impotent feminine sensibility is a basic structure of the novel, representing one of the important ways that the novel embodies the basic structures of this society, would suggest more generally that the achievement of female autonomy must have radical implications not only politically but also for the very forms and categories of all our thinking. Yet as students of this thinking, we are not only implicated in it but many of us committed to much of it. Literary criticism especially, because it addresses the best this thinking has produced, exposes this paradox in all its painful complexity—while also revealing the extraordinary possibility of our seeing the old world from a genuinely new perspective.

This analysis of novelistic form has been speculative, of course, a way of setting the issues of women's writing in the context of the whole literature in order to illustrate the uses of a comparative viewpoint as an alternative footing at the critical distance needed for re-vision. It has also been an exercise in joining rather than avoiding the contradiction between ideological and appreciative criticism on the supposition that the crucial issues manifest themselves precisely at the points of contradiction. As a method this has further implications I cannot pursue here. Let me suggest only that to focus on points of contradiction as the places where we can see the whole structure of our world most clearly implies the immanent relativity of all perception and knowledge. Thus, what appears first as a methodological contradiction, then becomes a subject in itself, seems finally to be shaping something like a new epistemology. But then, it is only right that feminism, as rethinking, rethink thinking itself.

Humanities Division
State University of New York College at Purchase

What Became of God the Mother?
Conflicting Images of God in
Early Christianity

Elaine H. Pagels

Unlike many of his contemporaries among the deities of the ancient Near East, the God of Israel shares his power with no female divinity, nor is he the divine Husband or Lover of any.[1] He scarcely can be characterized in any but masculine epithets: King, Lord, Master, Judge, and Father.[2] Indeed, the absence of feminine symbolism of God marks Judaism, Christianity, and Islam in striking contrast to the world's other religious traditions, whether in Egypt, Babylonia, Greece, and Rome or Africa, Polynesia, India, and North America. Jewish, Christian, and Islamic theologians, however, are quick to point out that God is not to be considered in sexual terms at all. Yet the actual language they use daily in worship and prayer conveys a different message and gives the distinct impression that God is thought of in exclusively *masculine* terms. And while it is true that Catholics revere Mary as the mother of Jesus, she cannot be identified as divine in her own right: if she is "mother of God," she is not "God the Mother" on an equal footing with God the Father.

Christianity, of course, added the trinitarian terms to the Jewish description of God. And yet of the three divine "Persons," two—the Father and Son—are described in masculine terms, and the third—the

This inquiry began as a short talk delivered at the Conference on Women at Bryn Mawr College, initiated by Clare Wofford; it was developed for delivery at "The Scholar and the Feminist III: The Search for Origins," a conference sponsored by the Barnard Women's Center and organized by Jane Gould, Hester Eisenstein, and Emily Kofron. I am grateful for their invitations and for criticism and suggestions offered by many colleagues, especially Cyril Richardson, Wayne Meeks, Nelle Morton, and Rayna R. Reiter.

1. Where the God of Israel is characterized as husband and lover in the Old Testament (OT), his spouse is described as the community of Israel (i.e., Isa. 50:1, 54:1–8; Jer. 2:2–3, 20–25, 3:1–20; Hos. 1–4, 14) or as the land of Israel (cf. Isa. 62:1–5).

2. One may note several exceptions to this rule: Deut. 32:11; Hos. 11:1; Isa. 66:12 ff; Num. 11:12.

Spirit—suggests the sexlessness of the Greek neuter term *pneuma.* This is not merely a subjective impression. Whoever investigates the early development of Christianity—the field called "patristics," that is, study of "the fathers of the church"—may not be surprised by the passage that concludes the recently discovered, secret *Gospel of Thomas:* "Simon Peter said to them [the disciples]: Let Mary be excluded from among us, for she is a woman, and not worthy of Life. Jesus said: Behold I will take Mary, and make her a male, so that she may become a living spirit, resembling you males. For I tell you truly, that every female who makes herself male will enter the Kingdom of Heaven."[3] Strange as it sounds, this only states explicitly what religious rhetoric often assumes: that the men form the legitimate body of the community, while women will be allowed to participate only insofar as their own identity is denied and assimilated to that of the men.

Further exploration of the texts which include this *Gospel*—written on papyrus, hidden in large clay jars nearly 1,600 years ago—has identified them as Jewish and Christian gnostic works which were attacked and condemned as "heretical" as early as A.D. 100–150. What distinguishes these "heterodox" texts from those that are called "orthodox" is at least partially clear: they abound in feminine symbolism that is applied, in particular, to God. Although one might expect, then, that they would recall the archaic pagan traditions of the Mother Goddess, their language is to the contrary specifically Christian, unmistakably related to a Jewish heritage. Thus we can see that certain gnostic Christians diverged even more radically from the Jewish tradition than the early Christians who described God as the "three Persons" or the Trinity. For instead of a monistic and masculine God, certain of these texts describe God as a dyadic being, who consists of *both* masculine and feminine elements. One such group of texts, for example, claims to have received a secret tradition from Jesus through James, and significantly, through Mary Magdalene.[4] Members of this group offer prayer to *both* the divine Father and Mother: "From Thee, Father, and through Thee, Mother, the two immortal names, Parents of the divine being, and thou, dweller in heaven, mankind of the mighty name. . . ."[5] Other texts indicate that their authors had pondered the nature of the beings to whom a single, masculine God proposed, "Let us make mankind in our image, after our likeness" (Gen. 1:26). Since the Genesis account goes on to say that mankind was created "male and female" (1:27), some concluded, apparently, that the God in whose image we are created likewise must be both masculine and feminine—both Father and Mother.

3. *The Gospel according to Thomas* (hereafter cited as *ET*), ed. A. Guillaumount, H. Ch. Puech, G. Quispel, W. Till, Yassah 'Abd-al-Masih (London: Collins, 1959), logion 113–114.

4. Hippolytus, *Refutationis Omnium Haeresium* (hereafter cited as *Ref*), ed. L. Dunker, F. Schneidewin (Göttingen, 1859), 5.7.

5. *Ref*, 5.6.

The characterization of the divine Mother in these sources is not simple since the texts themselves are extraordinarily diverse. Nevertheless, three primary characterizations merge. First, a certain poet and teacher, Valentinus, begins with the premise that God is essentially indescribable. And yet he suggests that the divine can be imagined as a Dyad consisting of two elements: one he calls the Ineffable, the Source, the Primal Father; the other, the Silence, the Mother of all things.[6] Although we might question Valentinus's reasoning that Silence is the appropriate complement of what is Ineffable, his equation of the former with the feminine and the latter with the masculine may be traced to the grammatical gender of the Greek words. Followers of Valentinus invoke this feminine power, whom they also call "Grace" (in Greek, the feminine term *charis*), in their own private celebration of the Christian eucharist: they call her "divine, eternal Grace, She who is before all things."[7] At other times they pray to her for protection as the Mother, "Thou enthroned with God, eternal, mystical Silence."[8] Marcus, a disciple of Valentinus, contends that "when Moses began his account of creation, he mentioned the Mother of all things at the very beginning, when he said, 'In the beginning God created the heavens and the earth,' "[9] for the word "beginning" (in Greek, the feminine *arche*) refers to the divine Mother, the source of the cosmic elements. When they describe God in this way different gnostic writers have different interpretations. Some maintain that the divine is to be considered masculo-feminine—the "great male-female power." Others insist that the terms are meant only as metaphors—for, in reality, the divine is *neither* masculine nor feminine. A third group suggests that one can describe the Source of all things in *either* masculine or feminine terms, depending on which aspect one intends to stress.[10] Proponents of these diverse views agree, however, that the divine is to be understood as consisting of a harmonious, dynamic relationship of opposites—a concept that may be akin to the eastern view of *yin* and *yang* but remains antithetical to orthodox Judaism and Christianity.

A second characterization of the divine Mother describes her as Holy Spirit. One source, the *Secret Book of John,* for example, relates how John, the brother of James, went out after the crucifixion with "great grief," and had a mystical vision of the Trinity: "As I was grieving . . . the heavens were opened, and the whole creation shone with an unearthly light, and the universe was shaken. I was afraid . . . and behold . . . a unity in three forms appeared to me, and I marvelled: how

6. Irenaeus, *Adversus Haereses* (hereafter cited as *AH*), ed. W. W. Harvey (Cambridge, 1857), 1.11.1.
7. Ibid., 1.13.2.
8. Ibid., 1.13.6.
9. Ibid., 1.18.2.
10. Ibid., 1.11.5.—21.1, 3; *Ref,* 6.29.

can a unity have three forms?" To John's question the vision answers: "It said to me, 'John, John, why do you doubt, or why do you fear? . . . I am the One who is with you always: I am the Father; I am the Mother; I am the Son.' "[11] John's interpretation of the Trinity—as Father, Mother, and Son—may not at first seem shocking but is perhaps the more natural and spontaneous interpretation. Where the Greek terminology for the Trinity, which includes the neuter term for spirit *(pneuma)*, virtually requires that the third "Person" of the Trinity be asexual, the author of the *Secret Book* looks to the Hebrew term for spirit, *ruah*—a feminine word. He thus concludes, logically enough, that the feminine "Person" conjoined with Father and Son must be the Mother! Indeed, the text goes on to describe the Spirit as Mother: ". . . the image of the invisible virginal perfect spirit. . . . She became the mother of the all, for she existed before them all, the mother-father [matropater]."[12] This same author, therefore, alters Genesis 1:2 ("the Spirit of God moved upon the face of the deep") to say "the Mother then was moved. . . ."[13] The secret *Gospel to the Hebrews* likewise has Jesus speak of "my Mother, the Spirit."[14] And in the *Gospel of Thomas*, Jesus contrasts his earthly parents, Mary and Joseph, with his divine Father—the Father of Truth—and his divine Mother, the Holy Spirit. The author interprets a puzzling saying of Jesus in the New Testament ("whoever does not hate his father and mother is not worthy of me") by adding: "Whoever does not love his father and his mother in my way cannot be my disciple; for my [earthly] mother gave me death but my true Mother gave me the Life."[15] Another secret gnostic gospel, the *Gospel of Phillip*, declares that whoever becomes a Christian "gains both a father and a mother."[16] The author refers explicitly to the feminine Hebrew term to describe the Spirit as "Mother of many."[17]

If these sources suggest that the Spirit constitutes the maternal element of the Trinity, the *Gospel of Phillip* makes an equally radical suggestion concerning the doctrine that later developed as the virgin birth. Here again the Spirit is praised as both Mother and Virgin, the counterpart—and consort—of the Heavenly Father: "If I may utter a mystery, the Father of the all united with the Virgin who came down,"[18] that is, with the Holy Spirit. Yet because this process is to be understood

11. *Apocryphon Johannis* (hereafter cited as *AJ*), ed. S. Giversen (Copenhagen: Prostant Apud Munksgaard, 1963), 47.20–48.14.
12. *AJ*, 52.34–53.6.
13. Ibid., 61.13–14.
14. Origen, *Commentary on John*, 2.12; *Hom. On Jeremiah*, 15.4.
15. *ET*, 101. The text of this passage is badly damaged; I follow here the reconstruction of G. MacRae of the Harvard Divinity School.
16. *L'Evangile selon Phillipe* (hereafter cited as *EP*), ed. J. E. Ménard (Leiden: Brill, 1967), logion 6.
17. *EP*, logion 36.
18. Ibid., logion 82.

symbolically, and not literally, the Spirit remains a virgin! The author explains that "for this reason, Christ was 'born of a virgin' "—that is, of the Spirit, his divine Mother. But the author ridicules those "literal-minded" Christians who mistakenly refer the virgin birth to Mary, Jesus' earthly mother, as if she conceived apart from Joseph: "Such persons do not know what they are saying; for when did a female ever impregnate a female?"[19] Instead, he argues, virgin birth refers to the mysterious union of the two divine powers, the Father of the All with the Holy Spirit.

Besides the eternal, mystical Silence, and besides the Holy Spirit, certain gnostics suggest a third characterization of the divine Mother as Wisdom. Here again the Greek feminine term for wisdom, *sophia,* like the term for spirit, *ruah,* translates a Hebrew feminine term, *hokhmah.* Early interpreters had pondered the meaning of certain biblical passages, for example, Proverbs: "God made the world in Wisdom." And they wondered if Wisdom could be the feminine power in which God's creation is "conceived"? In such passages, at any rate, Wisdom bears two connotations: first, she bestows the Spirit that makes mankind wise; second, she is a creative power. One gnostic source calls her the "first universal creator";[20] another says that God the Father was speaking to her when he proposed to "make mankind in our image."[21] The *Great Announcement,* a mystical writing, explains the Genesis account in the following terms: ". . . One Power that is above and below, self-generating, self-discovering, its own mother; its own father; its own sister; its own son: Father, Mother, unity, Root of all things."[22] The same author explains the mystical meaning of the Garden of Eden as a symbol of the womb: "Scripture teaches us that this is what is meant when Isaiah says, 'I am he that formed thee in thy mother's womb' [Isaiah 44:2]. The Garden of Eden, then, is Moses' symbolic term for the womb, and Eden the placenta, and the river which comes out of Eden the navel, which nourishes the fetus. . . ."[23] This teacher claims that the Exodus, consequently, symbolizes the exodus from the womb, "and the crossing of the Red Sea, they say, refers to the blood." Evidence for this view, he adds, comes directly from "the cry of the newborn," a spontaneous cry of praise for "the glory of the primal being, in which all the powers above are in harmonious embrace."[24]

The introduction of such symbolism in gnostic texts clearly bears implications for the understanding of human nature. The *Great An-*

---

19. Ibid., logion 17.
20. *Extraits de Théodote* (hereafter cited as *Exc*), ed. F. Sagnard, Sources chrétiennes 23 (Paris: Sources chrétiennes, 1948).
21. *AH*, 1.30.6.
22. *Ref,* 6.17.
23. Ibid., 6.14.
24. *AH*, 1.14.7–8.

nouncement for example, having described the Source as a masculo-feminine being, a "bisexual Power," goes on to say that "what came into being from that Power, that is, humanity, being one, is found to be two: a male-female being that bears the female within it."[25] This refers to the story of Eve's "birth" out of Adam's side (so that Adam, being one, is "discovered to be two," an androgyne who "bears the female within him"). Yet this reference to the creation story of Genesis 2—an account which inverts the biological birth process, and so effectively denies the creative function of the female—proves to be unusual in gnostic sources. More often, such sources refer instead to the first creation account in Genesis 1:26–27. ("And God said, let us make mankind in Our image, after Our image and likeness . . . in the image of God he created him: male and female he created them"). Rabbis in Talmudic times knew a Greek version of the passage, one that suggested to Rabbi Samuel bar Nahman that "when the Holy One . . . first created mankind, he created him with two faces, two sets of genitals, four arms, and legs, back to back: Then he split Adam in two, and made two backs, one on each side."[26] Some Jewish teachers (perhaps influenced by the story in Plato's *Symposium*) had suggested that Genesis 1:26–27 narrates an androgynous creation—an idea that gnostics adopted and developed. Marcus (whose prayer to the Mother is given above) not only concludes from this account that God is dyadic ("Let *us* make mankind"), but also that "mankind, which was formed according to the image and likeness of God [Father and Mother] was masculo-feminine."[27] And his contemporary, Theodotus, explains: "the saying that Adam was created 'male and female' means that the male and female elements together constitute the finest production of the Mother, Wisdom."[28] We can see, then, that the gnostic sources which describe God in both masculine and feminine terms often give a similar description of human nature as a dyadic entity, consisting of two equal male and female components.

All the texts cited above—secret "gospels," revelations, mystical teachings—are among those rejected from the select list of twenty-six that comprise the "New Testament" collection. As these and other writings were sorted and judged by various Christian communities, every one of these texts which gnostic groups revered and shared was rejected from the canonical collection as "heterodox" by those who called themselves "orthodox" (literally, straight-thinking) Christians. By the time this process was concluded, probably as late as the year A.D. 200, virtually all the feminine imagery for God (along with any suggestion of an an-

25. *Ref*, 6.18.
26. Genesis Rabba 8.1, also 17.6; cf. Levitius Rabba 14. For an excellent discussion of androgyny, see W. Meeks, "The Image of the Androgyne: Some Uses of a Symbol in Earliest Christianity," *History of Religions* 13 (1974): 165–208.
27. *AH*, 1.18.2.
28. *Exc*, 21.1.

drogynous human creation) had disappeared from "orthodox" Christian tradition.

What is the reason for this wholesale rejection? The gnostics themselves asked this question of their "orthodox" attackers and pondered it among themselves. Some concluded that the God of Israel himself initiated the polemics against gnostic teaching which his followers carried out in his name. They argued that he was a derivative, merely instrumental power, whom the divine Mother had created to administer the universe, but who remained ignorant of the power of Wisdom, his own Mother: "They say that the creator believed that he created everything by himself, but that, in reality, he had made them because his Mother, Wisdom, infused him with energy, and had given him her ideas. But he was unaware that the ideas he used came from her: He was even ignorant of his own Mother."[29] Folllowers of Valentinus suggested that the Mother herself encouraged the God of Israel to think that he was acting autonomously in creating the world; but, as one teacher adds, "It was because he was foolish and ignorant of his Mother that he said, 'I am God; there is none beside me.' "[30] Others attribute to him the more sinister motive of jealousy, among them the *Secret Book of John:* "He said, 'I am a jealous God, and you shall have no other God before me,' already indicating that another god does exist. For if there were no other god, of whom would he be jealous? Then the Mother began to be distressed. . . ."[31] A third gnostic teacher describes the Lord's shock, terror, and anxiety "when he discovered that he was not the God of the universe." Gradually his shock and fear gave way to wonder, and finally he came to welcome the teaching of Wisdom. The gnostic teacher concluded: "This is the meaning of the saying, 'The fear of the Lord is the beginning of wisdom.' "[32]

All of these are, of course, mythical explanations. To look for the actual, historical reasons why these gnostic writings were suppressed is an extremely difficult proposition, for it raises the much larger question of how (i.e., by what means and what criteria) certain ideas, including those expressed in the texts cited above, came to be classified as heretical and others as orthodox by the beginning of the third century. Although the research is still in its early stages, and this question is far from being solved, we may find one clue if we ask whether these secret groups derived any practical, social consequences from their conception of God—and of mankind—that included the feminine element? Here again, the answer is yes and can be found in the orthodox texts themselves. Irenaeus, an orthodox bishop, for example, notes with dismay that women in particular are attracted to heretical groups—especially to

29. *Ref,* 6.33.
30. *AH,* 1.5.4; *Ref,* 6.33.
31. *AJ,* 61.8–14.
32. *Ref,* 7.26.

Marcus's circle, in which prayers are offered to the Mother in her aspects as Silence, Grace, and Wisdom; women priests serve the eucharist together with men; and women also speak as prophets, uttering to the whole community what "the Spirit" reveals to them.[33] Professing himself to be at a loss to understand the attraction that Marcus's group holds, he offers only one explanation: that Marcus himself is a diabolically successful seducer, a magician who compounds special aphrodisiacs to "deceive, victimize, and defile" these "many foolish women!" Whether his accusation has any factual basis is difficult, probably impossible, to ascertain. Nevertheless, the historian notes that accusations of sexual license are a stock-in-trade of polemical arguments.[34] The bishop refuses to admit the possibility that the group might attract Christians—especially women—for sound and comprehensible reasons. While expressing his own moral outrage, Tertullian, another "father of the church," reveals his fundamental desire to keep women out of religion: "These heretical women—how audacious they are! They have no modesty: they are bold enough to teach, to engage in argument, to enact exorcisms, to undertake cures, and, it may be, even to baptize!"[35] Tertullian directs yet another attack against "that viper"—a woman teacher who led a congregation in North Africa.[36] Marcion had, in fact, scandalized his "orthodox" contemporaries by appointing women on an equal basis with men as priests and bishops among his congregations.[37] The teacher Marcillina also traveled to Rome to represent the Carpocratian group, an esoteric circle that claimed to have received secret teaching from Mary, Salome, and Martha.[38] And among the Montanists, a radical prophetic circle, the prophet Philumene was reputed to have hired a male secretary to transcribe her inspired oracles.[39]

Other secret texts, such as the *Gospel of Mary Magdalene* and the *Wisdom of Faith,* suggest that the activity of such women leaders challenged and therefore was challenged by the orthodox communities who regarded Peter as their spokesman. The *Gospel of Mary* relates that Mary tried to encourage the disciples after the crucifixion and to tell them what the Lord had told her privately. Peter, furious at the suggestion, asks, "Did he then talk secretly with a woman, instead of to us? Are we to go and learn from *her* now? Did he love her more than us?" Distressed at his rage, Mary then asks Peter: "What do you think? Do you think I made this up in my heart? Do you think I am lying about the Lord?" Levi

33. *AH,* 1.13.7.

34. Ibid., 1.13.2–5.

35. Tertullian, *De Praescriptione Haereticorum* (hereafter cited as *DP*), ed. E. Oehler (Lipsius, 1853–54), p. 41.

36. *De Baptismo* 1. I am grateful to Cyril Richardson for calling my attention to this passage and to the three subsequent ones.

37. Epiphanes, *De Baptismo,* 42.5.

38. *AH,* 1.25.6.

39. *DP,* 6.30.

breaks in at this point to mediate the dispute: "Peter, you are always irascible. You object to the woman as our enemies do. Surely the Lord knew her very well, and indeed, he loved her more than us. . . ." Then he and the others invite Mary to teach them what she knows.[40] Another argument between Peter and Mary occurs in *Wisdom of Faith*. Peter complains that Mary is dominating the conversation, even to the point of displacing the rightful priority of Peter himself and his brethren; he urges Jesus to silence her—and is quickly rebuked. Later, however, Mary admits to Jesus that she hardly dares to speak freely with him, because "Peter makes me hesitate: I am afraid of him, because he hates the female race." Jesus replies, that whoever receives inspiration from the Spirit is divinely ordained to speak, whether man or woman.[41]

As these texts suggest, then, women were considered equal to men, they were revered as prophets, and they acted as teachers, traveling evangelists, healers, priests, and even bishops. In some of these groups they played leading roles and were *excluded* from them in the orthodox churches, at least by A.D. 150–200. Is it possible, then, that the recognition of the feminine element in God and the recognition of mankind as a male and female entity bore within it the explosive social possibility of women acting on an equal basis with men in positions of authority and leadership? If this were true it might lead to the conclusion that these gnostic groups, together with their conception of God and human nature, were suppressed only because of their positive attitude toward women. But such a conclusion would be a mistake—a hasty and simplistic reading of the evidence. In the first place, orthodox Christian doctrine is far from wholly negative in its attitude toward women. Second, many other elements of the gnostic sources diverge in fundamental ways from what came to be accepted as orthodox Christian teaching. To examine this process in detail would require a much more extensive discussion than is possible here. Nevertheless the evidence does indicate that two very different patterns of sexual attitudes emerged in orthodox and gnostic circles. In simplest form, gnostic theologians correlate their description of God in both masculine and feminine terms with a complementary description of human nature. Most often they refer to the creation account of Genesis 1, which suggests an equal (or even androgynous) creation of mankind. This conception carries the principle of equality between men and women into the practical social and political structures of gnostic communities. The orthodox pattern is strikingly different: it describes God in exclusively masculine terms, and often uses Genesis 2 to describe how Eve was created from Adam and for his fulfillment. Like the gnostic view, the orthodox also translates into sociological practice: by the late second century, orthodox Christians

40. *The Gospel according to Mary,* Codex Berolinensis, *BG,* 8502,1.7.1–1.19.5, ed., intro., and trans. G. MacRae, unpublished manuscript.

41. *Pistis Sophia,* ed. Carl Schmidt (Berlin: Academie-Verlag, 1925), 36 (57), 71 (161).

came to accept the domination of men over women as the proper, God-given order—not only for the human race, but also for the Christian churches. This correlation between theology, anthropology, and sociology is not lost on the apostle Paul. In his letter to the disorderly Corinthian community, he reminds them of a divinely ordained chain of authority: as God has authority over Christ, so the man has authority over the woman, argues Paul citing Genesis 2: "The man is the image and glory of God, but the woman is the glory of man. For man is not from woman, but woman from man; and besides, the man was not created for the woman's sake, but the woman for the sake of the man."[42] Here the three elements of the orthodox pattern are welded into one simple argument: the description of God corresponds to a description of human nature which authorizes the social pattern of male domination.

A striking exception to this orthodox pattern occurs in the writings of one revered "father of the church," Clement of Alexandria. Clement identifies himself as orthodox, although he knows members of gnostic groups and their writings well; some scholars suggest that he was himself a gnostic initiate. Yet his own works demonstrate how all three elements of what we have called the "gnostic pattern" could be worked into fully "orthodox" teaching. First, Clement characterizes God not only in masculine but also in feminine terms: "The Word is everything to the child, both father and mother, teacher and nurse. . . . The nutriment is the milk of the Father . . . and the Word alone supplies us children with the milk of love, and only those who suck at this breast are truly happy. . . . For this reason seeking is called sucking; to those infants who seek the Word, the Father's loving breasts supply milk."[43] Second, in describing human nature, he insists that "men and women share equally in perfection, and are to receive the same instruction and discipline. For the name 'humanity' is common to both men and women; and for us 'in Christ there is neither male nor female.' "[44] Even in considering the active participation of women with men in the Christian community Clement offers a list—unique in orthodox tradition—of women whose achievements he admires. They range from ancient examples, like Judith, the assassin who destroyed Israel's enemy, to Queen Esther, who rescued her people from genocide, as well as others who took radical political stands. He speaks of Arignole the historian, of Themisto the Epicurean philosopher, and of many other women philosophers including two who studied with Plato and one trained by Socrates. Indeed, he cannot con-

---

42. 1 Cor. 11:7–9. For discussion, see R. Scroggs, "Paul and the Eschatological Woman," *Journal of the American Academy of Religion* 40 (1972): 283–303; R. Scroggs, "Paul and the Eschatological Woman: Revisited," *Journal of the American Academy of Religion* 42 (1974): 532–37; and E. Pagels, "Paul and Women: A Response to Recent Discussion," *Journal of the American Academy of Religion* 42 (1972): 538–49.

43. Clement Alexandrinus, *Paidegogos*, ed. O. Stählin (Leipzig, 1905), 1.6.

44. Ibid., 1.4.

tain his praise: "What shall I say? Did not Theano the Pythagoran make such progress in philosophy than when a man, staring at her, said, 'Your arm is beautiful,' she replied, 'Yes, but it is not on public display.' "[45] Clement concludes his list with famous women poets and painters.

If the work of Clement, who taught in Egypt before the lines of orthodoxy and heresy were rigidly drawn (ca. A.D. 160–80) demonstrates how gnostic principles could be incorporated even into orthodox Christian teaching, the majority of communities in the western empire headed by Rome did not follow his example. By the year A.D. 200, Roman Christians endorsed as "canonical" the pseudo-Pauline letter to Timothy, which interpreted Paul's views: "Let a woman learn in silence with full submissiveness. I do not allow any woman to teach or to exercise authority over a man; she is to remain silent, *for* [note Gen. 2!] Adam was formed first, then Eve and furthermore, Adam was not deceived, but the woman was utterly seduced and came into sin. . . ."[46] How are we to account for this irreversible development? The question deserves investigation which this discussion can only initiate. For example, one would need to examine how (and for what reasons) the zealously patriarchal traditions of Israel were adopted by the Roman (and other) Christian communities. Further research might disclose how social and cultural forces converged to suppress feminine symbolism—and women's participation—from western Christian tradition. Given such research, the history of Christianity never could be told in the same way again.

Department of Religion
Barnard College

45. Ibid., 1.19.
46. 2 Tim. 2:11–14.

Feminism and Science

Evelyn Fox Keller

In recent years, a new critique of science has begun to emerge from a number of feminist writings. The lens of feminist politics brings into focus certain masculinist distortions of the scientific enterprise, creating, for those of us who are scientists, a potential dilemma. Is there a conflict between our commitment to feminism and our commitment to science? As both a feminist and a scientist, I am more familiar than I might wish with the nervousness and defensiveness that such a potential conflict evokes. As scientists, we have very real difficulties in thinking about the kinds of issues that, as feminists, we have been raising. These difficulties may, however, ultimately be productive. My purpose in the present essay is to explore the implications of recent feminist criticism of science for the relationship between science and feminism. Do these criticisms imply conflict? If they do, how necessary is that conflict? I will argue that those elements of feminist criticism that seem to conflict most with at least conventional conceptions of science may, in fact, carry a liberating potential for science. It could therefore benefit scientists to attend closely to feminist criticism. I will suggest that we might even use feminist thought to illuminate and clarify part of the substructure of science (which may have been historically conditioned into distortion) in order to preserve the things that science has taught us, in order to be more objective. But first it is necessary to review the various criticisms that feminists have articulated.

The range of their critique is broad. Though they all claim that science embodies a strong androcentric bias, the meanings attached to this charge vary widely. It is convenient to represent the differences in meaning by a spectrum that parallels the political range characteristic of feminism as a whole. I label this spectrum from right to left, beginning somewhere left of center with what might be called the liberal position. From the liberal critique, charges of androcentricity emerge that are relatively easy to correct. The more radical critique calls for correspondingly more radical changes; it requires a reexamination of the underlying assumptions of scientific theory and method for the presence of male bias. The difference between these positions is, however, often obscured by a knee-jerk reaction that leads many scientists to regard all such criticism as a unit—as a challenge to the neutrality of science. One of the points I wish to emphasize here is that the range of meanings attributed to the claim of androcentric bias reflects very different levels of challenge, some of which even the most conservative scientists ought to be able to accept.

First, in what I have called the liberal critique, is the charge that is essentially one of unfair employment practices. It proceeds from the observation that almost all scientists are men. This criticism is liberal in the sense that it in no way conflicts either with traditional conceptions of science or with current liberal, egalitarian politics. It is, in fact, a purely political criticism, and one which can be supported by all of us who are in favor of equal opportunity. According to this point of view, science itself would in no way be affected by the presence or absence of women.

A slightly more radical criticism continues from this and argues that the predominance of men in the sciences has led to a bias in the choice and definition of problems with which scientists have concerned themselves. This argument is most frequently and most easily made in regard to the health sciences. It is claimed, for example, that contraception has not been given the scientific attention its human importance warrants and that, furthermore, the attention it has been given has been focused primarily on contraceptive techniques to be used by women. In a related complaint, feminists argue that menstrual cramps, a serious problem for many women, have never been taken seriously by the medical profession. Presumably, had the concerns of medical research been articulated by women, these particular imbalances would not have arisen.[1] Similar biases in sciences remote from the subject of women's bodies are more

1. Notice that the claim is not that the mere presence of women in medical research is sufficient to right such imbalances, for it is understood how readily women, or any "outsiders" for that matter, come to internalize the concerns and values of a world to which they aspire to belong.

difficult to locate—they may, however, exist. Even so, this kind of criticism does not touch our conception of what science is, nor our confidence in the neutrality of science. It may be true that in some areas we have ignored certain problems, but our definition of science does not include the choice of problem—that, we can readily agree, has always been influenced by social forces. We remain, therefore, in the liberal domain.

Continuing to the left, we next find claims of bias in the actual design and interpretation of experiments. For example, it is pointed out that virtually all of the animal-learning research on rats has been performed with male rats.[2] Though a simple explanation is offered—namely, that female rats have a four-day cycle that complicates experiments—the criticism is hardly vitiated by the explanation. The implicit assumption is, of course, that the male rat represents the species. There exist many other, often similar, examples in psychology. Examples from the biological sciences are somewhat more difficult to find, though one suspects that they exist. An area in which this suspicion is particularly strong is that of sex research. Here the influence of heavily invested preconceptions seems all but inevitable. In fact, although the existence of such preconceptions has been well documented historically,[3] a convincing case for the existence of a corresponding bias in either the design or interpretation of experiments has yet to be made. That this is so can, I think, be taken as testimony to the effectiveness of the standards of objectivity operating.

But evidence for bias in the interpretation of observations and experiments is very easy to find in the more socially oriented sciences. The area of primatology is a familiar target. Over the past fifteen years women working in the field have undertaken an extensive reexamination of theoretical concepts, often using essentially the same methodological tools. These efforts have resulted in some radically different formulations. The range of difference frequently reflects the powerful influence of ordinary language in biasing our theoretical formulations. A great deal of very interesting work analyzing such distortions has been done.[4] Though I cannot begin to do justice to that work here, let me offer, as a single example, the following description of a single-male troop of animals that Jane Lancaster provides as a substitute for the familiar concept of "harem": "For a female, males are a

2. I would like to thank Lila Braine for calling this point to my attention.
3. D. L. Hall and Diana Long, "The Social Implications of the Scientific Study of Sex," *Scholar and the Feminist* 4 (1977): 11–21.
4. See, e.g., Donna Haraway, "Animal Sociology and a Natural Economy of the Body Politic, Part I: A Political Physiology of Dominance"; and "Animal Sociology and a Natural Economy of the Body Politic, Part II: The Past Is the Contested Zone: Human Nature and Theories of Production and Reproduction in Primate Behavior Studies," *Signs: Journal of Women in Culture and Society* 4, no. 1 (Autumn 1978): 21–60.

resource in her environment which she may use to further the survival of herself and her offspring. If environmental conditions are such that the male role can be minimal, a one-male group is likely. Only one male is necessary for a group of females if his only role is to impregnate them."[5]

These critiques, which maintain that a substantive effect on scientific theory results from the predominance of men in the field, are almost exclusively aimed at the "softer," even the "softest," sciences. Thus they can still be accommodated within the traditional framework by the simple argument that the critiques, if justified, merely reflect the fact that these subjects are not sufficiently scientific. Presumably, fair-minded (or scientifically minded) scientists can and should join forces with the feminists in attempting to identify the presence of bias—equally offensive, if for different reasons, to both scientists and feminists—in order to make these "soft" sciences more rigorous.

It is much more difficult to deal with the truly radical critique that attempts to locate androcentric bias even in the "hard" sciences, indeed in scientific ideology itself. This range of criticism takes us out of the liberal domain and requires us to question the very assumptions of objectivity and rationality that underlie the scientific enterprise. To challenge the truth and necessity of the conclusions of natural science on the grounds that they too reflect the judgment of men is to take the Galilean credo and turn it on its head. It is not true that "the conclusions of natural science are true and necessary, and the judgement of man has nothing to do with.them";[6] it is the judgment of woman that they have nothing to do with.

The impetus behind this radical move is twofold. First, it is supported by the experience of feminist scholars in other fields of inquiry. Over and over, feminists have found it necessary, in seeking to reinstate women as agents and as subjects, to question the very canons of their fields. They have turned their attention, accordingly, to the operation of patriarchal bias on ever deeper levels of social structure, even of language and thought.

But the possibility of extending the feminist critique into the foundations of scientific thought is created by recent developments in the history and philosophy of science itself.[7] As long as the course of scientific thought was judged to be exclusively determined by its own logi-

5. Jane Lancaster, *Primate Behavior and the Emergence of Human Culture* (New York: Holt, Rinehart & Winston, 1975), p. 34.

6. Galileo Galilei, *Dialogue on the Great World Systems,* trans. T. Salusbury, ed. G. de Santillana (Chicago: University of Chicago Press, 1953), p. 63.

7. The work of Russell Hanson and Thomas S. Kuhn was of pivotal importance in opening up our understanding of scientific thought to a consideration of social, psychological, and political influences.

cal and empirical necessities, there could be no place for any signature, male or otherwise, in that system of knowledge. Furthermore, any suggestion of gender differences in our thinking about the world could argue only too readily for the further exclusion of women from science. But as the philosophical and historical inadequacies of the classical conception of science have become more evident, and as historians and sociologists have begun to identify the ways in which the development of scientific knowledge has been shaped by its particular social and political context, our understanding of science as a social process has grown. This understanding is a necessary prerequisite, both politically and intellectually, for a feminist theoretic in science.

Joining feminist thought to other social studies of science brings the promise of radically new insights, but it also adds to the existing intellectual danger a political threat. The intellectual danger resides in viewing science as pure social product; science then dissolves into ideology and objectivity loses all intrinsic meaning. In the resulting cultural relativism, any emancipatory function of modern science is negated, and the arbitration of truth recedes into the political domain.[8] Against this background, the temptation arises for feminists to abandon their claim for representation in scientific culture and, in its place, to invite a return to a purely "female" subjectivity, leaving rationality and objectivity in the male domain, dismissed as products of a purely male consciousness.[9]

Many authors have addressed the problems raised by total relativism;[10] here I wish merely to mention some of the special problems added by its feminist variant. They are several. In important respects, feminist relativism is just the kind of radical move that transforms the political spectrum into a circle. By rejecting objectivity as a masculine ideal, it simultaneously lends its voice to an enemy chorus and dooms women to residing outside of the realpolitik modern culture; it exacerbates the very problem it wishes to solve. It also nullifies the radical potential of feminist criticism for our understanding of science. As I see it, the task of a feminist theoretic in science is twofold: to distinguish that which is parochial from that which is universal in the scientific impulse,

---

8. See, e.g., Paul Feyerabend, *Against Method* (London: New Left Books, 1975); and *Science in a Free Society* (London: New Left Books, 1978).

9. This notion is expressed most strongly by some of the new French feminists (see Elaine Marks and Isabelle de Courtivron, eds., *New French Feminisms: An Anthology* [Amherst: University of Massachusetts Press, 1980]), and is currently surfacing in the writings of some American feminists. See, e.g., Susan Griffin, *Woman and Nature: The Roaring Inside Her* (New York: Harper & Row, 1978).

10. See, e.g., Steven Rose and Hilary Rose, "Radical Science and Its Enemies," *Socialist Register 1979*, ed. Ralph Miliband and John Saville (Atlantic Highlands, N.J.: Humanities Press, 1979), pp. 317–35. A number of the points made here have also been made by Elizabeth Fee in "Is Feminism a Threat to Objectivity?" (paper presented at the American Association for the Advancement of Science meeting, Toronto, January 4, 1981).

reclaiming for women what has historically been denied to them; and to legitimate those elements of scientific culture that have been denied precisely because they are defined as female.

It is important to recognize that the framework inviting what might be called the nihilist retreat is in fact provided by the very ideology of objectivity we wish to escape. This is the ideology that asserts an opposition between (male) objectivity and (female) subjectivity and denies the possibility of mediation between the two. A first step, therefore, in extending the feminist critique to the foundations of scientific thought is to reconceptualize objectivity as a dialectical process so as to allow for the possibility of distinguishing the objective effort from the objectivist illusion. As Piaget reminds us:

> Objectivity consists in so fully realizing the countless intrusions of the self in everyday thought and the countless illusions which result—illusions of sense, language, point of view, value, etc.—that the preliminary step to every judgement is the effort to exclude the intrusive self. Realism, on the contrary, consists in ignoring the existence of self and thence regarding one's own perspective as immediately objective and absolute. Realism is thus anthropocentric illusion, finality—in short, all those illusions which teem in the history of science. So long as thought has not become conscious of self, it is a prey to perpetual confusions between objective and subjective, between the real and the ostensible.[11]

In short, rather than abandon the quintessentially human effort to understand the world in rational terms, we need to refine that effort. To do this, we need to add to the familiar methods of rational and empirical inquiry the additional process of critical self-reflection. Following Piaget's injunction, we need to "become conscious of self." In this way, we can become conscious of the features of the scientific project that belie its claim to universality.

The ideological ingredients of particular concern to feminists are found where objectivity is linked with autonomy and masculinity, and in turn, the goals of science with power and domination. The linking of objectivity with social and political autonomy has been examined by many authors and shown to serve a variety of important political functions.[12] The implications of joining objectivity with masculinity are less well understood. This conjunction also serves critical political functions. But an understanding of the sociopolitical meaning of the entire constellation requires an examination of the psychological processes

---

11. Jean Piaget, *The Child's Conception of the World* (Totowa, N.J.: Littlefield, Adams & Co., 1972).

12. Jerome R. Ravetz, *Scientific Knowledge and Its Social Problems* (London: Oxford University Press, 1971); and Hilary Rose and Steven Rose, *Science and Society* (London: Allen Lane, 1969).

through which these connections become internalized and perpetuated. Here psychoanalysis offers us an invaluable perspective, and it is to the exploitation of that perspective that much of my own work has been directed. In an earlier paper, I tried to show how psychoanalytic theories of development illuminate the structure and meaning of an interacting system of associations linking objectivity (a cognitive trait) with autonomy (an affective trait) and masculinity (a gender trait).[13] Here, after a brief summary of my earlier argument, I want to explore the relation of this system to power and domination.

Along with Nancy Chodorow and Dorothy Dinnerstein, I have found that branch of psychoanalytic theory known as object relations theory to be especially useful.[14] In seeking to account for personality development in terms of both innate drives and actual relations with other objects (i.e., subjects), it permits us to understand the ways in which our earliest experiences—experiences in large part determined by the socially structured relationships that form the context of our developmental processes—help to shape our conception of the world and our characteristic orientations to it. In particular, our first steps in the world are guided primarily by the parents of one sex—our mothers; this determines a maturational framework for our emotional, cognitive, and gender development, a framework later filled in by cultural expectations.

In brief, I argued the following: Our early maternal environment, coupled with the cultural definition of masculine (that which can never appear feminine) and of autonomy (that which can never be compromised by dependency) leads to the association of female with the pleasures and dangers of merging, and of male with the comfort and loneliness of separateness. The boy's internal anxiety about both self and gender is echoed by the more widespread cultural anxiety, thereby encouraging postures of autonomy and masculinity, which can, indeed may, be designed to defend against that anxiety and the longing that generates it. Finally, for all of us, our sense of reality is carved out of the same developmental matrix. As Piaget and others have emphasized, the capacity for cognitive distinctions between self and other (objectivity) evolves concurrently and interdependently with the development of psychic autonomy; our cognitive ideals thereby become subject to the same psychological influences as our emotional and gender ideals. Along with autonomy the very act of separating subject from object—objectivity itself—comes to be associated with masculinity. The combined psycho-

13. Evelyn Fox Keller, "Gender and Science," *Psychoanalysis and Contemporary Thought* 1 (1978): 409–33.

14. Nancy Chodorow, *The Reproduction of Mothering: Psychoanalysis and the Sociology of Gender* (Berkeley: University of California Press, 1978); and Dorothy Dinnerstein, *The Mermaid and the Minotaur: Sexual Arrangements and Human Malaise* (New York: Harper & Row, 1976).

logical and cultural pressures lead all three ideals—affective, gender, and cognitive—to a mutually reinforcing process of exaggeration and rigidification.[15] The net result is the entrenchment of an objectivist ideology and a correlative devaluation of (female) subjectivity.

This analysis leaves out many things. Above all it omits discussion of the psychological meanings of power and domination, and it is to those meanings I now wish to turn. Central to object relations theory is the recognition that the condition of psychic autonomy is double edged: it offers a profound source of pleasure, and simultaneously of potential dread. The values of autonomy are consonant with the values of competence, of mastery. Indeed competence is itself a prior condition for autonomy and serves immeasurably to confirm one's sense of self. But need the development of competence and the sense of mastery lead to a state of alienated selfhood, of denied connectedness, of defensive separateness? To forms of autonomy that can be understood as protections against dread? Object relations theory makes us sensitive to autonomy's range of meanings; it simultaneously suggests the need to consider the corresponding meanings of competence. Under what circumstances does competence imply mastery of one's own fate and under what circumstances does it imply mastery over another's? In short, are control and domination essential ingredients of competence, and intrinsic to selfhood, or are they correlates of an alienated selfhood?

One way to answer these questions is to use the logic of the analysis summarized above to examine the shift from competence to power and control in the psychic economy of the young child. From that analysis, the impulse toward domination can be understood as a natural concomitant of defensive separateness—as Jessica Benjamin has written, "A way of repudiating sameness, dependency and closeness with another person, while attempting to avoid the consequent feelings of aloneness."[16] Perhaps no one has written more sensitively than psychoanalyst D. W. Winnicott of the rough waters the child must travel in negotiating the transition from symbiotic union to the recognition of self and other as autonomous entities. He alerts us to a danger that others have missed—a danger arising from the unconscious fantasy that the subject has actually destroyed the object in the process of becoming separate. Indeed, he writes, "It is the destruction of the object that places the

15. For a fuller development of this argument, see n. 12 above. By focusing on the contributions of individual psychology, I in no way mean to imply a simple division of individual and social factors, or to set them up as alternative influences. Individual psychological traits evolve in a social system and, in turn, social systems reward and select for particular sets of individual traits. Thus if particular options in science reflect certain kinds of psychological impulses or personality traits, it must be understood that it is in a distinct social framework that those options, rather than others, are selected.

16. Jessica Benjamin has discussed this same issue in an excellent analysis of the place of domination in sexuality. See "The Bonds of Love: Rational Violence and Erotic Domination," *Feminist Studies* 6, no. 1 (Spring 1980): 144–74, esp. 150.

object outside the area of control. . . . . After 'subject relates to object' comes 'subject destroys object' (as it becomes external); then may come '*object survives* destruction by the subject.' But there may or may not be survival." When there is, "because of the survival of the object, the subject may now have started to live a life in the world of objects, and so the subject stands to gain immeasurably; but the price has to be paid in acceptance of the ongoing destruction in unconscious fantasy relative to object-relating."[17] Winnicott, of course, is not speaking of actual survival but of subjective confidence in the survival of the other. Survival in that sense requires that the child maintain relatedness; failure induces inevitable guilt and dread. The child is poised on a terrifying precipice. On one side lies the fear of having destroyed the object, on the other side, loss of self. The child may make an attempt to secure this precarious position by seeking to master the other. The cycles of destruction and survival are reenacted while the other is kept safely at bay, and as Benjamin writes, "the original self assertion is . . . converted from innocent mastery to mastery over and against the other."[18] In psychodynamic terms, this particular resolution of preoedipal conflicts is a product of oedipal consolidation. The (male) child achieves his final security by identification with the father—an identification involving simultaneously a denial of the mother and a transformation of guilt and fear into aggression.

Aggression, of course, has many meanings, many sources, and many forms of expression. Here I mean to refer only to the form underlying the impulse toward domination. I invoke psychoanalytic theory to help illuminate the forms of expression that impulse finds in science as a whole, and its relation to objectification in particular. The same questions I asked about the child I can also ask about science. Under what circumstances is scientific knowledge sought for the pleasures of knowing, for the increased competence it grants us, for the increased mastery (real or imagined) over our own fate, and under what circumstances is it fair to say that science seeks actually to dominate nature? Is there a meaningful distinction to be made here?

In his work *The Domination of Nature* William Leiss observes, "The necessary correlate of domination is the consciousness of subordination in those who must obey the will of another; thus properly speaking only other men can be the objects of domination."[19] (Or women, we might add.) Leiss infers from this observation that it is not the domination of physical nature we should worry about but the use of our knowledge of physical nature as an instrument for the domination of human nature. He therefore sees the need for correctives, not in science but in its uses. This is his point of departure from other authors of the Frankfurt

17. D. W. Winnicott, *Playing and Reality* (New York: Basic Books, 1971), pp. 89–90.
18. Benjamin, p. 165.
19. William Leiss, *The Domination of Nature* (Boston: Beacon Press, 1974), p. 122.

school, who assume the very logic of science to be the logic of domination. I agree with Leiss's basic observation but draw a somewhat different inference. I suggest that the impulse toward domination does find expression in the goals (and even in the theories and practice) of modern science, and argue that where it finds such expression the impulse needs to be acknowledged as projection. In short, I argue that not only in the denial of interaction between subject and other but also in the access of domination to the goals of scientific knowledge, one finds the intrusion of a self we begin to recognize as partaking in the cultural construct of masculinity.

The value of consciousness is that it enables us to make choices—both as individuals and as scientists. Control and domination are in fact intrinsic neither to selfhood (i.e., autonomy) nor to scientific knowledge. I want to suggest, rather, that the particular emphasis Western science has placed on these functions of knowledge is twin to the objectivist ideal. Knowledge in general, and scientific knowledge in particular, serves two gods: power and transcendence. It aspires alternately to mastery over and union with nature.[20] Sexuality serves the same two gods, aspiring to domination and ecstatic communion—in short, aggression and eros. And it is hardly a new insight to say that power, control, and domination are fueled largely by aggression, while union satisfies a more purely erotic impulse.

To see the emphasis on power and control so prevalent in the rhetoric of Western science as projection of a specifically male consciousness requires no great leap of the imagination. Indeed, that perception has become a commonplace. Above all, it is invited by the rhetoric that conjoins the domination of nature with the insistent image of nature as female, nowhere more familiar than in the writings of Francis Bacon. For Bacon, knowledge and power are one, and the promise of science is expressed as "leading to you Nature with all her children to bind her to your service and make her your slave,"[21] by means that do not "merely exert a gentle guidance over nature's course; they have the power to conquer and subdue her, to shake her to her foundations."[22] In the context of the Baconian vision, Bruno Bettelheim's conclusion appears inescapable: "Only with phallic psychology did aggressive manipulation of nature become possible."[23]

20. For a discussion of the different roles these two impulses play in Platonic and in Baconian images of knowledge, see Evelyn Fox Keller, "Nature as 'Her'" (paper delivered at the Second Sex Conference, New York Institute for the Humanities, September 1979).

21. B. Farrington, *"Temporis Partus Masculus:* An Untranslated Writing of Francis Bacon," *Centaurus* 1 (1951): 193–205, esp. 197.

22. Francis Bacon, "Description of the Intellectual Globe," in *The Philosophical Works of Francis Bacon*, ed. J. H. Robertson (London: Routledge & Sons, 1905), p. 506.

23. Quoted in Norman O. Brown, *Life against Death* (New York: Random House, 1959), p. 280.

The view of science as an oedipal project is also familiar from the writings of Herbert Marcuse and Norman O. Brown.[24] But Brown's preoccupation, as well as Marcuse's, is with what Brown calls a "morbid" science. Accordingly, for both authors the quest for a nonmorbid science, an "erotic" science, remains a romantic one. This is so because their picture of science is incomplete: it omits from consideration the crucial, albeit less visible, erotic components already present in the scientific tradition. Our own quest, if it is to be realistic rather than romantic, must be based on a richer understanding of the scientific tradition, in all its dimensions, and on an understanding of the ways in which this complex, dialectical tradition becomes transformed into a monolithic rhetoric. Neither the oedipal child nor modern science has in fact managed to rid itself of its preoedipal and fundamentally bisexual yearnings. It is with this recognition that the quest for a different science, a science undistorted by masculinist bias, must begin.

The presence of contrasting themes, of a dialectic between aggressive and erotic impulses, can be seen both within the work of individual scientists and, even more dramatically, in the juxtaposed writings of different scientists. Francis Bacon provides us with one model;[25] there are many others. For an especially striking contrast, consider a contemporary scientist who insists on the importance of "letting the material speak to you," of allowing it to "tell you what to do next"—one who chastises other scientists for attempting to "impose an answer" on what they see. For this scientist, discovery is facilitated by becoming "part of the system," rather than remaining outside; one must have a "feeling for the organism."[26] It is true that the author of these remarks is not only from a different epoch and a different field (Bacon himself was not actually a scientist by most standards), she is also a woman. It is also true that there are many reasons, some of which I have already suggested, for thinking that gender (itself constructed in an ideological context) actually does make a difference in scientific inquiry. Nevertheless, my point here is that neither science nor individuals are totally bound by ideology. In fact, it is not difficult to find similar sentiments expressed by male scientists. Consider, for example, the following remarks: "I have often had cause to feel that my hands are cleverer than my head. That is a crude way of characterizing the dialectics of experimentation. When it is going well, it is like a quiet conversation with Nature."[27] The difference

24. Brown; and Herbert Marcuse, *One Dimensional Man* (Boston: Beacon Press, 1964).

25. For a discussion of the presence of the same dialectic in the writings of Francis Bacon, see Evelyn Fox Keller, "Baconian Science: A Hermaphrodite Birth," *Philosophical Forum* 11, no. 3 (Spring 1980): 299–308.

26. Barbara McClintock, private interviews, December 1, 1978, and January 13, 1979.

27. G. Wald, "The Molecular Basis of Visual Excitation," *Les Prix Nobel en 1967* (Stockholm: Kungliga Boktryckerlet, 1968), p. 260.

between conceptions of science as "dominating" and as "conversing with" nature may not be a difference primarily between epochs, nor between the sexes. Rather, it can be seen as representing a dual theme played out in the work of all scientists, in all ages. But the two poles of this dialectic do not appear with equal weight in the history of science. What we therefore need to attend to is the evolutionary process that selects one theme as dominant.

Elsewhere I have argued for the importance of a different selection process.[28] In part, scientists are themselves selected by the emotional appeal of particular (stereotypic) images of science. Here I am arguing for the importance of selection within scientific thought—first of preferred methodologies and aims, and finally of preferred theories. The two processes are not unrelated. While stereotypes are not binding (i.e., they do not describe all or perhaps any individuals), and this fact creates the possibility for an ongoing contest within science, the first selection process undoubtedly influences the outcome of the second. That is, individuals drawn by a particular ideology will tend to select themes consistent with that ideology.

One example in which this process is played out on a theoretical level is in the fate of interactionist theories in the history of biology. Consider the contest that has raged throughout this century between organismic and particulate views of cellular organization—between what might be described as hierarchical and nonhierarchical theories. Whether the debate is over the primacy of the nucleus or the cell as a whole, the genome or the cytoplasm, the proponents of hierarchy have won out. One geneticist has described the conflict in explicitly political terms:

> Two concepts of genetic mechanisms have persisted side by side throughout the growth of modern genetics, but the emphasis has been very strongly in favor of one of these. . . . The first of these we will designate as the "Master Molecule" concept. . . . This is in essence the Theory of the Gene, interpreted to suggest a totalitarian government. . . . The second concept we will designate as the "Steady State" concept. By this term . . . we envision a dynamic self-perpetuating organization of a variety of molecular species which owes its specific properties not to the characteristic of any one kind of molecule, but to the functional interrelationships of these molecular species.[29]

Soon after these remarks, the debate between "master molecules" and dynamic interactionism was foreclosed by the synthesis provided by

28. Keller, "Gender and Science."
29. D. L. Nanney, "The Role of the Cyctoplasm in Heredity," in *The Chemical Basis of Heredity*, ed. William D. McElroy and Bentley Glass (Baltimore: Johns Hopkins University Press, 1957), p. 136.

DNA and the "central dogma." With the success of the new molecular biology such "steady state" (or egalitarian) theories lost interest for almost all geneticists. But today, the same conflict shows signs of reemerging—in genetics, in theories of the immune system, and in theories of development.

I suggest that method and theory may constitute a natural continuum, despite Popperian claims to the contrary, and that the same processes of selection may bear equally and simultaneously on both the means and aims of science and the actual theoretical descriptions that emerge. I suggest this in part because of the recurrent and striking consonance that can be seen in the way scientists work, the relation they take to their object of study, and the theoretical orientation they favor. To pursue the example cited earlier, the same scientist who allowed herself to become "part of the system," whose investigations were guided by a "feeling for the organism," developed a paradigm that diverged as radically from the dominant paradigm of her field as did her methodological style.

In lieu of the linear hierarchy described by the central dogma of molecular biology, in which the DNA encodes and transmits all instructions for the unfolding of a living cell, her research yielded a view of the DNA in delicate interaction with the cellular environment—an organismic view. For more important than the genome as such (i.e., the DNA) is the "overall organism." As she sees it, the genome functions "only in respect to the environment in which it is found."[30] In this work the program encoded by the DNA is itself subject to change. No longer is a master control to be found in a single component of the cell; rather, control resides in the complex interactions of the entire system. When first presented, the work underlying this vision was not understood, and it was poorly received.[31] Today much of that work is undergoing a renaissance, although it is important to say that her full vision remains too radical for most biologists to accept.[32]

This example suggests that we need not rely on our imagination for a vision of what a different science—a science less restrained by the impulse to dominate—might be like. Rather, we need only look to the thematic pluralism in the history of our own science as it has evolved. Many other examples can be found, but we lack an adequate understanding of the full range of influences that lead to the acceptance or rejection not only of particular theories but of different theoretical orientations. What I am suggesting is that if certain theoretical inter-

---

30. McClintock, December 1, 1978.

31. McClintock, "Chromosome Organization and Genic Expression," *Cold Spring Harbor Symposium of Quantitative Biology* 16 (1951): 13–44.

32. McClintock's most recent publication on this subject is "Modified Gene Expressions Induced by Transposable Elements," in *Mobilization and Reassembly of Genetic Information*, ed. W. A. Scott, R. Werner, and J. Schultz (New York: Academic Press, 1980).

pretations have been selected against, it is precisely in this process of selection that ideology in general, and a masculinist ideology in particular, can be found to effect its influence. The task this implies for a radical feminist critique of science is, then, first a historical one, but finally a transformative one. In the historical effort, feminists can bring a whole new range of sensitivities, leading to an equally new consciousness of the potentialities lying latent in the scientific project.

Visiting Professor of Mathematics and Humanities
Northeastern University

Animal Sociology and a Natural Economy of the Body Politic, Part I: A Political Physiology of Dominance

Donna Haraway

> "I want to do something very important. Like fly into the past and make it come out right." [Dawn, from MARGE PIERCY, *Woman on the Edge of Time*]

The concept of the body politic is not new. Elaborate organic images for human society were richly developed by the Greeks. They conceived the citizen, the city, and the cosmos to be built according to the same principles. To perceive the body politic as an organism, as fundamentally alive and as part of a large cosmic organism, was central for them.[1] To see the structure of human groups as a mirror of natural forms has remained imaginatively and intellectually powerful. Throughout the early period of the Industrial Revolution, a particularly important development of the theory of the body politic linked natural and political economy on multiple levels. Adam Smith's theory of the market and of the division of labor as keystones of future capitalist economic thought, with Thomas Malthus's supposed law of the relation of population and resources, together symbolize the junction of natural forces and economic progress in the formative years of capitalist industrialism. The permeation of Darwin's evolutionary theory with this form of political economy has been a subject of considerable analysis from the nineteenth century to the present.[2] Without question, the modern evolutionary concept of a population, as the fundamental natural group, owes much to classical ideas of the body politic, which in turn are inextricably interwoven with the social relationships of production and reproduction.

The union of the political and physiological is the focus of this essay.

1. R. G. Collingwood, *The Idea of Nature* (Oxford: Clarendon Press, 1945).
2. R. M. Young, "Malthus and the Evolutionists: The Common Context of Biological and Society Theory," *Past and Present* 43 (1969): 109–41.

That union has been a major source of ancient and modern justifications of domination, especially of domination based on differences seen as natural, given, inescapable, and therefore moral. It has also been transformed by the modern biobehavioral sciences in ways we must understand if we are to work effectively for societies free from domination. The degree to which the principle of domination is deeply embedded in our natural sciences, especially in those disciplines that seek to explain social groups and behavior, must not be underestimated. In evading the importance of dominance as a part of the theory and practice of contemporary sciences, we bypass the crucial and difficult examination of the *content* as well as the social function of science. We leave this central, legitimating body of skill and knowledge to undermine our efforts, to render them utopian in the worst sense. Nor must we lightly accept the damaging distinction between pure and applied science, between use and abuse of science, and even between nature and culture. All are versions of the philosophy of science that exploits the rupture between subject and object to justify the double ideology of firm scientific objectivity and mere personal subjectivity. This antiliberation core of knowledge and practice in our sciences is an important buttress of social control.[3]

Recognition of that fact has been a major contribution by feminist theorists. Women know very well that knowledge from the natural sciences has been used in the interests of our domination and not our liberation, birth control propagandists notwithstanding. Moreover, general exclusion from science has only made our exploitation more acute. We have learned that both the exclusion and the exploitation are fruits of our position in the social division of labor and not of natural incapacities.[4] But if we have not often underestimated the principle of domination in the sciences, if we have been less mesmerized than many by the claims to value-free truth by scientists as we most frequently encounter them—in the medical marketplace[5]—we have allowed our

3. R. M. Young, "Science *Is* Social Relations," *Radical Science Journal* 5 (1977): 65–129. This essay has an exceptionally useful bibliography of radical critique of science. See also E. A. Burtt, *The Metaphysical Foundations of Modern Science* (New York: Humanities Press, 1952); Herbert Marcuse, *One Dimensional Man: Studies in the Ideology of Advanced Industrial Society* (Boston: Beacon Press, 1968); Karl Marx and Frederick Engels, *The German Ideology* (New York: International Publishers, 1970).

4. Harry Braverman, *Labor and Monopoly Capital: The Degradation of Work in the Twentieth Century* (New York: Monthly Review Press, 1974). Braverman situates the female work force in the center of his powerful Marxist analysis of modern labor, scientific management, and the deskilling of working people in a period of increasing scientific and technical expertise.

5. Linda Gordon, *Women's Body, Women's Right: A Social History of Birth Control in America* (New York: Viking Press, 1976). Excerpts from this important book may be found in a two-part series by Linda Gordon ("Birth Control: An Historical Study," *Science for the People* 9, no. 1 [1977]: 10–16, "Birth Control and the Eugenicists," ibid., 9, no. 2 [1977]: 8–15). See also James Reed, *From Private Vice to Public Virtue: The Birth Control Movement and American Society since 1830* (New York: Basic Books, 1978).

distance from science and technology to lead us to misunderstand the status and function of natural knowledge. We have accepted at face value the traditional liberal ideology of social scientists in the twentieth century that maintains a deep and necessary split between nature and culture and between the forms of knowledge relating to these two putatively irreconcilable realms. We have allowed the theory of the body politic to be split in such a way that natural knowledge is reincorporated covertly into techniques of social control instead of being transformed into sciences of liberation. We have challenged our traditional assignment to the status of natural objects by becoming antinatural in our ideology in a way which leaves the life sciences untouched by feminist needs.[6] We have granted science the role of a fetish, an object human beings make only to forget their role in creating it, no longer responsive to the dialectical interplay of human beings with the surrounding world in the satisfaction of social and organic needs. We have perversely worshiped science as a reified fetish in two complementary ways: (1) by completely rejecting scientific and technical discipline and developing feminist social theory totally apart from the natural sciences, and (2) by agreeing that "nature" is our enemy and that we must control our "natural" bodies (by techniques given us by biomedical science) at all costs to enter the hallowed kingdom of the cultural body politic as defined by liberal (and radical) theorists of political economy, instead of by ourselves. This cultural body politic was clearly identified by Marx: the marketplace that remakes all things and people into commodities.

A concrete example may help explain what I see as our dangerous misunderstanding, an example which takes us back to the point of union of the political and physiological. In *Civilization and Its Discontents,*[7] Freud developed a theory of the body politic that based human social development on progressive domination of nature, particularly of human sexual energies. Sex as danger and as nature are central to Freud's system, which repeats rather than initiates the traditional reduction of the body politic to physiological starting points. The body politic is in the first

6. Sherry B. Ortner, "Is Female to Male as Nature Is to Culture?" in *Women, Culture, and Society,* ed. Michelle Zimbalist Rosaldo and Louise Lamphere (Stanford, Calif.: Stanford University Press, 1974), pp. 67–87; Simone de Beauvoir, *The Second Sex* (London: Jonathan Cope, 1953). Both Ortner, from the point of view of structuralist anthropology, and de Beauvoir, from the perspective of existentialism, allow the ideology of the nature-culture split to dominate their feminist analyses. Carol P. MacCormack ("Biological Events and Cultural Control," *Signs* 3 [1977]: 93–100) has made use of anthropological theories of Mary Douglas (*Purity and Danger* [London: Routledge & Kegan Paul, 1966] and *Rules and Meanings* [London: Penguin Books, 1973]) in order to challenge the nature-culture distinction. MacCormack analyzes the female Sande sodality of Sierra Leone to stress women's collective construction of their own bodies for assuming their active roles in the body politic. The organicism and functionalism in MacCormack's framework should be critically explored.

7. Sigmund Freud, *Civilization and Its Discontents* (New York: W. W. Norton & Co., 1962).

instance seen to be founded on natural individuals whose instincts must be conquered to make possible the cultural group. Two recent neo-Freudian and neo-Marxist theorists have ironically reworked Freud's position in illuminating ways for the thesis of this essay: one is Norman O. Brown, the other Shulamith Firestone. Freud, Brown, and Firestone are useful tools in a dissection of the theories of the political and physiological organs of the body politic because they all begin their explanations with sexuality, add a dynamic of cultural repression, and then attempt to liberate again the personal and collective body.

Brown, in *Love's Body*, [8] developed an elaborate metaphorical play between the individual and political bodies to show the extraordinary patriarchal and authoritarian structure of our conceptions and experiences of both. The phallus, the head; the state, the body; the brothers, the rebellious overthrow of kingship only to establish the tyranny of the fraternal liberal market—these are Brown's themes. If only the father was head, only the brothers may be citizens. The only escape from the domination that Brown explored was through fantasy and ecstasy, leaving the body politic unchallenged in its fundamental male supremacy and in its reduction to the dynamic of repression of nature. Brown rejected civilization (the body politic) in order to save the body; the solution was necessitated by his root acceptance of the Freudian sexual reductionism and ensuing logic of domination. He turned nature into a fetish worshiped by total return to it (polymorphous perversity). He betrayed the socialist possibilities of a dialectical theory of the body politic that neither worships nor rejects natural science, that refuses to make nature and its knowledge a fetish.

Firestone, in the *Dialectic of Sex*, [9] also faces the implications of Freud's biopolitical theory of patriarchy and repression but tries to transform it to yield a feminist and socialist theory of liberation. She has been immensely important to feminists in this task. I think, however, that she committed the same mistake that Brown did, that of "physiological reduction of the body politic to sex," which fundamentally blocks a liberating socialism that neither fatalistically exploits the techniques given by sciences (while despairing of transforming their content) nor rejects a technical knowledge altogether for fantasy. Firestone located the flaw in women's position in the body politic in our own bodies, in our subservience to the organic demands of reproduction. In that critical sense she accepted a historical materialism based on reproduction and lost the possibility for a feminist-socialist theory of the body politic that would not see our personal bodies as the ultimate enemy. In that step she prepared for the logic of domination of technology—total control of now alienated bodies in a machine-determined future. She made the basic mistake of reducing social relations to natural objects, with the

8. Norman O. Brown, *Love's Body* (New York: Random House, 1966).
9. Shulamith Firestone, *Dialectic of Sex* (New York: William Morrow & Co., 1970).

logical consequence of seeing technical control as a solution. She certainly did not underestimate the principle of domination in the biobehavioral sciences, but she did misunderstand the status of scientific knowledge and practice. That is, she accepted that there are natural objects (bodies) separate from social relations. In that context, liberation remains subject to supposedly natural determinism, which can only be avoided in an escalating logic of counterdomination.

I think it is possible to build a socialist-feminist theory of the body politic that avoids physiological reductionism in both its forms: (1) capitulating to theories of biological determinism of our social position, and (2) adopting the basically capitalist ideology of culture against nature and thereby denying our responsibility to rebuild the life sciences. I understand Marxist humanism to mean that the fundamental position of the human being in the world is the dialectical relation with the surrounding world involved in the satisfaction of needs and thus in the creation of use values. The labor process constitutes the fundamental human condition. Through labor, we make ourselves individually and collectively in a constant interaction with all that has not yet been humanized. Neither our personal bodies nor our social bodies may be seen as natural, in the sense of outside the self-creating process called human labor. What we experience and theorize as nature and as culture are transformed by our work. All we touch and therefore know, including our organic and our social bodies, is made possible for us through labor. Therefore, culture does not dominate nature, nor is nature an enemy. The dialectic must not be made into a dynamic of growing domination.[10] The position, a historical materialism based on production, contrasts fundamentally with the ironically named historical materialism based on reproduction that I have tried to outline above.

One area of the biobehavioral sciences has been unusually important in the construction of oppressive theories of the body political: animal sociology, or the science of animal groups. To reappropriate the biosocial sciences for new practices and theories, a critical history of the physiological politics based on domination that have been central in animal sociology is important. The biosocial sciences have not simply been sexist mirrors of our own social world. They have also been tools in the reproduction of that world, both in supplying legitimating ideologies and in enhancing material power. There are three main reasons for choosing to focus on the science of animal, especially primate, groups.

First, its subject and procedures developed so as to span the nature-

10. Nancy Hartsock, "Objectivity and Revolution: Problems of Knowledge in Marxist Theory," and "Social Science, Praxis, and Political Action" (manuscripts available from author, Political Science Department, Johns Hopkins University). Because of the well-developed feminist analysis and avoidance of sexual reductionism, these papers are more useful for a critique of the theory and practice of scientific objectivity than those of Jürgen Habermas or Herbert Marcuse. See J. Habermas, *Toward a Rational Society: Student Protest, Science, and Politics* (Boston: Beacon Press, 1970).

culture split at precisely the same time in American intellectual history, between 1920 and 1940, when the ideology of the autonomy of the social sciences had at last gained acceptance, that is, when the liberal theory of society (based on functionalism and hierarchical systems theories) was being established in the universities. Intrinsic to the new liberal relations of natural and social disciplines was the project of human engineering— that is, the project of design and management of human material for efficient, rational functioning in a scientifically ordered society. Animals played an important role in this project. On one hand, they were plastic raw material of knowledge, subject to exact laboratory discipline. They could be used to construct and test model systems for both human physiology and politics. A model system of, for example, menstrual physiology or socialization processes did not necessarily imply reductionism. It was precisely direct reduction of human to natural sciences that the post-Spencerian, postevolutionary naturalist new ordering of knowledge forbade. The management sciences of the 1930s and after have been strict on that point. It is part of the nature-culture split. On the other hand, animals have continued to have a special status as natural objects that can show people their origin, and therefore their prerational, premanagement, precultural essence. That is, animals have been ominously ambiguous in their place in the doctrine of autonomy of human and natural sciences. So, despite the claims of anthropology to be able to understand human beings solely with the concept of culture and of sociology to need nothing but the idea of the human social group, animal societies have been extensively employed in rationalization and naturalization of the oppressive orders of domination in the human body politic.[11] They have provided the point of union of the physiological and political for modern liberal theorists while they continue to accept the ideology of the split between nature and culture.

Second, animal sociology has been central in the development of the most thorough naturalization of patriarchal division of authority in the body politic and in reduction of the body politic to sexual physiology. Thus this area of the natural sciences is one we need to understand thoroughly and tranform completely to produce a science that might express the social relations of liberation without committing the vulgar Marxist mistake of deriving directly the substance of knowledge from material conditions. We need to understand how and why animal groups have been used in theories of the evolutionary origin of human beings, of "mental illness," of the natural basis of cultural cooperation and competition, of language and other forms of communication, of technology, and especially of the origin and role of human forms of sex

11. See, for example, the University of Chicago 50th anniversary celebration symposium jointly produced by the biological and social sciences departments: Robert Redfield, ed., *Levels of Integration in Biological and Social Systems* (Lancaster, Pa.: Jaques Cattell Press, 1942).

and the family. In short, we need to know the animal science of the body politic as it has been and might be.[12] I believe the result of a liberating science of animal groups would better express who the animals are as well; we might free nature in freeing ourselves.

Third, the levels at which domination has formed an analytical principle in animal sociology allow a critique of the embodiment of social relations in the content and basic procedures of a natural science in such a way as to expose the fallacies of the claim to objectivity, but not in such a way as to permit facile rejection of scientific discipline in our knowledge of animals. We cannot dismiss the layers of domination in the science of animal groups as a film of unfortunate bias or ideology that can be peeled off the healthy objective strata of knowledge below. Neither can we think just anything we please about animals and their meaning for us. We come face to face with the necessity of a dialectical understanding of scientific labor in producing for us our knowledge of nature.

I will restrict my analysis primarily to a few years around World War II and to work on a single group of animals—the primates, in particular, the rhesus monkey, native to Asia but present in droves in scientific laboratories and research stations worldwide. I will focus principally on the work of one person, Clarence Ray Carpenter, who helped found the first major research station for free-ranging monkeys as part of the school of tropical medicine affiliated with Columbia University off Puerto Rico on the tiny island of Cayo Santiago in the late 1930s. These monkeys and their descendants have been central actors in dramatic reconstructions of natural society. Their affiliation with tropical medicine in a neocolonial holding of the United States, which has been so extensively used as an experiment station for capitalist fertility management policies, adds an ironic backdrop appropriate to our subject.

Men like Carpenter moved within a complex scientific world in which it would be incorrect to label most individuals or theories as sexist or whatever. It is not to attach simplistic labels but to unwind the specific social and theoretical structures of an area of life science that we need to examine the interconnections of laboratory heads, students, funding agencies, research stations, experimental designs, and historical setting. Carpenter earned his Ph.D. at Stanford for a study of the effects on sexual behavior of the removal of the gonads of male pigeons in mated pairs. He then received a National Research Council Fellowship in 1931 to study social behavior of primates under the direction of Robert M. Yerkes of the Laboratories of Comparative Psychobiology at Yale University. Yerkes had recently established the first comprehensive research

12. For important comparison and contrast of anarchist and Marxist socialisms on the meaning of nature for the body politic, see Peter Kropotkin, *Mutual Aid* (London: William Heinemann, 1902), and Frederick Engels, *Dialectics of Nature* (New York: International Publishers, 1940).

institution for the psychobiological study of anthropoid apes in the world. For Yerkes, apes were perfect models of human beings. They played a major part in his sense of mission to promote scientific management of every phase of society, an idea typical of his generation. "It has always been a feature for the use of the chimpanzee as an experimental animal to shape it intelligently to specification instead of trying to preserve its natural characteristics. We have believed it important to convert the animal into as nearly ideal a subject for biological research as is practicable. And with this intent has been associated the hope that eventual success might serve as an effective demonstration of the possibility of re-creating man himself in the image of a generally acceptable ideal."[13] He, then, designed primates as scientific objects in relation to his ideal of human progress through human engineering.

Yerkes was interested in the apes in two main regards—their intelligence and their social-sexual life. For him intelligence was the perfect expression of evolutionary position. He saw every living object in terms of the outstanding problem of experimental comparative psychology in America since its inception around 1900: the intelligence test. Species, racial, and individual qualities were fundamentally tied to the central index of intelligence, revealed on the one hand through behavior testing and on the other through the neural sciences. He had designed the army intelligence tests administered to recruits in World War I, tests seen to provide a rational basis for assignment and promotion, to indicate natural merit fitting men for command.[14] His role in the war was entirely compatible with his role as an entrepreneur in primate studies. In both cases he saw himself and his scientific peers working to foster a rational society based on science and preserved from old ignorance, embodied especially in religion and politics.

The social-sexual life of primates was for Yerkes thoroughly inter-

13. R. M. Yerkes, *Chimpanzees: A Laboratory Colony* (New Haven, Conn.: Yale University Press, 1943), p. 10. I am currently working on a book-length treatment of the history of primate studies in the twentieth century. Yerkes is a critical figure in linking foundations, universities, neurophysiology and endocrinology, personnel management, psychopathology, educational testing, personality studies, social and sexual hygiene—in short, the whole complex of science and society in his lifetime. James Reed is undertaking a comprehensive biography of Yerkes.

14. R. M. Yerkes, "What Psychology Contributed to the War," in *The New World of Science* (New York: Century Co., 1920). See also Daniel Kevles, "Testing the Army's Intelligence: Psychologists and the Military in World War I," *Journal of American History* 55 (1968): 565–81. Yerkes and his peers were not using "human engineering" simply as a metaphor. They explicitly saw physiological, biopsychological, and social sciences as key parts of rational management in advanced monopoly capitalism. The sciences inventoried raw materials, and the laboratory functioned as a pilot plant for human engineering (see R. M. Yerkes, "What Is Personnel Research?" *Journal of Personnel Research* 1 [1922]: 56–63). For a history of the project of human engineering, see David F. Noble, *America by Design: Science, Technology and the Rise of Corporate Capitalism* (New York: Alfred A. Knopf, Inc., 1977), esp. chap. 10.

twined with their intelligence. Mind would order and rule lower functions to create society. In a classic study of the origin of the body politic, Yerkes observed that female chimpanzees who were sexually receptive were allowed by the dominant males to have food and "privileges" to which they were ordinarily not entitled.[15] Primate intelligence allowed sexual states to stimulate the beginnings of human concepts of social right and privilege. The sexual reductionism hardly needs emphasis. His study linking sex and power was typical of work in the 1930s, and hardly different from much to this day. In an early feminist critique, Ruth Herschberger[16] marvellously imagined the perspective of Josie, the female chimpanzee whose psychosexual life was of such concern to Yerkes. Josie seems not to have seen her world in terms of trading sex for "privilege," but to Yerkes that economic link of physiology and politics seemed to have been scientifically confirmed to life at the organic base of civilization.

In addition to direct investigation of physiological sex and social behavior in human beings' closest relatives, Yerkes exercised, along with his peers, a tremendous influence on the overall direction of scientific study of sex in this country. He was for twenty-five years chairman of the Rockefeller Foundation–funded National Research Council Committee for Research on Problems of Sex (CRPS). This committee, from 1922 until well after the Second World War when federal funding became massively available for science, provided the financial base for the transformation of human sex into a scientific problem. Fundamental work on hormones and behavior, sex-linked differences in mental and emotional qualities, marital happiness, and finally the Kinsey studies was all funded by the Committee for Research on Problems of Sex. It played a key role in opening up sexual topics for polite discussion and respectable investigation in an era of undoubted prurience and ignorance.[17]

However, the opening was double edged; the committee, in its practice and ideological expressions, was structured on several levels according to the principle of the primacy of sex in organic and social processes. To make sex a scientific problem also made it an object for medical

15. R. M. Yerkes, "Social Dominance and Sexual Status in the Chimpanzee," *Quarterly Review of Biology* 14, no. 2 (1939): 115–36.

16. Ruth Herschberger, *Adam's Rib* (New York: Pellegrine & Cudhay, 1948).

17. See Emma Goldman's *Living My Life* (New York: Alfred A. Knopf, Inc., 1931) for her keen analysis of the effects of sexual ignorance on working-class women. See Diana Long Hall ("Biology, Sex Hormones and Sexism in the 1920s," *Philosophical Forum* 5 [1974]: 81–96) for general background on the political context of sex research. She is currently completing an important book on the history of endocrinology, the Committee for Research in Problems of Sex, and related subjects in American society to 1940. For an insiders' discussion, see Sophie Aberle and George W. Corner, *Twenty-five Years of Sex Research: History of the National Research Council Committee for Research in Problems of Sex, 1922–47* (Philadelphia: W. B. Saunders Co., 1953). The complicated network of scientific communities emerges clearly from Diana Long Hall's work.

therapy for all kinds of sexual "illness," most certainly including homosexuality and unhappy marriages. The biochemical and physiological basis of the therapeutic claims immensely strengthened the legitimating power of scientific managers over women's lives. The committee closed the escape holes for those who rejected Freud's kind of sexual reductionism: whether from the psychoanalytic or physical-chemical directions, sex was safely in the care of scientific-medical managers. Monkeys and apes were enlisted in this task in central roles; as natural objects unobscured by culture, they would show most plainly the organic base in relation to which culture emerged. That these "natural objects" were thoroughly designed according to the many-leveled meanings of an ideal of human engineering has hardly been noticed.

Carpenter arrived at Yale's primate laboratories already enmeshed in the web of funding and practice represented by the CRPS. His Ph.D work had been funded by the committee, his postdoctoral fellowship granted by essentially the same men, and his host, Yerkes, was the central figure in a very important network of scientific assumptions and practices. Those scientific networks crucially determined who did science and what science was considered good. From his education, funding, and social environment, there was little reason for Carpenter to reject the basic assumptions that identified reproduction and dominance based on sex with the fundamental organizing principles of a natural body politic. What Carpenter added, however, was significant. Methodologically, he established the demanding skill of naturalistic observation of wild primates in two extraordinarily careful field studies, one on New World howler monkeys and one on Asian gibbons. These studies have deeply influenced the techniques and interpretations of animal sociology. They are worthy of note because they are simultaneously excellent, commanding work and fully reflective of social relations based on dominance in the human world of scientists.[18] Theoretically, Carpenter tied the interpretations of the laboratory disciplines of comparative psychology and sexual physiology to evolutionary and ecological field biology centered on the concepts of population and community. In short, he started to link the elements of natural and political economy in new and important ways. The classic Darwinian conception of natural political economy of populations began to be integrated with the physiological and psychological sciences that greatly

18. C. R. Carpenter, *Naturalistic Behavior of Nonhuman Primates* (University Park: Pennsylvania State University Press, 1964). This book is a collection of Carpenter's major papers covering work from the 1930s on. Carpenter moved from primate studies to concern with educational television in American rural and Third World contexts. He brought into communications systems work the same functionalist, hierarchical conceptions of organization he used in analyzing primates. See also his "Concepts and Problems of Primate Sociometry," *Sociometry* 8 (1945): 56–61, and "The Applications of Less Complex Instructional Technologies," in *Quality Instructional Television*, ed. W. Schramm (Honolulu: Hawaii University Press, East-West Center, 1972), pp. 191–205.

flourished in the early twentieth century. The integration would be complete only after World War II, when Sherwood Washburn and his students transformed physical anthropology and primate studies by systematically exploiting the evolutionary functionalism of the neo-Darwinian synthesis and the social functionalism of Bronislaw Malinowski's theory of culture.

In addition to linking levels of psychobiological analysis to modern evolutionary theory, Carpenter analyzed primate groups with the tools of early systems theory that were simultaneously providing the technical base for the claim to scientific maturity of the social sciences based on concepts of culture and social group. Carpenter's early social functionalism—with all its remaining ties to an older comparative psychology and to developmental physiology (experimental embryology)—is crucial for examining the connecting chains from physiology to politics, from animal to human. Carpenter himself did not work within the doctrine of autonomy of natural and social sciences. Neither did he permit direct reduction of social to physiological or of human to animal. He elaborated analytical links between levels that were shared by both adherents and opponents of the crucial nature-culture distinction. Indeed, his primate sociology is a useful place to begin to unravel the many varieties of functionalism emerging within biological and social sciences between the two world wars, all based on principles of hierarchical order of the body and body politic. The functionalist disciplines underlay strong ideologies of social control and techniques of medical, educational, and industrial management.

A single experimental manipulation embodies in miniature all the layers of significance of the principle of dominance in Carpenter's seminal work on the animal body politic. In 1938 he collected about 400 rhesus monkeys in Asia and freed them on Cayo Santiago. After a period of social chaos, they organized themselves into six groups containing both sexes and ranging in size from three to 147 animals. The monkeys were allowed to range freely over the thirty-seven acre island and to divide space and other resources with little outside interference. The first major study undertaken of them was of their sexual behavior, including periodicity of estrus, homosexual, autoerotic, and "nonconformist" behavior. Carpenter's conclusions noted that intragroup dominance by males was strongly correlated with sexual activity, and so presumably with evolutionary advantage. All the sexist interpretations with which we have become monotonously familiar were present in the analysis of the study, including such renderings of animal activities as, "Homosexual females who play masculine roles attack females who play the feminine role prior to the formation of a female-female consort relation."[19]

19. Carpenter, *Naturalistic Behavior*, p. 339.

In harmony with the guiding notion of the ties of sex and dominance in the fundamental organization of the rhesus groups, Carpenter performed what on the surface is a very simple experiment, but one which represents the whole complex of layered explanation of the natural body politic from the physiological to the political. After watching the undisturbed group for one week as a control, he removed the "alpha male" (animal judged most dominant on the basis of priority access to food, sex, etc.), named Diablo, from his group. Carpenter then observed the remaining animals for one week, removed the number 2 male, waited another week, removed the number 3 male, waited, restored all three males to the group, and again observed the social behavior. He noted that removal of Diablo resulted in immediate restriction of the territorial range of the group on the island relative to other groups. Social order was seriously disrupted. "The group organization became more fluid and there was an increase in *intra-group conflict* and fights. . . . After a marked disruption lasting three weeks, the group was suddenly restructured when the dominant males were released."[20] Social order was restored, and the group regained its prior favorable position relative to other groups.

Several questions immediately arise. Why did Carpenter not use as a control the removal of other than dominant males from the group to test his organizing hypothesis about the source of social order? Literally, he removed the putative head from the collective animal body. What did this field experiment, this decapitation, mean to Carpenter?

First, it must be examined on a physiological level. Carpenter relied on biological concepts for understanding social bodies. He drew from theories of embryological development that tried to explain the formation of complex whole animals from simpler starting materials of fertilized eggs. One important embryological theory used the concept of fields organized by axes of activity called dominance gradients. A field was a spatial whole formed by the complex interaction of gradients. A gradient was conceived, in this theory, to consist of an ordered series of processes from low to high levels of activity measured, for example, by differential oxygen consumption. Note that at this basic level dominance was conceived as a purely physiological property that could be objectively measured. The slope of a gradient could be shallow or steep. Several gradients making up a field would be organized around a principal axis of greatest slope, the organization center. An organism grew in complexity through integrated multiplication of dominance systems. An appropriate experimental system within developmental physiology designed to test theories of fields, gradients, physiological dominance, and organization centers was the simple hydra. It had only one axis or possible gradient: head to tail. One could cut off the polyp's head, observe

20. Ibid., p. 362.

temporary disorganization of remaining tissue, and see ultimate re-establishment of a new head from among the physiologically "competing" cells. Further, one could remove much or little from the head portion of the activity gradient and test the extent of ensuing organic disorganization.[21]

Carpenter conceived social space to be like the organic space of a developing organism, and so he looked for gradients that organized the social field through time. He found such a physiological gradient of activity in the dominance hierarchy of the males of the social group. He performed the theoretically based experiment of head removal and "observed" ensuing physiological competition among cells or organs (i.e., other points—animals—on the activity-dominance gradient) to reestablish a chief organization center (achieve alpha male status) and restore social harmony. Several consequences flow from these identifications.

First, other groups of animals in the society could be ordered on activity axes as well; females, for example, were found to have a dominance hierarchy of less steepness or lower slope. Young animals had unstable dominance gradients; the observation underlying that interpretation was that ordinary dominance behavior could not be reliably seen and that immature animals did not show constant dominance relations to one another. As unseen "observations" became just as important as evidence as seen ones, a concept of latent dominance followed readily. From this point, it is an easy step to judgments about the amount of dominance that functions to organize social space (call that quantity leadership) and the amount that causes social disruption (call that pathological aggression). Throughout the period around World War II, similar studies of the authoritarian personality in human beings abounded; true social order must rest on a balance of dominance, interpreted as the foundation of cooperation. Competitive aggression became the chief form that organized other forms of social integration. Far from competition and cooperation being mutual opposites, the former is the precondition of the latter—on physiological grounds. If the most active (dominant) regions, the organization centers, of an organism are removed, other gradient systems compete to reestablish organic order: a period of fights and fluidity ensues within the body politic. The chief point is that without an organizing dominance hierarchy, social order supposedly is seen to break down into individualistic, unproductive competition. The control experiment of removing other animals than the dominant males was not done because it did not make sense within the whole complex of theory, analogies to individual organisms, and unexamined assumptions.

21. C. M. Child was the primary gradient field theorist whose ideas entered social theory (see C. M. Child, "Biological Foundations of Social Integration," *Publications of the American Sociological Society* 22 [1928]: 26–42).

The authoritarian personality studies bring us to the second level of explanation of the body politic implicit in Carpenter's experiment: the psychological. The idea of a dominance hierarchy was derived in the first instance from study of "peck orders" in domestic chickens and other birds initiated by the Norwegian Thorlief Schjelderup-Ebbe as early as 1913, but not incorporated into American comparative psychology in any important way until the 1930s. Then animal sociology and psychology, as well as human branches of the disciplines, focused great attention on ideas of competition and cooperation.[22] Society was derived from complex interactions of pairs of individuals, understood and measured by psychological techniques, which constituted the social field space. One looked for axes of dominance as organizing principles on both the physiological and psychological levels.

The third and last level implicit in Carpenter's manipulation is that of natural political economy. The group that loses its alpha male loses in the competitive struggle with other organized organic societies. The result would be reflected in less food, higher infant mortality, fewer offspring, and thus evolutionary disadvantage or even extinction. The market competition implicit in organic evolutionary theory surfaces here. The theory of the function of male dominance nicely joins the political economy aspect of the study of animal behavior and evolution (competitive, division of labor, resource allocation model) with the social integration aspect (cooperative coordination through leadership and social position) with the purely physiological understandings of reproductive and embryological phenomena. All three perspectives link functionalist equilibrium social models—established in social sciences of the period—to explicit ideological, political concerns with competition and cooperation (in labor struggles, for example).[23] Since animal societies are seen to have in simpler form all the characteristics of human societies and cultures, one may legitimately learn from them the base of supposedly natural, integrated community for humanity. Elton Mayo—the influential Harvard,

22. Thorlief Schjelderup-Ebbe, "Social Behavior of Birds," in *Handbook of Social Psychology*, ed. Carl Murchison (Worcester, Mass.: Clark University Press, 1935), 2:947–72.

23. Elton Mayo, *The Human Problems of Industrial Civilization* (New York: Macmillan Co., 1933). Stephen Cross, Johns Hopkins University History of Science Department, is writing a dissertation on industrial sociology-physiology developed in relation to L. J. Henderson's Pareto seminars in the 1930s at Harvard. See Barbara Heyl, "The Harvard Pareto Circle," *Journal of the History of Behavioral Sciences* 4 (1968): 316–34; L. J. Henderson, *Pareto's General Sociology: A Physiologist's Interpretation* (Cambridge, Mass.: Harvard University Press, 1935); and Talcott Parsons, "On Building Social System Theory: A Personal History," *Daedalus* (Fall 1970), pp. 826–81. The theme of cooperation-competition in anthropological focus on personality and culture in the 1930s was pervasive and crucial. See Margaret Mead, ed., *Cooperation and Competition among Primitive Peoples* (New York: McGraw-Hill Book Co., 1937); and Mark A. May and Leonard W. Dobb, *Competition and Cooperation* (New York: Social Science Research Council, 1937). This report was mainly a bibliography on the competition-cooperation theme in the 1930s.

anti-labor union, industrial psychologist-sociologist of the same period—called such a community the "Garden of Industry."[24]

The political principle of domination has been transformed here into the legitimating scientific principle of dominance as a natural property with a physical-chemical base. Manipulations, concepts, organizing principles—the entire range of tools of the science—must be seen to be penetrated by the principle of domination. Science cannot be reclaimed for liberating purposes by simply reinterpreting observations or changing terminology, a crass ideological exercise in any case, which denies a dialectical interaction with the animals in the project of self-creation through scientific labor. But the difficult process of remaking the biosocial and biobehavioral sciences for liberation has begun. Not surprisingly, one of the first steps has been to switch the focus from primates as models of human beings to a deeper look at the animals themselves—how they live and relate to their environments in ways that may have little to do with us and that will surely reform our sense of relation to nature in our theories of the body politic. These "revisionist" scientific theories and practices deserve serious attention. Of them, "feminist" perspectives in physical anthropology and primatology have stressed principles of organization for bodies and societies that do not depend on dominance hierarchies. Dominance structures are still seen and examined, but cease to be used as causal explanations of functional organization. Rather, the revisionists have stressed matrifocal groups, long-term social cooperation rather than short-term spectacular aggression, flexible process rather than strict structure, and so on.[25] The scientific and ideological issues are complex; the emerging work is justly controversial.

In our search for an understanding of a feminist body politic, we need the discipline of the natural and social sciences, just as we need every creative form of theory and practice. These sciences will have liberating functions insofar as we build them on social relations not

24. Leon Baritz, *Servants of Power* (Middletown, Conn.: Wesleyan University Press, 1960). This work develops Mayo's industrial mythology in the context of a general criticism of the subservient role to established power played by American social science (see esp. chaps. 5 and 6).

25. For further discussion of revisionist primatologists see the second part of my article, "The Past Is the Contested Zone," in this volume. Other revisionists include Shirley Strum, "Life with the Pumphouse Gang," *National Geographic* 147 (1975): 672–91; Glenn Hausfater, "Dominance and Reproduction in Baboons *(Papio Cynocephalus)*: A Quantitative Analysis" (Ph.D. diss., University of Chicago, 1974); Jane Lancaster, *Primate Behavior and the Emergence of Human Culture* (New York: Holt, Rinehart & Winston, 1975); and Cynthia Moss, *Portraits in the Wild: Behavior Studies of East African Mammals* (Boston: Houghton Mifflin Co., 1975). Moss is a science writer; Lancaster and Strum are part of Sherwood Washburn's remarkable lineage. Again, we must remember influential networks in the scientific community.

based on domination. A corollary of that requirement is the rejection of all forms of the ideological claims for pure objectivity rooted in the subject-object split that has legitimated our logics of domination of nature and ourselves. If our experience is of domination, we will theorize our lives according to principles of dominance. As we transform the foundations of our lives, we will know how to build natural sciences to underpin new relations with the world. We, like Dawn in Marge Piercy's *Woman on the Edge of Time*, want to fly into nature, as well as into the past, to make it come out all right. But the sciences are collective expressions and cannot be remade individually. Like Luciente and Hawk, in the same novel, feminists have been clear that "nobody can *make* things come out right," that "it isn't bad to want to help, to want to work, to seize history, . . . But to want to do it alone is less good. To hand history to someone like a cake you baked."[26]

Department of History of Science
Johns Hopkins University

26. Marge Piercy, *Woman on the Edge of Time* (New York: Alfred A. Knopf, Inc., 1976), pp. 188–89.

Compulsory Heterosexuality and Lesbian Existence

Adrienne Rich

I

Biologically men have only one innate orientation—a sexual one that draws them to women,—while women have two innate orientations, sexual toward men and reproductive toward their young.[1]

. . . I was a woman terribly vulnerable, critical, using femaleness as a sort of standard or yardstick to measure and discard men. Yes—

I want to mention, for this 1983 reprinting, some texts which have appeared since the writing of this article. Documentation on male violence against women has been accumulating. *Aegis, Magazine on Ending Violence against Women*, continues to be an important resource. Single copy is $3.25 from Feminist Alliance against Rape, P.O. Box 21033, Washington, D.C. 20009. See also Louise Armstrong, *Kiss Daddy Goodnight* (New York: Pocket Books, 1976); Sandra Butler, *Conspiracy of Silence: The Trauma of Incest* (San Francisco: New Glide Publications, 1978); F. Delacoste and F. Newman, eds., *Fight Back! Feminist Resistance to Male Violence* (Minneapolis: Cleis Press, 1981); Judy Freespirit, *Daddy's Girl: An Incest Survivor's Story* (Langlois, Oreg., Diaspora Distribution, 1982); Judith Herman, *Father-Daughter Incest* (Cambridge, Mass.: Harvard University Press, 1981); T. McNaron and Y. Morgan, eds., *Voices in the Night: Women Speaking about Incest* (Minneapolis: Cleis Press, 1982); Florence Rush, *The Best-Kept Secret* (New York: McGraw-Hill Book Co., 1980); Diana Russell, *Rape in Marriage* (New York: Macmillan Publishing Co., 1982); and Betsy Warrior's richly informative, multipurpose compilation of essays, statistics, listings, and facts, the *Battered Women's Directory* (formerly titled *Working on Wife Abuse*; 8th ed. [1982], obtainable at $9.50 from Directory, Betsy Warrior, 46 Pleasant St., Cambridge, MA 02139). See also Wini Breines and Linda Gordon, "The New Scholarship on Family Violence," *Signs: Journal of Women in Culture and Society* 8, no. 3 (Spring 1983): 490–531. For more recent literature which depicts woman-bonding and woman-identification as a basis for female survival, see, among others, Gloria Anzaldúa and Cherríe Moraga, eds., *This Bridge Called My Back: Writings by Radical Women of Color* (Watertown, Mass.: Persephone Press, 1981); Juanita Ramos and Mirtha Quintinales, eds., *Compañeras: Antología Lesbiana Latina, Latina Lesbian Anthology* (tentatively from Kitchen Table/Women of Color Press, 1984); J. R. Roberts, *Black Lesbians: An Annotated Bibliography* (Tallahassee, Fla.: Naiad Press, 1981); Barbara Smith, ed., *Home Girls: A Black Feminist Anthology* (Kitchen Table/Women of Color Press, 1983). For accounts of contemporary Jewish lesbian existence, see E. T. Beck, ed., *Nice Jewish Girls: A Lesbian Anthology* (Watertown, Mass.: Persephone Press, 1982). See also Elly Bulkin, ed., *Lesbian Fiction: An Anthology* (Watertown, Mass.: Persephone Press, 1981). The earliest formulation that I know of heterosexuality as institution was in the lesbian-feminist paper the *Furies*, founded in 1971. For a collection of articles from that paper, see Nancy Myron and Charlotte Bunch, eds., *Lesbianism and the Women's Movement* (Oakland, Calif.: Diana Press, 1975; distributed by Crossing Press, Trumansburg, N.Y. 14886). EDITOR'S NOTE: This is a revised and updated version of the note that appeared in the Summer 1980 issue of *Signs: Journal of Women in Culture and Society*.

1. Alice Rossi, "Children and Work in the Lives of Women" (paper delivered at the University of Arizona, Tucson, February 1976).

something like that. I was an Anna who invited defeat from men
without ever being conscious of it. (But I am conscious of it. And
being conscious of it means I shall leave it all behind me and
become—but what?) I was stuck fast in an emotion common to
women of our time, that can turn them bitter, or Lesbian, or solitary. Yes, that Anna during that time was . . .

[Another blank line across the page:][2]

The bias of compulsory heterosexuality, through which lesbian experience is perceived on a scale ranging from deviant to abhorrent, or simply
rendered invisible, could be illustrated from many other texts than the
two just preceding. The assumption made by Rossi, that women are
"innately sexually oriented" toward men, or by Lessing, that the lesbian
choice is simply an acting-out of bitterness toward men, are by no means
theirs alone; they are widely current in literature and in the social sciences.

I am concerned here with two other matters as well: first, how and
why women's choice of women as passionate comrades, life partners,
co-workers, lovers, tribe, has been crushed, invalidated, forced into hiding and disguise; and second, the virtual or total neglect of lesbian existence in a wide range of writings, including feminist scholarship. Obviously there is a connection here. I believe that much feminist theory and
criticism is stranded on this shoal.

My organizing impulse is the belief that it is not enough for feminist
thought that specifically lesbian texts exist. Any theory or cultural/
political creation that treats lesbian existence as a marginal or less "natural" phenomenon, as mere "sexual preference," or as the mirror image
of either heterosexual or male homosexual relations, is profoundly
weakened thereby, whatever its other contributions. Feminist theory can
no longer afford merely to voice a toleration of "lesbianism" as an
"alternative life-style," or make token allusion to lesbians. A feminist
critique of compulsory heterosexual orientation for women is long over-
due. In this exploratory paper, I shall try to show why.

I will begin by way of examples, briefly discussing four books that
have appeared in the last few years, written from different viewpoints
and political orientations, but all presenting themselves, and favorably
reviewed, as feminist.[3] All take as a basic assumption that the social

---

2. Doris Lessing, *The Golden Notebook* (New York: Bantam Books [1962] 1977), p. 480.
3. Nancy Chodorow, *The Reproduction of Mothering* (Berkeley: University of California
Press, 1978); Dorothy Dinnerstein, *The Mermaid and the Minotaur: Sexual Arrangements and
the Human Malaise* (New York: Harper & Row, 1976); Barbara Ehrenreich and Deirdre
English, *For Her Own Good: 150 Years of the Experts' Advice to Women* (Garden City, N.Y.:
Doubleday & Co., Anchor Press, 1978); Jean Baker Miller, *Toward a New Psychology of
Women* (Boston: Beacon Press, 1976).

relations of the sexes are disordered and extremely problematic, if not disabling, for women; all seek paths toward change. I have learned more from some of these books than from others; but on this I am clear: each one might have been more accurate, more powerful, more truly a force for change, had the author felt impelled to deal with lesbian existence as a reality, and as a source of knowledge and power available to women; or with the institution of heterosexuality itself as a beachhead of male dominance.[4] In none of them is the question ever raised, whether in a different context, or other things being equal, women would *choose* heterosexual coupling and marriage; heterosexuality is presumed as a "sexual preference" of "most women," either implicitly or explicitly. In none of these books, which concern themselves with mothering, sex roles, relationships, and societal prescriptions for women, is compulsory heterosexuality ever examined as an institution powerfully affecting all these; or the idea of "preference" or "innate orientation" even indirectly questioned.

In *For Her Own Good: 150 Years of the Experts' Advice to Women* by Barbara Ehrenreich and Deirdre English, the authors' superb pamphlets, *Witches, Midwives and Nurses: A History of Women Healers,* and *Complaints and Disorders: The Sexual Politics of Sickness,* are developed into a provocative and complex study. Their thesis in this book is that the advice given American women by male health professionals, particularly in the areas of marital sex, maternity, and child care, has echoed the dictates of the economic marketplace and the role capitalism has needed women to play in production and/or reproduction. Women have become the consumer victims of various cures, therapies, and normative judgments in different periods (including the prescription to middle-class

4. I could have chosen many other serious and influential recent books, including anthologies, which would illustrate the same point: e.g., *Our Bodies, Ourselves,* the Boston Women's Health Collective's best-seller (New York: Simon & Schuster, 1976), which devotes a separate (and inadequate) chapter to lesbians, but whose message is that heterosexuality is most women's life preference; Berenice Carroll, ed., *Liberating Women's History: Theoretical and Critical Essays* (Urbana: University of Illinois Press, 1976), which does not include even a token essay on the lesbian presence in history, though an essay by Linda Gordon, Persis Hunt, et al. notes the use by male historians of "sexual deviance" as a category to discredit and dismiss Anna Howard Shaw, Jane Addams, and other feminists ("Historical Phallacies: Sexism in American Historical Writing"); and Renate Bridenthal and Claudia Koonz, eds., *Becoming Visible: Women in European History* (Boston: Houghton Mifflin Co., 1977), which contains three mentions of male homosexuality but no materials that I have been able to locate on lesbians. Gerda Lerner, ed., *The Female Experience: An American Documentary* (Indianapolis: Bobbs-Merrill Co., 1977), contains an abridgment of two lesbian/feminist position papers from the contemporary movement but no other documentation of lesbian existence. Lerner does note in her preface, however, how the charge of deviance has been used to fragment women and discourage women's resistance. Linda Gordon, in *Woman's Body, Woman's Right: A Social History of Birth Control in America* (New York: Viking Press, Grossman, 1976), notes accurately that: "It is not that feminism has produced more lesbians. There have always been many lesbians, despite high levels of repression; and most lesbians experience their sexual preference as innate . . ." (p. 410).

women to embody and preserve the sacredness of the home—the "scientific" romanticization of the home itself). None of the "experts'" advice has been either particularly scientific or women-oriented; it has reflected male needs, male fantasies about women, and male interest in controlling women—particularly in the realms of sexuality and motherhood—fused with the requirements of industrial capitalism. So much of this book is so devastatingly informative and is written with such lucid feminist wit, that I kept waiting as I read for the basic prescription against lesbianism to be examined. It never was.

This can hardly be for lack of information. Jonathan Katz's *Gay American History*[5] tells us that as early as 1656 the New Haven Colony prescribed the death penalty for lesbians. Katz provides many suggestive and informative documents on the "treatment" (or torture) of lesbians by the medical profession in the nineteenth and twentieth centuries. Recent work by the historian Nancy Sahli documents the crackdown on intense female friendships among college women at the turn of the present century.[6] The ironic title, *For Her Own Good*, might have referred first and foremost to the economic imperative to heterosexuality and marriage and to the sanctions imposed against single women and widows—both of whom have been and still are viewed as deviant. Yet, in this often enlightening Marxist-feminist overview of male prescriptions for female sanity and health, the economics of prescriptive heterosexuality go unexamined.[7]

Of the three psychoanalytically based books, one, Jean Baker Miller's *Toward a New Psychology of Women,* is written as if lesbians simply do not exist, even as marginal beings. Given Miller's title I find this astonishing. However, the favorable reviews the book has received in feminist journals, including *Signs* and *Spokeswoman,* suggest that Miller's heterocentric assumptions are widely shared. In *The Mermaid and the Minotaur: Sexual Arrangements and the Human Malaise,* Dorothy Dinnerstein makes an impassioned argument for the sharing of parenting between women and men and for an end to what she perceives as the male/female symbiosis of "gender arrangements," which she feels are leading the species further and further into violence and self-extinction. Apart from other problems that I have with this book (including her silence on the institutional and random terrorism men have practiced on women—and children—throughout history, amply documented by

5. Jonathan Katz, *Gay American History* (New York: Thomas Y. Crowell Co., 1976).

6. Nancy Sahli, "Smashing: Women's Relationships before the Fall," *Chrysalis: A Magazine of Women's Culture* 8 (1979): 17–27. A version of the article was presented at the Third Berkshire Conference on the History of Women, June 11, 1976.

7. This is a book which I have publicly endorsed. I would still do so, though with the above caveat. It is only since beginning to write this article that I fully appreciated how enormous is the unasked question in Ehrenreich and English's book.

Barry, Daly, Griffin, Russell and van de Ven, and Brownmiller,[8] and her obsession with psychology to the neglect of economic and other material realities that help to create psychological reality), I find utterly ahistorical Dinnerstein's view of the relations between women and men as "a collaboration to keep history mad." She means by this, to perpetuate social relations which are hostile, exploitive, and destructive to life itself. She sees women and men as equal partners in the making of "sexual arrangements," seemingly unaware of the repeated struggles of women to resist oppression (our own and that of others) and to change our condition. She ignores, specifically, the history of women who—as witches, *femmes seules,* marriage resisters, spinsters, autonomous widows, and/or lesbians—have managed on varying levels *not* to collaborate. It is this history, precisely, from which feminists have so much to learn and on which there is overall such blanketing silence. Dinnerstein acknowledges at the end of her book that "female separatism," though "on a large scale and in the long run wildly impractical," has something to teach us: "Separate, women could in principle set out to learn from scratch— undeflected by the opportunities to evade this task that men's presence has so far offered—what intact self-creative humanness is."[9] Phrases like "intact self-creative humanness" obscure the question of what the many forms of female separatism have actually been addressing. The fact is that women in every culture and throughout history *have* undertaken the task of independent, nonheterosexual, woman-connected existence, to the extent made possible by their context, often in the belief that they were the "only ones" ever to have done so. They have undertaken it even though few women have been in an economic position to resist marriage altogether; and even though attacks against unmarried women have ranged from aspersion and mockery to deliberate gynocide, including the burning and torturing of millions of widows and spinsters during the witch persecutions of the fifteenth, sixteenth, and seventeenth centuries in Europe, and the practice of suttee on widows in India.[10]

Nancy Chodorow does come close to the edge of an acknowledgment of lesbian existence. Like Dinnerstein, Chodorow believes that the fact that women, and women only, are responsible for child care in the sexual division of labor has led to an entire social organization of gender inequality, and that men as well as women must become primary carers for children if that inequality is to change. In the process of examining, from a psychoanalytic perspective, how mothering-by-women affects the psychological development of girl and boy children, she offers documentation that men are "emotionally secondary" in women's lives; that

8. Susan Brownmiller, *Against Our Will: Men, Women and Rape* (New York: Simon & Schuster, 1975).

9. Dinnerstein, p. 272.

10. Daly, pp. 184–85; 114–33.

"women have a richer, ongoing inner world to fall back on. . . . men do not become as emotionally important to women as women do to men."[11] This would carry into the late twentieth century Smith-Rosenberg's findings about eighteenth- and nineteenth-century women's emotional focus on women. "Emotionally important" can of course refer to anger as well as to love, or to that intense mixture of the two often found in women's relationships with women: one aspect of what I have come to call the "double-life of women" (see below). Chodorow concludes that because women have women as mothers, "The mother remains a primary internal object [*sic*] to the girl, so that heterosexual relationships are on the model of a nonexclusive, second relationship for her, whereas for the boy they recreate an exclusive, primary relationship." According to Chodorow, women "have learned to deny the limitations of masculine lovers for both psychological and practical reasons."[12]

But the practical reasons (like witch burnings, male control of law, theology, and science, or economic nonviability within the sexual division of labor) are glossed over. Chodorow's account barely glances at the constraints and sanctions which, historically, have enforced or insured the coupling of women with men and obstructed or penalized our coupling or allying in independent groups with other women. She dismisses lesbian existence with the comment that "lesbian relationships do tend to re-create mother-daughter emotions and connections, but most women are heterosexual" (implied: more mature, having developed beyond the mother-daughter connection). She then adds: "This heterosexual preference and taboos on homosexuality, in addition to objective economic dependence on men, make the option of primary sexual bonds with other women unlikely—though more prevalent in recent years."[13] The significance of that qualification seems irresistible—but Chodorow does not explore it further. Is she saying that lesbian existence has become more visible in recent years (in certain groups?), that economic and other pressures have changed (under capitalism, socialism, or both?), and that consequently more women are rejecting the heterosexual "choice"? She argues that women want children because their heterosexual relationships lack richness and intensity, that in having a child a woman seeks to re-create her own intense relationship with her mother. It seems to be that on the basis of her own findings, Chodorow leads us implicitly to conclude that heterosexuality is *not* a "preference" for women; that, for one thing, it fragments the erotic from the emotional in a way that women find impoverishing and painful. Yet her book participates in mandating it. Neglecting the covert socializations and the overt forces which have channelled women into marriage and heterosexual romance,

11. Chodorow, pp. 197–98.
12. Ibid., pp. 198–99.
13. Ibid., p. 200.

pressures ranging from the selling of daughters to postindustrial economics to the silences of literature to the images of the television screen,
she, like Dinnerstein, is stuck with trying to reform a man-made
institution—compulsory heterosexuality—as if, despite profound emotional impulses and complementarities drawing women toward women,
there is a mystical/biological heterosexual inclination, a "preference" or
"choice" which draws women toward men.

Moreover, it is understood that this "preference" does not need to
be explained, unless through the tortuous theory of the female Oedipus
complex or the necessity for species reproduction. It is lesbian sexuality
which (usually, and, incorrectly, "included" under male homosexuality)
is seen as requiring explanation. This assumption of female heterosexuality seems to me in itself remarkable: it is an enormous assumption to
have glided so silently into the foundations of our thought.

The extension of this assumption is the frequently heard assertion
that in a world of genuine equality, where men were nonoppressive and
nurturing, everyone would be bisexual. Such a notion blurs and sen-
timentalizes the actualities within which women have experienced sexuality; it is the old liberal leap across the tasks and struggles of here and
now, the continuing process of sexual definition which will generate its
own possibilities and choices. (It also assumes that women who have
chosen women have done so simply because men are oppressive and
emotionally unavailable: which still fails to account for women who continue to pursue relationships with oppressive and/or emotionally unsatisfying men.) I am suggesting that heterosexuality, like motherhood,
needs to be recognized and studied as a *political institution*—even, or
especially, by those individuals who feel they are, in their personal experience, the precursors of a new social relation between the sexes.

II

If women are the earliest sources of emotional caring and physical
nurture for both female and male children, it would seem logical, from a
feminist perspective at least, to pose the following questions: whether the
search for love and tenderness in both sexes does not originally lead
toward women; *why in fact women would ever redirect that search;* why
species-survival, the means of impregnation, and emotional/erotic relationships should ever have become so rigidly identified with each
other; and why such violent strictures should be found necessary to
enforce women's total emotional, erotic loyalty and subservience to
men. I doubt that enough feminist scholars and theorists have taken the
pains to acknowledge the societal forces which wrench women's emotional and erotic energies away from themselves and other women and

from woman-identified values. These forces, as I shall try to show, range from literal physical enslavement to the disguising and distorting of possible options.

I do not, myself, assume that mothering-by-women is a "sufficient cause" of lesbian existence. But the issue of mothering-by-women has been much in the air of late, usually accompanied by the view that increased parenting by men would minimize antagonism between the sexes and equalize the sexual imbalance of power of males over females. These discussions are carried on without reference to compulsory heterosexuality as a phenomenon let alone as an ideology. I do not wish to psychologize here, but rather to identify sources of male power. I believe large numbers of men could, in fact, undertake child care on a large scale without radically altering the balance of male power in a male-identified society.

In her essay "The Origin of the Family," Kathleen Gough lists eight characteristics of male power in archaic and contemporary societies which I would like to use as a framework: "men's ability to deny women sexuality or to force it upon them; to command or exploit their labor to control their produce; to control or rob them of their children; to confine them physically and prevent their movement; to use them as objects in male transactions; to cramp their creativeness; or to withhold from them large areas of the society's knowledge and cultural attainments."[14] (Gough does not perceive these power-characteristics as specifically enforcing heterosexuality; only as producing sexual inequality.) Below, Gough's words appear in italics; the elaboration of each of her categories, in brackets, is my own.

Characteristics of male power include:

the power of men

1. *to deny women* [our own] *sexuality*
   [by means of clitoridectomy and infibulation; chastity belts; punishment, including death, for female adultery; punishment, including death, for lesbian sexuality; psychoanalytic denial of the clitoris; strictures against masturbation; denial of maternal and postmenopausal sensuality; unnecessary hysterectomy; pseudolesbian images in media and literature; closing of archives and destruction of documents relating to lesbian existence];
2. *or to force it* [male sexuality] *upon them*
   [by means of rape (including marital rape) and wife beating; father-daughter, brother-sister incest; the socialization of women to feel that male sexual "drive" amounts to a right;[15] idealization

14. Kathleen Gough, "The Origin of the Family," in *Toward an Anthropology of Women*, ed. Rayna [Rapp] Reiter (New York: Monthly Review Press, 1975), pp. 69–70.
15. Barry, pp. 216–19.

of heterosexual romance in art, literature, media, advertising, etc.; child marriage; arranged marriage; prostitution; the harem; psychoanalytic doctrines of frigidity and vaginal orgasm; pornographic depictions of women responding pleasurably to sexual violence and humiliation (a subliminal message being that sadistic heterosexuality is more "normal" than sensuality between women)];

3. *to command or exploit their labor to control their produce*
[by means of the institutions of marriage and motherhood as unpaid production; the horizontal segregation of women in paid employment; the decoy of the upwardly mobile token woman; male control of abortion, contraception, and childbirth; enforced sterilization; pimping; female infanticide, which robs mothers of daughters and contributes to generalized devaluation of women];

4. *to control or rob them of their children*
[by means of father-right and "legal kidnapping";[16] enforced sterilization; systematized infanticide; seizure of children from lesbian mothers by the courts; the malpractice of male obstetrics; use of the mother as "token torturer"[17] in genital mutilation or in binding the daughter's feet (or mind) to fit her for marriage];

5. *to confine them physically and prevent their movement*
[by means of rape as terrorism, keeping women off the streets; purdah; foot-binding; atrophying of women's athletic capabilities; haute couture, "feminine" dress codes; the veil; sexual harassment on the streets; horizontal segregation of women in employment; prescriptions for "full-time" mothering; enforced economic dependence of wives];

6. *to use them as objects in male transactions*
[use of women as "gifts"; bride-price; pimping; arranged marriage; use of women as entertainers to facilitate male deals, e.g., wife-hostess, cocktail waitress required to dress for male sexual titillation, call girls, "bunnies," geisha, *kisaeng* prostitutes, secretaries];

7. *to cramp their creativeness*
[witch persecutions as campaigns against midwives and female healers and as pogrom against independent, "unassimilated" women;[18] definition of male pursuits as more valuable than female within any culture, so that cultural values become embodiment of male subjectivity; restriction of female self-fulfillment to marriage and motherhood; sexual exploitation of women by male artists and teachers; the social and economic

16. Anna Demeter, *Legal Kidnapping* (Boston: Beacon Press, 1977), pp. xx, 126–28.
17. Daly, pp. 132, 139–41, 163–65.
18. Barbara Ehrenreich and Deirdre English, *Witches, Midwives and Nurses: A History of Women Healers* (Old Westbury, N.Y.: Feminist Press, 1973); Andrea Dworkin, *Woman Hating* (New York: E. P. Dutton, 1974), pp. 118–54; Daly, pp. 178–222.

disruption of women's creative aspirations;[19] erasure of female tradition];[20] and

8. *to withhold from them large areas of the society's knowledge and cultural attainments*
   [by means of noneducation of females (60% of the world's illiterates are women); the "Great Silence" regarding women and particularly lesbian existence in history and culture;[21] sex-role stereotyping which deflects women from science, technology, and other "masculine" pursuits; male social/professional bonding which excludes women; discrimination against women in the professions].

These are some of the methods by which male power is manifested and maintained. Looking at the schema, what surely impresses itself is the fact that we are confronting not a simple maintenance of inequality and property possession, but a pervasive cluster of forces, ranging from physical brutality to control of consciousness, which suggests that an enormous potential counterforce is having to be restrained.

Some of the forms by which male power manifests itself are more easily recognizable as enforcing heterosexuality on women than are others. Yet each one I have listed adds to the cluster of forces within which women have been convinced that marriage, and sexual orientation toward men, are inevitable, even if unsatisfying or oppressive components of their lives. The chastity belt; child marriage; erasure of lesbian existence (except as exotic and perverse) in art, literature, film; idealization of heterosexual romance and marriage—these are some fairly obvious forms of compulsion, the first two exemplifying physical force, the second two control of consciousness. While clitoridectomy has been assailed by feminists as a form of woman-torture,[22] Kathleen Barry first pointed out that it is not simply a way of turning the young girl into a "marriageable" woman through brutal surgery: it intends that women in the intimate proximity of polygynous marriage will not form sexual relationships with each other; that—from a male, genital-fetishist perspective—female erotic connections, even in a sex-segregated situation, will be literally excised.[23]

19. See Virginia Woolf, *A Room of One's Own* (London: Hogarth Press, 1929), and *Three Guineas* (New York: Harcourt Brace & Co., [1938] 1966); Tillie Olsen, *Silences* (Boston: Delacorte Press, 1978); Michelle Cliff, "The Resonance of Interruption," *Chrysalis: A Magazine of Women's Culture* 8 (1979): 29–37.

20. Mary Daly, *Beyond God the Father* (Boston: Beacon Press, 1973), pp. 347–51; Olsen, pp. 22–46.

21. Daly, *Beyond God the Father*, p. 93.

22. Fran P. Hosken, "The Violence of Power: Genital Mutilation of Females," *Heresies: A Feminist Journal of Art and Politics* 6 (1979): 28–35; Russell and van de Ven, pp. 194–95.

23. Barry, pp. 163–64.

The function of pornography as an influence on consciousness is a major public issue of our time, when a multibillion-dollar industry has the power to disseminate increasingly sadistic, women-degrading visual images. But even so-called soft-core pornography and advertising depict women as objects of sexual appetite devoid of emotional context, without individual meaning or personality: essentially as a sexual commodity to be consumed by males. (So-called lesbian pornography, created for the male voyeuristic eye, is equally devoid of emotional context or individual personality.) The most pernicious message relayed by pornography is that women are natural sexual prey to men and love it; that sexuality and violence are congruent; and that for women sex is essentially masochistic, humiliation pleasurable, physical abuse erotic. But along with this message comes another, not always recognized: that enforced submission and the use of cruelty, if played out in heterosexual pairing, is sexually "normal," while sensuality between women, including erotic mutuality and respect, is "queer," "sick," and either pornographic in itself or not very exciting compared with the sexuality of whips and bondage.[24] Pornography does not simply create a climate in which sex and violence are interchangeable; *it widens the range of behavior considered acceptable from men in heterosexual intercourse*—behavior which reiteratively strips women of their autonomy, dignity, and sexual potential, including the potential of loving and being loved by women in mutuality and integrity.

In her brilliant study, *Sexual Harassment of Working Women: A Case of Sex Discrimination*, Catharine A. MacKinnon delineates the intersection of compulsory heterosexuality and economics. Under capitalism, women are horizontally segregated by gender and occupy a structurally inferior position in the workplace; this is hardly news, but MacKinnon raises the question why, even if capitalism "requires some collection of individuals to occupy low-status, low-paying positions . . . such persons must be biologically female," and goes on to point out that "the fact that male employers often do not hire qualified women, *even when they could pay them less than men* suggests that more than the profit motive is implicated" [emphasis added].[25] She cites a wealth of material documenting the fact that women are not only segregated in low-paying, service jobs (as secretaries, domestics, nurses, typists, telephone operators, child-care workers, waitresses) but that "sexualization of the woman" is part of the job. Central and intrinsic to the economic realities of women's lives is the requirement that women will "market sexual attractiveness to men, who

24. The issue of "lesbian sadomasochism" needs to be examined in terms of the dominant cultures' teachings about the relation of sex and violence, and also of the acceptance by some lesbians of male homosexual mores. I believe this to be another example of the "double-life" of women.

25. Catharine A. MacKinnon, *Sexual Harassment of Working Women: A Case of Sex Discrimination* (New Haven, Conn.: Yale University Press, 1979), pp. 15–16.

tend to hold the economic power and position to enforce their pre-dilections." And MacKinnon exhaustively documents that "sexual harassment perpetuates the interlocked structure by which women have been kept sexually in thrall to men at the bottom of the labor market. Two forces of American society converge: men's control over women's sexuality and capital's control over employees' work lives."[26] Thus, women in the workplace are at the mercy of sex-as-power in a vicious circle. Economically disadvantaged, women—whether waitresses or professors—endure sexual harassment to keep their jobs and learn to behave in a complaisantly and ingratiatingly heterosexual manner be-cause they discover this is their true qualification for employment, what-ever the job description. And, MacKinnon notes, the woman who too decisively resists sexual overtures in the workplace is accused of being "dried-up" and sexless, or lesbian. This raises a specific difference be-tween the experiences of lesbians and homosexual men. A lesbian, clos-eted on her job because of heterosexist prejudice, is not simply forced into denying the truth of her outside relationships or private life; her job depends on her pretending to be not merely heterosexual but a hetero-sexual *woman*, in terms of dressing and playing the feminine, deferential role required of "real" women.

MacKinnon raises radical questions as to the qualitative differences between sexual harassment, rape, and ordinary heterosexual inter-course. ("As one accused rapist put it, he hadn't used 'any more force than is usual for males during the preliminaries.'") She criticizes Susan Brownmiller[27] for separating rape from the mainstream of daily life and for her unexamined premise that "rape is violence, intercourse is sexual-ity," removing rape from the sexual sphere altogether. Most crucially she argues that "taking rape from the realm of 'the sexual,' placing it in the realm of 'the violent,' allows one to be against it without raising any questions about the extent to which the institution of heterosexuality has defined force as a normal part of 'the preliminaries.'"[28] "Never is it asked whether, under conditions of male supremacy, the notion of 'con-sent' has any meaning."[29]

The fact is that the workplace, among other social institutions, is a place where women have learned to accept male violation of our psychic and physical boundaries as the price of survival; where women have been educated—no less than by romantic literature or by

---

26. Ibid., p. 174.

27. Brownmiller (n. 8 above).

28. MacKinnon, p. 219. Susan Schecter writes: "The push for heterosexual union at whatever cost is so intense that . . . it has become a cultural force of its own that creates battering. The ideology of romantic love and its jealous possession of the partner as property provide the masquerade for what can become severe abuse" (*Aegis: Magazine on Ending Violence against Women* [July–August 1979], pp. 50–51).

29. MacKinnon, p. 298.

pornography—to perceive ourselves as sexual prey. A woman seeking to escape such casual violations along with economic disadvantage may well turn to marriage as a form of hoped-for-protection, while bringing into marriage neither social or economic power, thus entering that institution also from a disadvantaged position. MacKinnon finally asks:

> What if inequality is built into the social conceptions of male and female sexuality, of masculinity and femininity, of sexiness and heterosexual attractiveness? Incidents of sexual harassment suggest that male sexual desire itself may be aroused by female vulnerability. . . . Men feel they can take advantage, so they want to, so they do. Examination of sexual harassment, precisely because the episodes appear commonplace, forces one to confront the fact that sexual intercourse normally occurs between economic (as well as physical) unequals . . . the apparent legal requirement that violations of women's sexuality appear out of the ordinary before they will be punished helps prevent women from defining the ordinary conditions of their own consent.[30]

Given the nature and extent of heterosexual pressures, the daily "eroticization of women's subordination" as MacKinnon phrases it,[31] I question the more or less psychoanalytic perspective (suggested by such writers as Karen Horney, H. R. Hayes, Wolfgang Lederer, and most recently, Dorothy Dinnerstein) that the male need to control women sexually results from some primal male "fear of women" and of women's sexual insatiability. It seems more probable that men really fear, not that they will have women's sexual appetites forced on them, or that women want to smother and devour them, but that women could be indifferent to them altogether, that men could be allowed sexual and emotional—therefore economic—access to women *only* on women's terms, otherwise being left on the periphery of the matrix.

The means of assuring male sexual access to women have recently received a searching investigation by Kathleen Barry.[32] She documents extensive and appalling evidence for the existence, on a very large scale, of international female slavery, the institution once known as "white slavery" but which in fact has involved, and at this very moment involves, women of every race and class. In the theoretical analysis derived from her research, Barry makes the connection between all enforced conditions under which women live subject to men: prostitution, marital rape, father-daughter and brother-sister incest, wife-beating, pornography, bride-price, the selling of daughters, purdah, and genital mutilation. She sees the rape paradigm—where the victim of sexual assault is held responsible for her own victimization—as leading to the rationaliza-

30. Ibid., p. 220.
31. Ibid., p. 221.
32. Kathleen Barry, *Female Sexual Slavery* (see unnumbered n. above).

tion and acceptance of other forms of enslavement, where the woman is presumed to have "chosen" her fate, to embrace it passively, or to have courted it perversely through rash or unchaste behavior. On the contrary, Barry maintains, "female sexual slavery is present in ALL situations where women or girls cannot change the conditions of their existence; where regardless of how they got into those conditions, e.g., social pressure, economic hardship, misplaced trust or the longing for affection, they cannot get out; and where they are subject to sexual violence and exploitation."[33] She provides a spectrum of concrete examples, not only as to the existence of a widespread international traffic in women, but also as to how this operates—whether in the form of a "Minnesota pipeline" funneling blonde, blue-eyed midwestern runaways to Times Square, or the purchasing of young women out of rural poverty in Latin America or Southeast Asia, or the providing of *maisons d'abattage* for migrant workers in the eighteenth arrondissement of Paris. Instead of "blaming the victim" or trying to diagnose her presumed pathology, Barry turns her floodlight on the pathology of sex colonization itself, the ideology of "cultural sadism" represented by the vast industry of pornography and by the overall identification of women primarily as "sexual beings whose responsibility is the sexual service of men."[34]

Barry delineates what she names a "sexual domination perspective" through whose lens, purporting objectivity, sexual abuse and terrorism of women by men has been rendered almost invisible by treating it as natural and inevitable. From its point of view, women are expendable as long as the sexual and emotional needs of the male can be satisfied. To replace this perspective of domination with a universal standard of basic freedom for women from gender-specific violence, from constraints on movement, and from male right of sexual and emotional access is the political purpose of her book. Like Mary Daly in *Gyn/Ecology*, Barry rejects structuralist and other cultural-relativist rationalizations for sexual torture and antiwoman violence. In her opening chapter, she asks of her readers that they refuse all handy escapes into ignorance and denial. "The only way we can come out of hiding, break through our paralyzing defenses, is to know it all—the full extent of sexual violence and domination of women. . . . In *knowing*, in facing directly, we can learn to chart our course out of this oppression, by envisioning and creating a world which will preclude female sexual slavery."[35]

"Until we name the practice, give conceptual definition and form to it, illustrate its life over time and in space, those who are its most obvious victims will also not be able to name it or define their experience."[36]

33. Ibid., p. 33.
34. Ibid., p. 103.
35. Ibid., p. 5.
36. Ibid., p. 100.

But women are all, in different ways and to different degrees, its victims; and part of the problem with naming and conceptualizing female sexual slavery is, as Barry clearly sees, compulsory heterosexuality. Compulsory heterosexuality simplifies the task of the procurer and pimp in worldwide prostitution rings and "eros centers," while, in the privacy of the home, it leads the daughter to "accept" incest/rape by her father, the mother to deny that it is happening, the battered wife to stay on with an abusive husand. "Befriending or love" is a major tactic of the procurer whose job it is to turn the runaway or the confused young girl over to the pimp for seasoning. The ideology of heterosexual romance, beamed at her from childhood out of fairy tales, television, films, advertising, popular songs, wedding pageantry, is a tool ready to the procurer's hand and one which he does not hesitate to use, as Barry amply documents. Early female indoctrination in "love" as an emotion may be largely a Western concept; but a more universal ideology concerns the primacy and uncontrollability of the male sexual drive. This is one of many insights offered by Barry's work:

As sexual power is learned by adolescent boys through the social experience of their sex drive, so do girls learn that the locus of sexual power is male. Given the importance placed on the male sex drive in the socialization of girls as well as boys, early adolescence is probably the first significant phase of male identification in a girl's life and development. . . . As a young girl becomes aware of her own increasing sexual feelings . . . she turns away from her heretofore primary relationships with girlfriends. As they become secondary to her, recede in importance in her life, her own identity also assumes a secondary role and she grows into male identification.[37.]

We still need to ask why some women never, even temporarily, "turn away from heretofore primary relationships" with other females? And why does male-identification—the casting of one's social, political, and intellectual allegiances with men—exist among lifelong sexual lesbians? Barry's hypothesis throws us among new questions, but it clarifies the diversity of forms in which compulsory heterosexuality presents itself. In the mystique of the overpowering, all-conquering male sex drive, the penis-with-a-life-of-its-own, is rooted the law of male sex-right to women, which justifies prostitution as a universal cultural assumption on the one hand, while defending sexual slavery within the family on the basis of "family privacy and cultural uniqueness" on the other.[38] The adolescent male sex drive, which, as both young women and men are

37. Ibid., p. 218.
38. Ibid., p. 140.

taught, once triggered cannot take responsibility for itself or take no for an answer, becomes, according to Barry, the norm and rationale for adult male sexual behavior: a condition of *arrested sexual development.* Women learn to accept as natural the inevitability of this "drive" because we receive it as dogma. Hence marital rape, hence the Japanese wife resignedly packing her husband's suitcase for a weekend in the *kisaeng* brothels of Taiwan, hence the psychological as well as economic imbalance of power between husband and wife, male employer and female worker, father and daughter, male professor and female student.

The effect of male-identification means

> internalizing the values of the colonizer and actively participating in carrying out the colonization of one's self and one's sex. . . . Male identification is the act whereby women place men above women, including themselves, in credibility, status, and importance in most situations, regardless of the comparative quality the women may bring to the situation. . . . Interaction with women is seen as a lesser form of relating on every level.[39]

What deserves further exploration is the double-think many women engage in and from which no woman is permanently and utterly free: However woman-to-woman relationships, female support networks, a female and feminist value system, are relied on and cherished, indoctrination in male credibility and status can still create synapses in thought, denials of feeling, wishful thinking, a profound sexual and intellectual confusion.[40] I quote here from a letter I received the day I was writing this passage: "I have had very bad relationships with men—I am now in the midst of a very painful separation. I am trying to find my strength through women—without my friends, I could not survive." How many times a day do women speak words like these, or think them, or write them, and how often does the synapse reassert itself?

Barry summarizes her findings:

> . . . Considering the arrested sexual development that is understood to be normal in the male population, and considering the numbers of men who are pimps, procurers, members of slavery gangs, corrupt officials participating in this traffic, owners, operators, employees of brothels and lodging and entertainment facilities, por-

39. Ibid., p. 172.
40. Elsewhere I have suggested that male identification has been a powerful source of white women's racism, and that it has been women who were seen as "disloyal" to male codes and systems who have actively battled against it (Adrienne Rich, "Disloyal to Civilization: Feminism, Racism, Gynephobia," in *On Lies, Secrets, and Silence: Selected Prose, 1966–1978* [New York: W. W. Norton & Co., 1979]).

nography purveyors, associated with prostitution, wife beaters, child molesters, incest perpetrators, johns (tricks) and rapists, one cannot but be momentarily stunned by the enormous male population engaging in female sexual slavery. The huge number of men engaged in these practices should be cause for declaration of an international emergency, a crisis in sexual violence. But what should be cause for alarm is instead accepted as normal sexual intercourse.[41]

Susan Cavin, in her rich and provocative, if highly speculative, dissertation, suggests that patriarchy becomes possible when the original female band, which includes children but ejects adolescent males, becomes invaded and outnumbered by males; that not patriarchal marriage, but the rape of the mother by the son, becomes the first act of male domination. The entering wedge, or leverage, which allows this to happen is not just a simple change in sex ratios; it is also the mother-child bond, manipulated by adolescent males in order to remain within the matrix past the age of exclusion. Maternal affection is used to establish male right of sexual access, which, however, must ever after be held by force (or through control of consciousness) since the original deep adult bonding is that of woman for woman.[42] I find this hypothesis extremely suggestive, since one form of false consciousness which serves compulsory heterosexuality is the maintenance of a mother-son relationship between women and men, including the demand that women provide maternal solace, nonjudgmental nurturing, and compassion for their harassers, rapists, and batterers (as well as for men who passively vampirize them). How many strong and assertive women accept male posturing from no one but their sons?

But whatever its origins, when we look hard and clearly at the extent and elaboration of measures designed to keep women within a male sexual purlieu, it becomes an inescapable question whether the issue we have to address as feminists is, not simple "gender inequality," nor the domination of culture by males, nor mere "taboos against homosexuality," but the enforcement of heterosexuality for women as a means of assuring male right of physical, economical, and emotional access.[43] One of many means of enforcement is, of course, the rendering invisible of the lesbian possibility, an engulfed continent which rises fragmentedly to view from time to time only to become submerged again. Feminist research and theory that contributes to lesbian invisibility or marginality is

41. Barry, p. 220.
42. Susan Cavin, "Lesbian Origins," Ph.D. diss., Rutgers University, 1978.
43. For my perception of heterosexuality as an economic institution I am indebted to Lisa Leghorn and Katherine Parker, who allowed me to read the unpublished manuscript of their book, *Woman's Worth: Sexual Economics and the World of Women* (London and Boston: Routledge & Kegan Paul, 1981).

actually working against the liberation and empowerment of woman as a group.[44]

The assumption that "most women are innately heterosexual" stands as a theoretical and political stumbling block for many women. It remains a tenable assumption, partly because lesbian existence has been written out of history or catalogued under disease; partly because it has been treated as exceptional rather than intrinsic; partly because to acknowledge that for women heterosexuality may not be a "preference" at all but something that has had to be imposed, managed, organized, propagandized, and maintained by force, is an immense step to take if you consider yourself freely and "innately" heterosexual. Yet the failure to examine heterosexuality as an institution is like failing to admit that the economic system called capitalism or the caste system of racism is maintained by a variety of forces, including both physical violence and false consciousness. To take the step of questioning heterosexuality as a "preference" or "choice" for women—and to do the intellectual and emotional work that follows—will call for a special quality of courage in heterosexually identified feminists but I think the rewards will be great: a freeing-up of thinking, the exploring of new paths, the shattering of another great silence, new clarity in personal relationships.

III

I have chosen to use the terms *lesbian existence* and *lesbian continuum* because the word *lesbianism* has a clinical and limiting ring. *Lesbian existence* suggests both the fact of the historical presence of lesbians and our continuing creation of the meaning of that existence. I mean the term *lesbian continuum* to include a range—through each woman's life and throughout history—of woman-identified experience; not simply the fact that a woman has had or consciously desired genital sexual experience with another woman. If we expand it to embrace many more forms of primary intensity between and among women, including the sharing

44. I would suggest that lesbian existence has been most recognized and tolerated where it has resembled a "deviant" version of heterosexuality; e.g., where lesbians have, like Stein and Toklas, played heterosexual roles (or seemed to in public) and have been chiefly identified with male culture. See also Claude E. Schaeffer, "The Kuterai Female Berdache: Courier, Guide, Prophetess and Warrior," *Ethnohistory* 12, no. 3 (Summer 1965): 193–236. (Berdache: "an individual of a definite physiological sex [m. or f.] who assumes the role and status of the opposite sex and who is viewed by the community as being of one sex physiologically but as having assumed the role and status of the opposite sex" [Schaeffer, p. 231].) Lesbian existence has also been relegated to an upper-class phenomenon, an elite decadence (as in the fascination with Paris salon lesbians such as Renée Vivien and Natalie Clifford Barney), to the obscuring of such "common women" as Judy Grahn depicts in her *The Work of a Common Woman* (Oakland, Calif.: Diana Press, 1978) and *True to Life Adventure Stories* (Oakland, Calif.: Diana Press, 1978).

of a rich inner life, the bonding against male tyranny, the giving and receiving of practical and political support; if we can also hear in it such associations as *marriage resistance* and the "haggard" behavior identified by Mary Daly (obsolete meanings: "intractable," "willful," "wanton," and "unchaste" . . . "a woman reluctant to yield to wooing")[45]—we begin to grasp breadths of female history and psychology which have lain out of reach as a consequence of limited, mostly clinical, definitions of "lesbianism."

Lesbian existence comprises both the breaking of a taboo and the rejection of a compulsory way of life. It is also a direct or indirect attack on male right of access to women. But it is more than these, although we may first begin to perceive it as a form of nay-saying to patriarchy, an act of resistance. It has of course included role playing, self-hatred, breakdown, alcoholism, suicide, and intrawoman violence; we romanticize at our peril what it means to love and act against the grain, and under heavy penalties; and lesbian existence has been lived (unlike, say, Jewish or Catholic existence) without access to any knowledge of a tradition, a continuity, a social underpinning. The destruction of records and memorabilia and letters documenting the realities of lesbian existence must be taken very seriously as a means of keeping heterosexuality compulsory for women, since what has been kept from our knowledge is joy, sensuality, courage, and community, as well as guilt, self-betrayal, and pain.[46]

Lesbians have historically been deprived of a political existence through "inclusion" as female versions of male homosexuality. To equate lesbian existence with male homosexuality because each is stigmatized is to deny and erase female reality once again. To separate those women stigmatized as "homosexual" or "gay" from the complex continuum of female resistance to enslavement, and attach them to a male pattern, is to falsify our history. Part of the history of lesbian existence is, obviously, to be found where lesbians, lacking a coherent female community, have shared a kind of social life and common cause with homosexual men. But this has to be seen against the differences: women's lack of economic and cultural privilege relative to men; qualitative differences in female and male relationships, for example, the prevalence of anonymous sex and the justification of pederasty among male homosexuals, the pronounced ageism in male homosexual standards of

45. Daly, *Gyn/Ecology*, p. 15.
46. "In a hostile world in which women are not supposed to survive except in relation with and in service to men, entire communities of women were simply erased. History tends to bury what it seeks to reject" (Blanche W. Cook," "'Women Alone Stir My Imagination': Lesbianism and the Cultural Tradition," *Signs: Journal of Women in Culture and Society* 4, no. 4 [Summer 1979]: 719–20). The Lesbian Herstory Archives in New York City is one attempt to preserve contemporary documents on lesbian existence—a project of enormous value and meaning, still pitted against the continuing censorship and obliteration of relationships, networks, communities, in other archives and elsewhere in the culture.

sexual attractiveness, etc. In defining and describing lesbian existence I would hope to move toward a dissociation of lesbian from male homosexual values and allegiances. I perceive the lesbian experience as being, like motherhood, a profoundly *female* experience, with particular oppressions, meanings, and potentialities we cannot comprehend as long as we simply bracket it with other sexually stigmatized existences. Just as the term "parenting" serves to conceal the particular and significant reality of being a parent who is actually a mother, the term "gay" serves the purpose of blurring the very outlines we need to discern, which are of crucial value for feminism and for the freedom of women as a group.

As the term "lesbian" has been held to limiting, clinical associations in its patriarchal definition, female friendship and comradeship have been set apart from the erotic, thus limiting the erotic itself. But as we deepen and broaden the range of what we define as lesbian existence, as we delineate a lesbian continuum, we begin to discover the erotic in female terms: as that which is unconfined to any single part of the body or solely to the body itself, as an energy not only diffuse but, as Audre Lorde has described it, omnipresent in "the sharing of joy, whether physical, emotional, psychic," and in the sharing of work; as the empowering joy which "makes us less willing to accept powerlessness, or those other supplied states of being which are not native to me, such as resignation, despair, self-effacement, depression, self-denial."[47] In another context, writing of women and work, I quoted the autobiographical passage in which the poet H.D. described how her friend Bryher supported her in persisting with the visonary experience which was to shape her mature work:

> . . . I knew that this experience, this writing-on-the-wall before me, could not be shared with anyone except the girl who stood so bravely there beside me. This girl had said without hesitation, "Go on." It was she really who had the detachment and integrity of the Pythoness of Delphi. But it was I, battered and dissociated . . . who was seeing the pictures, and who was reading the writing or granted the inner vision. Or perhaps, in some sense, we were "seeing" it together, for without her, admittedly, I could not have gone on. . . .[48]

If we consider the possibility that all women—from the infant suckling her mother's breast, to the grown woman experiencing orgasmic sensations while suckling her own child, perhaps recalling her mother's

47. Audre Lorde, *Uses of the Erotic: The Erotic as Power*, Out & Out Books Pamphlet no. 3 (New York: Out & Out Books [476 2d Street, Brooklyn, New York 11215], 1979).

48. Adrienne Rich, "Conditions for Work: The Common World of Women," in *On Lies, Secrets and Silence* (p. 209); H. D., *Tribute to Freud* (Oxford: Carcanet Press, 1971), pp. 50–54.

milk-smell in her own; to two women, like Virginia Woolf's Chloe and Olivia, who share a laboratory;[49] to the woman dying at ninety, touched and handled by women—exist on a lesbian continuum, we can see ourselves as moving in and out of this continuum, whether we identify ourselves as lesbian or not. It allows us to connect aspects of woman-identification as diverse as the impudent, intimate girl-friendships of eight- or nine-year olds and the banding together of those women of the twelth and fifteenth centuries known as Beguines who "shared houses, rented to one another, bequeathed houses to their room-mates . . . in cheap subdivided houses in the artisans' area of town," who "practiced Christian virtue on their own, dressing and living simply and not associating with men," who earned their livings as spinners, bakers, nurses, or ran schools for young girls, and who managed—until the Church forced them to disperse—to live independent both of marriage and of conventual restrictions.[50] It allows us to connect these women with the more celebrated "Lesbians" of the women's school around Sappho of the seventh century B.C.; with the secret sororities and economic networks reported among African women; and with the Chinese marriage resistance sisterhoods—communities of women who refused marriage, or who if married often refused to consummate their marriages and soon left their husbands—the only women in China who were not footbound and who, Agnes Smedley tells us, welcomed the births of daughters and organized successful women's strikes in the silk mills.[51] It allows us to connect and compare disparate individual instances of marriage resistance: for example, the type of autonomy claimed by Emily Dickinson, a nineteenth-century white woman genius, with the strategies available to Zora Neale Hurston, a twentieth-century black woman genius. Dickinson never married, had tenuous intellectual friendships with men, lived self-convented in her genteel father's house, and wrote a lifetime of passionate letters to her sister-in-law Sue Gilbert and a smaller group of such letters to her friend Kate Scott Anthon. Hurston married twice but soon left each husband, scrambled her way from Florida to Harlem to

49. Woolf, *A Room of One's Own*, p. 126.

50. Gracia Clark, "The Beguines: A Mediaeval Women's Community," *Quest: A Feminist Quarterly* 1, no. 4 (1975): 73–80.

51. See Denise Paulmé, ed., *Women of Tropical Africa* (Berkeley: University of California Press, 1963), pp. 7, 266–67. Some of these sororities are described as "a kind of defensive syndicate against the male element"—their aims being "to offer concerted resistance to an oppressive patriarchate," "independence in relation to one's husband and with regard to motherhood, mutual aid, satisfaction of personal revenge." See also Audre Lorde, "Scratching the Surface: Some Notes on Barriers to Women and Loving," *Black Scholar* 9, no. 7 (1978): 31–35; Marjorie Topley, "Marriage Resistance in Rural Kwangtung," in *Women in Chinese Society*, ed. M. Wolf and R. Witke (Stanford, Calif.: Stanford University Press, 1978), pp. 67–89; Agnes Smedley, *Portraits of Chinese Women in Revolution*, ed. J. MacKinnon and S. MacKinnon (Old Westbury, N.Y.: Feminist Press, 1976), pp. 103–10.

Columbia University to Haiti and finally back to Florida, moved in and out of white patronage and poverty, professional success, and failure; her survival relationships were all with women, beginning with her mother. Both of these women in their vastly different circumstances were marriage resisters, committed to their own work and selfhood, and were later characterized as "apolitical." Both were drawn to men of intellectual quality; for both of them women provided the on-going fascination and sustenance of life.

If we think of heterosexuality as the "natural" emotional and sensual inclination for women, lives such as these are seen as deviant, as pathological, or as emotionally and sensually deprived. Or, in more recent and permissive jargon, they are banalized as "life-styles." And the work of such women—whether merely the daily work of individual or collective survival and resistance, or the work of the writer, the activist, the reformer, the anthropologist, or the artist—the work of self-creation—is undervalued, or seen as the bitter fruit of "penis envy," or the sublimation of repressed eroticism, or the meaningless rant of a "manhater." But when we turn the lens of vision and consider the degree to which, and the methods whereby, heterosexual "preference" has actually been imposed on women, not only can we understand differently the meaning of individual lives and work, but we can begin to recognize a central fact of women's history: that women have always resisted male tyranny. A feminism of action, often, though not always, without a theory, has constantly reemerged in every culture and in every period. We can then begin to study women's struggle against powerlessness, women's radical rebellion, not just in male-defined "concrete revolutionary situations"[52] but in all the situations male ideologies have not perceived as revolutionary: for example, the refusal of some women to produce children, aided at great risk by other women; the refusal to produce a higher standard of living and leisure for men (Leghorn and Parker show how both are part of women's unacknowledged, unpaid, and ununionized economic contribution); that female antiphallic sexuality which, as Andrea Dworkin notes, has been "legendary," which, defined as "frigidity" and "puritanism," has actually been a form of subversion of male power—"an ineffectual rebellion, but . . . rebellion nonetheless."[53] We can no longer have patience with Dinnerstein's view that women have simply collaborated with men in the "sexual arrangements" of history; we begin to observe behavior, both in history and in individual biography, that has hitherto been invisible or misnamed; behavior which often constitutes, given the limits of the counterforce exerted in a given time and place, radical rebellion. And we can connect these re-

52. See Rosalind Petchesky, "Dissolving the Hyphen: A Report on Marxist-Feminist Groups 1–5," in *Capitalist Patriarchy and the Case for Socialist Feminism*, ed. Zillah Eisenstein (New York: Monthly Review Press, 1979), p. 387.

53. Andrea Dworkin, *Pornography: Men Possessing Women* (New York: Putnam/Peridgee Books, 1981).

bellions and the necessity for them with the physical passion of woman for woman which is central to lesbian existence: the erotic sensuality which has been, precisely, the most violently erased fact of female experience.

Heterosexuality has been both forcibly and subliminally imposed on women, yet everywhere women have resisted it, often at the cost of physical torture, imprisonment, psychosurgery, social ostracism, and extreme poverty. "Compulsory heterosexuality" was named as one of the "crimes against women" by the Brussels Tribunal on Crimes against Women in 1976. Two pieces of testimony, from women from two very different cultures, suggest the degree to which persecution of lesbians is a global practice here and now. A report from Norway relates:

> A lesbian in Oslo was in a heterosexual marriage that didn't work, so she started taking tranquillizers and ended up at the health sanatorium for treatment and rehabilitation. . . . The moment she said in family group therapy that she believed she was a lesbian, the doctor told her she was not. He knew from "looking into her eyes," he said. She had the eyes of a woman who wanted sexual intercourse with her husband. So she was subjected to so-called "couch therapy." She was put into a comfortably heated room, naked, on a bed, and for an hour her husband was to . . . try to excite her sexually. . . . The idea was that the touching was always to end with sexual intercourse. She felt stronger and stronger aversion. She threw up and sometimes ran out of the room to avoid this "treatment." The more strongly she asserted that she was a lesbian, the more violent the forced heterosexual intercourse became. This treatment went on for about six months. She escaped from the hospital, but she was brought back. Again she escaped. She has not been there since. In the end she realized that she had been subjected to forcible rape for six months.

(This, surely, is an example of female sexual slavery according to Barry's definition.) And from Mozambique:

> I am condemned to a life of exile because I will not deny that I am a lesbian, that my primary commitments are, and will always be to other women. In the new Mozambique, lesbianism is considered a left-over from colonialism and decadent Western civilization. Lesbians are sent to rehabilitation camps to learn through self-criticism the correct line about themselves. . . . If I am forced to denounce my own love for women, if I therefore denounce myself, I could go back to Mozambique and join forces in the exciting and hard struggles of rebuilding a nation, including the struggle for the emancipation of Mozambiquan women. As it is, I either risk the rehabilitation camps, or remain in exile.[54]

---

54. Russell and van de Ven, pp. 42–43, 56–57.

Nor can it be assumed that women like those in Carroll Smith-Rosenberg's study, who married, stayed married, yet dwelt in a profoundly female emotional and passional world, "preferred" or "chose" heterosexuality. Women have married because it was necessary, in order to survive economically, in order to have children who would not suffer economic deprivation or social ostracism, in order to remain respectable, in order to do what was expected of women because coming out of "abnormal" childhoods they wanted to feel "normal," and because heterosexual romance has been represented as the great female adventure, duty, and fulfillment. We may faithfully or ambivalently have obeyed the institution, but our feelings—and our sensuality—have not been tamed or contained within it. There is no statistical documentation of the numbers of lesbians who have remained in heterosexual marriages for most of their lives. But in a letter to the early lesbian publication, *Ladder,* the playwright Lorraine Hansberry had this to say:

> I suspect that the problem of the married woman who would prefer emotional-physical relationships with other women is proportionally much higher than a similar statistic for men. (A statistic surely no one will ever really have.) This because the estate of woman being what it is, how could we ever begin to guess the numbers of women who are not prepared to risk a life alien to what they have been taught all their lives to believe was their "natural" destiny—AND—their only expectation for ECONOMIC security. It seems to be that this is why the question has an immensity that it does not have for male homosexuals. . . . A woman of strength and honesty may, if she chooses, sever her marriage and marry a new male mate and society will be upset that the divorce rate is rising so—but there are few places in the United States, in any event, where she will be anything remotely akin to an "outcast." Obviously this is not true for a woman who would end her marriage to take up life with another woman.[55]

This *double-life*—this apparent acquiescence to an institution founded on male interest and prerogative—has been characteristic of female experience: in motherhood, and in many kinds of heterosexual behavior, including the rituals of courtship; the pretense of asexuality by the nineteenth-century wife; the simulation of orgasm by the prostitute, the courtesan, the twentieth-century "sexually liberated" woman.

Meridel LeSueur's documentary novel of the Depression, *The Girl,* is arresting as a study of female double-life. The protagonist, a waitress in a St. Paul working-class speakeasy, feels herself passionately attracted to

55. I am indebted to Jonathan Katz's *Gay American History* (n. 5 above) for bringing to my attention Hansberry's letters to *Ladder* and to Barbara Grier for supplying me with copies of relevant pages from *Ladder,* quoted here by permission of Barbara Grier. See also the reprinted series of *Ladder,* ed. Jonathan Katz et al. (New York: Arno Press); and Deirdre Carmody, "Letters by Eleanor Roosevelt Detail Friendship with Lorena Hickok," *New York Times* (October 21, 1979).

the young man Butch, but her survival relationships are with Clara, an older waitress and prostitute, with Belle, whose husband owns the bar, and with Amelia, a union activist. For Clara and Belle and the unnamed protagonist, sex with men is in one sense an escape from the bedrock misery of daily life; a flare of intensity in the grey, relentless, often brutal web of day-to-day existence:

> ... It was like he was a magnet pulling me. It was exciting and powerful and frightening. He was after me too and when he found me I would run, or be petrified, just standing in front of him like a zany. And he told me not to be wandering with Clara to the Marigold where we danced with strangers. He said he would knock the shit out of me. Which made me shake and tremble, but it was better than being a husk full of suffering and not knowing why.[56]

Throughout the novel the theme of double-life emerges; Belle reminisces of her marriage to the bootlegger Hoinck:

> You know, when I had that black eye and said I hit it on the cupboard, well he did it the bastard, and then he says don't tell anybody. ... He's nuts, that's what he is, nuts, and I don't see why I live with him, why I put up with him a minute on this earth. But listen kid, she said, I'm telling you something. She looked at me and her face was wonderful. She said, Jesus Christ, Goddam him I love him that's why I'm hooked like this all my life, Goddam him I love him.[57]

After the protagonist has her first sex with Butch, her women friends care for her bleeding, give her whiskey, and compare notes.

> My luck, the first time and I got into trouble. He gave me a little money and I come to St. Paul where for ten bucks they'd stick a huge vet's needle into you and you start it and then you were on your own. ... I never had no child. I've just had Hoinck to mother, and a hell of a child he is.[58]

> Later they made me go back to Clara's room to lie down. ... Clara lay down beside me and put her arms around me and wanted me to tell her about it but she wanted to tell about herself. She said she started it when she was twelve with a bunch of boys in an old shed. She said nobody had paid any attention to her before and she became very popular. ... They like it so much, she said, why shouldn't

---

56. Meridel LeSueur, *The Girl* (Cambridge, Mass.: West End Press, 1978), pp. 10–11. LeSueur describes, in an afterword, how this book was drawn from the writings and oral narrations of women in the Workers Alliance who met as a writers' group during the Depression.

57. Ibid., p. 20.

58. Ibid., pp. 53–54.

you give it to them and get presents and attention? I never cared anything for it and neither did my mama. But it's the only thing you got that's valuable. . . . [59]

Sex is thus equated with attention from the male, who is charismatic though brutal, infantile, or unreliable. Yet it is the women who make life endurable for each other, give physical affection without causing pain, share, advise, and stick by each other. *(I am trying to find my strength through women—without my friends, I could not survive.)* LeSueur's *The Girl* parallels Toni Morrison's remarkable *Sula,* another revelation of female double-life:

> Nel was the one person who had wanted nothing from her, who had accepted all aspects of her. . . . Nel was one of the reasons [Sula] had drifted back to Medallion. . . . The men . . . had merged into one large personality: the same language of love, the same entertainments of love, the same cooling of love. Whenever she introduced her private thoughts into their rubbings and goings, they hooded their eyes. They taught her nothing but love tricks, shared nothing but worry, gave nothing but money. She had been looking all along for a friend, and it took her a while to discover that a lover was not a comrade and could never be—for a woman.

But Sula's last thought at the second of her death is, "Wait'll I tell Nel." And after Sula's death, Nel looks back on her own life:

> "All that time, all that time, I thought I was missing Jude." And the loss pressed down on her chest and came up into her throat. "We was girls together," she said as though explaining something. "O Lord, Sula," she cried, "Girl, girl, girlgirlgirl!" It was a fine cry— loud and long—but it had no bottom and it had no top, just circles and circles of sorrow.[60]

The Girl and *Sula* are both novels which reveal the lesbian continuum in contrast to the shallow or sensational "lesbian scenes" in recent commercial fiction.[61] Each shows us woman-identification untarnished (till the end of LeSueur's novel) by romanticism; each depicts the competition of heterosexual compulsion for women's attention, the diffusion and frustration of female bonding that might, in a more conscious form, reintegrate love with power.

59. Ibid., p. 55.
60. Toni Morrison, *Sula* (New York: Bantam Books, 1973), pp. 103–4. I am indebted to to Lorraine Bethel's essay, " 'This Infinity of Conscious Pain': Zora Neale Hurston and the Black Female Literary Tradition," in *All the Women Are White, All the Blacks Are Men, But Some of Us Are Brave: Black Women's Studies,* ed. Gloria T. Hull, Patricia Bell Scott, and Barbara Smith (Old Westbury, N.Y.: Feminist Press, 1982).
61. See Maureen Brady and Judith McDaniel, "Lesbians in the Mainstream: The Image of Lesbians in Recent Commercial Fiction," *Conditions,* vol. 6 (1979).

IV

Woman-identification is a source of energy, a potential springhead of female power, violently curtailed and wasted under the institution of heterosexuality. The denial of reality and visibility to women's passion for women, women's choice of women as allies, life companions, and community; the forcing of such relationships into dissimulation and their disintegration under intense pressure have meant an incalculable loss to the power of all women *to change the social relations of the sexes, to liberate ourselves and each other.* The lie of compulsory female heterosexuality today afflicts not just feminist scholarship, but every profession, every reference work, every curriculum, every organizing attempt, every relationship or conversation over which it hovers. It creates, specifically, a profound falseness, hypocrisy, and hysteria in the heterosexual dialogue, for every heterosexual relationship is lived in the queasy strobelight of that lie. However we chose to identify ourselves, however we find ourselves labeled, it flickers across and distorts our lives.[62]

The lie keeps numberless women psychologically trapped, trying to fit mind, spirit, and sexuality into a prescribed script because they cannot look beyond the parameters of the acceptable. It pulls on the energy of such women even as it drains the energy of "closeted" lesbians—the energy exhausted in the double-life. The lesbian trapped in the "closet," the woman imprisoned in prescriptive ideas of the "normal," share the pain of blocked options, broken connections, lost access to self-definition freely and powerfully assumed.

The lie is many-layered. In Western tradition, one layer—the romantic—asserts that women are inevitably, even if rashly and tragically, drawn to men; that even when that attraction is suicidal (e.g., *Tristan und Isolde,* Kate Chopin's *The Awakening*) it is still an organic imperative. In the tradition of the social sciences it asserts that primary love between the sexes is "normal," that women *need* men as social and economic protectors, for adult sexuality, and for psychological completion; that the heterosexually constituted family is the basic social unit; that women who do not attach their primary intensity to men must be, in functional terms, condemned to an even more devastating outsiderhood than their outsiderhood as women. Small wonder that lesbians are reported to be a more hidden population than male homosexuals. The black lesbian/feminist critic, Lorraine Bethel, writing on Zora Neale Hurston, remarks that for a black woman—already twice an outsider—to choose to assume still another "hated identity" is problematic indeed. Yet the lesbian continuum has been a lifeline for black women both in Africa and the United States.

62. See Russell and van de Ven, p. 40: " . . . few heterosexual women realize their lack of free choice about their sexuality, and few realize how and why compulsory heterosexuality is also a crime against them."

Black women have a long tradition of bonding together . . . in a
Black/women's community that has been a source of vital survival
information, psychic and emotional support for us. We have a distinct Black woman-identified folk culture based on our experiences
as Black women in this society; symbols, language and modes of
expression that are specific to the realities of our lives. . . . Because
Black women were rarely among those Blacks and females who
gained access to literary and other acknowledged forms of artistic
expression, this Black female bonding and Black woman-
identification has often been hidden and unrecorded except in the
individual lives of Black women through our own memories of our
particular Black female tradition.[63]

Another layer of the lie is the frequently encountered implication
that women turn to women out of hatred for men. Profound skepticism,
caution, and righteous paranoia about men may indeed be part of any
healthy woman's response to the woman-hatred embedded in male-
dominated culture, to the forms assumed by "normal" male sexuality,
and to *the failure even of "sensitive" or "political" men to perceive or find these
troubling.* Yet woman-hatred is so embedded in culture, so "normal" does
it seem, so profoundly is it neglected as a social phenomenon, that many
women, even feminists and lesbians, fail to identify it until it takes, in
their own lives, some permanently unmistakable and shattering form.
Lesbian existence is also represented as mere refuge from male abuses,
rather than as an electric and empowering charge between women. I
find it interesting that one of the most frequently quoted literary passages on lesbian relationship is that in which Colette's Renée, in *The
Vagabond,* describes "the melancholy and touching image of two weak
creatures who have perhaps found shelter in each other's arms, there to
sleep and weep, safe from man who is often cruel, and there to taste
*better than any pleasure, the bitter happiness of feeling themselves akin, frail and
forgotten* [emphasis added]."[64] Colette is often considered a lesbian writer;
her popular reputation has, I think, much to do with the fact that she
writes about lesbian existence as if for a male audience; her earliest
"lesbian" novels, the Claudine series, were written under compulsion for
her husband and published under both their names. At all events, except
for her writings on her mother, Colette is a far less reliable source on
lesbian existence than, I would think, Charlotte Brontë, who understood
that while women may, indeed must, be one another's allies, mentors,

63. Lorraine Bethel.
64. Dinnerstein, the most recent writer to quote this passage, adds ominously: "But
what has to be added to her account is that these 'women enlaced' are sheltering each other
not just from what men want to do to them, but also from what they want to do to each
other" (Dinnerstein, p. 103). The fact is, however, that woman-to-woman violence is a
minute grain in the universe of male-against-female violence perpetrated and rationalized
in every social institution.

and comforters in the female struggle for survival, there is quite extraneous delight in each other's company and attraction to each others' minds and character, which proceeds from a recognition of each others' strengths.

By the same token, we can say that there is a *nascent* feminist political content in the act of choosing a woman lover or life partner in the face of institutionalized heterosexuality.[65] But for lesbian existence to realize this political content in an ultimately liberating form, the erotic choice must deepen and expand into conscious woman-identification—into lesbian/feminism.

The work that lies ahead, of unearthing and describing what I call here "lesbian existence" is potentially liberating for all women. It is work that must assuredly move beyond the limits of white and middle-class Western women's studies to examine women's lives, work, and groupings within every racial, ethnic, and political structure. There are differences, moreover, between "lesbian existence" and the "lesbian continuum"—differences we can discern even in the movement of our own lives. The lesbian continuum, I suggest, needs delineation in light of the "double-life" of women, not only women self-described as heterosexual but also of self-described lesbians. We need a far more exhaustive account of the forms the double-life has assumed. Historians need to ask at every point how heterosexuality as institution has been organized and maintained through the female wage scale, the enforcement of middle-class women's "leisure," the glamorization of so-called sexual liberation, the withholding of education from women, the imagery of "high art" and popular culture, the mystification of the "personal" sphere, and much else. We need an economics which comprehends the institution of heterosexuality, with its doubled workload for women and its sexual divisions of labor, as the most idealized of economic relations.

The question inevitably will arise: Are we then to condemn all heterosexual relationships, including those which are least oppressive? I believe this question, though often heartfelt, is the wrong question here. We have been stalled in a maze of false dichotomies which prevents our apprehending the institution as a whole: "good" versus "bad" marriages; "marriage for love" versus arranged marriage; "liberated" sex versus prostitution; heterosexual intercourse versus rape; Liebeschmerz versus humiliation and dependency. Within the institution exist, of course, qualitative differences of experience; but the absence of choice remains the great unacknowledged reality, and in the absence of choice, women will remain dependent upon the chance or luck of particular relationships and will have no collective power to determine the meaning and place of sexuality in their lives. As we address the institution itself, moreover, we begin to perceive a history of female resistance which has

65. Conversation with Blanche W. Cook, New York City, March 1979.

never fully understood itself because it has been so fragmented, mis-
called, erased. It will require a courageous grasp of the politics and
economics, as well as the cultural propaganda, of heterosexuality to
carry us beyond individual cases or diversified group situations into the
complex kind of overview needed to undo the power men everywhere
wield over women, power which has become a model for every other
form of exploitation and illegitimate control.

Montague, Massachusetts

A Response to Inequality: Black Women, Racism, and Sexism

Diane K. Lewis

Introduction

The women's liberation movement has generated a number of theories about female inequality. Because the models usually focus exclusively upon the effects of sexism, they have been of limited applicability to minority women subjected to the constraints of both racism and sexism.[1] In addition, black women have tended both to see racism as a more powerful cause of their subordinate position than sexism and to view the women's liberation movement with considerable mistrust.[2]

Yet there are recent indications that a growing number of black women have become more responsive to the issue of women's rights.[3]

I am indebted to Oscar Berland and Naomi Katz for comments on an earlier draft of this paper.

1. For example, *Women, Culture and Society*, ed. Michelle Z. Rosaldo and Louise Lamphere (Stanford, Calif.: Stanford University Press, 1974), proposes several models of female subordination, but none considers fully the structural position and theoretical implications of women subject to both racism and sexism.

2. See Linda J. M. LaRue, "Black Liberation and Women's Lib," *Transaction* 8 (November–December 1970): 59–64; Nathan and Julia Hare, "Black Women 1970," ibid., pp. 68, 90; Jean Cooper, "Women's Liberation and the Black Woman," *Journal of Home Economics* 63 (October 1971): 521–23; Toni Cade, ed., *The Black Woman* (New York: New American Library, Signet Books, 1970); Mae C. King, "The Politics of Sexual Stereotypes," *Black Scholar* 4 (March–April 1973): 12; Inez Smith Reid, *"Together" Black Women* (New York: Third Press, 1972).

3. A 1972 poll showed that black women were more sympathetic than white women to efforts to upgrade women's status in society (62 percent to 45 percent, respectively) and that black women were also more supportive than white women of the attempts by women's liberation groups to do so (67 percent and 35 percent, respectively) (see Louis Harris & Associates, *The 1972 Virginia Slims American Women's Opinion Poll: A Survey of the Attitudes of Women on Their Roles in Politics and the Economy*, pp. 2, 4). Interestingly, Lucy Komisar notes that black organizations such as the Urban League and the National Association for the

During the past few years black women's organizations have emerged whose specific aim is to combat both sexism and racism. In January 1973 fifteen women formed the San Francisco–based Black Women Organized for Action (BWOA). It now has between 300 and 400 members.[4] In December 1973 the first conference of the National Black Feminist Organization (NBFO) met on the east coast in New York. It attracted 400 women. Though its leadership acknowledged difficulties in organizing black women around feminist issues,[5] the group stressed that many goals central to the women's liberation movement—day care, abortions, maternity leaves—were of critical importance to black women. Indeed, some were of greater intrinsic concern to them than to white women because of their more severe economic disadvantage.

This paper attempts to explain the initial rejection and then more favorable reaction to the women's movement on the part of black women. To do so, it develops a model of inequality which may illuminate the situation of women in complex societies who experience discrimination because of race and sex. A trend toward a greater acceptance of feminism may be due to changes in black women's perception of oppression, which in turn reflects changes in the social order. In the 1960s the black liberation movement began to generate important structural shifts in the relationship between blacks and whites in America. Blacks began to participate more fully in public activities previously reserved for whites. In such domains they encountered patterns of sexual discrimination. As the bulk of the higher-status, authoritative positions meted to

---

Advancement of Colored People, which formerly had little interest in feminist issues, have, in recent years, worked jointly with the National Organization of Women to further both minority and women's rights (see Lucy Komisar, "Where Feminism Will Lead," *Civil Rights Digest* 6 [Spring 1974]: 9).

4. Patsy G. Fulcher, Aileen C. Hernandez, and Eleanor R. Spikes, "Sharing the Power and the Glory," *Contact* 4 (Fall, 1974): 52. Eleanor Spikes, a cofounder of the organization, gave the recent estimate of membership (personal communication, April 1976) (see also, *What It Is,* the BWOA Newsletter which can be obtained from P.O. Box 10572, San Francisco, California 94115). Other black women's groups recently organized to eliminate both racism and sexism are League of Black Women (in Chicago), Black Women Concerned (in Baltimore), National Black Women's Political Leadership Caucus (in Detroit), and Sisters Getting Ourselves Together (in Davis, Calif.). (List compiled by Hernandez Associates, 4444 Geary Boulevard, San Francisco, California 94118). The BWOA is dedicated to involving black women in the political process, to helping them get jobs, and to supporting them in business, the arts, and all areas where they face discrimination and. exclusion.

5. For example, when Eleanor Holmes Norton, Commissioner of Human Rights for New York City and a NBFO board member stated, "Five years ago you couldn't have gotten five women to come here," a welfare mother said, "Five years ago! . . . We tried to start a consciousness raising group four months ago and nobody was interested" (see "Feminism: 'The Black Nuance,' " *Newsweek* [December 17, 1973], p. 89).

blacks went to black men, a number of black women, particularly in the middle class, became more sensitive to the obstacle of sexism and to the relevance of the women's movement.[6]

Structural Inequality and Black Americans

Michelle Rosaldo has offered a model of female inequality. It proposes that (a) women are universally subordinate to men, (b) men are dominant due to their participation in public life and their relegation of women to the domestic sphere, and (c) the differential participation of men and women in public life gives rise not only to universal male authority over women but to a higher valuation of male over female roles.[7] The point that female inequality is inseparable from differential male/female activity in the public sphere is well taken. Nevertheless, a careful look at the relationship between black men and women and between blacks and whites in this society casts doubt on the full validity of Rosaldo's model.

Historically, black men, like black women, have been excluded from participation in the dominant society's politico-jural sphere and denied access to authority. Moreover, special measures have been needed to reaffirm black male inferiority. Since slavery coexisted with male dominance in the wider society, black men, as men, constituted a potential threat to the established order of white superiority. Laws were formulated that specifically denied black men normal adult prerogatives.[8] Such covertly sanctioned acts as lynchings and the rape and sexual exploitation of black women further intensified black male powerlessness.

Stringent institutionalized barriers to male participation continued for almost 100 years after slavery. These included the refusal of membership in national trade unions, which effectively barred black men from the job market;[9] prejudicial welfare laws, which undermined the

6. Eudora Pettigrew concluded more bluntly: "The black man grapples to achieve social justice and parity with the white male—essentially to attain white male power, privilege and status—while black women are shoved to the back of the bus." Quoted in Geraldine Rickman, "A Natural Alliance: The New Role for Black Women," *Civil Rights Digest* 6 (Spring 1974): 62 (see also Pauli Murray, "The Liberation of Black Women," in *Women: A Feminist Perspective,* ed. Jo Freeman [Palo Alto, Calif.: Mayfield Publishing Co., 1975], p. 354).

7. Rosaldo, "Women, Culture and Society: A Theoretical Overview," in Rosaldo and Lamphere, pp. 17–42.

8. Even Moynihan notes that black exclusionary laws were aimed primarily at defining and keeping the black *man* in his place (see Daniel Moynihan, *The Negro Family: The Case for National Action* [Washington, D.C.: Department of Labor, 1965], p. 62; Lerone Bennett, Jr., *Before the Mayflower* [Baltimore: Pelican Books, 1968], pp. 70–71, 92–93).

9. Andrew Billingsley, *Black Families in White America* (Englewood Cliffs, N.J.: Prentice-Hall, Inc., 1968), pp. 85–90.

man's status as husband and father;[10] and vigorous tactics to block black
participation in the political process.[11] The systematic exclusion of black
men from the public sphere suggests that black sex-role relationships cannot be adequately explained by the notion of a structural opposition between the domestic and public spheres or the differential participation of
men and women in the public sphere.[12]

Rosaldo also suggests that egalitarian sex relationships can only develop in a society at a time when both sexes share equal participation in
the public and domestic spheres.[13] There is growing evidence of strong
egalitarianism in black sex-role relationships.[14] However, black men and

10. For a discussion of how modern public welfare functions to replace the male in
low-income families, a process which affects a still-sizable number of blacks on welfare, see
Helen Icken Safa, "The Female-based Household in Public Housing," *Human Organization*
24 (Summer 1965): 135–39 (see also Johnnie Tillmon, "Welfare Is a Woman's Issue," in
Marriage and the Family: A Critical Analysis and Proposals for Change, ed. Carolyn C. Perrucci
and Dena B. Targ [New York: David McKay Co., 1974], p. 109).

11. In the past, this took the form of intimidation and poll tax laws in the South and
gerrymandering and cooptation in the North. For an analysis of other establishment bars
to effective black political participation, see Stokely Carmichael and Charles V. Hamilton,
Black Power: The Politics of Liberation in America (New York: Random House, Vintage Books,
1967).

12. Among racially oppressed groups it is important to distinguish between the public
life of the dominant and the dominated societies. Using this framework, we recognize a
range of male participation from token admittance to the public life of the dominant
society to its attempts to destroy the public life within a dominated society. Mexican-
American men, for example, have played strong public roles in their own dominated
society, and, in fact, as Mexican-Americans have become more assimilated to the dominant
society, sex roles have become less hierarchical (see Leo Grebler, Joan W. Moore, and
Ralph C. Guzman, *The Mexican American People: The Nation's Second Largest Minority* [New
York: Free Press, 1970], pp. 361–72). On the other hand, Afro-American men historically
faced attempts at exclusion, enforced by the dominant society, from participation in a
public life even among their own people (see Bennett, pp. 70–71, 92–93, and also Robert
Staples, "The Myth of the Impotent Black Male," *Black Scholar* 2 [June 1971]: 3).

13. Rosaldo, pp. 40–42.

14. Virginia Heyer Young, "Family and Childhood in a Southern Negro Community," *American Anthropologist* 72 (April 1970): 269–88; Peter Kunkel and Sara Sue Ken-
nard, *Spout Spring: A Black Community* (New York: Holt, Rinehart & Winston, 1971); Diane
K. Lewis, "The Black Family: Socialization and Sex Roles," *Phylon* 36 (September 1975):
221–37; Robert B. Hill, *The Strengths of Black Families* (New York: Emerson Hall, 1972), p.
18. It has been pointed out that the notion of women's universal inferiority may be a
reflection of our own Western cultural bias (see Nancy Tanner, "Matrifocality in Indonesia
and Africa and among Black Americans," in Rosaldo and Lamphere, pp. 129–56, and
Ruby Rohrlich Leavitt, *Peaceable Primates and Gentle People: Anthropological Approaches to
Women's Studies* [New York: Harper & Row, 1975]). After developing most of the ideas in
this paper, I was interested to see further critiques of the thesis of worldwide female
inequality by the contributors to *Women Cross-culturally: Change and Challenge*, ed. Ruby
Rohrlich Leavitt (The Hague: Mouton & Co., 1975), particularly the articles "Women,
Knowledge and Power," by Constance Sutton, Susan Makiesky, Daisy Dwyer, and Laura
Klein (pp. 581–600), and "Class, Commodity, and the Status of Women," by Eleanor
Leacock (pp. 601–16).

women shared equal exclusion from, rather than equal participation in, the public sphere. What the black experience suggests is that differential participation in the public sphere is a symptom rather than a cause of structural inequality. While inequality is *manifested* in the exclusion of a group from public life, it is actually *generated* in the group's unequal access to power and resources in a hierarchically arranged social order. Relationships of dominance and subordination, therefore, emerge from a basic structural opposition between groups which is reflected in exclusion of the subordinate group from public life. This process may be further accentuated by increasing differentiation between the public and domestic spheres.[15] Members of a subordinate group, moreover, constitute a potential common-interest group whose interests derive from their shared powerlessness.[16] Their interests remain latent, however, until the power relations between themselves and a dominant group begin to shift and the structural opposition between them erupts into conflict.

Black women, due to their membership in two subordinate groups that lack access to authority and resources in society, are in structural opposition with a dominant racial and a dominant sexual group. In each subordinate group they share potential common interests with group comembers, black men on the one hand and white women on the other. Ironically, each of these is a member of the dominant group: black men as men, white women as whites. Thus, the interests which bind black women together with and pull them into opposition against comembers crosscut one another in a manner which often obscures one set of interests over another. Historically, their interests as blacks have taken precedence over their interests as women. A shift in the power relations between the races had to come before changes in the structural relationship between the sexes.

It has been noted that the latent interests shared by members of a subordinate group become manifest when they have been formulated into a conscious ideology.[17] Ideology, I suggest, articulates increasing

15. See Louise Lamphere, "Strategies, Cooperation and Conflict among Women in Domestic Groups," in Rosaldo and Lamphere, p. 100; and Leacock, pp. 610–11. Lamphere notes the relationship between sex egalitarianism and the merging of public and private spheres, and Leacock suggests that it is the imposition of hierarchical social forms that give rise to a division between public and domestic domains.

16. This model derives from ideas in Ralf Dahrendorf, "Toward a Theory of Social Conflict" in *Social Change: Sources, Patterns, Consequences,* ed. Amitai Etzioni and Eva Etzioni (New York: Basic Books, 1964), pp. 98–111, and in Denton E. Morrison, "Some Notes toward Theory on Relative Deprivation, Social Movements, and Social Change," *American Behavioral Scientist* 14 (May 1971): 675–90. "Power" here refers to "having great influence or control over others" (*The American Heritage Dictionary* [New York: Houghton Mifflin Co., 1969], p. 1027); "interests" refers to common values, objectives, and definitions of a situation.

17. See Dahrendorf, p. 107.

discontent, which emerges as a group's members perceive that their legitimate expectations are being frustrated. Frustration arises as they experience a sense of relative deprivation vis-à-vis other groups, a process occurring when (1) members of a subordinate group perceive the possibility of their own improved, more equitable position in the social system by comparing themselves with another group of structurally equivalent status whose members are improving their positions, and (2) members of a dominant group continue to frustrate their legitimate expectations for improved position while granting privileges and resources to members of the other subordinate group. The set of potential interests most clearly perceived as illegitimately blocked will become manifest first through the process of structural conflict. The black women's reactions to the black liberation and feminist movements described below reflect, I feel, their changing interests as they have become manifest through shifts in power relations between the races and between the sexes. Their response suggests that, as a subordinate group's interests change, the lines of conflict and structural opposition between groups tend to shift correspondingly.

The Structural Position of Black Women and White Women in America

Both white and black women in America have been excluded from the politico-jural domain and from positions of authority and prestige which have been reserved mainly for white men. Their joint exclusion as women would place them structurally in the same subordinate group, sharing potential common interests. Yet, due to racism, black women have occupied a structural position subordinate to white women in society.[18] They have had less access to deference, power, and authority. Sanday, noting the difference between deference and power as a basis of women's position, finds that Western women may receive deference in their "often highly valued roles as helpmate, sex object, the 'driving force behind every successful man,' etc." She contrasts this with women

18. Class, a third mitigating factor, is purposely omitted from this section in order to highlight the contrasts between white and black women which stem from racism. That white women represent on the whole a far more privileged group than black women is shown in census data which reveal that 64 percent of employed white women but only 42 percent of black and other minority women hold professional, clerical, or sales jobs, while 19 percent of white women and 37 percent of black and other minority women work in low-paying service-related and domestic occupations (see U.S. Bureau of the Census, *The Social and Economic Status of the Black Population in the United States, 1974*, Current Population Reports, Series P-23, No. 54 [Washington, D.C.: Government Printing Office, 1975], table 49, p. 74). Thus, while poor white women occupy a subordinate position, a greater percentage of black women are poor, and their inequality is compounded by race as well as class and sex.

who, playing important economic roles in other societies, may have power over critical resources but who lack deference and may be resented and feared by their husbands.[19] Black women, on account of male exclusion from the job market, have been forced to share with black men marginal participation in the public work world of the dominant society through menial and ill-paying jobs. Their economic contributions have often been essential to their families. Their important economic role has assured them power over the limited resources available to a racially excluded group. On the basis of power over crucial resources, black women have held a relatively high position within a dominated society.[20] This contrasts with the deference accorded white women in the dominant society. For, unlike white women, black women have lacked deference in the dominant society principally because of the stigma of race. Within the dominated society, their source of power has become one basis of denial of deference. Black writers have noted that black men, unable to get and keep jobs, display resentment toward black women who assume the role of "provider."[21] Concomitantly, the roles played by white women which are highly valued, that is, "the driving force behind every successful man," the valued sex object, are frequently denied black women: the first because of the exclusion of black men from the public world, and the second because of the impossibility of attaining a white standard of beauty.

19. Peggy R. Sanday, "Female Status in the Public Domain," in Rosaldo and Lamphere (n. 1 above), p. 191.

20. See Clyde W. Franklin, Jr., and Laurel R. Walum, "Toward a Paradigm of Substructural Relations: An Application to Sex and Race in the United States," *Phylon* 33 (Fall 1972): 249.

21. For example, William A. Blakey, a black man who is Director of Congressional Liaison for the U.S. Commission on Civil Rights, writes that the attitude of many black men toward black women is one of disrespect and a desire to dominate. He suggests that black men feel they must persecute black women in order to repudiate the myth of the " 'castrating' black matriarch" (see William A. Blakey, "Everybody Makes the Revolution: Some Thoughts on Racism and Sexism," *Civil Rights Digest* 6 [Spring 1974]: 19). Alice Walker also noted the prevailing antagonism of black men when she stated: "Black women are called matriarchs, called castraters of the men, and all kinds of things by black men. . . . [However black women] don't [*sic*] realize that they were all these ugly things that people said they were. They thought they were just providing for their families, that they were just surviving" (see Alice Walker, quoted in "Women on Women," *American Scholar* 972 [Autumn 1972]: 601–2. See also Frances Beale, "Double Jeopardy: To Be Black and Female," in Cade (n. 2 above), p. 92; Toni Cade, "On the Issue of Roles," ibid., p. 106; W. H. Grier and Price M. Cobb, *Black Rage* (New York: Basic Books, 1968). The contrast between female power over resources and male attitudes toward women that vary from resentment to lack of deferential treatment, which is characteristic not only of black Americans but of a number of other societies as well (e.g., Nupe, Iroquois; see Sanday, p. 191), suggests the complex factors involved in assessing sex-role relationships. Thus, structural egalitarianism may or may not be paralleled by mutual respect and deference just as male dominance may coexist with female deference or with women's fear and resentment toward men.

White women have not only been given deference. They have also had some access to power and authority.[22] While they themselves lacked authority in the dominant society, they have had a route to power through their kinship and marital ties with men (e.g., fathers, husbands, and sons) who do exercise authority in the public sphere. Moreover, white women, as members of the dominant group, formerly held both considerable authority and power vis-á-vis the subordinate racial group.

The variance in deference and access to power and authority between black and white women have proven to be critical factors underlying the black woman's perception of common group interests with black men and distrust of white women. During the long period of male exclusion from the public sphere, black women shared the experience of racial oppression with black men. From their perspective as members of a subordinate and powerless racial group, white women wielded greater power and garnered more respect than black men and far more than black women. In fact, attributes of the white woman's status currently criticized by many feminists as examples of sexism were seen (and are still seen) by many black women as representative of the unique privileges of women of the dominant group. For example, women who were forced to take menial jobs (often, in the past, and still to some extent in the present, as domestics in white women's homes) and who were unable to care for their own children or to rely on men for economic support contrasted themselves with white women who were not required to work outside their own homes and who were well provided for by their husbands.

A Response to Inequality

During the protest political movements of the sixties, radical white women became discontented at the subordinate position assigned them by white male activists. They formulated an ideology of female liberation to express their common interests as members of a powerless group in conflict with men, whom they perceived as blocking their legitimate aspirations to authority and resources in society.[23] Significantly, their sense of deprivation grew as they saw black people demanding and acquiring an improved and more equitable position in the wider society. The women's liberation movement emerged, in part, to acquire for women the same

22. Authority can be defined as the legitimate right to make decisions and command obedience. It contrasts with power where influence and control over others are not institutionalized but rest informally with individuals or their roles (see Rosaldo, p. 21, n. 2).

23. Jo Freeman, "The Origins of the Women's Liberation Movement," in *Changing Women in a Changing Society,* ed. Joan Huber (Chicago: University of Chicago Press, 1973), pp. 37–39.

access to authority and resources that the civil rights movement was fighting to obtain for blacks.[24]

The reaction of white women to traditional female subordination did not go unnoticed by black women. They, however, initially began to crystallize their interests as women at the same time that they continued to perceive obstacles to their most legitimate interests primarily in racial terms. In the remarkable anthology edited by Toni Cade, black women warn that the patterning of sex roles in white society offers a dangerous and stultifying model for blacks.[25] They note the detrimental effect of the dominant society on black man-woman relations.[26] They clearly establish that their aim is not so much to demand rights as women as to clarify issues or to "demand rights as Blacks first, women second."[27] In fact, the shared interests of black women seem to have little in common with white women. Cade asks: "How relevant are the truths, the experiences, the findings of White women to Black women? I don't know that our priorities are the same, that our concerns and methods are the same."[28]

Three years after publication of the Cade anthology, however, black women began clearly to formulate their interests as women concomitantly with their interests as members of an oppressed racial group. At the NBFO conference in 1973 a participant stated: "While we share with our men a history of toil and dignity, it is categorically different to be Black and a woman in this society than it has been to be Black and male."[29] The emergence of a feminist movement among black women, signaled by formation of the NBFO, the BWOA, and other organizations concerned with the special problems of being female and black,[30] indicates that some contemporary black women have begun to perceive the way both sex inequality and race inequality affect their lives.

In order to understand the structural factors which account for the black women's growing responsiveness to feminism it is necessary to

24. Catharine Stimpson, " 'Thy Neighbor's Wife, Thy Neighbor's Servants': Women's Liberation and Black Civil Rights," in *Women in Sexist Society*, ed. Vivian Gornick and Barbara K. Moran (New York: New American Library, Signet Books, 1971), pp. 622–57.

25. E.g., Cade, "On the Issue of Roles," pp. 102–3.

26. Beale, pp. 90–92.

27. "Preface," in Cade, *The Black Woman*, p. 10.

28. Ibid., p. 9.

29. Eleanor H. Norton, quoted on p. 86 in Bernette Golden, "Black Women's Liberation," *Essence* 4 (February 1974): 35–36, 75–76, 86.

30. Patricia Bell Scott, "Black Female Liberation and Family Action Programs: Some Considerations" (unpublished paper, n.d., p. 4), suggests that most black women's organizations are now concerned with the issue of black feminism, that is, the plight of black women who are oppressed by both sexism and racism. Among groups she cites, in addition to the NBFO, are the National Welfare Rights Organization, the National Committee on Household Employment, Domestics United of North Carolina, and the Black Women's Community Development Foundation.

analyze the effect of the race struggle on the position of black women. The worldwide black struggle against oppression heightened the discontent of American blacks at their subordinate position. As African countries gained independence from European colonizers, Afro-Americans experienced a growing sense of relative deprivation and perceived the possibility of changing power relationships between whites and blacks in the United States. While for many years the conflict between black and white was waged at the covert level and expressed in an ideology of gradual "race" advancement, black Americans became increasingly impatient at obstacles to their legitimately perceived expectations. Their interests became manifest, their ideology "militant." Civil rights activity in the 1950s spawned the "Black Power" movement, aimed at direct black participation in the political process, and the "Black Is Beautiful" movement, focused on a legitimation of black standards of beauty and physical worth. While black women easily perceived their own interests expressed in these political and cultural ideologies, and while they played a critical role in civil rights activities,[31] these movements, significantly, were seen as primarily male inspired and male led. According to some, the black woman's alleged place was "a step behind" the man's, and her proper role was the bearing and rearing of warriors for the struggle. Many women activists interpreted this attitude as an understandable reaction by black men, who had been duped by proposed white models of black matriarchy and male castration. They counseled patience and conciliation at what they perceived as deliberate divisive tactics by the dominant society.[32] Consequently, Pauli Murray noted, in spite of the black women's broad participation in the civil rights movement ". . . the aspirations of the black community have been articulated almost exclusively by black males. There has been very little public discussion of the problems, objectives or concerns of black women."[33] The black liberation movement resulted in the passage of such federal laws as the Civil Rights Act of 1964 and the Voting Rights Act of 1965. They were to provide institutional support for the termination of black exclusion from the public sphere. The laws, which had a dominoes effect, began to knock down barriers in many American institutions. Edu-

31. For a discussion of some of the significant contributions of black women to the black liberation movement, see Phyl Garland, "Builders of a New South," *Ebony* 21 (August 1966): 27–30, 34–37.
32. See Beale, p. 93; Cade, "On the Issues of Roles," pp. 107–8; Jean Carey Bond and Patricia Perry, "Is the Black Male Castrated," in Cade, *The Black Woman*, pp. 113–18; and Gwen Patton, "Black People and the Victorian Ethos," ibid., pp. 143–48. Francis Beale in a 1970 newspaper interview noted: "Often, as a way of escape . . . black men have turned their hostility toward their women. But this is what we have to understand about him . . . as black women we have to have a conciliatory attitude" (see Charlayne Hunter, "Many Blacks Wary of Women's Liberation Movement in U.S.," *New York Times* [November 17, 1970], p. 47).
33. Murray (n. 6 above), p. 354.

cation, direct political participation, and jobs began to become more accessible to "upwardly mobile" blacks. However, as blacks began to participate in the wider society they moved into a public arena sharply characterized by sex inequality. This situation, together with male domination of the black movement, signaled a significant differentiation in the participation of black men and women in the public sphere. Observing this situation, another black women, corroborating Murray, notes: "It is clear that when translated into actual opportunities for employment and promotional and educational benefits the civil rights movement really meant rights for black men. . . ."[34]

This differentiation is apparent in a comparison of the relative educational levels of black men and women. Education for blacks appears to have shifted in favor of men during the past few years, preceding apace with greater black inclusion in institutions of higher learning. Formerly, sociological studies of black communities showed that black women had higher rates of literacy and more years of schooling than males.[35] They were expected to go into higher education more often than men and had different aspirations,[36] which were linked primarily to the job market for adult blacks in the past. For example, in the South in the 1940s black men aspired to some independence through working their own farms or learning a skilled trade like bricklaying, plastering, or painting, skills transmitted from father to son. Black women, however, were offered higher education so they could become schoolteachers in the segregated school systems of the South and thereby get "out of the white folk's kitchen," the only other job possibility for black females.[37]

In the past, black women were also given greater educational opportunities than men by their families because "educational achievement for black men did not mean the opening up of economic opportunities."[38] Census data show that black women have more median years of schooling and more often graduate from high school than black men. The median years of formal education for black women and men twenty-five years of age and older between 1940 and 1970 are given in table 1.

In 1966, for blacks between twenty-five and thirty-four years of age women more often had a college degree than men; 5.2 percent of the men and 6.1 percent of the women had completed four or more years of

34. Constance M. Carroll, "Three's a Crowd: The Dilemma of the Black Woman in Higher Education," in *Academic Women on the Move*, ed. Alice Rossi and Ann Calderwood (New York: Russell Sage Foundation, 1973), p. 177.

35. Charles Johnson, *Shadow of the Plantation* (Chicago: University of Chicago Press, 1969), pp. 129–30.

36. Hylan Lewis, *Blackways of Kent* (New Haven, Conn.: College and University Press, 1964), pp. 105–6.

37. Ibid.

38. Gerda Lerner, ed., *Black Women in White America: A Documentary History* (New York: Random House, Pantheon Books, 1972), p. 220.

college. However, by 1974 the situation had reversed, and 8.8 percent of the men and 7.6 percent of the women had achieved that level of education.[39] Recent figures also show a sharp rise in the numbers of black men currently enrolled in college. While in 1970 16 percent of black men and 15 percent of black women between eighteen and twenty-four years of age were enrolled in college, by 1974 the figures were 20 percent and 16 percent, respectively.[40] The data indicate a decided shift in favor of black men in higher education over the past few years.[41]

Even in the late 1960s, however, when black women were enrolled in college in somewhat greater proportions than black men, black men were more likely to obtain graduate degrees beyond the M.A. than black women.[42] Jackson's 1968 study of black institutions found that 91 percent of the professional degrees granted in the combined fields of medicine, dentistry, law, veterinary medicine, and theology went to black

Table 1

Median Years of Schooling for Ages 25 and Over

Year	Black Women	Black Men
1940	6.1	5.3
1960	8.5	7.9
1970	10.0	9.3

SOURCES.—Figures for 1940 are from U.S. Department of Commerce, Bureau of the Census, *Sixteenth Census of the United States: 1940. Population: Characteristics of the Nonwhite Population by Race* (Washington, D.C.: Government Printing Office, 1943), table 6, p. 34; for 1960 are for "nonwhite" and are from U.S. Bureau of the Census, *U.S. Census of Population: 1960. Educational Attainment of the Population of the United States: 1960.* Supplementary Reports PC (S1)-37. (Washington, D.C.: Government Printing Office, 1972), table 173, p. 6; for 1970 are from U.S. Bureau of the Census, *Census of Population: 1970. Subject Reports. Educational Attainment.* Final Report PC(2)-5B (Washington, D.C.: Government Printing Office, 1973), table 1, pp. 3, 6.

39. U.S. Bureau of the Census (n. 18 above), table 68, p. 97.
40. Ibid., table 65, p. 94.
41. See Cynthia Fuchs Epstein, "Positive Effects of the Multiple Negative: Explaining the Success of Black Professional Women," in Huber (n. 23 above), pp. 152–53. See also a study by Elias Blake, Linda Jackson Lambert, and Joseph L. Martin, "Degrees Granted and Enrollment Trends in Historically Black Colleges: An Eight Year Study" (Washington, D.C.: Institute for Services to Education, 1974), table 9a, p. 31, which shows that in black four-year colleges, as well, black male enrollment has gradually increased from 45.4 percent in 1966 to 47.8 percent in 1973.
42. Carroll, pp. 174–75.

men and only 9 percent to black women.[43] Two surveys of blacks with doctorates in all fields from all institutions in 1969 and 1970 suggest that black women hold roughly 21 percent of these advanced degrees.[44] Moreover, black men attend more prestigious institutions than black women, and this factor, along with their greater monopoly of advanced professional degrees, affects occupational patterns.[45]

For, according to figures of the U.S. Census Bureau, black women are the poorest paid in the occupational structure. Black men earn more than both black women and white women. The median earnings for year-round, full-time workers in 1963, 1970, and 1974 show an interesting trend over the eleven-year span (see table 2). Note that the wage differential between black women's and black men's salaries went from $1,739 in 1963 to $2,334 in 1974. Although the gap between the dollar earnings of black women and black men widened, there was some improvement in the ratio of female to male income, black women earning 57 percent of the income of black men in 1963 and 74 percent in 1974. In the past, the low pay of black women was related to their frequent employment as domestics. In 1963, as shown in table 3, one out of three black women was a private household worker, but by 1974 only 11 per-

Table 2

Median Earnings Year-round Full-Time Workers
($)

Group	1963	1970	1974
White males	6,245	9,447	12,434
Black males	4,019	6,435	8,705
White females	3,687	5,536	7,021
Black females	2,280	4,536	6,371

SOURCES.—Figures for 1963 are from U.S. Bureau of the Census, *Income of Families and Persons in the United States, 1963*, Current Population Reports, Series P-60, No. 43 (Washington, D.C.: Government Printing Office, 1964), table 18, p. 34 (the table compares whites and nonwhites; the latter are predominantly black); for 1970 are from U.S. Bureau of the Census, *Money Income in 1973 of Families and Persons in the United States*, Current Population Reports, Series P-60, No. 97 (Washington, D.C.: Government Printing Office, 1975), table F, p. 12; for 1974 are from U.S. Bureau of the Census, *Money Income in 1974 of Families and Persons in the United States*, Current Population Reports, Series P-60, No. 101 (Washington, D.C.: Government Printing Office, 1975), pp. 106–7.

43. Jacqueline J. Jackson, "Black Women and Higher Education" (unpublished paper, 1973), cited ibid., table 9.1, p. 174. Jackson's figures show that 62 percent of these professional degrees were in the fields of medicine and law and that 85.6 percent of the M.D.'s and 90.4 percent of the LL.B.'s were granted to black men.

44. See Kent G. Mommsen, "Career Patterns of Black American Doctorates" (Ph.D. diss., Florida State University, 1970), table 1, p. 41.

45. Jacqueline J. Jackson, "But Where Are the Men?" *Black Scholar* 3 (December 1971): 30–41.

Table 3

Occupation of Men and Women, 1963, 1970, 1974 (Annual Averages, in Percentages)

| | 1963 | | | | 1970 | | | | 1974 | | | |
| | Women | | Men | | Women | | Men | | Women | | Men | |
	White	Negro and Other Races*	White	Negro and Other Races*	White	Negro and Other Races*	White	Negro and Other Races*	White	Negro and Other Races*	White	Negro and Other Races*
White-collar workers:	61	21	41	15	64	36	43	22	64	42	42	24
Professional and technical	14	8	13	5	15	11	15	8	15	12	15	9
Managers and administrators except farm	5	2	15	4	5	2	15	5	5	3	15	5
Sales workers	8	2	6	2	8	3	6	2	7	2	6	2
Clerical workers	34	10	7	5	36	21	7	7	36	25	6	7
Blue-collar workers:	17	15	46	57	16	19	46	60	15	20	46	57
Craft and kindred workers	1	0.5	20	11	1	1	21	14	2	1	21	16
Operatives, including transport	15	14	20	25	14	17	19	28	13	17	18	26
Non-farm laborers	0.3	0.7	6	21	...	1	6	18	1	1	7	15
Service workers	15	22	6	16	15	26	6	13	17	26	7	15
Private household workers	5	34	...	...	3	18	...	...	3	11	...	...
Farm workers	3	7	8	11	2	2	8	6	2	1	5	4

SOURCES.—Figures for 1963 taken from U.S. Bureau of the Census, *The Social and Economic Status of the Black Population in the United States, 1973*, Current Population Reports, Special Studies Series P-23, No. 48 (Washington, D.C.: Government Printing Office, 1974), table 38, p. 54 and table 39, p. 55; for 1970 and 1974 taken from U.S. Bureau of the Census, *The Social and Economic Status of the Black Population in the United States, 1974*, Current Population Reports, Series P-23, No. 54 (Washington, D.C.: Government Printing Office, 1975), table 48, p. 73, and table 49, p. 74.

*Nearly 90 percent are Negro.

cent of black women were domestics. However, a comparison of jobs held by black women with those held by black men in 1974 shows that while black women have been moving out of domestic work 37 percent or over one-third were still in low-paying service and household jobs not covered by the federal minimum wage, as compared with only 15 percent of black men. Moreover, while black women white-collar workers relative to black men have been highly represented in teaching, nursing, and social work—occupations which are extensions of their domestic roles and traditional careers for women—black men, as they have moved into the public sphere, have been more often found than women in the more prestigious and better-paid professions of medicine, law, science, and college teaching.[46]

Figures showing gradual black inclusion in the field of higher education clearly indicate that black women are either poorly represented or relegated to the lower-status and lower-paid jobs. For example, Carroll found that at the University of Pittsburgh in 1970 black and white women were disproportionately represented in nontenured academic positions and that black men, as well as white men, in relationship to their total numbers, monopolized the higher and tenured ranks (see table 4). Carroll notes that for the University of Pittsburgh, "Clearly, sex is more of a handicap than race . . . and the disproportion between the sexes is far greater for blacks than for whites."[47] Five years later, the occupational profile of the University of California, one of the largest educational complexes in the United States, shows that continued recruitment of blacks and other minorities has resulted in a marked sex inequality in high-level positions. The figures for April 1975 show employment in administration and in tenured and nontenured ladder-faculty positions for black men and women in the nine-campus system (see table 5).[48]

Table 4

Full-Time Professional Staff at University of Pittsburgh, 1970

Rank	White Men	White Women	Minority Men	Minority Women
Full professor	420	25	21	0
Associate professor	355	42	17	1
Nontenured	792	268	83	31

SOURCE.—Figures compiled from Constance M. Carroll, "Three's a Crowd: The Dilemma of the Black Woman in Higher Education," in *Academic Women on the Move*, ed. Alice Rossi and Ann Calderwood (New York: Russell Sage Foundation, 1973), table 9.3, p. 175.
NOTE.—"Minority" refers to predominantly black.

46. See Epstein, pp. 153–54, and Jackson, "But Where Are the Men?" p. 32.

47. Carroll, pp. 174–75 (see also William Moore, Jr., and Lonnie H. Wagstaff, *Black Educators in White Colleges* [San Francisco: Jossey-Bass, Inc., 1974], pp. 154–77).

48. It should be stressed that blacks and other minorities (Asian/Asian-Americans, American Indians and Mexican/Spanish-Americans) are still greatly underrepresented in

Information on black law-faculty members, nationwide, shows a similar skewing in favor of black men. The 1976 directory of minority law professors reveals that there are 226 blacks and thirty-eight nonwhite women out of a total of 282 minority professors. A check of the directory turned thirty-seven women who could be identified by name and judging by surname the majority of these were probably black (see table 6).

The situation in institutions of higher learning is paralleled in government jobs and in the business world generally. In 1974 black women were 19.8 percent of all women and 63.7 percent of all blacks working full time as GS-graded federal employees. While they were generally underrepresented among women in the higher-level jobs, among blacks they were both markedly overrepresented in the lower-ranking jobs and underrepresented in the higher-ranking jobs, as shown in table 7.

Similarly, the 1975 California State Personnel Board's report to the governor and legislature on state employees, which gave monthly salary by sex and race, showed that while the percentages of black men and women were approximately the same (i.e., 3.7 and 3.4 percent, respectively, of the total numbers employed) black men were more highly represented than black women at the higher salary ranges (see table 8). A recent survey of minorities in the mass-media industry indicates that 82 percent were males.[49] In the business-management training field as well, men, regardless of race, have been given a decided preference over women.[50]

---

higher education. The point here is that their gradual inclusion into the system has been proceeding along sex discriminatory lines. This was especially evident in the employment figures for April 1974 (see the table below for figures for April 1974). Comparison with table 5 shows that there has been some improvement for minority women over the ensuing eighteen months. A total of twelve additional black women were hired while seven "other minority" women were added.

	Black Men	Black Women	Other Minority Men	Other Minority Women
Deans and provosts	5	1	1	...
Tenured faculty	41	...	178	7
Nontenured ladder faculty	51	9	84	21

SOURCE.—University of California computer printout, PER 1096, "Summary of Ethnic and Sex Employment, as of April 30, 1974," pp. 1–3.

49. Abigail Jones Nash, Marilyn Jackson-Beeck, Leverne Tracy Regan, and Vernon A. Stone, "Minorities and Women in Broadcast News: Two National Surveys" (paper presented at the annual convention of the Association for Education in Journalism, San Diego, 1974), p. 7.

50. See Bird McCord, "Identifying and Developing Women for Management Positions," *Training and Development Journal* 25 (November 1971): 2.

Table 5

Total Minorities at the University of California, October 1975

Rank	Black Men	Black Women	Other Minority Men	Other Minority Women	Total Men	Total Women
Deans and provosts	6	1	1	2	155	16
Full professors	24	3	126	...	2,947	124
Associate professors	21	3	82	10	1,398	135
Nontenured ladder faculty	47	15	91	23	1,146	290

Source.—University of California Computer printout, PER 1023, "Summary of Ethnic and Sex Employment, Academic Group/Rank, All Campuses, as of October 31, 1975," pp. 1–3.

Table 6

Minority Law-Faculty Members

Rank	Total Blacks	Minority Women
Professor	37	4
Associate professor	39	6
Assistant professor	51	8
Administrator	24	6
Teacher/administrator	22	5
Part time	49	6
Teaching fellow	4	2
Total	226	37

SOURCE.—*1976 Directory of Minority Law Faculty Members,* Section on Minority Groups, Association of American Law Schools, pp. 9, 25–48.

Table 7

Full-Time Federal Employment of Black Women

General Schedule Grade Grouping	Total Black	Black Women		
		N	All Blacks (%)	All Women (%)
GS-1–4	66,999	50,143	74.8	12.7
GS-5–8	67,316	45,147	67.1	19.5
GS-9–11	20,772	8,591	41.4	15.8
GS-12–15	11,429	2,206	19.3	12.2
GS-16–18	149	16	10.7	13.3
Total	166,665	106,103	63.7	19.8

SOURCE.—From U.S. Bureau of the Census, *The Social and Economic Status of the Black Population in the United States, 1974* (see table 3 above), table 53, p. 78.

Direct black participation in the political process through election to office has increased over the past five years. While blacks are still woefully underrepresented in government, they moved from 1,230 to 2,630 elected officials between 1969 and 1974. However, movement of blacks into politics, as into higher-paying jobs generally, replicates the wider societal pattern of unequal female inclusion in the politico-jural domain. In 1974, while 2,293 black men were elected officials only 337 black women held that position.[51] This is a significant shift toward disparity, given the tradition of egalitarianism between the sexes and the former importance of women in black public life.[52]

51. U.S. Bureau of the Census, *The Social and Economic Status of the Black Population in the United States, 1973,* Current Population Reports, Special Studies Series P-23, No. 48, (Washington, D.C.: Government Printing Office, 1974), table 74, p. 103. In 1974 blacks held 0.5 of 1 percent of the elective offices (see Herrington J. Bryce and Alan E. Warrick, "Black Women in Elective Offices," *Black Scholar* 6 [October 1974]: 17–20).

52. Lerner (n. 38 above), pp. 319–22, shows that in the past black women, although not holders of elective office, were active in politics.

Table 8

California State Employees: Percentage Distribution
of Monthly Salary for Black Workers, March 1975

Monthly Salary Rate ($)	Black Men	Black Women
Under 500	3.6	12.5
500–699	2.6	7.9
700–899	5.2	5.3
900–1,099	5.7	2.8
1,100–1,299	2.9	1.1
1,300–1,599	2.4	0.9
1,600–2,099	2.4	0.7
Over 2,099	1.8	0.2

SOURCE.—"Minority Women: Triple Discrimination," *Affirmative Action in Progress* 2 (April 1976): 6.

If, as an aftermath of the 1960s, a number of black men were recruited into higher-paying, more authoritative, and prestigious positions, black women generally moved into the lower-status and lower-paying jobs traditionally reserved for women in the dominant society. During this process they made significant strides relative to white women. Although the difference in earnings between black men and women has widened, the income gap between black women and white women has tended to narrow (see table 9). Black women earned 62 percent of the median income of white women in 1963; this increased to 90 percent in 1974.[53] Similarly, recent census data indicate that the overall occupational distribution of black women has improved relative to white women. Since 1963 black women have moved out of domestic work and into clerical positions in greater numbers. Thus, in 1963, 34 percent of black women were domestics, and only 10 percent were clerical workers; in 1974, 11 percent were domestics and 25 percent were clerical workers. Since the percentages for white women clerical workers have remained relatively stable between 1963 and 1974 (34 percent and

Table 9

Wage Differential between Black Women, Black Men
and White Women
($)

	1963	1970	1974
Between black women and black men	1,739	1,899	2,334
Between black women and white women	1,407	1,000	650

53. For a comparison of increases in the ratio of black to white median income from 1967 to 1973 for men and women, see U.S. Bureau of the Census, *Money Income in 1973 of Families and Persons in the United States,* Current Population Reports, Series P-60, No. 97 (Washington, D.C.: Government Printing Office, 1975), table F, p. 12.

36 percent, respectively), black women appear to be moving toward parity with white women in that occupation (see table 3). Although the position of black women has improved in relationship to white women, the data show that for women as a whole sexism continues to constitute a major barrier in the wider society. In fact, the ratio of white female to white male earnings has *decreased* slightly between 1963 and 1974, women earning 59 percent of the male's median income in 1963 and only 56 percent in 1975 (computed from table 3). The existence of sex bias in the wider society explains the observation that the civil rights movement elicited active efforts to provide career opportunities for black men, while little attention was paid to the employment needs of black women.[54]

Class and Sexism

The black liberation movement began to generate important structural changes in the relationship between blacks and whites in American society. For black women, these changes serve to heighten their perception of sexism, since they experience deep-seated sex discrimination as they engage in increased participation in the public sphere. Middle-class black women, in particular, are becoming more sensitive to the obstacle of sexism as racial barriers begin to fall and as the bulk of the higher-status, authoritative positions reserved for blacks have gone to black men. Nevertheless, if the leadership of black organizations recently formed to combat both racism and sexism appears to be middle class, the membership in these black women's groups seems to crosscut class lines. Thus the BWOA notes that its members include welfare recipients, maids, and the unemployed as well as high-income earners. In recognition of this diversity, the organization has adopted a flexible membership policy.[55] Similarly, the NBFO conference attracted domestic workers, welfare mothers, and other poor black women as well as students, housewives, and professionals. As one participant put it, "We were able to do what white feminists have failed to do: transcend class lines and eradicate labels."[56]

A further examination of the structural position of black women suggests why not only upwardly mobile black women but also poor black women will become more responsive to feminist issues. They, along with

54. See Pauli Murray, "Jim Crow and Jane Crow," in Lerner, p. 596.

55. Dues are computed on a sliding scale from $5.00 to $25.00 a year, but members pay when and what they can. Moreover, a woman can become a member *either* by paying dues *or* attending meetings *or* working on a committee (see Fulcher et al. [n. 4 above], pp. 52, 63).

56. Ashaki Habiba Taha, letter *MS* 3 (August 1974): 12 (see also Golden [n. 29 above], p. 36).

middle-class black women, are seriously affected by sex discrimination on the job. For example, Dietrich and Greiser in a study of black blue-collar workers found sexism to be an important factor in black poverty.[57] Furthermore, demographic and occupational trends, which affect all black women, should also elicit among them a sense of common interest which crosscuts class lines. There has been a steadily declining sex ratio from 95.0 in 1940 to 90.8 in 1970.[58] This probably contributes to the fact that black women are more often single than white women, more often work, and are more often heads of household. Thus, in 1974 about one half of minority women worked compared with 44 percent of white women.[59] In 1973, while 77 percent of white women who were fourteen years old and over and ever married were married and living with their husbands, only 54 percent of black women in the same category were married and residing with their spouses.[60] In 1975, while only 11 percent of white families were female headed, 35 percent of black families were supported by women.[61] Black women with preschool-aged children were also more likely to work than white mothers; in 1973, 49 percent of black women as compared with 32 percent of white women with small children were in the labor force.[62]

Black women, then, are more often self-supporting than white women and far more likely to carry single-handedly responsibilities for dependent children. These factors, together with their continued greater concentration in lower-paying service-related jobs than either white women or black men, cause poor black women, particularly, to be vitally affected by matters of inadequate income and child-care facilities, both major issues in the women's movement. For poor women, as a black welfare mother notes, women's liberation is "a matter of survival," a perception increasingly held by such groups devoted to removing obstacles to the legitimate interests of poor black women as the National Welfare Rights Organization.[63]

Since both poor and middle-class black women participate in and have been aware of some of the successes of the black liberation move-

57. Kathryn Dietrich and Lee Greiser, "The Influence of Sex on Wage-Income of Black, Blue-Collar Workers in Selected Non-metropolitan and Metropolitan Areas of Texas" (paper presented at the annual meeting of the Southern Association of Agricultural Scientists, Memphis, Tennessee, February 1974).

58. Jackson, "But Where Are the Men?" table 3, p. 39. The sex ratio among whites has also declined steadily but in 1970 was, at 95.3, far more favorable for whites.

59. U.S. Bureau of the Census, *The Social and Economic Status of the Black Population in the United States, 1973*, p. 93.

60. Ibid., table 64, p. 90.

61. U.S. Bureau of the Census, *The Social and Economic Status of the Black Population in the United States, 1974*, table 72, p. 107.

62. U.S. Bureau of the Census, *The Social and Economic Status of the Black Population in the United States, 1973*, table 68, p. 95.

63. Tillmon (n. 10 above), pp. 108, 109, 111.

ment, their expectations of greater access to resources have been raised. As these expectations have been frustrated, a sense of common interest is beginning to emerge which may increasingly include all classes of black women. A study of race and class factors affecting women's attitudes toward the women's liberation movement in Cleveland found that white working-class women were far less likely than white middle-class women to be interested in women's rights, while black working-class women were somewhat *more* receptive than black middle-class women to efforts to change women's status[64] (see table 10).

The shared experience of racism has also tended to blur class lines among blacks. This, too, probably will contribute to a greater tendency for both poor and middle-class black women to agree regarding women's rights. For example, middle-class black families are in a more precarious position than middle-class white families because of racism. Especially in times of economic recession and high unemployment, they may find themselves in economic straits similar to lower-class blacks.[65]

Whether black women develop a sense of common interests that is manifested more in opposition to sexism or to racism will depend upon the structural relationship between the sexes and between the races. With growing black participation in the wider society some black women, experiencing frustration of their interests primarily as women, now probably share the viewpoint a member of NBFO expressed. "White women are our natural allies; we can't take on the system alone."[66] Middle-class black women will increasingly feel their interests as women illegitimately frustrated if a combination of factors continues: (1) the

Table 10

Percentage of Black and White Women Manifesting a High or
Low Degree of Interest in Women's Rights

Degree of Interest	Black Women		White Women	
	Middle Class	Working Class	Middle Class	Working Class
High	44	48	54	27
Low	56	52	46	73

Source.—From Willa Mae Hemmons, "Toward an Understanding of Attitudes Held by Black Women on the Women's Liberation Movement" (Ph.D. diss., Case Western Reserve University, 1973), tables 7 and 8, p. 101.

64. Willa Mae Hemmons, "Toward an Understanding of Attitudes Held by Black Women on the Women's Liberation Movement" (Ph.D. diss., Case Western Reserve University, 1973). Her sample for this exploratory study was a purposive one, including eighty-three women, forty-five black and thirty-seven white. She notes that she sought women from different classes and residential and occupational areas; however the size of her sample makes her results more suggestive than conclusive (see her discussion of the sample, pp. 80–86).

65. Cf. Billingsley (n. 9 above), pp. 10–15.

66. Eleanor H. Norton, quoted in Golden, p. 86.

income gap between themselves and white women narrows even more, (2) the overall position of women remains low, and (3) the white male hierarchy persists in admitting minority males but excluding minority females from equitable participation in the wider society. Middle-class black women, even more than middle-class white women, occupy a structural position likely to generate a pervasive sense of relative deprivation and an ideology of discontent.

However, on the other hand, black women may see that racism still affects a considerable number of blacks, including black men. Jessie Bernard, analyzing occupations and earnings for black and white men and women for the period 1939–70, concluded: ". . . racism tends to be more serious for black men than black women . . . (and) sexism tends to be more serious for black women than racism."[67] While some middle-class black men have made significant advances, a careful inspection of the trends of the ratio of black to white earnings shows that black men, as a whole, are making much slower headway in closing the income gap between them and white men than are black women relative to white women. Black men earned 64 percent of the median income of white men in 1967; 67 percent of the income of white men in 1973.[68] This would appear to matter to black women. For example, if they marry, there will probably be more pressure on them to work in order to supplement the family income than on married white women. Indeed, now black married women are more likely to work outside the home than their white counterparts.[69]

Perpetuation of a situation in which all black men, irrespective of their socioeconomic status, are subject to racism, might well propel increasing numbers of black women, irrespective of their class backgrounds into overt opposition to both sexism and racism. Their way of doing so, however, might involve organizations concerned with women's rights, but limited to blacks and strongly racially oriented.[70] The concern with racism would preclude too exclusive a concern with sexism.

Department of Anthropology
University of California, Santa Cruz

67. Jessie Bernard, "The Impact of Sexism and Racism on Employment Status and Earnings, with Addendum," Module 25 (New York: MSS Modular Publications, Inc., 1974), p. 5.

68. U.S. Bureau of the Census, *Money Income in 1973 of Families and Persons in the United States*, table F, p. 12. This was similar to the rate of growth of black female income to the black male's, i.e., black women earned 67 percent of the income of black men in 1967 and 70 percent of the income of black men in 1973.

69. U.S. Bureau of of the Census, *The Social and Economic Status of the Black Population in the United States, 1973*, table 67, p. 95.

70. For an alternate thesis on the possible direction of change in the relationship between blacks and whites, males and females, see Franklin and Walum (n. 20 above), pp. 247–52. See also Rickman (n. 6 above), pp. 57–65, for an interesting discussion of the black professional woman's structural position which enables her to act as catalyst for change in the position of both women and blacks.

Capitalism, Patriarchy, and Job Segregation by Sex

Heidi Hartmann

The division of labor by sex appears to have been universal throughout human history. In our society the sexual division of labor is hierarchical, with men on top and women on the bottom. Anthropology and history suggest, however, that this division was not always a hierarchical one. The development and importance of a sex-ordered division of labor is the subject of this paper. It is my contention that the roots of women's present social status lie in this sex-ordered division of labor. It is my belief that not only must the hierarchical nature of the division of labor between the sexes be eliminated, but the very division of labor between the sexes itself must be eliminated if women are to attain equal social status with men and if women and men are to attain the full development of their human potentials.

The primary questions for investigation would seem to be, then, first, how a more sexually egalitarian division became a less egalitarian one, and second, how this hierarchical divison of labor became extended to wage labor in the modern period. Many anthropological studies suggest that the first process, sexual stratification, occurred together with the increasing productiveness, specialization, and complexity of society;

I would like to thank many women at the New School for sharing their knowledge with me and offering encouragement and debate, in particular, Amy Hirsch, Christine Gailey, Nadine Felton, Penny Ciancanelli, Rayna Reiter, and Viana Muller. I would also like to thank Amy Bridges, Carl Degler, David Gordon, Fran Blau, Grace Horowitz, Linda Gordon, Suad Joseph, Susan Strasser, and Tom Vietorisz for helpful comments.

for example, through the establishment of settled agriculture, private property, or the state. It occurred as human society emerged from the primitive and became "civilized." In this perspective capitalism is a relative latecomer, whereas patriarchy,[1] the hierarchical relation between men and women in which men are dominant and women are subordinate, was an early arrival.

I want to argue that, before capitalism, a patriarchal system was established in which men controlled the labor of women and children in the family, and that in so doing men learned the techniques of hierarchical organization and control. With the advent of public-private separations such as those created by the emergence of state apparatus and economic systems based on wider exchange and larger production units, the problem for men became one of maintaining their control over the labor power of women. In other words, a direct personal system of control was translated into an indirect, impersonal system of control, mediated by society-wide institutions. The mechanisms available to men were (1) the traditional division of labor between the sexes, and (2) techniques of hierarchical organization and control. These mechanisms were crucial in the second process, the extension of a sex-ordered division of labor to the wage-labor system, during the period of the emergence of capitalism in Western Europe and the United States.

The emergence of capitalism in the fifteenth to eighteenth centuries threatened patriarchal control based on institutional authority as it destroyed many old institutions and created new ones, such as a "free" market in labor. It threatened to bring all women and children into the

1. I define patriarchy as a set of social relations which has a material base and in which there are hierarchical relations between men, and solidarity among them, which enable them to control women. Patriarchy is thus the system of male oppression of women. Rubin argues that we should use the term "sex-gender system" to refer to that realm outside the economic system (and not always coordinate with it) where gender stratification based on sex differences is produced and reproduced. Patriarchy is thus only one form, a male dominant one, of a sex-gender system. Rubin argues further that patriarchy should be reserved for pastoral nomadic societies as described in the Old Testament where male power was synonomous with fatherhood. While I agree with Rubin's first point, I think her second point makes the usage of patriarchy too restrictive. It is a good label for most male-dominant societies (see Gayle Rubin, "The Traffic in Women," in *Toward an Anthropology of Women*, ed. Rayna Reiter [New York: Monthly Review Press, 1975]). Muller offers a broader definition of patriarchy "as a social system in which the status of women is defined primarily as wards of their husbands, fathers, and brothers," where wardship has economic and political dimensions (see Viana Muller, "The Formation of the State and the Oppression of Women: A Case Study in England and Wales," mimeographed [New York: New School for Social Research, 1975], p. 4, n. 2). Muller relies on Karen Sacks, "Engels Revisited: Women, the Organization of Production, and Private Property," in *Woman, Culture and Society*, ed. Michelle Z. Rosaldo and Louise Lamphere (Stanford, Calif.: Stanford University Press, 1974). Patriarchy as a system between and among men as well as between men and women is further explained in a draft paper, "The Unhappy Marriage of Marxism and Feminism: Towards a New Union," by Amy Bridges and Heidi Hartmann.

labor force and hence to destroy the family and the basis of the power of men over women (i.e., the control over their labor power in the family).[2] If the theoretical tendency of pure capitalism would have been to eradicate all arbitrary differences of status among laborers, to make all laborers equal in the marketplace, why are women still in an inferior position to men in the labor market? The possible answers are legion; they range from neoclassical views that the process is not complete or is hampered by market imperfections to the radical view that production requires hierarchy even if the market nominally requires "equality."[3] All of these explanations, it seems to me, ignore the role of men—ordinary men, men as men, men as workers—in maintaining women's inferiority in the labor market. The radical view, in particular, emphasizes the role of men as capitalists in creating hierarchies in the production process in order to maintain their power. Capitalists do this by segmenting the labor market (along race, sex, and ethnic lines among others) and playing workers off against each other. In this paper I argue that male workers have played and continue to play a crucial role in maintaining sexual divisions in the labor process.

Job segregation by sex, I will argue, is the primary mechanism in capitalist society that maintains the superiority of men over women, because it enforces lower wages for women in the labor market. Low wages keep women dependent on men because they encourage women to marry. Married women must perform domestic chores for their husbands. Men benefit, then, from both higher wages and the domestic division of labor. This domestic division of labor, in turn, acts to weaken women's position in the labor market. Thus, the hierarchical domestic division of labor is perpetuated by the labor market, and vice versa. This process is the present outcome of the continuing interaction of two interlocking systems, capitalism and patriarchy. Patriarchy, far from being vanquished by capitalism, is still very virile; it shapes the form modern capitalism takes, just as the development of capitalism has transformed patriarchal institutions. The resulting mutual accommodation between patriarchy and capitalism has created a vicious circle for women.

My argument contrasts with the traditional views of both neoclas-

---

2. Marx and Engels perceived the progress of capitalism in this way, that it would bring women and children into the labor market and thus erode the family. Yet despite Engels's acknowledgment in *The Origin of the Family, Private Property, and the State* (New York: International Publishers, 1972), that men oppress women in the family, he did not see that oppression as based on the control of women's labor, and, if anything, he seems to lament the passing of the male-controlled family (see his *The Condition of the Working Class in England* [Stanford, Calif.: Stanford University Press, 1968], esp. pp. 161–64).

3. See Richard C. Edwards, David M. Gordon, and Michael Reich, "Labor Market Segmentation in American Capitalism," draft essay, and the book they edited, *Labor Market Segmentation* (Lexington, Mass.: Lexington Books, 1975) for an explication of this view.

sical and Marxist economists. Both ignore patriarchy, a social system with a material base. The neoclassical economists tend to exonerate the capitalist system, attributing job segregation to exogenous *ideological* factors, like sexist attitudes. Marxist economists tend to attribute job segregation to capitalists, ignoring the part played by male workers and the effect of centuries of patriarchal social relations. In this paper I hope to redress the balance. The line of argument I have outlined here and will develop further below is perhaps incapable of proof. This paper, I hope, will establish its plausibility rather than its incontrovertibility.

The first part of this paper briefly reviews evidence and explanations offered in the anthropological literature for the creation of dominance-dependence relations between men and women. The second part reviews the historical literature on the division of labor by sex during the emergence of capitalism and the Industrial Revolution in England and the United States. This part focuses on the extension of male-female dominance-dependence relations to the wage-labor market and the key role played by men in maintaining job segregation by sex and hence male superiority.

Anthropological Perspectives on the Division of Labor by Sex

Some anthropologists explain male dominance by arguing that it existed from the very beginning of human society. Sherry Ortner suggests that indeed "female is to male as nature is to culture."[4] According to Ortner, culture devalues nature; females are associated with nature, are considered closer to nature in all cultures,[5] and are thus devalued. Her view is compatible with that of Rosaldo,[6] who emphasizes the public-private split, and that of Lévi-Strauss, who assumes the subordination of women during the process of the creation of society.

4. Sherry B. Ortner, "Is Female to Male as Nature Is to Culture?" *Feminist Studies* 1, no. 2 (Fall 1972): 5–31. "The universality of female subordination, the fact that it exists within every type of social and economic arrangement, and in societies of every degree of complexity, indicates to me that we are up against something very profound, very stubborn, something that cannot be remedied merely by rearranging a few tasks and roles in the social system, nor even by rearranging the whole economic structure" (pp. 5–6).

5. Ortner specifically rejects a biological basis for this association of women with nature and the concomitant devaluation of both. Biological differences "only take on significance of superior/inferior within the framework of culturally defined value systems" (ibid., p. 9). The biological explanation is, of course, the other major explanation for the universality of female subordination. I, too, deny the validity of this explanation and will not discuss it in this paper. Female physiology does, however, play a role in supporting a cultural view of women as closer to nature, as Ortner argues persuasively, following DeBeauvoir (ibid., pp. 12–14). Ortner's article was reprinted in *Woman, Culture, and Society* in slightly revised form.

6. Michelle Z. Rosaldo, "Woman, Culture, and Society: A Theoretical Overview," in *Woman, Culture, and Society.*

According to Lévi-Strauss, culture began with the exchange of women by men to cement bonds between families—thereby creating *society*.[7] In fact, Lévi-Strauss sees a fundamental tension between the family (i.e., the domestic realm in which women reside closer to nature) and society, which requires that families break down their autonomy to exchange with one another. The exchange of women is a mechanism that enforces the interdependence of families and that creates society. By analogy, Lévi-Strauss suggests that the division of labor between the sexes is the mechanism which enforces "a reciprocal state of dependency between the sexes."[8] It also assures heterosexual marriage. "When it is stated that one sex must perform certain tasks, this also means that the other sex is forbidden to do them."[9] Thus the existence of a sexual division of labor is a universal of human society, though the exact division of the tasks by sex varies enormously.[10] Moreover, following Lévi-Strauss, because it is men who exchange women and women who are exchanged in creating social bonds, men benefit more than women from these social bonds, and the division of labor between the sexes is a hierarchical one.[11]

While this first school of anthropological thought, the "universalists," is based primarily on Lévi-Strauss and the exchange of women, Chodorow, following Rosaldo and Ortner, emphasizes women's confinement to the domestic sphere. Chodorow locates this confinement in the mothering role. She constructs the universality of patriarchy on the universal fact that women mother. Female mothering reproduces itself via the creation of gender-specific personality structures.[12]

Two other major schools of thought on the origins of the sexual divison of labor merit attention. Both reject the universality, at least in

7. Claude Lévi-Strauss, "The Family," in *Man, Culture and Society*, ed. by Harry L. Shapiro (New York: Oxford University Press, 1971).

8. Ibid., p. 348.

9. Ibid., pp. 347–48. "One of the strongest field recollections of this writer was his meeting, among the Bororo of central Brazil, of a man about thirty years old: unclean, ill-fed, sad, and lonesome. When asked if the man was seriously ill, the natives' answer came as a shock: what was wrong with him?–nothing at all, he was just a bachelor. And true enough, in a society where labor is systematically shared between men and women and where only the married status permits the man to benefit from the fruits of woman's work, including delousing, body painting, and hair-plucking as well as vegetable food and cooked food (since the Bororo woman tills the soil and makes pots), a bachelor is really only half a human being" (p. 341).

10. For further discussion of both the universality and variety of the division of labor by sex, see Melville J. Herskovits, *Economic Anthropology* (New York: W. W. Norton & Co., 1965), esp. chap. 7; Theodore Caplow, *The Sociology of Work* (New York: McGraw-Hill Book Co., 1964), esp. chap. 1.

11. For more on the exchange of women and its significance for women, see Rubin.

12. Nancy Chodorow, *Family Structure and Feminine Personality: The Reproduction of Mothering* (Berkeley: University of California Press, forthcoming). Chodorow offers an important alternative interpretation of the Oedipus complex (see her "Family Structure and Feminine Personality" in *Woman, Culture, and Society*).

theory if not in practice, of the sex-ordered division of labor. One is the "feminist-revisionist" school which argues that we cannot be certain that the division of labor is male supremacist; it may be separate but equal (as Lévi-Strauss occasionally seems to indicate), but we will never know because of the bias of the observers which makes comparisons impossible. This school is culturally relativist in the extreme, but it nevertheless contributes to our knowledge of women's work and status by stressing the accomplishments of females in their part of the division of labor.[13]

The second school also rejects the universality of sex-ordered division of labor but, unlike relativists, seeks to compare societies to isolate the variables which coincide with greater or lesser autonomy of women. This school, the "variationist," is subdivided according to the characteristics members emphasize: the contribution of women to subsistence and their control over their contribution, the organization of tribal versus state societies, the requirements of the mode of production, the emergence of wealth and private property, the boundaries of the private and public spheres.[14] A complete review of these approaches is impossible here, but I will cite a few examples from this literature to illustrate the relevance of these variables for the creation of a sex-ordered division of labor.

Among the !Kung, a hunting and gathering people in South West Africa, the women have a great deal of autonomy and influence.[15] Draper argues that this is the result of (1) the contribution of 60–80 percent of the community's food by the women and their retention of control over its distribution; (2) equal absence from the camp and equal range and mobility of the male hunters and the female gatherers (the women are not dependent on the men for protection in their gathering range); (3) the flexibility of sex roles and the willingness of adults to do the work of the opposite sex (with the exception that women did not hunt and men did not remove nasal mucous or feces from children!); (4) the absence of physical expression of aggression; (5) the small size (seventeen to sixty-five) of and flexible membership in living groups; (6)

13. Several of the articles in the Rosaldo and Lamphere collection are of this variety (see particularly Collier and Stack). Also, see Ernestine Friedl, "The Position of Women: Appearance and Reality," *Anthropological Quarterly* 40, no. 3 (July 1967): 97–108.

14. For an example of one particular emphasis, Leavitt states: "The most important clue to woman's status anywhere is her degree of participation in economic life and her control over property and the products she produces, both of which factors appear to be related to the kinship system of a society" (Ruby B. Leavitt, "Women in Other Cultures," in *Woman and Sexist Society,* ed. Vivian Gornick and Barbara K. Moran [New York: New American Library, 1972], p. 396). In a historical study which also seeks to address the questions of women's status, Joanne McNamara and Suzanne Wemple ("The Power of Woman through the Family in Medieval Europe: 500–1100," *Feminist Studies* 1, nos 3–4 [Winter–Spring 1973]: 126–41) emphasize the private-public split in their discussion of women's loss of status during this period.

15. Patricia Draper, "!Kung Women: Contrasts in Sexual Egalitarianism in Foraging and Sedentary Contexts," in *Toward an Anthropology of Women.*

a close, public settlement arrangement, in which the huts were situated in a circle around the campfire.

In the late 1960s when Draper did her fieldwork, some of the !Kung were beginning to settle in small villages where the men took up herding and the women agriculture, like other groups (e.g., the Bantu) who were already settled. The agriculture and the food preparation were more time consuming for the women than gathering had been and, while they continued to gather from time to time, the new agricultural pursuits kept the women closer to home. The men, in contrast, through herding, remained mobile and had greater contact with the world outside the !Kung: the Bantus, politics, wage work, and advanced knowledge (e.g., about domesticated animals). These sex roles were maintained with more rigidity. Boys and girls came to be socialized differently, and men began to feel their work superior to the women's. Men began to consider property theirs (rather than jointly owned with the women), and "[r]anking of individuals in terms of prestige and differential worth ha[d] begun. . . ."[16] Houses, made more permanent and private, were no longer arranged in a circle. The women in particular felt that the group as a whole had less ability to observe, and perhaps to sanction, the behavior of people in married couples. Doubtless these changes occurred partly because of the influence of the male-dominated Western culture on the !Kung. The overall result, according to Draper, was a decrease in the status and influence of women, the denigration of their work, and an increase, for women, in the importance of the family unit at the expense of the influence of the group as a whole. The delineation of public and private spheres placed men in the public and women in the private sphere, and the public sphere came to be valued more.

Boserup, in *Woman's Role in Economic Development,* writes extensively of the particular problems caused for women when Third World tribal groups came into contact with Western colonial administrations.[17] The usual result was the creation or strengthening of male dominance as, for example, where administrations taught men advanced agricultural techniques where women were farmers, or schooled men in trading where women were traders. The Europeans encouraged men to head and support their families, superseding women's traditional responsibilities. Previous to colonization, according to Leavitt: "In regions like Africa and Southeast Asia, where shifting agriculture and the female farmer predominate, the women work very hard and receive limited support from their husbands, but they also have some economic independence, considerable freedom of movement, and an important place in the community. . . . In traditional African marriages the woman is expected to support herself and her children and to feed the family,

16. Ibid., p. 108.
17. Ester Boserup, *Woman's Role in Economic Development* (London: George Allen & Unwin, 1970).

including her husband, with the food she grows."[18] Boserup supports this view of the economic role of women before the influence of Europeans began to be felt.

Europeans also entrusted local governance to male leaders and ignored women's traditional participation in tribal society. That the women had highly organized and yet nonhierarchical governmental structures, which were unknown and ignored by the colonists, is illustrated by the case of the Igbo in Nigeria. Allen reports that Igbo women held *mikiri*, or meetings, which were democratic discussions with no official leaders and "which articulated women's interests *as opposed to* those of men."[19] The women needed these meetings because they lived in patrilocal villages and had few kinship ties with each other, and because they had their own separate economic activities, their own crops, and their own trading, which they needed to protect from men. When a man offended the women, by violating the women's market rules or letting his cows into the women's yam fields, the women often retaliated as a group by "sitting on a man"—carrying on loudly at his home late at night and "perhaps demolishing his hut or plastering it with mud and roughing him up a bit."[20] Women also sometimes executed collective strikes and boycotts. With the advent of the British administrators, and their inevitably unfavorable policies toward women, the Igbo women adapted their tactics and used them against the British. For example, in response to an attempt to tax the women farmers, tens of thousands of women were involved in riots at administrative centers over an area of 6,000 square miles containing a population of 2 million people. The "Women's War," as it was called, was coordinated through the market *mikiri* network.[21] Allen continues to detail the distintegration of the *mikiri* in the face of British colonial and missionary policies.

In a study of a somewhat different process of state formation, Muller looks at the decline of Anglo-Saxon and Welsh tribal society and the formation of the English nation-state, a process which occurred from the eighth to the fifteenth century. Muller writes:

> The transition from tribe to state is historically probably the greatest watershed in the decline in the status of women. . . . This is not to deny that in what we call "tribal," that is, pre-state, society there is not a wide variation in the status of women and even that in certain pre-state societies, women may be in what we would consider an abject position *vis à vis* the men in that society. . . . We

18. Leavitt, pp. 412, 413.

19. Judith Van Allen, " 'Sitting on a Man': Colonialism and the Lost Political Institutions of Igbo Women," *Canadian Journal of African Studies* 6, no. 2 (1972): 169.

20. Ibid., p. 170.

21. Ibid., pp. 174–75. The British naturally thought the women were directed in their struggle by the men, though very few men participated in the riots.

believe that the causes for these variations in status can be found, as in the case of State Societies, in the material conditions which give rise to the social and economic positions therein.[22]

Muller stresses that, in the Welsh and Anglo-Saxon tribes, "the right of individual maintenance was so well entrenched that these rights were not entrusted to a patriarchal head of a nuclear family, but were, rather, vested in the larger social group of the *gwely* [four-generation kinship group]."[23] Both men and women upon adulthood received a share of cattle from the *gwely*. The cattle provided their personal maintenance and prevented an individual from becoming dependent upon another. Thus, although in the tribal system land inheritance was patrilineal and residence patrilocal, a married woman had her own means of economic subsistence. Women were political participants both in their husbands' and in their natal lineages. Like a man, a woman was responsible for her children's crimes, and she and her natal lineages (*not* her spouse's) were responsible for her crimes. Tribal customs were, however, undermined by the emergence of the state. ". . . we can observe the development of public—as opposed to social—male authority, through the political structure imposed by the emerging state. Since the state is interested in the alienation of the tribal resource base—its land and its labor power —it finds it convenient to use the traditional gender division of labor and resources in tribal society and places them in a hierarchical relationship both internally (husband over wife and children) and externally (lords over peasants and serfs)."[24] The king established regional administrative units without regard to tribal jurisdictions, appointed his own administrators, bypassed the authority of the tribal chiefs, and levied obligations on the males as "heads" of individual households. Tribal groups lost collective responsibility for their members, and women and children lost their group rights and came under the authority of their husbands. Woman's work became private for the benefit of her husband, rather than public for the benefit of the kin group. As Muller points out, there must have been tendencies evident in tribal society that created the preconditions for a hierarchical, male-dominated state, for it was not equally likely that the emerging state would be female. Among these tendencies, for example, were male ownership of land and greater male participation in military expeditions, probably especially those farther away.[25]

22. Muller, p. 1. I am very grateful to Viana Muller for allowing me to summarize parts of her unpublished paper.
23. Ibid., p. 14.
24. Ibid., p. 25.
25. The examples of the !Kung, the Igbo, the Anglo-Saxons, and the groups discussed by Boserup all suggest that the process of expansion of state or emerging-state societies and the conquest of other peoples was an extremely important mechanism for

This summary of several studies from the third school of an-thropology, the variationist school, points to a number of variables that help to explain a decrease in woman's social status. They suggest that increased sexual stratification occurs along with a general process of social stratification (which at least in some versions seems to depend on and foster an increase in social surplus—to support the higher groups in the hierarchy). As a result, a decrease in the social status of woman occurs when (1) she loses control of subsistence through a change in production methods and devaluation of her share of the division of labor; (2) her work becomes private and family centered rather than social and kin focused; and/or (3) some men assert their power over other men through the state mechanism by elevating these subordinate men in their families, using the nuclear family against the kin group.[26] In this way the division of labor between men and women becomes a more hierarchical one. Control over women is maintained directly in the family by the man, but it is sustained by social institutions, such as the state and religion.

The work in this school of anthropology suggests that patriarchy did not always exist, but rather that it emerged as social conditions changed. Moreover, men participated in this transformation. Because it benefited men relative to women, men have had a stake in reproducing patriarchy. Although there is a great deal of controversy among an-thropologists about the origins of patriarchy, and more work needs to be done to establish the validity of this interpretation, I believe the weight of the evidence supports it. In any case, most anthropologists agree that patriarchy emerged long before capitalism, even if they disagree about its origins.

In England, as we have seen, the formation of the state marks the end of Anglo-Saxon tribal society and the beginning of feudal society. Throughout feudal society the tendencies toward the privatization of family life and the increase of male power within the family appear to strengthen, as does their institutional support from church and state. By the time of the emergence of capitalism in the fifteenth through eigh-

---

spreading hierarchy and male domination. In fact, the role of warfare and imperialism raises the question of whether the state, to establish itself, creates the patriarchal family, or the patriarchal family creates the state (Thomas Vietorisz, personal communication). Surely emerging patriarchal social relations in prestate societies paved the way for both male public power (i.e., male control of the state apparatus) and the privatization of patriarchal power in the family. Surely also this privatization—and the concomitant decline of tribal power—strengthened, and was strengthened by, the state.

26. This point is stressed especially by Muller but is also illustrated by the !Kung. Muller states: "The men, although lowered from clansmen to peasants, were elevated to heads of nuclear families, with a modicum of both public power [through the state and religion] and a measure of private power through the decree of the Church-State that they were to be lords over their wives" (p. 35).

teenth centuries, the nuclear, patriarchal peasant family had become the basic production unit in society.[27]

The Emergence of Capitalism and the Industrial Revolution in England and the United States

The key process in the emergence of capitalism was primitive accumulation, the prior accumulation that was necessary for capitalism to establish itself.[28] Primitive accumulation was a twofold process which set the preconditons for the expansion of the scale of production: first, free laborers had to be accumulated; second, large amounts of capital had to be accumulated. The first was achieved through enclosures and the removal of people from the land, their subsistence base, so that they were forced to work for wages. The second was achieved through both the growth of smaller capitals in farms and shops amassed through banking facilities, and vast increases in merchant capital, the profits from the slave trade, and colonial exploitation.

The creation of a wage-labor force and the increase in the scale of production that occurred with the emergence of capitalism had in some ways a more severe impact on women than on men. To understand this impact let us look at the work of women before this transition occurred and the changes which took place as it occurred.[29] In the 1500s and 1600s, agriculture, woolen textiles (carried on as a by-industry of ag-

27. Both Hill and Stone describe England during this period as a patriarchal society in which the institutions of the nuclear family, the state, and religion, were being strengthened (see Christopher Hill, *Society and Puritanism* [New York: Schocken Books, 1964], esp. chap. 13; Lawrence Stone, *The Crisis of the Aristocracy, 1558–1641*, abridged ed. [New York: Oxford University Press, 1967], esp. chap. 11). Recent demographic research verifies the establishment of the nuclear family prior to the industrial revolution (see Peter Laslett, ed., *Household and Family in Past Time* [Cambridge: Cambridge University Press, 1972]). Because of limitations of my knowledge and space, and because I sought to discuss, first, the concept and establishment of patriarchy and second, its transformation in a wage-labor society, I am skipping over the rise and fall of feudal society and the emergence of family-centered petty commodity production and focusing in the next section on the disintegration of this family-centered production, creation of the wage-labor force, and the maintenance of job segregation in a capitalist context.

28. See Karl Marx, "The So-called Primitive Accumulation," in *Capital*, 3 vols. (New York: International Publishers, 1967), vol. 1, pt. 8; Stephen Hymer, "Robinson Crusoe and the Secret of Primitive Accumulation," *Monthly Review* 23, no. 4 (September 1971): 11–36.

29. This account relies primarily on that of Alice Clark, *The Working Life of Women in the Seventeenth Century* (New York: Harcourt, Brace & Howe, 1920). Her account is supported by many others, such as B. L. Hutchins, *Women in Modern Industry* (London: G. Bell & Sons, 1915); Georgiana Hill, *Women in English Life from Medieval to Modern Times*, 2 vols. (London: Richard Bentley & Son, 1896); F. W. Tickner, *Women in English Economic History* (New York: E. P. Dutton & Co., 1923); Ivy Pinchbeck, *Women Workers and the Industrial Revolution, 1750–1850* (London: Frank Cass & Co., 1930; reprinted 1969).

riculture), and the various crafts and trades in the towns were the major sources of livelihood for the English population. In the rural areas men worked in the fields on small farms they owned or rented and women tended the household plots, small gardens and orchards, animals, and dairies. The women also spun and wove. A portion of these products were sold in small markets to supply the villages, towns, and cities, and in this way women supplied a considerable proportion of their families' cash income, as well as their subsistence in kind. In addition to the tenants and farmers, there was a small wage-earning class of men and women who worked on the larger farms. Occasionally tenants and their wives worked for wages as well, the men more often than the women.[30] As small farmers and cottagers were displaced by larger farmers in the seventeenth and eighteenth centuries, their wives lost their main sources of support, while the men were able to continue as wage laborers to some extent. Thus women, deprived of these essential household plots, suffered relatively greater unemployment, and the families as a whole were deprived of a large part of their subsistence.[31]

In the 1700s, the demand for cotton textiles grew, and English merchants found they could utilize the labor of the English agricultural population, who were already familiar with the arts of spinning and weaving. The merchants distributed materials to be spun and woven, creating a domestic industrial system which occupied many displaced farm families. This putting-out system, however, proved inadequate. The complexities of distribution and collection and, perhaps more important, the control the workers had over the production process (they could take time off, work intermittently, steal materials) prevented an increase in the supply of textiles sufficient to meet the merchants' needs. To solve these problems first spinning, in the late 1700s, and then weaving, in the early 1800s, were organized into factories. The textile factories were located in the rural areas, at first, in order both to take advantage of the labor of children and women, by escaping the restric-

30. Women and men in England had been employed as agricultural laborers for several centuries. Clark found that by the seventeenth century the wages of men were higher than women's and the tasks done were different, though similar in skill and strength requirements (Clark 1920, p. 60). Wages for agricultural (and other work) were often set by local authorities. These wage differentials reflected the relative social status of men and women and the social norms of the time. Women were considered to require lower wages because they ate less, for example, and were expected to have fewer luxuries, such as tobacco (see Clark and Pinchbeck throughout for substantiation of women's lower standard of living). Laura Oren has substantiated this for English women during the period 1860–1950 (see n. 60 below).

31. The problem of female unemployment in the countryside was a generally recognized one which figured prominently in the debate about poor-law reform, for example. As a remedy, it was suggested that rural families be allowed to retain small household plots, that women be used more in agricultural wage labor and also in the putting-out system, and that men's wages be adjusted upward (see Ivy Pinchbeck, *Women Workers and the Industrial Revolution, 1750–1850*, pp. 69–84).

tions of the guilds in the cities, and to utilize waterpower. When spinning was industrialized, women spinners at home suffered greater unemployment, while the demand for male handloom weavers increased. When weaving was mechanized, the need for handloom weavers fell off as well.[32]

In this way, domestic industry, created by emerging capitalism, was later superseded and destroyed by the progress of capitalist industrialization. In the process, women, children, and men in the rural areas all suffered dislocation and disruption, but they experienced this in different ways. Women, forced into unemployment by the capitalization of agriculture more frequently than men, were more available to labor, both in the domestic putting-out system and in the early factories. It is often argued both that men resisted going into the factories because they did not want to lose their independence and that women and children were more docile and malleable. If this was in fact the case, it would appear that these "character traits" of women and men were already established before the advent of the capitalistic organization of industry, and that they would have grown out of the authority structure prevailing in the previous period of small-scale, family agriculture. Many historians suggest that within the family men were the heads of households, and women, even though they contributed a large part of their families' subsistence, were subordinate.[33]

We may never know the facts of the authority structure within the preindustrial family, since much of what we know is from prescriptive literature or otherwise class biased, and little is known about the point of view of the people themselves. Nevertheless, the evidence on family life and on relative wages and levels of living suggests that women were subordinate within the family. This conclusion is consonant with the anthropological literature, reviewed in Part I above, which describes the emergence of patriarchial social relations along with early societal

32. See Stephen Marglin, "What Do Bosses Do? The Origins and Functions of Hierarchy in Capitalist Production," *Review of Radical Political Economics* 6, no. 2 (Summer 1974): 60–112, for a discussion of the transition from putting out to factories. The sexual division of labor changed several times in the textile industry. Hutchins writes that the further back one goes in history, the more was the industry controlled by women. By the seventeenth century, though, men had become professional handloom weavers, and it was often claimed that men had superior strength or skill—which was required for certain types of weaves or fabrics. Thus, the increase in demand for handloom weavers in the late 1700s brought increased employment for men. When weaving was mechanized in the factories women operated the power looms, and male handloom weavers became unemployed. When jenny and waterframe spinning were replaced by mule spinning, supposedly requiring more strength, men took that over and displaced women spinners. A similar transition occurred in the United States. It is important to keep in mind that as a by-industry, both men and women engaged in various processes of textile manufacture, and this was intensified under putting out (see Pinchbeck 1969, chaps. 6–9).

33. See Clark; Pinchbeck; E. P. Thompson, *The Making of the English Working Class* (New York: Vintage Books, 1963).

stratification. Moreover, the history of the early factories suggests that capitalists took advantage of this authority structure, finding women and children more vulnerable, both because of familial relations and because they were simply more desperate economically due to the changes in agriculture which left them unemployed.[34]

The transition to capitalism in the cities and towns was experienced somewhat differently than in the rural areas, but it tends to substantiate the line of argument just set out: men and women had different places in the familial authority structure, and capitalism proceeded in a way that built on that authority structure. In the towns and cities before the transition to capitalism a system of family industry prevailed: a family of artisans worked together at home to produce goods for exchange. Adults were organized in guilds, which had social and religious functions as well as industrial ones. Within trades carried on as family industries women and men generally performed different tasks: in general, the men worked at what were considered more skilled tasks, the women at processing the raw materials or finishing the end product. Men, usually the heads of the production units, had the status of master artisans. For though women usually belonged to their husbands' guilds, they did so as appendages; girls were rarely apprenticed to a trade and thus rarely become journeymen or masters. Married women participated in the production process and probably acquired important skills, but they usually controlled the production process only if they were widowed, when guilds often gave them the right to hire apprentices and journeymen. Young men may have married within their guilds (i.e., the daughters of artisans in the same trade). In fact, young women and girls had a unique and very important role as extra or casual laborers in a system where the guilds prohibited hiring additional workers from outside the family, and undoubtedly they learned skills which were useful when they married.[35] Nevertheless, girls appear not to have been trained as carefully as boys were and, as adults, not to have attained the same status in the guilds.

Although in most trades men were the central workers and women the assistants, other trades were so identified by sex that family industry did not prevail.[36] Carpentry and millinery were two such trades. Male carpenters and female milliners both hired apprentices and assistants

34. In fact, the earliest factories utilized the labor of poor children, already separated from their families, who were apprenticed to factory owners by parish authorities. They were perhaps the most desperate and vulnerable of all.

35. Hutchins, p. 16 (see also Olive J. Jocelyn, *English Apprenticeship and Child Labor* [London: T. Fisher Unwin, 1912], pp. 149–50, on the labor of girls, and Clark, chap. 5, on the organization of family industry in towns).

36. The seventeenth century already found the crafts and trades sex divided. Much work needs to be done on the development of guilds from the point of view of shedding light on the sexual division of labor and on the question of the nature of women's organizations. Such work would enable us to trace more accurately the decline in women's status from the tribal period, through feudalism, to the emergence of capitalism.

and attained the status of master craftspersons. According to Clark, although some women's trades, such as millinery, were highly skilled and organized in guilds, many women's trades were apparently difficult to organize in strong guilds, because most women's skills could not be easily monopolized. All women, as part of their home duties, knew the arts of textile manufacturing, sewing, food processing, and to some extent, trading.

In the seventeenth and eighteenth centuries the family industry system and the guilds began to break down in the face of the demand for larger output. Capitalists began to organize production on a larger scale, and production became separated from the home as the size of establishments grew. Women were excluded from participation in the industries in which they had assisted men as they no longer took place at home, where married women apparently tended to remain to carry on their domestic work. Yet many women out of necessity sought work in capitalistically organized industry as wage laborers. When women entered wage labor they appear to have been at a disadvantage relative to men. First, as in agriculture, there was already a tradition of lower wages for women (in the previously limited area of wage work). Second, women appear to have been less well trained than men and obtained less desirable jobs. And third, they appear to have been less well organized than men.

Because I think the ability of men to organize themselves played a crucial role in limiting women's participation in the wage-labor market, I want to offer, first, some evidence to support the assertion that men were better organized and, second, some plausible reasons for their superiority in this area. I am not arguing that men had greater organizational abilities at all times and all places, or in all areas or types of organization, but am arguing here that it is plausible that they did in England during this period, particularly in the area of economic production. As evidence of their superiority, we have the guilds themselves, which were better organized among men's trades than women's, and in which, in joint trades, men had superior positions—women were seldom admitted to the hierarchical ladder of progression. Second, we have the evidence of the rise of male professions and the elimination of female ones during the sixteenth and seventeenth centuries. The medical profession, male from its inception, established itself through hierarchical organization, the monopolization of new, "scientific" skills, and the assistance of the state. Midwifery was virtually wiped out by the men. Brewing provides another example. Male brewers organized a fellowship, petitioned the king for monopoly rights (in exchange for a tax on every quart they brewed), and succeeded in forcing the numerous small-scale brewsters to buy from them.[37] Third, throughout the formative period

37. See Clark, pp. 221–31, for the brewers, and pp. 242–84, for the medical profession.

of industrial capitalism, men appear to have been better able to organize themselves as wage workers. And as we shall see below, as factory production became established men used their labor organizations to limit women's place in the labor market.

As to why men might have had superior organizational ability during this transitional period, I think we must consider the development of patriarchal social relations in the nuclear family, as reinforced by the state and religion, a process briefly described above for Anglo-Saxon England. Since men's superior position was reinforced by the state, and men acted in the political arena as heads of households and in the households as heads of production units, it seems likely that men would develop more organizational structures beyond their households. Women, in an inferior position at home and without the support of the state, would be less likely to be able to do this. Men's organizational knowledge, then, grew out of their position in the family and in the division of labor. Clearly, further investigation of organizations before and during the transition period is necessary to establish the mechanisms by which men came to control this public sphere.

Thus, the capitalistic organization of industry, in removing work from the home, served to increase the subordination of women, since it served to increase the relative importance of the area of men's domination. But it is important to remember that men's domination was already established and that it clearly influenced the direction and shape that capitalist development took. As Clark has argued, with the separation of work from the home men became less dependent on women for industrial production, while women became more dependent on men economically. From a position much like that of the African women discussed in Part I above, English married women, who had supported themselves and their children, became the domestic servants of their husbands. Men increased their control over technology, production, and marketing, as they excluded women from industry, education, and political organization.[38]

When women participated in the wage-labor market, they did so in a position as clearly limited by patriarchy as it was by capitalism. Men's control over women's labor was altered by the wage-labor system, but it was not eliminated. In the labor market the dominant position of men was maintained by sex-ordered job segregation. Women's jobs were lower paid, considered less skilled, and often involved less exercise of

38. Ibid., chap. 7. Eli Zaretsky ("Capitalism, the Family, and Personal Life," *Socialist Revolution*, nos. 13, 14 [1973]), follows a similar interpretation of history and offers different conclusions. Capitalism exacerbated the sexual division of labor and created the *appearance* that women work for their husbands; in reality, women who did domestic work at home were working for capital. Thus according to Zaretsky the present situation has its roots more in capitalism than in patriarchy. Although capitalism may have increased the consequence for women of the domestic division of labor, surely patriarchy tells us more about why men didn't stay home. That women worked for men in the home, as well as for capital, is also a reality.

authority or control.[39] Men acted to enforce job segregation in the labor market; they utilized trade-union associations and strengthened the domestic division of labor, which required women to do housework, child care, and related chores. Women's subordinate position in the labor market reinforced their subordinate position in the family, and that in turn reinforced their labor-market position.

The process of industrialization and the establishment of the factory system, particularly in the textile industry, illustrate the role played by men's trade-union associations. Textile factories employed children at first, but as they expanded they began to utilize the labor of adult women and of whole families. While the number of married women working has been greatly exaggerated,[40] apparently enough married women had followed their work into the factories to cause both their husbands and the upper classes concern about home life and the care of children. Smelser has argued that in the early factories the family industry system and male control could often be maintained. For example, adult male spinners often hired their own or related children as helpers, and whole families were often employed by the same factory for the same length of working day.[41] Technological change, however, increasingly made this difficult, and factory legislation which limited the hours of children, but not of adults, further exacerbated the difficulties of the "family factory system."

The demands of the factory laborers in the 1820s and 1830s had

39. William Lazonick argues in his dissertation, "Marxian Theory and the Development of the Labor Force in England" (Ph.D. diss., Harvard University, 1975), that the degree of authority required of the worker was often decisive in determining the sex of the worker. Thus handloom weavers in cottage industry were men because this allowed them to control the production process and the labor of the female spinners. In the spinning factories, mule spinners were men because mule spinners were required to supervise the labor of piecers, usually young boys. Men's position as head of the family established their position as heads of production units, and vice versa. While this is certainly plausible, I think it requires further investigation. Lazonick's work in this area (see chap. 4, "Segments of the Labour Force: Women, Children, and Irish") is very valuable.

40. Perhaps 25 percent of female textile factory workers were married women (see Pinchbeck, p. 198; Margaret Hewitt, *Wives and Mothers in Victorian Industry* [London: Rockliff, 1958], pp. 14 ff.). It is important to remember also that factory employment was far from the dominant employment of women. Most women worked as domestic servants.

41. Neil Smelser, *Social Change and the Industrial Revolution* (Chicago: University of Chicago Press, 1959), chaps. 9–11. Other researchers have also established that in some cases there was a considerable degree of familial control over some aspects of the work process. See Tamara Hareven's research on mills in New Hampshire; e.g., "Family Time and Industrial Time: The Interaction between Family and Work in a Planned Corporation Town, 1900–1924," *Journal of Urban History* 1, no. 3 (May 1975): 365–89. Michael Anderson, *Family Structure in Nineteenth Century Lancashire* (Cambridge: Cambridge University Press, 1971), argues, based on demographic data, that the "practice of allowing operatives to employ assistants, though widespread, can at no period have resulted in a predominantly parent-child pattern of employment" (p. 116). Also see Amy Hirsch's treatment of this question in her "Capitalism and the Working Class Family in British Textile Industries during the Industrial Revolution," mimeographed (New York: New School for Social Research, 1975).

been designed to maintain the family factory system,[42] but by 1840 male factory operatives were calling for limitations on the hours of work of children between nine and thirteen to eight a day, and forbidding the employment of younger children. According to Smelser this caused parents difficulty in training and supervising their children, and to remedy it male workers and the middle and upper classes began to recommend that women, too, be removed from the factories.[43]

The upper classes of the Victorian Age, the age that elevated women to their pedestals, seem to have been motivated by moral outrage and concern for the future of the English race (and for the reproduction of the working class): "In the male," said Lord Shaftesbury, "the moral effects of the system are very sad, but in the female they are infinitely worse, not alone upon themselves, but upon their families, upon society, and, I may add, upon the country itself. It is bad enough if you corrupt the man, but if you corrupt the woman, you poison the waters of life at the very fountain."[44] Engels, too, appears to have been outraged for similar reasons: ". . . we find here precisely the same features reappearing which the Factories' Report presented,—the work of women up to the hour of confinement, incapacity as housekeepers, neglect of home and children, indifference, actual dislike to family life, and demoralization; further the crowding out of men from employment, the constant improvement of machinery, early emancipation of children, husbands supported by their wives and children, etc., etc."[45] Here, Engels has

42. "[The factory operatives'] agitation in the 1820's and 1830's was one avenue taken to protect the traditional relationship between adult and child, to perpetuate the structure of wages, to limit the recruitment of labourers into industry, and to maintain the father's economic authority" (Smelser, p. 265). Lazonick argues that the workers' main interest were not in maintaining their familial dominance in industry but in maintaining their family life outside industry. According to Smelser, agitation before 1840 sought to establish equal length days for all workers, which would tend to maintain the family in the factory, whereas after 1840 male workers came to accept the notion that married women and children should stay at home.

43. The question of the motives of the various groups involved in passing the factory acts is indeed a thorny one. Women workers themselves may have favored the legislation as an improvement in their working conditions, but some undoubtedly needed the incomes longer hours enabled. Most women working in the mills were young, single women who perhaps benefited from the protection. Single women, though "liberated" by the mills from direct domination in their families (about which there was much discussion in the 1800s), were nevertheless kept in their place by the conditions facing them in the labor market. Because of their age and sex, job segregation and lower wages assured their inability to be completely self-sufficient. Ruling-class men, especially those associated with the larger firms, may have had an interest in factory legislation in order to eliminate unfair competition. Working-class and ruling-class men may have cooperated to maintain men's dominant position in the labor market and in the family.

44. From Mary Merryweather, *Factory Life,* cited in *Women in English Life from Medieval to Modern Times,* 2: 200. The original is recorded in *Hansard Parliamentary Debates,* 3d ser., House of Commons, June 7, 1842.

45. Frederick Engels, *The Condition of the Working Class in England in 1844* (London: Geo. Allen & Unwin, 1892), p. 199.

touched upon the reasons for the opposition of the male workers to the situation. Engels was apparently ambivalent about whose side he was on, for, while he often seems to share the attitudes of the men and of the upper classes, he also referred to the trade unions as elite organizations of grown-up men who achieved benefits for themselves but not for the unskilled, women, or children.[46]

That male workers viewed the employment of women as a threat to their jobs is not surprising, given an economic system where competition among workers was characteristic. That women were paid lower wages exacerbated the threat. But why their response was to attempt to exclude women rather than to organize them is explained, not by capitalism, but by patriarchal relations between men and women: men wanted to assure that women would continue to perform the appropriate tasks at home.

Engels reports an incident which probably occurred in the 1830s. Male Glasgow spinners had formed a secret union: "The Committee put a price on the heads of all blacklegs [strikebreakers] . . . and deliberately organized arson in factories. One factory to be set on fire had women blacklegs on the premises who had taken the places of men at the spinning machines. A certain Mrs. MacPherson, the mother of one of these girls, was murdered and those responsible were shipped off to America at the expense of the union."[47] Hostility to the competition of young females, almost certainly less well trained and lower paid, was common enough. But if anything, the wage work of married women was thought even less excusable.

In 1846 the *Ten Hours' Advocate* stated clearly that they hoped for the day when such threats would be removed altogether: ". . . It is needless for us to say, that all attempts to improve the morals and physical condition of female factory workers will be abortive, unless their hours are materially reduced. Indeed we may go so far as to say, that married females would be much better occupied in performing the domestic duties of the household, than following the never-tiring motion of machinery. We therefore hope the day is not distant, when the husband will be able to provide for his wife and family, without sending the former to endure the drudgery of a cotton mill."[48] Eventually, male trade unionists realized that women could not be removed altogether, but their attitude was still ambivalent. One local wrote to the Women's Trade Union League, organized in 1889 to encourage unionization among women workers: "Please send an organizer to this town as we

46. Ibid., p. xv.

47. Engels, *The Condition of the Working Class in England in 1844* (Stanford, Calif.: Stanford University Press, 1968), p. 251.

48. Smelser, p. 301. Similarly, Pinchbeck quotes from a deputation of the West Riding Short-Time Committee which demands "the gradual withdrawal of all females from the factories" because "home, its cares, its employments, is woman's true sphere." Gladstone thought this a good suggestion, easily implemented by appropriate laws, e.g., "forbidding a female to work in a factory after her marriage and during the life-time of her husband" (Pinchbeck, p. 200, n. 3, from the *Manchester and Salford Advertiser* [January 8, 15, 1842]).

have decided that if the women here cannot be organized they must be exterminated."[49]

The deplorable situation of women in the labor market was explained in a variety of ways by British historians and economists writing in the early twentieth century. Some accepted the logic of the male unions that women belonged at home if possible and men's wages should be increased. Ivy Pinchbeck, for example, stated: ". . . the industrial revolution marked a real advance, since it led to the assumption that men's wages should be paid on a family basis, and prepared the way for the more modern conception that in the rearing of children and in homemaking, the married woman makes an adequate economic contribution."[50] Others argued that this system would only perpetuate women's low economic status. Examining the literature from this period, especially the Webb-Rathbone-Fawcett-Edgeworth series in the *Economic Journal*, is important because it sets the framework for nearly all the explanations of women's position in the labor market that have been used since. In addition, this literature tends to support the argument, delineated in this paper, that job segregation was detrimental to women and that male unions tended to enforce it.

Several writers who focused on job segregation and noncompeting groups as the central mechanism discussed the actions of male unionists as well. Webb offered as a justification for the lower wages women received the explanation that they rarely did the same grade of work, even when engaged in the same occupation or industry. He cited cigar making, where men made fancy cigars and women made cheap ones requiring less skill.[51] Yet he also acknowledged the role male unions played in preventing women from gaining skills and admitted the possibility that, even for equal work, women received lower wages.[52]

49. Quoted in G. D. H. Cole and Raymond Postgate, *The Common People, 1746–1946*, 4th ed. (London: Methuen, 1949), p. 432.

50. Pinchbeck, pp. 312–13. The history of the emergence of capitalism and the Industrial Revolution clearly shows that the "family wage" is a recent phenomenon. Before the late 1800s, it was expected that working-class (and earlier, middle- and upper-class) married women would support themselves. Andrew Ure, a manufacturer, wrote in 1835: "Factory females have also in general much lower wages than males, and they have been pitied on this account with perhaps an injudicious sympathy, since the low price of their labour here tends to make household duties their most profitable as well as agreeable occupation, and prevents them from being tempted by the mill to abandon the care of their offspring at home. Thus Providence effects its purposes with a wisdom and efficacy which should repress the short-sighted presumption of human devices" (*The Philosophy of Manufacturers* [London: C. Knight, 1835], p. 475). The development of the family wage is discussed in somewhat greater detail in Heidi Hartmann, "Capitalism and Women's Work in the Home, 1900–1930" (Ph.D. diss., Yale University, 1974). More work needs to be done on this concept.

51. Sidney Webb, "The Alleged Differences in the Wages Paid to Men and Women for Similar Work," *Economic Journal* 1, no. 4 (December 1891): 639.

52. The competition between men and women in industry is, indeed, not so much a direct underselling in wages as a struggle to secure the better paid kinds of work (ibid., p. 658).

Millicent Fawcett argued that equal pay for equal work was a fraud for women, since having been kept from obtaining equal skills their work (at the same jobs) was, in fact, not equal.[53] The essence of trade-union policy, she felt, was to exclude women if they were less efficient and, furthermore, to keep them less efficient.[54] As Eleanor Rathbone put it in 1917, male union leaders will support equal pay as "an effective way of maintaining the exclusion of women while appearing as the champions of equality between the sexes." Many of the followers, she thought, "are obviously rather shocked in their hearts at the idea of a woman earning a man's pay."[55]

Rathbone also considered seriously the different family responsibilities of women. They are a reality, she insisted; men do support their families more often than women do, and men want sufficient money to do this. But she did not necessarily agree with this arrangement; she simply acknowledged that most people considered it "a fundamental part of the social structure":

> The line of argument I have been following usually either irritates or depresses all women who have the interests of their own sex at heart, because it seems to point to an impasse. If the wages of men and women are really based upon fundamentally different conditions, and if these conditions cannot be changed, then it would seem . . . that women are the eternal blacklegs, doomed despite themselves to injure the prospects of men whenever they are brought into competition with them. . . . If that were really so, then it would seem as if men were justified in treating women, as in practice they have treated them—as a kind of industrial lepers, segregated in trades which men have agreed to abandon to them, permitted to occupy themselves in making clothes or in doing domestic services for each other, and in performing those subsidiary processes in the big staple trades, which are so monotonous or unskilled that men do not care to claim them.[56]

World War I, however, had raised women's expectations, and women were not likely to go back to their place willingly—even though the male

---

53. Millicent G. Fawcett, "Mr. Sidney Webb's Article on Women's Wages," *Economic Journal* 2, no. 1 (March 1892): 173–76.

54. In her review of *Women in the Printing Trades,* ed. J. Ramsay Mac Donald, Fawcett wrote that a trade union in Scotland "decided that women must either be paid the same rates as men or got rid of altogether" (p. 296). She cites "the constant and vigilant opposition of Trades Unions to the employment and the technical training of women in the better paid and more skilled branches of trade" (p. 297). As one example, she cites the London Society of Journeymen Bookbinders who tried to get the highly skilled job of laying gold leaf—a women's job—assigned to the male union members (*Economic Journal* 14, no. 2 [June 1904]: 295–99).

55. Eleanor F. Rathbone, "The Remuneration of Women's Services," *Economic Journal* 27, no. 1 (March 1917): 58.

56. Ibid., pp. 62, 63.

unions had been promised that the women's jobs were only
temporary—especially since in addition to their wages, married women
whose husbands were at war received government allowances according
to family size. Rathbone wrote: ". . . the future solution of the problem is
doubtful and difficult, and . . . it opens up unpleasant possibilities of
class antagonism and sex antagonism; . . . for women especially it seems
to offer a choice between being exploited by capitalists or dragooned
and oppressed by trade unionists. It is a dismal alternative."[57] She rec-
ommended the continuation of allowances after the war because they
would insure that families would not have to rely on men's wages, that
women who stayed at home would be paid for their work, and that
women in the labor market could complete equally with men since their
"required" wages would not be different. By 1918, Fawcett also thought
equal pay for equal work a realizable goal. Advancement in the labor
market required equal pay in order not to undercut the men's wages.
The main obstacles, she argued, were the male unions and social customs. Both led to overcrowding in the women's jobs.[58]

In 1922, Edgeworth formalized Fawcett's job segregation and overcrowding model; job segregation by sex causes overcrowding in female
sectors, which allows men's wages to be higher and forces women's wages
to be lower, than they would be otherwise. Edgeworth agreed that male
unions were the main cause of overcrowding.[59] He argued that men
should have an advantage because of their family responsibilities, and the
corollary, that since women do not have the same family responsibilities
as men, and may even be subsidized by men, their participation will tend
to pull wages down. And he seemed to suggest that equal competition in
the job market would result in lower wages even for single women
vis-à-vis single men, because women required 20 percent less food for
top efficiency. In this last, Edgeworth was simply taking seriously what
many had remarked upon—that women have a lower standard of living
than men and are willing to work for less.[60] Edgeworth concluded that
restrictions on women's work should be removed but that, since unfet-

57. Ibid., p. 64.

58. Millicent G. Fawcett, "Equal Pay for Equal Work," *Economic Journal* 28, no. 1
(March 1918): 1–6.

59. "The pressure of male trade unions appears to be largely responsible for that
crowding of women into comparatively few occupations, which is universally recognized as
a main factor in the depression of their wages" (F. Y. Edgeworth, "Equal Pay to Men and
Women for Equal Work," *Economic Journal* 32, no. 4 [December 1922]: 439).

60. While this reasoning may sound circular, I believe it is quite valid. As Marx said,
wages are determined by the value of the socially necessary commodities required to
maintain the worker, and what is necessary is the product of historical development, of
customs of comfort, of trade union activity, etc. (*Capital*, 1: 171). Laura Oren has examined
the literature on the level of living of work-class families and found that, indeed, within the
family, women have less food, less leisure, and less pocket money ("The Welfare of Women
in Laboring Families: England, 1860–1950," *Feminist Studies* 1, nos. 3–4 [Winter-Spring
1973]: 107–25). That women, like immigrant groups, can reproduce themselves on less,
and have for centuries, is a contributing factor in their lower wages.

tered competition would probably drag down the wages of men for the reasons noted above, men and families should be compensated for their losses due to the increased participation of women.[61]

The main explanation the English literature offers for lower wages is job segregation by sex, and for both lower wages and the existence of job segregation it offers several interdependent explanations: (1) the exclusionary policies of male unions, (2) the financial responsibility of men for their families, (3) the willingness of women to work for less (and their inability to get more) because of subsidies or a lower standard of living, and (4) women's lack of training and skills. The English historical literature strongly suggests that job segregation by sex is patriarchal in origin, rather longstanding, and difficult to eradicate. Men's ability to organize in labor unions—stemming perhaps from a greater knowledge of the technique of hierarchical organization—appears to be key in their ability to maintain job segregation and the domestic division of labor.

Turning to the United States experience provides an opportunity, first, to explore shifts in the sex composition of jobs, and, second, to consider further the role of unions, particularly in establishing protective legislation. The American literature, especially the works of Abbott and Baker,[62] emphasizes sex shifts in jobs and, in contrast to the English literature, relies more heavily on technology as an explanatory phenomenon.

Conditions in the United States differed from those in England. First, the division of labor within colonial farm families was probably more rigid, with men in the fields and women producing manufactured articles at home. Second, the early textile factories employed young single women from the farms of New England; a conscious effort was made, probably out of necessity, to avoid the creation of a family labor system and to preserve the labor of men for agriculture.[63] This changed, however, with the eventual dominance of manufacture over agriculture as the leading sector in the economy and with immigration. Third, the shortage of labor and dire necessity in colonial and frontier America perhaps created more opportunities for women in nontraditional pursuits outside the family; colonial women were engaged in a wide variety

61. Edgeworth's conclusions are typical of those of neoclassical economists. In furthering Fawcett's analysis he further abstracted from reality. Whereas Fawcett had realized that women were not less efficient than men, and Rathbone had argued similarly, Edgeworth clung to the notion that men deserved more and sought to justify it theoretically. He opposed family allowances, also with neoclassical reasoning because they would raise taxes, discourage investment, encourage the reproduction of the poorer classes, and remove the incentive for men to work. Edgeworth reports the comment of a lady-inspector: "I almost agree with the social worker who said that if the husband got out of work the only thing that the wife should do is to sit down and cry, because if she did anything else he would remain out of work" (p. 453).

62. Edith Abbott, *Women in Industry* (New York: Arno Press, 1969); Elizabeth F. Baker, *Technology and Woman's Work* (New York: Columbia University Press, 1964).

63. See Abbott, esp. chap. 4.

of occupations.[64] Fourth, shortages of labor continued to operate in women's favor at various points throughout the nineteenth and twentieth centuries. Fifth, the constant arrival of new groups of immigrants created an extremely heterogeneous labor force, with varying skill levels and organizational development and rampant antagonisms.[65]

Major shifts in the sex composition of employment occurred in boot and shoe manufacture, textile manufacture, teaching, cigar making, and clerical work.[66] In all of these, except textiles, the shift was toward more women. New occupations opened up for both men and women, but men seemed to dominate in most of them, even though there were exceptions. Telephone operating and typing for example, became women's jobs.

In all of the cases of increase in female employment, the women were partially stimulated by a sharp rise in the demand for the service or product. During the late 1700s and early 1800s, domestic demand for ready-made boots went up because of the war, a greater number of slaves, general population expansion, and the settling of the frontier. Demand for teachers increased rapidly before, during, and after the Civil War as public education spread. The demand for cheap, machine-made cigars grew rapidly at the end of the nineteenth century. The upward shift in the numbers of clerical workers came between 1890 and 1930, when businesses grew larger and became more centralized, requiring more administration, distribution, transportation, marketing, and communication.

In several cases the shift to women was accompanied by technical innovations, which allowed increased output and sometimes reduced the skill required of the worker. By 1800, boot- and shoemakers had devised a division of labor which allowed women to work on sewing the uppers at home. In the 1850s, sewing machines were applied to boots and shoes in factories. In the 1870s, the use of wooden molds, rather than hand bunching, simplified cigar making, and in the 1880s, machinery was brought in. And in clerical work, the typewriter, of course, greatly increased the productivity of clerical labor. The machinery introduced in textiles, mule spinners, was traditionally operated by males. In printing, where male unions were successful in excluding women, the unions insisted on staffing the new linotypes.[67]

64. Ibid., chap. 2.

65. These antagonisms were often increased by employers. During a cigar-makers strike in New York City in 1877 employers brought in unskilled native American girls. By printing on the boxes, "These cigars were made by American girls," they sold many more boxes of the imperfect cigars than they had expected to (Abbott, p. 207).

66. This summary is based on Abbott and is substantiated by both Baker and Helen L. Sumner, *History of Women in Industry in the United States, 1910,* United States Bureau of Labor, *Report on Condition of Women and Child Wage-Earners in the United States* (Washington, D.C.: Government Printing Office, 1911), vol. 9.

67. Baker and Abbott rely heavily on technological factors coupled with biological sex differences as explanations of shifts in the sex composition of jobs. Increased speed of

The central purposes of subdividing the labor process, simplifying tasks, and introducing machines were to raise production, to cheapen it, and to increase management's control over the labor process. Subdivision of the labor process ordinarily allowed the use of less skilled labor in one or more subportions of the task. Cheapening of labor power and more control over labor were the motive forces behind scientific management and earlier efforts to reorganize labor.[68] Machinery was an aid in the process, not a motive force. Machinery, unskilled labor, and women workers often went together.

In addition to greater demand and technical change, often a shortage of the usual supply of labor contributed to a change in the labor force. In textiles, for example, in the 1840s the young New England farm women were attracted to new job opportunities for middle-class women, such as teaching. Their places in the mills were taken by immigrants. In boots and shoes the increased demand could not be met by the available trained shoemakers. And in clerical work the supply of high school educated males was not equal to the increase in demand. Moreover, in clerical work in particular the changes that occurred in the job structure reduced its attractiveness to men—with expansion, the jobs became dead-end ones—while for women the opportunities compared favorably with their opportunities elsewhere.[69]

Cigar making offers ample opportunity to illustrate both the opposition of male unionists to impending sex changes in labor-force composition in their industries and the form that opposition took: protective

---

machines and sometimes increased heaviness are cited as favoring men, who are stronger and have longer endurance, etc. Yet often each cites statistics which indicate that the same types of machines are used by both sexes; e.g., mule spinning machines. I would argue that these perceived differences are merely rationalizations used to justify the current sex assignment of tasks. Social pressures were powerful mechanisms of enforcement. Abbott gives several examples of this. A woman had apparently learned the mule in Lawrence and went to Waltham when mules were introduced there. She had to leave, however, because according to a male operative: "The men made unpleasant remarks and it was too hard for her, being the only woman" (p. 92). And: "Some of the oldest employees in the New England mills to-day [1910] say they can remember when weaving was so universally considered women's work that a 'man weaver' was held up to public ridicule for holding a 'woman's job' " (p. 95).

68. See Harry Braverman, *Labor and Monopoly Capital* (New York: Monthly Review Press, 1974), esp. chaps. 3–5.

69. Elyce J. Rotella, "Occupational Segregation and the Supply of Women to the American Clerical Labor Force, 1870–1930" (paper presented at the Berkshire Conference on the History of Women, Radcliffe College, October 25–27, 1974). Despite the long-standing recognition of job segregation and shifts in sex composition, there are surprisingly few studies of the process of shifting. In addition to Rotella for clerical workers there is Margery Davies, "Woman's Place Is at the Typewriter," *Radical America* 8, no. 4 (July-August 1974): 1–28. Valerie K. Oppenheimer discusses the shift in elementary teaching in *The Female Labor Force in the United States* (Berkeley: Institute of International Studies, University of California, 1970). And Abbott and Baker discuss several shifts.

legislation.[70] Cigar making was a home industry before 1800, when women on farms in Connecticut and elsewhere made rather rough cigars and traded them at village stores. Early factories employed women, but they were soon replaced by skilled male immigrants whose products could compete with fancy European cigars. By 1860, women were only 9 percent of the employed in cigar making. This switch to men was followed by one to women, but not without opposition from the men. In 1869, the wooden mold was introduced, and so were Bohemian immigrant women (who had been skilled workers in cigar factories in Austria-Hungary).[71] The Bohemian women, established by tobacco companies in tenements, perfected a division of labor in which young girls (and later their husbands)[72] could use the molds. Beginning in 1873 the Cigarmakers International Union agitated vociferously against home work, which was eventually restricted (for example, in New York in 1894). In the late 1880s machinery was introduced into the factories, and women were used as strikebreakers. The union turned to protective legislation.

The attitude of the Cigarmakers International Union toward women was ambivalent at best. The union excluded women in 1864, but admitted them in 1867. In 1875 it prohibited locals from excluding women, but apparently never imposed sanctions on offending locals.[73] In 1878 a Baltimore local wrote Adolph Strasser, the union president: "We have combatted from its incipiency the movement of the introduction of female labor in any capacity whatever, be it bunch maker, roller, or what not."[74] Lest these ambiguities be interpreted as national-local conflicts, let Strasser speak for himself (1879): "We cannot drive the females out of the trade, but we can restrict their daily quota of labor through factory laws. No girl under 18 should be employed more than eight hours per day; all overwork should be prohibited. . . ."[75]

70. This account is based primarily on Abbott, chap. 9, and Baker, pp. 31–36.

71. According to Abbott, Samuel Gompers claimed the Bohemian women were brought in for the express purpose of strikebreaking (p. 197, n.).

72. Bohemian women came to America first, leaving their husbands behind to work on the fields. Their husbands, who were unskilled at the cigar trade, came over later (ibid., p. 199).

73. In 1877 a Cincinnati local struck to exclude women and was apparently successful. The Cincinnati Inquirer said: "The men say the women are killing the industry. It would seem that they hope to retaliate by killing the women" (ibid., p. 207).

74. Baker, p. 34.

75. John B. Andrews and W. D. P. Bliss, History of Women in Trade Unions in Report on Condition of Woman and Child Wage-Earners in the United States, vol. 10. Although the proportion of women in cigar making did increase eventually, in many other manufacturing industries the proportion of women decreased over time. Textiles and clothing are the outstanding examples (see Abbott, p. 320, and her "The History of Industrial Employment of Women in the United States," Journal of Political Economy 14 [October 1906]: 461–501). Sumner, cited in U.S. Bureau of Labor Statistics, Bulletin 175, concluded that men had taken over the skilled jobs in

Because women are unskilled workers, it may be erroneous to interpret this as animosity to *women* per se. Rather it is the fear of the skilled for the unskilled. Yet male unions denied women skills, while they offered them to young boys. This is quite clear in the case of printing.[76]

Women had been engaged as typesetters in printing from colonial times. It was a skilled trade, but required no heavy work. Abbott attributed the jealousy of the men in the trade to the fact that it was a trade "suited" to women. In any case, male unions seem to have been hostile to the employment of women from the beginning. In 1854 the National Typographical Union resolved not to "encourage by its act the employment of female compositors."[77] Baker suggests that the unions discouraged girls from learning the trade, and so women learned what they could in nonunion shops or as strikebreakers.[78] In 1869, at the annual convention of the National Labor Union, of which the National Typographical Union was a member, a struggle occurred over the seating of Susan B. Anthony, because she had allegedly used women compositors as strikebreakers. She had, she admitted, because they could learn the trade no other way.[79] in 1870 the Typographical Union charted a women's local in New York City. Its president, Augusta Lewis, who was also corresponding secretary of the National Typographical Union did not think the women's union could hold out for very long, because, although the union women supported the union men, the union men did not support the union women: "It is the general opinion of female compositors that they are more justly treated by what is termed 'rat' foremen, printers, and employers than they are by union men."[80] The women's local eventually folded in 1878.

Apparently, the general lack of support was successful from the men's point of view, for, in 1910, Abbott claimed that: "Officers of other trade unions frequently refer to the policy of the printers as an example of the way in which trade union control may be successful in checking or preventing the employment of women."[81] The Typographical Union

---

women's traditional fields, and women had to take unskilled work wherever they could find it (p. 28).

76. This account is based primarily on Abbott and Baker. The hostility to training women seems generalizable. The International Molders Union resolved: "Any member, honorary or active, who devotes his time in whole or in part to the instruction of female help in the foundry, or in any branch of the trade shall be expelled from the Union" (Gail Falk, "Women and Unions: A Historical View," mimeographed [New Haven, Conn.: Yale Law School, 1970]. Published in somewhat shortened form in *Women's Rights Law Reporter* 1 [Spring 1973]: 54–65).

77. Abbott, pp. 252–3.

78. Baker, pp. 39–40.

79. See Falk.

80. Eleanor Flexner, *Century of Struggle* (New York: Atheneum Publishers, 1970), p. 136.

81. Abbott, p. 260.

strongly backed equal pay for equal work as a way to protect the men's wage scale, not to encourage women. Women who had fewer skills could not demand, and expect to receive, equal wages.[82]

Unions excluded women in many ways,[83] not the least among them protective legislation. In this the unions were aided by the prevailing social sentiment about work for women, especially married women, which was seen as a social evil which ideally should be wiped out,[84] and by a strong concern on the part of "social feminists"[85] and others that women workers were severely exploited because they were unorganized. The social feminists did not intend to exclude women from desirable occupations but their strategy paved the way for this exclusion, because, to get protection for working women—which they felt was so desperately needed—they argued that women, as a sex, were weaker than men and more in need of protection.[86] Their strategy was successful in 1908 in *Muller* v. *Oregon*, when the Supreme Court upheld maximum hours laws

82. Baker observed that the testimony on the Equal Pay Act in 1963 was about evenly divided between those emphasizing women's needs and those emphasizing the protection of men (p. 419).

83. Falk noted that unions used constitutional exclusion, exclusion from apprenticeship, limitation of women to helper categories or nonladder apprenticeships, limitation of proportion of union members who could be women, i.e., quotas, and excessively high fees. Moreover, the craft unions of this period, pre-1930, had a general hostility toward organizing the unskilled, even those attached to their crafts.

84. Such a diverse group as Caroll Wright, first U.S. Labor Commissioner (Baker, p. 84), Samuel Gompers and Mother Mary Jones, traditional and radical labor organizers, respectively (Falk), James L. Davis, U.S. Secretary of Labor, 1922 (Baker, p. 400), Florence Kelley, head of the National Consumers League (Hill), all held views which were variations of this theme. (Hill is Ann C. Hill, "Protective Labor Legislation for Women: Its Origin and Effect," mimeographed [New Haven, Conn: Yale Law School, 1970], parts of which have been published in Barbara A. Babcock, Ann E. Freedman, Eleanor H. Norton, and Susan C. Ross, *Sex Discrimination and the Law: Causes and Remedies* [Boston: Little, Brown & Co., 1975], a law text which provides an excellent analysis of protective legislation, discrimination against women, etc.)

85. William O'Neill characterized those women who participated in various reform movements in the late nineteenth and early twentieth centuries "social feminists" to distinguish them from earlier feminists like Stanton and Anthony. The social feminists came to support women's rights because they thought it would help advance the cause of their reforms; they were not primarily interested in advancing the cause of women's rights (*Everyone Was Brave* [Chicago: Quadrangle Books, 1969], esp. chap. 3). William H. Chafe, *The American Woman* (New York: Oxford University Press, 1972), also provides an excellent discussion of the debate around protective laws.

86. What was achievable, from the legislatures and the courts, was what the social feminists aimed for. Because in Ritchie v. People (155 Ill 98 [1895]), the court had held that sex alone was not a valid basis for a legislature to abridge the right of an adult to contract for work and, thus, struck down a maximum-hours law for women, and because a maximum-hours law for baking employees had been struck down by the U.S. Supreme Court (Lockner), advocates of protective labor legislation believed their task would be difficult. The famous "Brandeis Brief" compiled hundreds of pages on the harmful effects of long hours of work and argued that women needed "especial protection" (see Babcock et al.).

for women, saying: "The two sexes differ in structure of body, in the capacity for long-continued labor particularly when done standing, the influence of vigorous health upon the future well-being of the race, the self-reliance which enables one to assert full rights, and in the capacity to maintain the struggle for subsistence. This difference justifies a difference in legislation and upholds that which is designed to compensate for some of the burdens which rest upon her."[87]

In 1916 in *Bunting* v. *Oregon* Brandeis used virtually the same data on the ill effects of long hours of work to argue successfully for maximum-hours laws for men as well as women. *Bunting* was not, however, followed by a spate of maximum-hours law for men, the way *Muller* had been followed by laws for women. In general, unions did not support protective legislation for men, although they continued to do so for women. Protective legislation, rather than organization, was the preferred strategy only for women.[88]

The effect of the laws was limited by their narrow coverage and inadequate enforcement, but despite their limitations, in those few occupations where night work or long hours were essential, such as printing, women were effectively excluded.[89] While the laws may have protected women in the "sweated" trades, women who were beginning to get established in "men's jobs" were turned back.[90] Some of these women fought back successfully, but the struggle is still being waged today along many of the same battle lines. As Ann C. Hill argued, the effect of these laws, psychically and socially, has been devastating. They confirmed woman's "alien" status as a worker.[91]

Throughout the above discussion of the development of the wage-labor force in England and the United States, I have emphasized the role of male workers in restricting women's sphere in the labor market. Although I have emphasized the role of men, I do not think that of employers was unimportant. Recent work on labor-market segmentation theory provides a framework for looking at the role of employers.[92] According to this model, one mechanism which creates segmentation is

87. Ibid., p. 32.

88. In 1914 the AFL voted to abandon the legislative road to reform (see Ann C. Hill).

89. Some states excluded women entirely from certain occupations: mining, meter reading, taxicab driving, core making, streetcar conducting, elevator operating, etc. (ibid.).

90. These conclusions are based on Ann C. Hill and are also supported by Baker.

91. At the same time that women were being excluded from certain skilled jobs in the labor force and otherwise protected, the home duties of women were emphasized in popular literature, through the home economics movement, in colleges and high schools, etc. A movement toward the stabilization of the nuclear family with one breadwinner, the male, is discernible (see Hartmann).

92. Edwards, Gordon, and Reich use labor-market segmentation to refer to a process in which the labor market becomes divided into different submarkets, each with its own characteristic behaviors; these segments can be different layers of a hierarchy or different groups within one layer.

the conscious, though not necessarily conspiratorial, action of capitalists; they act to exacerbate existing divisions among workers in order to further divide them, thus weakening their class unity and reducing their bargaining power.[93] The creation of complex internal job structures is itself part of this attempt. In fact, the whole range of different levels of jobs serves to obfuscate the basic two-class nature of capitalist society.[94] This model suggests, first, that sex segregation is one aspect of the labor-market segmentation inherent in advanced capitalism, and, second, capitalists have consciously attempted to exacerbate sex divisions. Thus, if the foregoing analysis has emphasized the continuous nature of job segregation by sex—present in all stages of capitalism and before [95]—and the conscious actions of male workers, it is important to note that the actions of capitalists may have been crucial in calling forth those responses from male workers.

Historically, male workers have been instrumental in limiting the participation of women in the labor market. Male unions have carried out the policies and attitudes of the earlier guilds, and they have continued to reap benefits for male workers. Capitalists inherited job segregation by sex, but they have quite often been able to use it to their own advantage. If they can supersede experienced men with cheaper women, so much the better; if they can weaken labor by threatening to do so, that's good, too; or, if failing that, they can use those status differences to reward men, and buy their allegiance to capitalism with patriarchal benefits, that's okay too.[96]

But even though capitalists' actions are important in explaining the current virility of sex segregation, labor-market-segmentation theory overemphasizes the role of capitalists and ignores the actions of workers themselves in perpetuating segmentation. Those workers in the more desirable jobs act to hang onto them, their material rewards, and their

93. Michael Reich's thesis, "Racial Discrimination and the White Income Distribution" (Ph.D. diss., Harvard University, 1973), sets forth this divide-and-rule model more thoroughly. In the labor-market-segmentation model there is another tendency toward segmentation in addition to the divide-and-rule mechanism. It arises out of the uneven development of advanced capitalism, i.e., the process of creation of a core and a peripheral economy. In fact, in the Edwards, Gordon, and Reich view, labor-market segmentation only comes to the fore under monopoly capitalism, as large corporations seek to extend control over their labor markets.

94. Thomas Vietorisz, "From Class to Hierarchy: Some Non-Price Aspects on the Transformation Problem" (paper presented at the Conference on Urban Political Economy, New School for Social Research, New York, February 15–16, 1975).

95. The strong divisions of the labor market by sex and race that existed even in the competitive phase of capitalism call into question the dominance of labor homogenization during that phase—as presented by Gordon, Edwards, and Reich.

96. Capitalists are not always able to use patriarchy to their advantage. Men's ability to retain as much of women's labor in the home as they have may hamper capitalist development during expansive phases. Men's resistance to female workers whom capitalists want to utilize also undoubtedly slows down capitalist advance.

subjective benefits.[97] Workers, through unions, have been parties to the creation and maintenance of hierarchical and parallel (i.e., separate but unequal) job structures. Perhaps the relative importance of capitalists and male workers in instituting and maintaining job segregation by sex has varied in different periods. Capitalists during the transition to capitalism, for example, seemed quite able to change the sex composition of jobs—when weaving was shifted to factories equipped with power looms women wove, even though most handloom weavers had been men, and mule spinning was introduced with male operators even though women had used the earlier spinning jennies and water frames. As industrialization progressed and conditions stabilized somewhat, male unions gained in strength and were often able to preserve or extend male arenas. Nevertheless, in times of overwhelming social or economic necessity, occasioned by vast increases in the demand for labor, such as in teaching or clerical work, male capitalists were capable of overpowering male workers. Thus, in periods of economic change, capitalists' actions may be more instrumental in instituting or changing a sex-segregated labor force—while workers fight a defensive battle. In other periods male workers may be more important in maintaining sex-segregated jobs; they may be able to prevent the encroachment of, or even to drive out, cheaper female labor, thus increasing the benefits to their sex.[98]

Conclusion

The present status of women in the labor market and the current arrangement of sex-segregated jobs is the result of a long process of interaction between patriarchy and capitalism. I have emphasized the actions of male workers throughout this process because I believe that emphasis to be correct. Men will have to be forced to give up their favored positions in the division of labor—in the labor market and at home—both if women's subordination is to end and if men are to begin to escape class oppression and exploitation.[99] Capitalists have indeed

97. Engels, Marx, and Lenin all recognized the *material* rewards the labor aristocracy reaps. It is important not to reduce these to *subjective* benefits, for then the problems arising out of intraclass divisions will be minimized. Castles and Kosack appear to make this error (see their "The Function of Labour Immigration in Western European Capitalism," *New Left Review*, no. 73 [May–June 1972], pp. 3–12, where references to Marx et al. can be found).

98. David Gordon suggested to me this "cyclical model" of the relative strengths of employer and workers.

99. Most Marxist-feminist attempts to deal with the problems in Marxist analysis raised by the social position of women seem to ignore these basic conflicts between the sexes, apparently in the interest of stressing the underlying class solidarity that should obtain among women and men workers. Bridges and Hartmann's draft paper (n. 1 above)

used women as unskilled, underpaid labor to undercut male workers, yet this is only a case of the chickens coming home to roost—a case of men's co-optation by and support for patriarchal society, with its hierarchy among men, being turned back on themselves with a vengeance. Capitalism grew on top of patriarchy; patriarchal capitalism is stratified society par excellence. If non-ruling-class men are to be free they will have to recognize their co-optation by patriarchal capitalism and relinquish their patriarchal benefits. If women are to be free, they must fight against both patriarchal power and capitalist organization of society.

Because both the sexual division of labor and male domination are so long standing, it will be very difficult to eradicate them and impossible to eradicate the latter without the former. The two are now so inextricably intertwined that it is necessary to eradicate the sexual division of labor itself in order to end male domination.[100] Very basic changes at all levels of society and culture are required to liberate women. In this paper, I have argued that the maintenance of job segregation by sex is a key root of women's status, and I have relied on the operation of society-wide institutions to explain the maintenance of job segregation by sex. But the consequences of that division of labor go very deep, down to the level of the subconscious. The subconscious influences behavior patterns, which form the micro underpinnings (or complements) of social institutions and are in turn reinforced by those social institutions.

I believe we need to investigate these micro phenomena as well as the macro ones I have discussed in this paper. For example, it appears to be a very deeply ingrained behavioral rule that men cannot be subordinate to women of a similar social class. Manifestations of this rule have been noted in restaurants, where waitresses experience difficulty in giving orders to bartenders, unless the bartender can reorganize the situation to allow himself autonomy; among executives, where women executives are seen to be most successful if they have little contact with others at their level and manage small staffs; and among industrial workers, where female factory inspectors cannot successfully correct the work of male production workers.[101] There is also a deeply ingrained fear of

---

reviews this literature. A few months ago a friend (female) said, "We are much more likely to be able to get Thieu out of Vietnam than we are to get men to do the dishes." She was right.

100. In our society, women's jobs are synonymous with low-status, low-paying jobs: ". . . we may replace the familiar statement that women earn less because they are in low paying occupations with the statement that women earn less because they are in *women's jobs.* . . . As long as the labor market is divided on the basis of sex, it is likely that the tasks allocated to women will be ranked as less prestigious or important, reflecting women's lower social status in the society at large" (Francine Blau [Weisskoff], "Women's Place in the Labor Market," *American Economic Review* 62, no. 4 [May 1972]: 161).

101. Theodore Caplow, *The Sociology of Work* (New York: McGraw-Hill Book Co.,

being identified with the other sex. As a general rule, men and women must never do anything which is not masculine or feminine (respectively).[102] Male executives, for example, often exchange handshakes with male secretaries, a show of respect which probably works to help preserve their masculinity.

At the next deeper level, we must study the subconscious—both how these behavioral rules are internalized and how they grow out of personality structure.[103] At this level, the formation of personality, there have been several attempts to study the production of gender, the *socially* imposed differentiation of humans based on biological sex differences.[104] A materialist interpretation of reality, of course, suggests that gender production grows out of the extant division of labor between the sexes,[105] and, in a dialectical process, reinforces that very division of labor itself. In my view, because of these deep ramifications of the sexual division of labor we will not eradicate sex-ordered task division until we eradicate the socially imposed gender differences between us and, therefore, the very sexual division of labor itself.

In attacking both patriarchy and capitalism we will have to find ways to change both society-wide institutions and our most deeply ingrained habits. It will be a long, hard struggle.

New School for Social Research

1964), pp. 237 ff., discusses several behavioral rules and their impact. Harold Willensky, "Women's Work: Economic Growth, Ideology, Structure," *Industrial Relations* 7, no. 3 (May 1968): 235–48, also discusses the implication for labor-market phenomena of several behavioral rules.

102. "The use of tabooed words, the fostering of sports and other interests which women do not share, and participation in activities which women are intended to disapprove of—hard drinking, gambling, practical jokes, and sexual essays of various kinds—all suggest that the adult male group is to a large extent engaged in a reaction *against* feminine influence, and therefore cannot tolerate the presence of women without changing its character entirely" (Caplow, p. 239). Of course, the lines of division between masculine and feminine are constantly shifting. At various times in the nineteenth century, teaching, selling in retail stores, and office work were each thought to be totally unsuitable for women. This variability of the boundaries between men's jobs and women's jobs is one reason why an effort to locate basic behavioral principles would seem to make sense —though, ultimately, of course, these rules are shaped by the division of labor itself.

103. Caplow based his rules on the Freudian view that men identify freedom from female dominance with maturity, i.e., they seek to escape their mothers.

104. See Rubin (n. 1 above), and Juliet Mitchell, *Feminism and Psychoanalysis* (New York: Pantheon Books, 1974), who seek to re-create Freud from a feminist perspective. So does Shulamith Firestone, *The Dialectic of Sex* (New York: Bantam Books, 1971).

105. For example, the current domestic division of labor in which women nurture children profoundly affects (differentially) the personality structures of girls and boys. For a non-Freudian interpretation of this phenomenon, see Chodorow (n. 12 above).

Feminism, Marxism, Method, and the State: An Agenda for Theory

Catharine A. MacKinnon

Sexuality is to feminism what work is to marxism: that which is most one's own, yet most taken away. Marxist theory argues that society is fundamentally constructed of the relations people form as they do and make things needed to survive humanly. Work is the social process of shaping and transforming the material and social worlds, creating people as social beings as they create value. It is that activity by which people become who they are. Class is its structure, production its consequence, capital its congealed form, and control its issue.

Dedicated to the spirit of Shelly Rosaldo in us all.

The second part of this article, which will appear in a forthcoming issue of *Signs* as "Feminism, Marxism, Method, and the State: Toward Feminist Jurisprudence," applies the critique developed here to theories of the state and to legal materials. Both articles are parts of a longer work in progress. The argument of this essay on the relation between marxism and feminism has not changed since it was first written in 1973, but the argument on feminism itself has. In the intervening years, the manuscript has been widely circulated, in biannual mutations, for criticism. Reflecting on that process, which I hope publication will continue (this *is* "an agenda for theory"), I find the following people, each in their way, contributed most to its present incarnation: Sonia E. Alvarez, Douglas Bennett, Paul Brest, Ruth Colker, Robert A. Dahl, Karen E. Davis, Andrea Dworkin, Alicia Fernandez, Jane Flax, Bert Garskoff, Elbert Gates, Karen Haney, Kent Harvey, Linda Hoaglund, Nan Keohane, Duncan Kennedy, Bob Lamm, Martha Roper, Michelle Z. Rosaldo, Anne E. Simon, Sharon Silverstein, Valerie A. Tebbetts, Rona Wilensky, Gaye Williams, Jack Winkler, and Laura X. The superb work of Martha Freeman and Lu Ann Carter was essential to its production.

Implicit in feminist theory is a parallel argument: the molding, direction, and expression of sexuality organizes society into two sexes—women and men—which division underlies the totality of social relations. Sexuality is that social process which creates, organizes, expresses, and directs desire,[1] creating the social beings we know as women and men, as their relations create society. As work is to marxism, sexuality to feminism is socially constructed yet constructing, universal as activity yet historically specific, jointly comprised of matter and mind. As the organized expropriation of the work of some for the benefit of others defines a class—workers—the organized expropriation of the sexuality of some for the use of others defines the sex, woman. Heterosexuality is its structure, gender and family its congealed forms, sex roles its qualities generalized to social persona, reproduction a consequence, and control its issue.

Marxism and feminism are theories of power and its distribution: inequality. They provide accounts of how social arrangements of patterned disparity can be internally rational yet unjust. But their specificity is not incidental. In marxism to be deprived of one's work, in feminism of one's sexuality, defines each one's conception of lack of power per se. They do not mean to exist side by side to insure that two separate spheres of social life are not overlooked, the interests of two groups are not

---

I have rendered "marxism" in lower case and "Black" in upper case and have been asked by the publisher to explain these choices. It is conventional to capitalize terms that derive from a proper name. Since I wish to place marxism and feminism in equipoise, the disparate typography would weigh against my analytic structure. Capitalizing both would germanize the text. I also hope feminism, a politics authored by those it works in the name of, is never named after an individual. Black is conventionally (I am told) regarded as a color rather than a racial or national designation, hence is not usually capitalized. I do not regard Black as merely a color of skin pigmentation, but as a heritage, an experience, a cultural and personal identity, the meaning of which becomes specifically stigmatic and/or glorious and/or ordinary under specific social conditions. It is as much socially created as, and at least in the American context no less specifically meaningful or definitive than, any linguistic, tribal, or religious ethnicity, all of which are conventionally recognized by capitalization.

1. "Desire" is selected as a term parallel to "value" in marxist theory to refer to that substance felt to be primordial or aboriginal but posited by the theory as social and contingent. The sense in which I mean it is consonant with its development in contemporary French feminist theories, e.g., in Hélène Cixous, "The Laugh of Medusa: Viewpoint," trans. Keith Cohen and Paula Cohen, *Signs: Journal of Women in Culture and Society* 1, no. 4 (Summer 1976): 875–93; and in works by Gauthier, Irigaray, LeClerc, Duras, and Kristeva in *New French Feminisms: An Anthology*, ed. Elaine Marks and Isabelle de Courtivron (Amherst: University of Massachusetts Press, 1980). My use of the term is to be distinguished from that of Gilles Deleuze and Felix Guattari, *Anti-Oedipus: Capitalism and Schizophrenia* (New York: Viking Press, 1977); and Guy Hocquenghem, *Homosexual Desire* (London: Allison & Busby, 1978), for example.

obscured, or the contributions of two sets of variables are not ignored. They exist to argue, respectively, that the relations in which many work and few gain, in which some fuck and others get fucked,[2] are the prime moment of politics.

What if the claims of each theory are taken equally seriously, each on its own terms? Can two social processes be basic at once? Can two groups be subordinated in conflicting ways, or do they merely crosscut? Can two theories, each of which purports to account for the same thing—power as such—be reconciled? Or, is there a connection between the fact that the few have ruled the many and the fact that those few have been men?

Confronted on equal terms, these theories pose fundamental questions for each other. Is male dominance a creation of capitalism or is capitalism one expression of male dominance? What does it mean for class analysis if one can assert that a social group is defined and exploited through means largely independent of the organization of production, if in forms appropriate to it? What does it mean for a sex-based analysis if one can assert that capitalism would not be materially altered if it were sex integrated or even controlled by women? If the structure and interests served by the socialist state and the capitalist state differ in class terms, are they equally predicated upon sex inequality? To the extent their form and behavior resemble one another, could this be their commonality? Is there a relationship between the power of some classes over others and that of all men over all women?

Rather than confront these questions, marxists and feminists have usually either dismissed or, in what amounts to the same thing, subsumed each other. Marxists have criticized feminism as bourgeois in theory and in practice, meaning that it works in the interest of the ruling class. They argue that to analyze society in terms of sex ignores class divisions among women, dividing the proletariat. Feminist demands, it is claimed, could be fully satisfied within capitalism, so their pursuit undercuts and deflects the effort for basic change. Efforts to eliminate barriers to women's personhood—arguments for access to life chances without regard to sex—are seen as liberal and individualistic. Whatever women have in common is considered based in nature, not society; cross-cultural analyses of commonalities in women's social conditions are seen as ahistorical and lacking in cultural specificity. The women's movement's focus

---

2. I know no nondegraded English verb for the activity of sexual expression that would allow a construction parallel to, for example, "I am working," a phrase that could apply to nearly any activity. This fact of language may reflect and contribute to the process of obscuring sexuality's pervasiveness in social life. Nor is there *any* active verb meaning "to act sexually" that specifically envisions a woman's action. If language constructs as well as expresses the social world, these words support heterosexual values.

upon attitudes and feelings as powerful components of social reality is criticized as idealist; its composition, purportedly of middle-class educated women, is advanced as an explanation for its opportunism.

Feminists charge that marxism is male defined in theory and in practice, meaning that it moves within the world view and in the interest of men. Feminists argue that analyzing society exclusively in class terms ignores the distinctive social experiences of the sexes, obscuring women's unity. Marxist demands, it is claimed, could be (and in part have been) satisfied without altering women's inequality to men. Feminists have often found that working-class movements and the left undervalue women's work and concerns, neglect the role of feelings and attitudes in a focus on institutional and material change, denigrate women in procedure, practice, and everyday life, and in general fail to distinguish themselves from any other ideology or group dominated by male interests. Marxists and feminists thus accuse each other of seeking (what in each one's terms is) reform—changes that appease and assuage without addressing the grounds of discontent—where (again in each one's terms) a fundamental overthrow is required. The mutual perception, at its most extreme, is not only that the other's analysis is incorrect, but that its success would be a defeat.

Neither set of allegations is groundless. In the feminist view, sex, in analysis and in reality, does divide classes, a fact marxists have been more inclined to deny or ignore than to explain or change. Marxists, similarly, have seen parts of the women's movement function as a special interest group to advance the class-privileged: educated and professional women. To consider this group coextensive with "the women's movement" precludes questioning a definition of coalesced interest and resistance[3] which gives disproportionate visibility to the movement's least broadly based segment. But advocates of women's interests have not always been class conscious; some have exploited class-based arguments for advantage, even when the interests of working-class *women* were thereby obscured.

For example, in 1866, in an act often thought to inaugurate the first wave of feminism, John Stuart Mill petitioned the English parliament for women's suffrage with the following partial justification: "Under whatever conditions, and within whatever limits, men are admitted to suffrage, there is not a shadow of justification for not admitting women under the same. The majority of women of any class are not likely to differ in political opinion from the majority of men in the same class."[4] Perhaps Mill means that, to the extent class determines opinion, sex is

3. Accepting this definition has tended to exclude from "the women's movement" and make invisible the diverse ways that many women—notably Blacks and working-class women—have *moved* against their determinants.

4. John Stuart Mill, "The Subjection of Women," in *Essays on Sex Equality,* ed. Alice S. Rossi (Chicago: University of Chicago Press, 1970), pp. 184–85.

irrelevant. In this sense, the argument is (to some persuasively) narrow. It can also justify limiting the extension of the franchise to women who "belong to" men of the same class that already exercises it, to the further detriment of the excluded underclass, "their" women included.[5]

This kind of reasoning is confined neither to the issue of the vote nor to the nineteenth century. Mill's logic is embedded in a theoretical structure that underlies much contemporary feminist theory and justifies much of the marxist critique. That women should be allowed to engage in politics expressed Mill's concern that the state not restrict individuals' self-government, their freedom to develop talents for their own growth, and their ability to contribute to society for the good of humanity. As an empirical rationalist, he resisted attributing to biology what could be explained as social conditioning. As a utilitarian, he found most sex-based inequalities inaccurate or dubious, inefficient, and therefore unjust. The liberty of women as individuals to achieve the limits of self-development without arbitrary interference extended to women his meritocratic goal of the self-made man, condemning (what has since come to be termed) sexism as an interference with personal initiative and laissez-faire.

The hospitality of such an analysis to marxist concerns is problematic. One might extend Mill's argument to cover class as one more arbitrary, socially conditioned factor that produces inefficient development of talent and unjust distribution of resources among individuals. But although this might be in a sense materialist, it would not be a class analysis. Mill does not even allow for income leveling. Unequal distribution of wealth is exactly what laissez-faire and unregulated personal initiative produces. The individual concept of rights that this theory requires on a juridical level (especially but not only in the economic sphere), a concept which produces the tension between liberty for each and equality among all, pervades liberal feminism, substantiating the criticism that feminism is for the privileged few.

The marxist criticism that feminism focuses upon feelings and attitudes is also based on something real: the centrality of consciousness raising. Consciousness raising is the major technique of analysis, structure of organization, method of practice, and theory of social change of the women's movement.[6] In consciousness raising, often in groups, the

5. Mill personally supported universal suffrage. As it happened, working-class men got the vote before women of any class.
6. Feminists have observed the importance of consciousness raising without seeing it as method in the way developed here. See Pamela Allen, *Free Space: A Perspective on the Small Group in Women's Liberation* (New York: Times Change Press, 1970); Anuradha Bose, "Consciousness Raising," in *Mother Was Not a Person*, ed. Margaret Anderson (Montreal: Content Publishing, 1972); Nancy McWilliams, "Contemporary Feminism, Consciousness-Raising, and Changing Views of the Political," in *Women in Politics*, ed. Jane Jaquette (New York: John Wiley & Sons, 1974); Joan Cassell, *A Group Called Women: Sisterhood & Symbolism in the Feminist Movement* (New York: David McKay, 1977); and Nancy

impact of male dominance is concretely uncovered and analyzed through the collective speaking of women's experience, from the perspective of that experience. Because marxists tend to conceive of powerlessness, first and last, as concrete and externally imposed, they believe that it must be concretely and externally undone to be changed. Women's powerlessness has been found through consciousness raising to be both internalized and externally imposed, so that, for example, femininity is identity to women as well as desirability to men. The feminist concept of consciousness and its place in social order and change emerge from this practical analytic. What marxism conceives as change in consciousness is not a form of social change in itself. For feminism, it can be, but because women's oppression is not just in the head, feminist *consciousness* is not just in the head either. But the pain, isolation, and thingification of women who have been pampered and pacified into nonpersonhood—women "grown ugly and dangerous from being nobody for so long"[7]—is difficult for the materially deprived to see as a form of oppression, particularly for women whom no man has ever put on a pedestal.

Marxism, similarly, has not just been misunderstood. Marxist theory *has* traditionally attempted to comprehend all meaningful social variance in class terms. In this respect, sex parallels race and nation as an undigested but persistently salient challenge to the exclusivity—or even primacy—of class as social explanation. Marxists typically extend class to cover women, a division and submersion that, to feminism, is inadequate to women's divergent and common experience. In 1912 Rosa Luxemburg, for example, addressed a group of women on the issue of suffrage: "Most of these bourgeois women who act like lionesses in the struggle against 'male prerogatives' would trot like docile lambs in the camp of conservative and clerical reaction if they had the suffrage. Indeed, they would certainly be a good deal more reactionary than the male part of their class. Aside from the few who have taken jobs or professions, the bourgeoisie do not take part in social production. They are nothing but co-consumers of the surplus product their men extort

Hartsock, "Fundamental Feminism: Process and Perspective," *Quest: A Feminist Quarterly* 2, no. 2 (Fall 1975): 67–80.

7. Toni Cade (now Bambara) thus describes a desperate Black woman who has too many children and too little means to care for them or herself in "The Pill: Genocide or Liberation?" in *The Black Woman: An Anthology*, ed. Toni Cade (New York: Mentor, New American Library, 1970), p. 168. By using her phrase in altered context, I do not want to distort her meaning but to extend it. Throughout this essay, I have tried to see if women's condition is shared, even when contexts or magnitudes differ. (Thus, it is very different to be "nobody" as a Black woman than as a white lady, but neither is "somebody" by male standards.) This is the approach to race and ethnicity attempted throughout. I aspire to include all women in the term "women" in some way, without violating the particularity of any woman's experience. Whenever this fails, the statement is simply wrong and will have to be qualified or the aspiration (or the theory) abandoned.

from the proletariat. They are parasites of the parasites of the social body."[8] Her sympathies lay with "proletarian women" who derive their right to vote from being "productive for society like the men."[9] With a blind spot analogous to Mill's within her own perspective, Luxemburg defends women's suffrage on class grounds, although in both cases the vote would have benefited women without regard to class.

Women as women, across class distinctions and apart from nature, were simply unthinkable to Luxemburg, as to most marxists. Feminist theory asks marxism: What is class for women? Luxemburg, again like Mill in her own context, subliminally recognizes that women derive their class position, with concomitant privileges and restrictions, from their associations with men. For a feminist, this may explain why they do not unite against male dominance, but it does not explain that dominance, which cuts across class lines even as it takes forms peculiar to classes. What distinguishes the bourgeois woman from her domestic servant is that the latter is paid (if barely), while the former is kept (if contingently). But is this a difference in social productivity or only in its indices, indices which themselves may be products of women's undervalued status?[10] Luxemburg sees that the bourgeois woman of her time

8. Rosa Luxemburg, "Women's Suffrage and Class Struggle," in *Selected Political Writings*, ed. Dick Howard (New York: Monthly Review Press, 1971), pp. 219–20. It may or may not be true that women as a group vote more conservatively than men, on a conventional left-right spectrum. The apparently accurate suspicion that they do may have accounted for left ambivalence on women's suffrage as much as any principled view of the role of reform in a politics of radical change.

9. Ibid., p. 220.

10. This question is most productively explored in the controversy over wages for housework. See Margaret Benston, "The Political Economy of Women's Liberation," *Monthly Review*, vol. 21, no. 4 (September 1969), reprinted in *From Feminism to Liberation*, ed. Edith Hoshino Altbach (Cambridge, Mass.: Schenckman Publishing Co., 1971), pp. 199–210; Peggy Morton, "Women's Work Is Never Done," in *Women Unite* (Toronto: Canadian Women's Educational Press, 1972); Hodee Edwards, "Housework and Exploitation: A Marxist Analysis," *No More Fun and Games: A Journal of Female Liberation*, issue 4 (July 1971), pp. 92–100; and Mariarosa Dalla Costa and Selma James, *The Power of Women and the Subversion of the Community* (Bristol: Falling Wall Press, 1973). This last work situates housework in a broader theoretical context of wagelessness and potential political power while avoiding support of wages for housework as a program; its authors have since come to support wages for housework, deducing it from the perspective presented here. See also Sylvia Federici, *Wages against Housework* (Bristol: Falling Wall Press, 1973); Wally Seccombe, "The Housewife and Her Labor under Capitalism," *New Left Review* 83 (January–February 1974): 3–24; Carol Lopate, "Women and Pay for Housework," *Liberation* 18, no. 9 (May–June 1974): 11–19; Nicole Cox and Sylvia Federici, *Counter-Planning from the Kitchen—Wages for Housework: A Perspective on Capital and the Left* (Bristol: Falling Wall Press, 1975); Wendy Edmond and Suzi Fleming, eds., *All Work and No Pay: Women, Housework and the Wages Due* (Bristol: Falling Wall Press, 1975); Jeanette Silveira, *The Housewife and Marxist Class Analysis* (Seattle, Wash.: By the author, 1975) (pamphlet available from the author, P.O. Box 30541, Seattle, Wash. 98103); Jean Gardiner, "Women's Domestic Labor," *New Left Review* 89 (January–February 1975): 47–55; Beth Ingber and Cleveland Modern Times Group, "The Social Factory," *Falling Wall Review*, no. 5 (1976), pp. 1–7;

is a "parasite of a parasite" but fails to consider her commonality with the proletarian woman who is the slave of a slave. In the case of bourgeois women, to limit the analysis of women's relationship to capitalism to their relations through men is to see only its vicarious aspect. To fail to do this in the case of proletarian women is to miss its vicarious aspect.

Feminist observations of women's situation in socialist countries, although not conclusive on the contribution of marxist theory to understanding women's situation, have supported the theoretical critique.[11] In the feminist view, these countries have solved many social problems, women's subordination not included. The criticism is not that socialism has not automatically liberated women in the process of transforming production (assuming that this transformation is occurring). Nor is it to diminish the significance of such changes for women: "There is a difference between a society in which sexism is expressed in the form of female infanticide and a society in which sexism takes the form of unequal representation on the Central Committee. And the difference is worth dying for."[12] The criticism is rather that these countries do not make a priority of working for women that distinguishes them from nonsocialist societies. Capitalist countries value women in terms of their "merit" by male standards; in socialist countries women are invisible except in their capacity as "workers," a term that seldom includes women's distinctive work: housework, sexual service, childbearing. The con-

---

Joan Landes, "Wages for Housework: Subsidizing Capitalism?" *Quest: A Feminist Quarterly* 2, no. 2 (Fall 1975): 17–30; Batya Weinbaum and Amy Bridges, "The Other Side of the Paycheck: Monopoly Capital and the Structure of Conscription," *Monthly Review* 28, no. 3 (July–August 1976): 88–103.

11. These observations are complex and varied. Typically they begin with the recognition of the important changes socialism has made for women, qualified by reservations about its potential to make the remaining necessary ones. Delia Davin, "Women in the Countryside of China," in *Women in Chinese Society,* ed. Margery Wolf and Roxane Witke (Stanford, Calif.: Stanford University Press, 1974); Katie Curtin, *Women in China* (New York: Pathfinder Press, 1975); Judith Stacey, "When Patriarchy Kowtows: The Significance of the Chinese Family Revolution for Feminist Theory," *Feminist Studies* 2, no. 2/3 (1975): 64–112; Julia Kristeva, *About Chinese Women* (New York: Urizen Books, 1977); Hilda Scott, *Does Socialism Liberate Women? Experiences from Eastern Europe* (Cambridge, Mass.: Beacon Press, 1974); Margaret Randall, *Cuban Women Now* (Toronto: Women's Press, 1974) (an edited collation of Cuban women's own observations); and *Cuban Women Now: Afterword* (Toronto: Women's Press, 1974); Carollee Bengelsdorf and Alice Hageman, "Emerging from Underdevelopment: Women and Work in Cuba," in *Capitalist Patriarchy and the Case for Socialist Feminism,* ed. Zillah Eisenstein (New York: Monthly Review Press, 1979).

12. Barbara Ehrenreich, "What Is Socialist Feminism?" *Win* (June 3, 1976), reprinted in *Working Papers on Socialism and Feminism* (Chicago: New American Movement, n.d.). Counterpoint is provided by feminists who have more difficulty separating the two. Susan Brownmiller notes: "It seems to me that a country that wiped out the tsetse fly can by fiat put an equal number of women on the Central Committee" ("Notes of an Ex-China Fan," *Village Voice,* quoted in Batya Weinbaum, *The Curious Courtship of Women's Liberation and Socialism* [Boston: South End Press, 1978], p. 7).

cern of revolutionary leadership for ending women's confinement to traditional roles too often seems limited to making their labor available to the regime, leading feminists to wonder whose interests are served by this version of liberation. Women become as free as men to work outside the home while men remain free from work within it. This also occurs under capitalism. When woman's labor or militancy suits the needs of emergency, she is suddenly man's equal, only to regress when the urgency recedes.[13] Feminists do not argue that it means the same to women to be on the bottom in a feudal regime, a capitalist regime, and a socialist regime; the commonality argued is that, despite real changes, bottom is bottom.

Where such attitudes and practices come to be criticized, as in Cuba or China, changes appear gradual and precarious, even where the effort looks major. If seizures of state and productive power overturn work relations, they do not overturn sex relations at the same time or in the same way, as a class analysis of sex would (and in some cases did) predict.[14] Neither technology nor socialism, both of which purport to alter women's role at the point of production, have ever yet equalized women's-status relative to men. In the feminist view, nothing has. At minimum, a separate effort appears required—an effort that can be shaped by revolutionary regime and work relations—but a separate effort nonetheless. In light of these experiences, women's struggles, whether under capitalist or socialist regimes, appear to feminists to have more in common with each other than with leftist struggles anywhere.

Attempts to create a synthesis between marxism and feminism,

13. Stacey (n. 11 above); Janet Salaff and Judith Merkle, "Women and Revolution: The Lessons of the Soviet Union and China," *Socialist Revolution* 1, no. 4 (1970): 39–72; Linda Gordon, *The Fourth Mountain* (Cambridge, Mass.: Working Papers, 1973); Richard Stites, *The Women's Liberation Movement in Russia: Feminism, Nihilism, and Bolshevism* (Princeton, N.J.: Princeton University Press, 1978), pp. 392–421.

14. See Fidel Castro, *Women and the Cuban Revolution* (New York: Pathfinder Press, 1970); but compare Fidel's "Speech at Closing Session of the 2d Congress of the Federation of Cuban Women," November 29, 1974, *Cuba Review* 4 (December 1974): 17–23. Stephanie Urdang, *A Revolution within a Revolution: Women in Guinea-Bissau* (Boston: New England Free Press, n.d.). This is the general position taken by official documents of the Chinese revolution, as collected by Elisabeth Croll, ed., *The Women's Movement in China: A Selection of Readings, 1949–1973*, Modern China Series, no. 6 (London: Anglo-Chinese Educational Institute, 1974). Mao Tse-Tung recognized a distinctive domination of women by men (see discussion by Stuart Schram, *The Political Thought of Mao Tse-Tung* [New York: Praeger Publishers, 1969], p. 257), but interpretations of his thought throughout the revolution saw issues of sex as bourgeois deviation (see Croll, ed., pp. 19, 22, 32). The Leninist view which the latter documents seem to reflect is expressed in Clara Zetkin's account, "Lenin on the Woman Question," excerpted as appendix in *The Woman Question* (New York: International Publishers, 1951), p. 89. Engels earlier traced the oppression of women to the rise of class society, the patriarchal family, and the state, arguing that woman's status would be changed with the elimination of private property as a form of ownership and her integration into public production (Friedrich Engels, *Origin of the Family, Private Property and the State* [New York: International Publishers, 1942]).

termed socialist-feminism, have not recognized the depth of the antagonism or the separate integrity of each theory. These juxtapositions
emerge as unconfronted as they started: either feminist or marxist, usually the latter. Socialist-feminist practice often divides along the same
lines, consisting largely in organizational cross-memberships and mutual
support on specific issues.[15] Women with feminist sympathies urge attention to women's issues by left or labor groups; marxist women pursue
issues of class within feminist groups; explicitly socialist-feminist groups
come together and divide, often at the hyphen.[16]

Most attempts at synthesis attempt to integrate or explain the appeal
of feminism by incorporating issues feminism identifies as central—the
family, housework, sexuality, reproduction, socialization, personal
life—within an essentially unchanged marxian analysis.[17] According to

15. Sheila Rowbotham, *Hidden from History: Rediscovering Women in History from the
Seventeenth Century to the Present* (New York: Random House, 1973); Mary Jo Buhle,
"Women and the Socialist Party, 1901–1914," in Altbach, ed. (n. 10 above); Robert Shaffer,
"Women and the Communist Party, USA, 1930–1940," *Socialist Review* 45 (May–June
1979): 73–118. Contemporary attempts to create socialist-feminist groups and strategies
are exemplified in position papers: Chicago Women's Liberation Union, "Socialist
Feminism: A Strategy for the Women's Movement," mimeograph (Chicago, 1972) (available from Women's Liberation Union, Hyde Park Chapter, 819 W. George, Chicago, Ill.
60657); Berkeley-Oakland Women's Union, "Principles of Unity," *Socialist Revolution* 4, no.
1 (January–March 1974): 69–82; Lavender and Red Union, *The Political Perspective of the
Lavender and Red Union* (Los Angeles: Fanshen Printing Collective, 1975). Rosalind Petchesky, "Dissolving the Hyphen: A Report on Marxist-Feminist Groups 1–5," in Eisenstein,
ed. (n. 11 above), and Red Apple Collective, "Socialist-Feminist Women's Unions: Past and
Present," *Quest: A Feminist Quarterly* 4, no. 1 (1977): 88–96, reflect on the process.

16. Many attempts at unity began as an effort to justify women's struggles in marxist
terms, as if only that could make them legitimate. This anxiety lurks under many synthetic
attempts, although feminism has largely redirected its efforts from justifying itself within
any other perspective to developing its own.

17. While true from a feminist standpoint, this sweeping characterization does
minimize the wide varieties of marxist theories that have produced significantly different
analyses of women's situation. Juliet Mitchell, *Woman's Estate* (New York: Random House,
1971); Sheila Rowbotham, *Women, Resistance and Revolution: A History of Women and Revolution in the Modern World* (New York: Random House, 1972); Zillah Eisenstein, "Some Notes
on the Relations of Capitalist Patriarchy," in Eisenstein, ed. (n. 11 above); Eli Zaretsky, "Socialist Politics and the Family," *Socialist Revolution* 19 (January–March 1974): 83–99; Eli Zaretsky, "Capitalism, the Family and Personal Life," *Socialist Revolution* 3, nos. 1 and 2 (January–April 1973): 69–126, and no. 3 (May–June 1973): 19–70; Virginia Held, "Marx, Sex
and the Transformation of Society," in *Women and Philosophy: Toward a Theory of Liberation*,
ed. Carol C. Gould and Marx W. Wartofsky (New York: G. P. Putnam's Sons, 1976), pp.
168–84; Mihailo Marković, "Women's Liberation and Human Emancipation," ibid., pp.
145–67; Hal Draper, "Marx and Engels on Women's Liberation," in *Female Liberation*, ed.
Roberta Salper (New York: Alfred A. Knopf, Inc., 1972), pp. 83–107. No matter how
perceptive about the contributions of feminism or sympathetic to women's interests, these
attempts cast feminism, ultimately, as a movement *within* marxism: "I want to suggest that
the women's movement can provide the basis for building a new and authentic American
socialism" (Nancy Hartsock, "Feminist Theory and the Development of Revolutionary

the persuasion of the marxist, women become a caste, a stratum, a cultural group, a division in civil society, a secondary contradiction, or a nonantagonistic contradiction; women's liberation becomes a precondition, a measure of society's general emancipation, part of the superstructure, or an important aspect of the class struggle. Most commonly, women are reduced to some other category, such as "women workers," which is then treated as coextensive with all women.[18] Or, in what has become near reflex, women become "the family," as if this single form of women's confinement (then divided on class lines, then on racial lines) can be *presumed* the crucible of women's determination.[19] Or,

Strategy," in Eisenstein, ed. [n. 11 above], p. 57). Attempts at synthesis that push these limits include Gayle Rubin, "The Traffic in Women: Notes on the 'Political Economy' of Sex," in *Toward an Anthropology of Women,* ed. Rayna R. Reiter (New York: Monthly Review Press, 1975), pp. 157–210; Sheila Rowbotham, *Women's Liberation and the New Politics,* Spokesman Pamphlet, no. 17 (Bristol: Falling Wall Press, 1971); Annette Kuhn and AnnMarie Wolpe, "Feminism and Materialism," in *Feminism and Materialism: Women and Modes of Production,* ed. Annette Kuhn and AnnMarie Wolpe (London: Routledge & Kegan Paul, 1978); Ann Foreman, *Femininity as Alienation: Women and the Family in Marxism and Psychoanalysis* (London: Pluto Press, 1977); Meredith Tax and Jonathan Schwartz, "The Wageless Slave and the Proletarian," mimeograph (1972) (available from the author); Heidi I. Hartmann, "Capitalism, Patriarchy, and Job Segregation by Sex," *Signs: Journal of Women in Culture and Society* 1, no. 3, pt. 2 (Spring 1976): 137–69, and "The Unhappy Marriage of Marxism and Feminism: Towards a More Progressive Union," *Capital and Class* 8 (Summer 1979): 1–33; advocates of "wages for housework" mentioned in n. 10 above; and work by Linda Gordon, *Woman's Body, Woman's Right: A Social History of Birth Control in America* (New York: Grossman Publishers, 1976), pp. 403–18. Also see Linda Gordon, "The Struggle for Reproductive Freedom: Three Stages of Feminism," in Eisenstein, ed. (n. 11 above). Charlotte Bunch and Nancy Myron, *Class and Feminism* (Baltimore: Diana Press, 1974) exemplifies, without explicitly articulating, feminist method applied to class.

18. This tendency, again with important variations, is manifest in writings otherwise as diverse as Charnie Guettel, *Marxism and Feminism* (Toronto: Canadian Women's Education Press, 1974); Mary Alice Waters, "Are Feminism and Socialism Related?" in *Feminism and Socialism,* ed. Linda Jenness (New York: Pathfinder Press, 1972), pp. 18–26; Weather Underground, *Prairie Fire* (Underground, U.S.A.: Red Dragon Collective, 1975); Marjorie King, "Cuba's Attack on Women's Second Shift, 1974–1976," *Latin American Perspectives* 4, nos. 1 and 2 (Winter–Spring 1977): 106–19; Al Syzmanski, "The Socialization of Women's Oppression: A Marxist Theory of the Changing Position of Women in Advanced Capitalist Society," *Insurgent Sociologist* 6, no. 11 (Winter 1976): 31–58; "The Political Economy of Women," *Review of Radical Political Economics* 4, no. 3 (July 1972). See also Selma James, *Women, the Unions and Work, or What Is Not to Be Done* (Bristol: Falling Wall Press, 1976). This is true for "wages for housework" theory in the sense that it sees women as exploited because they do work—housework.

19. Engels (n. 14 above); Leon Trotsky, *Women and the Family,* trans. Max Eastman et al. (New York: Pathfinder Press, 1970); Evelyn Reed, *Woman's Evolution: From Matriarchal Clan to Patriarchal Family* (New York: Pathfinder Press, 1975); Lise Vogel, "The Earthly Family," *Radical America* 7, nos. 4–5 (July–October 1973): 9–50; Kollontai Collective, "The Politics of the Family: A Marxist View" (paper prepared for Socialist Feminist Conference at Yellow Springs, Ohio, July 4–6, 1975); Linda Limpus, *Liberation of Women: Sexual Repres-*

the marxist meaning of reproduction, the iteration of productive relations, is punned into an analysis of biological reproduction, as if women's bodily differences from men must account for their subordination to men; and as if this social analogue to the biological makes women's definition material, therefore based on a division of *labor* after all, therefore real, therefore (potentially) unequal.[20] Sexuality, if noticed at all, is, like "every day life,"[21] analyzed in gender-neutral terms, as if its social meaning can be presumed the same, or coequal, or complementary, for women and men.[22] Although a unified theory of social inequality is presaged in these strategies of subordination, staged progression, and assimilation of women's concerns to left concerns, at most an uneven

---

sion and the Family (Boston: New England Free Press, n.d.); Marlene Dixon, "On the Super-Exploitation of Women," *Synthesis* 1, no. 4 (Spring 1977): 1–11; David P. Levine and Lynn S. Levine, "Problems in the Marxist Theory of the Family," photocopied (Department of Economics, Yale University, July 1978). A common approach to treating women's situation as coterminous with the family is to make women's circumstances the incident or focus for a reconciliation of Marx with Freud. This approach, in turn, often becomes more Freudian than marxist, without yet becoming feminist in the sense developed here. Juliet Mitchell, *Psychoanalysis and Feminism: Freud, Reich, Laing and Women* (New York: Pantheon Books, 1974); Eli Zaretsky, "Male Supremacy and the Unconscious," *Socialist Revolution* 21, no. 22 (January 1975): 7–56; Nancy Chodorow, *The Reproduction of Mothering: Psychoanalysis and the Sociology of Gender* (Berkeley: University of California Press, 1978). See also Herbert Marcuse, "Socialist Feminism: The Hard Core of the Dream," *Edcentric: A Journal of Educational Change*, no. 31–32 (November 1974), pp. 7–44.

20. Sometimes "reproduction" refers to biological reproduction, sometimes to the "reproduction" of daily life, as housework, sometimes both. Political Economy of Women Group, "Women, the State and Reproduction since the 1930s," *On the Political Economy of Women*, CSE Pamphlet no. 2, Stage 1 (London: Conference of Socialist Economists, 1977). Family theories (n. 19 above) often analyze biological reproduction as a part of the family, while theories of women as workers often see it as work (n. 18 above). For an analysis of reproduction as an aspect of *sexuality*, in the context of an attempted synthesis, see Gordon, "The Struggle for Reproductive Freedom: Three Stages of Feminism" (n. 17 above).

21. Henri Lefebvre, *Everyday Life in the Modern World* (London: Penguin Books, 1971); Bruce Brown, *Marx, Freud and the Critique of Everyday Life: Toward a Permanent Cultural Revolution* (New York: Monthly Review Press, 1973).

22. Herbert Marcuse, *Eros and Civilization: A Philosophical Inquiry into Freud* (New York: Random House, 1955); Wilhelm Reich, *Sex-Pol: Essays, 1929–1934* (New York: Random House, 1972); Reimut Reiche, *Sexuality and Class Struggle* (London: New Left Books, 1970); Bertell Ollman, *Social and Sexual Revolution: Essays on Marx and Reich* (Boston: South End Press, 1979); Red Collective, *The Politics of Sexuality in Capitalism* (London: Red Collective, 1973). This is also true of Michel Foucault, *The History of Sexuality*, vol. 1, *An Introduction* (New York: Random House, 1980). Although Foucault understands that sexuality must be discussed at the same time as method, power, class, and the law, he does not systematically comprehend the specificity of gender—women's and men's relation to these factors—as a primary category for comprehending them. As one result, he cannot distinguish between the silence about sexuality that Victorianism has made into a noisy discourse and the silence that has *been* women's sexuality under conditions of subordination by and to men. Lacan notwithstanding, none of these theorists grasps sexuality (*including desire itself*) as social, nor the content of its determination as a sexist social order that eroticizes potency (as male) and victimization (as female).

combination is accomplished. However sympathetically, "the woman question" is always reduced to some other question, instead of being seen as *the* question, calling for analysis on its own terms.

Socialist-feminism stands before the task of synthesis as if nothing essential to either theory fundamentally opposes their wedding—indeed as if the union had already occurred and need only be celebrated. The failure to contain both theories on equal terms derives from the failure to confront each on its own ground: at the level of method. Method shapes each theory's vision of social reality. It identifies its central problem, group, and process, and creates as a consequence its distinctive conception of politics as such. Work and sexuality as concepts, then, derive their meaning and primacy from the *way* each theory approaches, grasps, interprets, and inhabits its world. Clearly, there is a relationship between how and what a theory sees: is there a marxist method without class? a feminist method without sex? Method in this sense organizes the apprehension of truth; it determines what counts as evidence and defines what is taken as verification. Instead of engaging the debate over which came (or comes) first, sex or class, the task for theory is to explore the conflicts and connections between the methods that found it meaningful to analyze social conditions in terms of those categories in the first place.[23]

23. Marxist method is not monolithic. Beginning with Marx, it has divided between an epistemology that embraces its own historicity and one that claims to portray a reality outside itself. In the first tendency, all thought, including social analysis, is ideological in the sense of being shaped by social being, the conditions of which are external to no theory. The project of theory is to create what Lukács described as "a theory of theory and a consciousness of consciousness" (Georg Lukács, "Class Consciousness," in *History and Class Consciousness: Studies in Marxist Dialectics* [Cambridge, Mass.: MIT Press, 1968], p. 47). Theory is a social activity engaged in the life situation of consciousness. See Jane Flax, "Epistemology and Politics: An Inquiry into Their Relation" (Ph.D. diss., Yale University, 1974). In the second tendency, theory is acontextual to the extent that it is correct. Real processes and thought processes are distinct; being has primacy over knowledge. The real can only be unified with knowledge of the real, as in dialectical materialism, because they have previously been separated. Nicos Poulantzas, *Political Power and Social Classes* (London: Verso, 1978), p. 14. Theory as a form of thought is methodologically set apart both from the illusions endemic to social reality—ideology—and from reality itself, a world defined as thinglike, independent of both ideology and theory. Ideology here means thought that is socially determined without being conscious of its determinations. Situated thought is as likely to produce "false consciousness" as access to truth. Theory, by definition, is, on the contrary, nonideological. Since ideology is interested, theory must be disinterested in order to penetrate myths that justify and legitimate the status quo. As Louis Althusser warned, "We know that a 'pure' science only exists on condition that it continually frees itself from ideology which occupies it, haunts it, or lies in wait for it" (*For Marx* [London: Verso, 1979], p. 170). When this attempt is successful, society is seen "from the point of view of class exploitation" (Louis Althusser, *Lenin and Philosophy* [New York: Monthly Review Press, 1971], p. 8). A theory that embraced its own historicity might see the scientific imperative itself as historically contingent. (On the objective standpoint, see text, pp. 537–42.) The problem with using scientific method to understand women's situation is that it is precisely unclear and crucial what is thought and what is thing, so that

Feminism has not been perceived as having a method, or even a central argument, with which to contend. It has been perceived not as a systematic analysis but as a loose collection of factors, complaints, and issues which, taken together, describe rather than explain the misfortunes of the female sex. The challenge is to demonstrate that feminism systematically converges upon a central explanation of sex inequality through an approach distinctive to its subject yet applicable to the whole of social life, including class.

Under the rubric of feminism, woman's situation has been explained as a consequence of biology[24] or of reproduction and mothering, social organizations of biology;[25] as caused by the marriage law[26] or, as

the separation itself becomes problematic. The second tendency grounds the marxist claim to be scientific; the first, its claim to capture as thought the flux of history. The first is more hospitable to feminism; the second has become the dominant tradition.

24. Simone de Beauvoir, *The Second Sex* (New York: Alfred A. Knopf, Inc., 1970). Her existential theory merges, in order to criticize, social meaning with biological determination in "anatomical destiny": "Here we have the key to the whole mystery. On the biological level a species is maintained only by creating itself anew; but this creation results only in repeating the same Life in more individuals. But man assures the repetition of Life while transcending Life through Existence; by this transcendence he creates values that deprive pure repetition of all value. . . . Her misfortune is to have been biologically destined for the repetition of Life when even in her own view Life does not carry within itself its reasons for being, reasons that are more important than life itself " (p. 59). She does not ask, for example, whether the social value placed upon "repetition of life," the fact that it is seen as iterative rather than generative, or the fact that women are more identified with it than are men, are themselves social artifacts of women's subordination, rather than existential derivations of biological fiat. Shulamith Firestone substitutes the contradiction of sex for class in a dialectical analysis, but nevertheless takes sex itself as presocial: "Unlike economic class, sex class sprang directly from a biological reality; men and women were created different, and not equally privileged. . . . The biological family is an inherently unequal power distribution" (*The Dialectic of Sex: The Case For Feminist Revolution* [New York: William Morrow & Co., 1972], p. 3). Her solutions are consistent: "The freeing of women from the tyranny of their reproductive biology by every means available, and the diffusion of childbearing and the childrearing role to the society as a whole, men as well as women" (p. 206). Susan Brownmiller (in *Against Our Will: Men, Women and Rape* [New York: Simon & Schuster, 1976]) expresses a biological theory of rape within a social critique of the centrality of rape to women's subordination: "Men's structural capacity to rape and woman's corresponding structural vulnerability are as basic to the physiology of both our sexes as the primal act of sex itself. Had it not been for this accident of biology, an accommodation requiring the locking together of two separate parts, penis and vagina, there would be neither copulation nor rape as we know it. . . . By anatomical fiat—the inescapable construction of their genital organs—the human male was a natural predator and the human female served as his natural prey" (pp. 4, 6). She does not seem to think it necessary to explain why women do not engulf men, an equal biological possibility. Criticizing the law for confusing intercourse with rape, she finds them biologically indistinguishable, leaving one wondering whether she, too, must alter or acquiesce in the biological.

25. Adrienne Rich, *Of Woman Born: Motherhood as Experience and Institution* (New York: W. W. Norton & Co., 1976); Chodorow (n. 19 above); Dorothy Dinnerstein, *The Mermaid and the Minotaur: Sexual Arrangements and Human Malaise* (New York: Harper & Row, 1977); Suzanne Arms, *Immaculate Deception: A New Look at Women and Childbirth in America* (Boston: Houghton Mifflin Co., 1975).

26. I take Mill's "The Subjection of Women" (n. 4 above) to be the original articulation

extensions, by the patriarchal family, becoming society as a "patriarchy";[27] or as caused by artificial gender roles and their attendant attitudes.[28] Informed by these attempts, but conceiving nature, law, the family, and roles as consequences, not foundations, I think that feminism fundamentally identifies sexuality as the primary social sphere of male power. The centrality of sexuality emerges not from Freudian conceptions[29] but from feminist practice on diverse issues, including abortion, birth control, sterilization abuse, domestic battery, rape, incest, lesbianism, sexual harassment, prostitution, female sexual slavery, and pornography. In all these areas, feminist efforts confront and change women's lives concretely and experientially. Taken together, they are producing a feminist political theory centering upon sexuality: its social determination, daily construction, birth to death expression, and ultimately male control.

Feminist inquiry into these specific issues began with a broad unmasking of the attitudes that legitimize and hide women's status, the ideational envelope that contains woman's body: notions that women desire and provoke rape, that girls' experiences of incest are fantasies, that career women plot and advance by sexual parlays, that prostitutes are lustful, that wife beating expresses the intensity of love. Beneath each of these ideas was revealed bare coercion and broad connections to woman's social definition as a sex. Research on sex roles, pursuing Simone de Beauvoir's insight that "one is not born, one rather becomes a woman,"[30] disclosed an elaborate process: how and what one learns to become one. Gender, cross-culturally, was found to be a learned quality, an acquired characteristic, an assigned status, with qualities that vary independent of biology and an ideology that attributes them to nature.[31]

---

of the theory, generalized in much contemporary feminism, that women are oppressed by "patriarchy," meaning a system originating in the household wherein the father dominates, the structure then reproduced throughout the society in gender relations.

27. In her "notes toward a theory of patriarchy" Kate Millett comprehends "sex as a status category with political implications," in which politics refers to "power-structured relationships, arrangements whereby one group of persons is controlled by another. . . . Patriarchy's chief institution is the family" (*Sexual Politics* [New York: Ballantine Books, 1969], pp. 32, 31, 45).

28. Sandra L. Bem and Daryl J. Bem, "Case Study of Nonconscious Ideology: Training the Woman to Know Her Place," in *Beliefs, Attitudes and Human Affairs*, ed. D. J. Bem (Belmont, Calif.: Brooks/Cole, 1970); Eleanor Emmons Maccoby and Carol Nagy Jacklin, *The Psychology of Sex Differences* (Stanford, Calif.: Stanford University Press, 1974); and Shirley Weitz, *Sex Roles: Biological, Psychological and Social Foundations* (New York: Oxford University Press, 1977).

29. Nor does it grow directly from Lacanian roots, although French feminists have contributed much to the developing theory from within that tradition.

30. De Beauvoir (n. 24 above), p. 249.

31. J. H. Block, "Conceptions of Sex Role: Some Cross-cultural and Longitudinal Perspectives," *American Psychologist* 28, no. 3 (June 1973): 512–26; Nancy Chodorow, "Being and Doing: A Cross-cultural Examination of the Socialization of Males and Females," in *Women in Sexist Society*, ed. V. Gornick and B. K. Moran (New York: Basic

The discovery that the female archetype is the feminine stereotype exposed "woman" as a social construction. Contemporary industrial society's version of her is docile, soft, passive, nurturant, vulnerable, weak, narcissistic, childlike, incompetent, masochistic, and domestic, made for child care, home care, and husband care. Conditioning to these values permeates the upbringing of girls and the images for emulation thrust upon women. Women who resist or fail, including those who never did fit—for example, black and lower-class women who cannot survive if they are soft and weak and incompetent,[32] assertively self-respecting women, women with ambitions of male dimensions—are considered less female, lesser women. Women who comply or succeed are elevated as models, tokenized by success on male terms or portrayed as consenting to their natural place and dismissed as having participated if they complain.

If the literature on sex roles and the investigations of particular issues are read in light of each other, each element of the female *gender* stereotype is revealed as, in fact, *sexual*. Vulnerability means the appearance/reality of easy sexual access; passivity means receptivity and disabled resistance, enforced by trained physical weakness; softness means pregnability by something hard. Incompetence seeks help as vulnerability seeks shelter, inviting the embrace that becomes the invasion, trading exclusive access for protection . . . from the same access. Domesticity nurtures the consequent progeny, proof of potency, and ideally waits at home dressed in saran wrap.[33] Woman's infantilization evokes pedophilia; fixation on dismembered body parts (the breast man, the leg man) evokes fetishism; idolization of vapidity, necrophilia. Narcissism insures that woman identifies with that image of herself that man holds up: "Hold still, we are going to do your portrait, so that you can begin looking like it right away."[34] Masochism means that pleasure in violation becomes her sensuality. Lesbians so violate the sexuality implicit in female gender stereotypes as not to be considered women at all.

Socially, femaleness means femininity, which means attractiveness

Books, 1971); R. R. Sears, "Development of Gender Role," in *Sex and Behavior*, ed. F. A. Beach (New York: John Wiley & Sons, 1965).

32. National Black Feminist Organization, "Statement of Purpose," *Ms.* (May 1974): "The black woman has had to be strong, yet we are persecuted for having survived" (p. 99). Johnnie Tillmon, "Welfare Is a Women's Issue," *Liberation News Service* (February 26, 1972), in *America's Working Women: A Documentary History, 1600 to the Present*, ed. Rosalyn Baxandall, Linda Gordon, and Susan Reverby (New York: Vintage Books, 1976): "On TV a woman learns that human worth means beauty and that beauty means being thin, white, young and rich. . . . In other words, an A.F.D.C. mother learns that being a 'real woman' means being all the things she isn't and having all the things she can't have" (pp. 357–58).

33. Marabel Morgan, *The Total Woman* (Old Tappan, N.J.: Fleming H. Revell Co., 1973). "Total Woman" makes blasphemous sexuality into a home art, redomesticating what prostitutes have marketed as forbidden.

34. Cixous (n. 1 above), p. 892.

to men, which means sexual attractiveness, which means sexual availability on male terms.[35] What defines woman as such is what turns men on. Good girls are "attractive," bad girls "provocative." Gender socialization is the process through which women come to identify themselves as sexual beings, as beings that exist for men. It is that process through which women internalize (make their own) a male image of their sexuality *as* their identity as women.[36] It is not just an illusion. Feminist inquiry into women's own experience of sexuality revises prior comprehensions of sexual issues and transforms the concept of sexuality itself—its determinants and its role in society and politics. According to this revision, one "becomes a woman"—acquires and identifies with the status of the female—not so much through physical maturation or inculcation into appropriate role behavior as through the experience of sexuality: a complex unity of physicality, emotionality, identity, and status affirmation. Sex as gender and sex as sexuality are thus defined in terms of each other, but it is sexuality that determines gender, not the other way around. This, the central but never stated insight of Kate Millett's *Sexual Politics*,[37] resolves the duality in the term "sex" itself: what women learn in order to "have sex," in order to "become women"— woman as gender—comes through the experience of, and is a condition for, "having sex"—woman as sexual object for man, the use of women's sexuality by men. Indeed, to the extent sexuality is social, women's sexuality *is* its use, just as our femaleness *is* its alterity.

Many issues that appear sexual from this standpoint have not been seen as such, nor have they been seen as defining a politics. Incest, for example, is commonly seen as a question of distinguishing the real evil, a crime against the family, from girlish seductiveness or fantasy. Contraception and abortion have been framed as matters of reproduction and fought out as proper or improper social constraints on nature. Or they are seen as private, minimizing state intervention into intimate relations. Sexual harassment was a nonissue, then became a problem of distinguishing personal relationships or affectionate flirtation from abuse of position. Lesbianism, when visible, has been either a perversion or not, to be tolerated or not. Pornography has been considered a question of freedom to speak and depict the erotic, as against the obscene or violent. Prostitution has been understood either as mutual lust and degradation or an equal exchange of sexual need for economic need. The issue in rape has been whether the intercourse was provoked/mutually

35. Indications are that this is true not only in Western industrial society; further cross-cultural research is definitely needed.

36. Love justifies this on the emotional level. Firestone (n. 24 above), chap. 6.

37. Millett's analysis is pervasively animated by the sense that women's status is sexually determined. It shapes her choice of authors, scenes, and themes and underlies her most pointed criticisms of women's depiction. Her explicit discussion, however, vacillates between clear glimpses of that argument and statements nearly to the contrary.

desired, or whether it was forced: was it sex or violence? Across and beneath these issues, sexuality itself has been divided into parallel provinces: traditionally, religion or biology; in modern transformation, morality or psychology. Almost never politics.

In a feminist perspective, the formulation of each issue, in the terms just described, expresses ideologically the same interest that the problem it formulates expresses concretely: the interest from the male point of view. Women experience the sexual events these issues codify[38] as a cohesive whole within which each resonates. The defining theme of that whole is the male pursuit of control over women's sexuality—men not as individuals nor as biological beings, but as a gender group characterized by maleness as socially constructed, of which this pursuit is definitive. For example, women who need abortions see contraception as a struggle not only for control over the biological products of sexual expression but over the social rhythms and mores of sexual intercourse. These norms often appear hostile to women's self-protection even when the technology is at hand. As an instance of such norms, women notice that sexual harassment looks a great deal like ordinary heterosexual initiation under conditions of gender inequality. Few women are in a position to refuse unwanted sexual initiatives. That consent rather than nonmutuality is the line between rape and intercourse further exposes the inequality in normal social expectations. So does the substantial amount of male force allowed in the focus on the woman's resistance, which tends to be disabled by socialization to passivity. If sex is ordinarily accepted as something men do *to* women, the better question would be whether consent is a meaningful concept. Penetration (often by a penis) is also substantially more central to both the legal definition of rape and the male definition of sexual intercourse than it is to women's sexual violation or sexual pleasure. Rape in marriage expresses the male sense of entitlement to access to women they annex; incest extends it. Although most women are raped by men they know, the closer the relation, the less women are allowed to claim it was rape. Pornography becomes difficult to distinguish from art and ads once it is clear that what is degrading to women is compelling to the consumer. Prostitutes sell the unilaterality that pornography advertises. That most of these issues codify behavior that is neither countersystemic nor exceptional is supported by women's experience as victims: these behaviors are either not illegal or are effectively permitted on a large scale. As women's experience blurs the lines between deviance and normalcy, it obliterates the distinction between abuses *of* women and the social definition of what a woman *is*.[39]

38. Each of these issues is discussed at length in the second part of this article "Toward Feminist Jurisprudence"), forthcoming.

39. On abortion and contraception, see Kristin Luker, *Taking Chances: Abortion and the Decision Not to Contracept* (Berkeley: University of California Press, 1975). On rape, see Diana E. H. Russell, *Rape: The Victim's Perspective* (New York: Stein & Day, 1977); Andrea

These investigations reveal rape, incest, sexual harassment, pornography, and prostitution as not primarily abuses of physical force, violence, authority, or economics. They are abuses of sex. They need not and do not rely for their coerciveness upon forms of enforcement other than the sexual; that those forms of enforcement, at least in this context, are themselves sexualized is closer to the truth. They are not the erotization *of* something else; eroticism *itself* exists in their form. Nor are they perversions of art and morality. They *are* art and morality from the male point of view. They are sexual because they express the relations, values, feelings, norms, and behaviors of the culture's sexuality, in which considering things like rape, pornography, incest, or lesbianism deviant, perverse, or blasphemous is part of their excitement potential.

Sexuality, then, is a form of power. Gender, as socially constructed, embodies it, not the reverse. Women and men are divided by gender, made into the sexes as we know them, by the social requirements of heterosexuality, which institutionalizes male sexual dominance and female sexual submission.[40] If this is true, sexuality is the linchpin of gender inequality.

A woman is a being who identifies and is identified as one whose sexuality exists for someone else, who is socially male. Women's sexuality is the capacity to arouse desire in that someone. If what is sexual about a woman is what the male point of view requires for excitement, have male requirements so usurped its terms as to have become them? Considering women's sexuality in this way forces confrontation with whether there is any such thing. Is women's sexuality its absence? If being *for* another is the whole of women's sexual construction, it can be no more escaped by separatism, men's temporary concrete absence, than eliminated or qualified by permissiveness, which, in this context, looks like women emulating male roles. As Susan Sontag said: "The question is: *what* sexuality are women to be liberated to enjoy? Merely to remove the onus placed upon the sexual expressiveness of women is a hollow victory if the sexuality they become freer to enjoy remains the old one that converts women into objects. . . . This already 'freer' sexuality mostly reflects a

Medea and Kathleen Thompson, *Against Rape* (New York: Farrar, Straus & Giroux, 1974); Lorenne N. G. Clark and Debra Lewis, *Rape: The Price of Coercive Sexuality* (Toronto: Women's Press, 1977); Susan Griffin, *Rape: The Power of Consciousness* (San Francisco: Harper & Row, 1979); Kalamu ya Salaam, "Rape: A Radical Analysis from the African-American Perspective," in his *Our Women Keep Our Skies from Falling* (New Orleans: Nkombo, 1980), pp. 25–40. On incest, see Judith Herman and Lisa Hirschman, "Father-Daughter Incest," *Signs: Journal of Women in Culture and Society* 2, no. 1 (Summer 1977): 735–56. On sexual harassment, see my *Sexual Harassment of Working Women* (New Haven, Conn.: Yale University Press, 1979). On pornography, see Andrea Dworkin, *Pornography: Men Possessing Women* (New York: G. P. Putnam's Sons, 1981).

40. Ellen Morgan, *The Erotization of Male Dominance/Female Submission* (Pittsburgh: Know, Inc., 1975); Adrienne Rich, "Compulsory Heterosexuality and Lesbian Existence," *Signs: Journal of Women in Culture and Society* 5, no. 4 (Summer 1980): 631–60.

spurious idea of freedom: the right of each person, briefly, to exploit and dehumanize someone else. Without a change in the very norms of sexuality, the liberation of women is a meaningless goal. Sex as such is not liberating for women. Neither is more sex."[41] Does removing or revising gender constraints upon sexual expression change or even challenge its norms?[42] This question ultimately is one of social determination in the broadest sense: its mechanism, permeability, specificity, and totality. If women are socially defined such that female sexuality cannot be lived or spoken or felt or even somatically sensed apart from its enforced definition, so that it *is* its own lack, then there is no such thing as a woman as such, there are only walking embodiments of men's projected needs. For feminism, asking whether there is, socially, a female sexuality is the same as asking whether women exist.

Methodologically, the feminist concept of the personal as political is an attempt to answer this question. Relinquishing all instinctual, natural, transcendental, and divine authority, this concept grounds women's sexuality on purely relational terrain, anchoring women's power and accounting for women's discontent in the same world they stand against. The personal as political is not a simile, not a metaphor, and not an analogy. It does not mean that what occurs in personal life is similar to, or comparable with, what occurs in the public arena. It is not an application of categories from social life to the private world, as when Engels (followed by Bebel) says that in the family the husband is the bourgeois and the wife represents the proletariat.[43] Nor is it an equation of two spheres which remain analytically distinct, as when Reich interprets state behavior in sexual terms,[44] or a one-way infusion of one sphere into the other, as when Lasswell interprets political behavior as the displacement

41. Susan Sontag, "The Third World of Women," *Partisan Review* 40, no. 2 (1973): 180–206, esp. 188.

42. The same question could be asked of lesbian sadomasochism: when women engage in ritualized sexual dominance and submission, does it express the male structure or subvert it? The answer depends upon whether one has a social or biological definition of gender and of sexuality and then upon the content of these definitions. Lesbian sex, simply as sex between women, does not by definition transcend the erotization of dominance and submission and their social equation with maculinity and femininity. Butch/femme as *sexual* (not just gender) role playing, together with parallels in lesbian sadomasochism's "top" and "bottom," suggest to me that sexual conformity extends far beyond gender object mores. For a contrary view see Pat Califia, *Sapphistry: The Book of Lesbian Sexuality* (Tallahassee, Fla.: Naiad Press, 1980); Gayle Rubin, "Sexual Politics, the New Right and the Sexual Fringe," in *What Color Is Your Handkerchief: A Lesbian S/M Sexuality Reader* (Berkeley, Calif.: Samois, 1979), pp. 28–35.

43. Engels (n. 14 above); August Bebel, *Women under Socialism*, trans. Daniel DeLeon (New York: New York Labor News Press, 1904).

44. Reich (n. 22 above). He examines fascism, for example, as a question of how the masses can be made to desire their own repression. This might be seen as a precursor to the feminist question of how female desire *itself* can become the lust for self-annihilation.

of personal problems into public objects.[45] It means that women's distinctive experience as women occurs within that sphere that has been socially lived as the personal—private, emotional, interiorized, particular, individuated, intimate—so that what it is to *know* the *politics* of woman's situation is to know women's personal lives.

The substantive principle governing the authentic politics of women's personal lives is pervasive powerlessness to men, expressed and reconstituted daily *as* sexuality. To say that the personal is political means that gender as a division of power is discoverable and verifiable through women's intimate experience of sexual objectification, which is definitive of and synonymous with women's lives as gender female. Thus, to feminism, the personal is epistemologically the political, and its epistemology is its politics.[46] Feminism, on this level, is the theory of women's point of view. It is the theory of Judy Grahn's "common woman"[47] speaking Adrienne Rich's "common language."[48] Consciousness raising is its quintessential expression. Feminism does not appropriate an existing method—such as scientific method—and apply it to a different sphere of society to reveal its preexisting political aspect. Consciousness raising not only comes to know different things as politics; it necessarily comes to know them in a different way. Women's experience of politics, of life as sex object, gives rise to its own method of appropriating that reality: feminist method.[49] As its own kind of social analysis,

45. Harold Lasswell, *Psychoanalysis and Politics* (Chicago: University of Chicago Press, 1930).

46. The aphorism "Feminism is the theory; lesbianism is the practice" has been attributed to TiGrace Atkinson by Anne Koedt, "Lesbianism and Feminism," in *Radical Feminism*, ed. Anne Koedt, Ellen Levine, and Anita Rapone (New York: New York Times Book Co., 1973), p. 246. See also Radicalesbians, "The Woman Identified Woman," ibid., pp. 24–45; TiGrace Atkinson, "Lesbianism & Feminism," *Amazon Odyssey: The First Collection of Writings by the Political Pioneer of the Women's Movement* (New York: Links Books, 1974), pp. 83–88; Jill Johnston, *Lesbian Nation: The Feminist Solution* (New York: Simon & Schuster, 1973), pp. 167, 185, 278. This aphorism accepts a simplistic view of the relationship between theory and practice. Feminism reconceptualizes the connection between being and thinking such that it may be more accurate to say that feminism is the epistemology of which lesbianism is an ontology. But see n. 56 below on this latter distinction as well.

47. Judy Grahn, *The Work of a Common Woman* (New York: St. Martin's Press, 1978). "The Common Woman" poems are on pp. 61–73.

48. Adrienne Rich, "Origins and History of Consciousness," in *The Dream of a Common Language: Poems, 1974–1977* (New York: W. W. Norton & Co., 1978), p. 7. This means that a women's movement exists wherever women identify collectively to resist/reclaim their determinants as such. This feminist redefinition of consciousness requires a corresponding redefinition of the process of mobilizing it: feminist *organizing*. The transformation from subordinate group to movement parallels Marx's distinction between a class "in itself " and a class "for itself." See Karl Marx, *The Poverty of Philosophy* (New York: International Publishers, 1963), p. 195.

49. In addition to the references in n. 1, see Sandra Lee Bartky, "Toward a

within yet outside the male paradigm just as women's lives are, it has a distinctive theory of the *relation* between method and truth, the individual and her social surroundings, the presence and place of the natural and spiritual in culture and society, and social being and causality itself.

Having been objectified as sexual beings while stigmatized as ruled by subjective passions, women reject the distinction between knowing subject and known object—the division between subjective and objective postures—as the means to comprehend social life. Disaffected from objectivity, having been its prey, but excluded from its world through relegation to subjective inwardness, women's interest lies in overthrowing the distinction itself. Proceeding connotatively and analytically at the same time, consciousness raising is at once common sense expression and critical articulation of concepts. Taking situated feelings and common detail (common here meaning both ordinary and shared) as the matter of political analysis, it explores the terrain that is most damaged, most contaminated, yet therefore most women's own, most intimately known, most open to reclamation. The process can be described as a collective "sympathetic internal experience of the gradual construction of [the] system according to its inner necessity,"[50] as a strategy for deconstructing it.

Through consciousness raising, women grasp the collective reality of women's condition from within the perspective of that experience, not from outside it. The claim that a sexual politics exists and is socially fundamental is grounded in the claim of feminism *to* women's perspective, not from it. Its claim to women's perspective *is* its claim to truth. In its account of itself, women's point of view contains a duality analogous

Phenomenology of Feminist Consciousness," in *Feminism and Philosophy*, ed. Mary Vetterling-Braggin et al. (Totowa, N.J.: Littlefield, Adams & Co., 1977). Susan Griffin reflects/creates the process: "We do not rush to speech. We allow ourselves to be moved. We do not attempt objectivity. . . . We said we had experienced this ourselves. I felt so much for her then, she said, with her head cradled in my lap, she said, I knew what to do. We said we were moved to see her go through what we had gone through. We said this gave us some knowledge" (*Woman and Nature: The Roaring Inside Her* [New York: Harper & Row, 1978],. p. 197). Assertions such as "our politics begin with our feelings" have emerged from the practice of consciousness raising. Somewhere between mirror-reflexive determination and transcendence of determinants, "feelings" are seen as both access to truth—at times a bit phenomenologically transparent—and an artifact of politics. There is both suspicion of feelings and affirmation of their health. They become simultaneously an inner expression of outer lies and a less contaminated resource for verification. See San Francisco Redstockings, "Our Politics Begin with Our Feelings," in *Masculine/Feminine: Readings in Sexual Mythology and the Liberation of Women*, ed. Betty Roszak and Theodore Roszak (New York: Harper & Row, 1969).

50. Fredric Jameson, *Marxism and Form* (Princeton, N.J.: Princeton University Press, 1971), p. xi. Jameson is describing dialectical method: "I have felt that the dialectical method can be acquired only by a concrete working through of detail, by a sympathetic internal experience of the gradual construction of a system according to its inner necessity."

to that of the marxist proletariat: determined by the reality the theory explodes, it thereby claims special access to that reality.[51] Feminism does not see its view as subjective, partial, or undetermined but as a critique of the purported generality, disinterestedness, and universality of prior accounts. These have not been half right but have invoked the wrong whole. Feminism not only challenges masculine partiality but questions the universality imperative itself. Aperspectivity is revealed as a strategy of male hegemony.[52]

"Representation of the world," de Beauvoir writes, "like the world itself, is the work of men; they describe it from their own point of view, which they confuse with the absolute truth."[53] The parallel between representation and construction should be sustained: men *create* the world from their own point of view, which then *becomes* the truth to be described. This is a closed system, not anyone's confusion. *Power to create the world from one's point of view is power in its male form.*[54] The male epistemological stance, which corresponds to the world it creates, is ob-

51. This distinguishes both feminism and at least a strain in marxism from Freud: "My self-analysis is still interrupted and I have realized the reason. I can only analyze my self with the help of knowledge obtained objectively (like an outsider). Genuine self-analysis is impossible, otherwise there would be no [neurotic] illness" (Sigmund Freud, Letter to Wilhelm Fleiss, #71, October 15, 1887, quoted in Mitchell, *Psychoanalysis and Feminism: Freud, Reich, Laing and Women* [n. 19 above], pp. 61–62, see also p. 271). Given that introspection is not analytically dispositive to Freud, the collective self-knowledge of feminism might be collective neurosis. Although it is interpersonal, it is still an insider to its world.

52. Feminist scholars are beginning to criticize objectivity from different disciplinary standpoints, although not as frontally as here, nor in its connection with objectification. Julia Sherman and Evelyn Torton Beck, eds., *The Prism of Sex: Essays in the Sociology of Knowledge* (Madison: University of Wisconsin Press, 1979); Margrit Eichler, *The Double Standard: A Feminist Critique of Feminist Social Science* (New York: St. Martin's Press, 1980); Evelyn Fox Keller, "Gender and Science," *Psychoanalysis and Contemporary Thought* 1, no. 3 (1978): 409–33. Adrienne Rich, "Toward a Woman-centered University," in *Woman and the Power to Change*, ed. Florence Howe (New York: McGraw-Hill Book Co., 1975).

53. De Beauvoir (n. 24 above). De Beauvoir had not pursued the analysis to the point I suggest here by 1979, either. See her "Introduction," in Marks and de Courtivron, eds. (n. 1 above), pp. 41–56.

54. This does not mean all men *have* male power equally. American Black men, for instance, have substantially less of it. But to the extent that they cannot create the world from their point of view, they find themselves unmanned, castrated, literally or figuratively. This supports rather than qualifies the sex specificity of the argument without resolving the relationship between racism and sexism, or the relation of either to class. Although historically receiving more attention, race and nation are otherwise analogous to sex in the place they occupy for, and the challenge they pose to, marxist theory. If the real basis of history and activity is class and class conflict, what, other than "false consciousness," is one to make of the historical force of sexism, racism, and nationalism? Similarly, positing a supra-class unit with true meaning, such as "Black people," is analytically parallel to positing a supra-class (and supra-racial) unit "women." Treating race, nation, and sex as lesser included problems has been the major response of marxist theory to such challenges. Any relationship *between* sex and race tends to be left entirely out of account, since they are considered parallel "strata." Attempts to confront the latter issue include Adrienne Rich,

jectivity: the ostensibly noninvolved stance, the view from a distance and from no particular perspective, apparently transparent to its reality. It does not comprehend its own perspectivity, does not recognize what it sees as subject like itself, or that the way it apprehends its world is a form of its subjugation and presupposes it. The objectively knowable is object. Woman through male eyes is sex object, that by which man knows himself at once as man and as subject.[55] What is objectively known corresponds to the world and can be verified by pointing to it (as science does) because the world itself is controlled from the same point of view.[56]

"Disloyal to Civilization: Feminism, Racism and Gynephobia," in *On Lies, Secrets and Silence: Selected Essays, 1966–1978* (New York: W. W. Norton & Co., 1979); Selma James, *Sex, Race and Class* (Bristol: Falling Wall Press, 1967); R. Coles and J. H. Coles, *Women of Crisis* (New York: Dell Publishing Co., Delacorte Press, 1978); Socialist Women's Caucus of Louisville, "The Racist Use of Rape and the Rape Charge" (Louisville, Ky., ca. 1977); Angela Davis, "The Role of Black Women in the Community of Slaves," *Black Scholar* 3, no. 4 (December 1971): 2–16; The Combahee River Collective, "A Black Feminist Statement," in Eisenstein, ed. (n. 11 above); Karen Getman, "Relations of Gender and Sexuality during the Period of Institutional Slavery in the Southern Colonies" (working paper, Yale University, 1980); E. V. Spelman, "Feminism, Sexism and Racism" (University of Massachusetts, 1981); Cherríe Moraga and Gloria Anzaldúa, eds., *This Bridge Called My Back: Writings of Radical Women of Color* (Watertown, Mass.: Persephone Press, 1981).

55. This suggests a way in which marxism and feminism may be reciprocally illuminating, without, for the moment, confronting the deep divisions between them. Marxism comprehends the *object* world's *social* existence: how objects are constituted, embedded in social life, infused with meaning, created in systematic and structural relation. Feminism comprehends the *social* world's *object* existence: how women are created in the image of, and as, things. The object world's social existence varies with the structure of production. Suppose that wherever the sexes are unequal, women are objects, but what it means to be an object varies with the productive relations that create objects as social. Thus, under primitive exchange systems, women are exchange objects. Under capitalism, women appear as commodities. That is, women's sexuality as object for men is valued as objects are under capitalism, namely as commodities. Under true communism, women would be collective sex objects. If women have universally been sex objects, it is also true that matter as the acted-upon in social life has a history. If women have always been things, it is also true that things have not always had the same meaning. Of course, this does not explain sex inequality. It merely observes, once that inequality exists, the way its dynamics may interact with the social organization of production. Sexual objectification may also have a separate history, with its own periods, forms, structures, technology, and, potentially, revolutions.

56. In a sense, this realization collapses the epistemology/ontology distinction altogether. What is purely an ontological category, a category of "being" free of social perception? Surely not the self/other distinction. Ultimately, the feminist approach turns social inquiry into political hermeneutics: inquiry into situated meaning, one in which the inquiry itself participates. A feminist political hermeneutics would be a theory of the answer to the question, What does it mean? that would comprehend that the first question to address is, To whom? within a context that comprehends gender as a social division of power. Useful general treatments of hermeneutical issues (which nevertheless proceed as if feminism, or a specific problematic of women, did not exist) include Josef Bleicher, *Contemporary Hermeneutics: Hermeneutics as Method, Philosophy and Critique* (London: Routledge & Kegan Paul, 1980); Hans-Georg Gadamer, *Philosophical Hermeneutics*, trans. David E. Linge (Berkeley: University of California Press, 1976); Rosalind Coward and John Ellis,

Combining, like any form of power, legitimation with force, male power extends beneath the representation of reality to its construction: it makes women (as it were) and so verifies (makes true) who women "are" in its view, simultaneously confirming its way of being and its vision of truth. The eroticism that corresponds to this is "the use of things to experience self."[57] As a coerced pornography model put it, "You do it, you do it, and you do it; then you become it."[58] The fetish speaks feminism.

Objectification makes sexuality a material reality of women's lives, not just a psychological, attitudinal, or ideological one.[59] It obliterates

---

Language and Materialism: Developments in Semiology and the Theory of the Subject (London: Routledge & Kegan Paul, 1977). Mary Daly approaches the ontological issue when she says that ontological theory without an understanding of sex roles can not be "really ontological" (*Beyond God the Father: Toward a Philosophy of Women's Liberation* [Boston: Beacon Press, 1973], p. 124). But both in this work, and more pervasively in *Gyn/Ecology: The Metaethics of Radical Feminism* (Boston: Beacon Press, 1978), the extent of the *creation* of women's *reality* by male epistemology, therefore the extent and nature of women's damage, is slighted in favor of a critique of its lies and distortions. Consider her investigation of suttee, a practice in which Indian widows are supposed to throw themselves upon their dead husband's funeral pyres in grief (and to keep pure), in which Daly focuses upon demystifying its alleged voluntary aspects. Women are revealed drugged, pushed, browbeaten, or otherwise coerced by the dismal and frightening prospect of widowhood in Indian society (Daly, *Gyn/Ecology*, pp. 113–33). Neglected—both as to the women involved and as to the implications for the entire diagnosis of sexism as illusion—are suttee's deepest victims: women who want to die when their husband dies, who volunteer for self-immolation because they believe their life is over when his is. See also Duncan Kennedy, "The Structure of Blackstone's Commentaries," *Buffalo Law Review* 28, no. 2 (1979): 211–12.

57. Dworkin (n. 39 above), p. 124. Explicitness is the aesthetic, the allowed sensibility, of objectified eroticism. Under this norm, written and pictured evocations of sexuality are compulsively literal. What it is to arouse sexuality through art is to recount events "objectively," i.e., verbally and visually to re-present who did what to whom. On the "dynamic of total explicitness" as stylization, explored in the context of the "foremost insight of the modern novel: the interweaving, the symbolic and structural interchange between economic and sexual relations," see George Steiner, "Eros and Idiom: 1975," in *On Difficulty and Other Essays* (New York: Oxford University Press, 1978), p. 100: "Chasteness of discourse [in George Eliot's work] acts not as a limitation but as a liberating privacy within which the character can achieve the paradox of autonomous life" (p. 107). This connects the lack of such liberating privacy for women—in life, law, or letters—with women's lack of autonomy and authentic erotic vocabulary.

58. Linda Lovelace, *Ordeal* (Secaucus, N.J.: Citadel Press, 1980). The same may be true for class. See Richard Sennett and Jonathan Cobb, *The Hidden Injuries of Class* (New York: Alfred A. Knopf, Inc., 1972). Marxism teaches that exploitation/degradation somehow necessarily produces resistance/revolution. Women's experience with sexual exploitation/degradation teaches that it also produces grateful complicity in exchange for survival and self-loathing to the point of the extinction of self, respect for which makes resistance conceivable. The problem here is not to explain why women acquiesce in their condition but why they ever do anything but.

59. The critique of sexual objectification first became visibly explicit in the American women's movement with the disruption of the Miss America Pageant in September 1968. Robin Morgan, "Women Disrupt the Miss America Pageant," *Rat* (September 1978), reprinted in *Going Too Far: The Personal Chronicle of a Feminist* (New York: Random House, 1977), pp. 62–67. The most compelling account of sexual objectification I know is con-

the mind/matter distinction that such a division is premised upon. Like the value of a commodity, women's sexual desirability is fetishized: it is made to appear a quality of the object itself, spontaneous and inherent, independent of the social relation which creates it, uncontrolled by the force that requires it. It helps if the object cooperates: hence, the vaginal

---

tained in the following description of women's depiction in art and the media: "According to usage and conventions which are at last being questioned but have by no means been overcome, the social presence of a woman is different in kind from that of a man. . . . A man's presence suggests what he is capable of doing to you or for you. By contrast, a woman's presence expresses her own attitude to herself, and *defines what can and cannot be done to her.* . . . To be born a woman has been to be born, within an allotted and confined space, into the keeping of men. The social presence of women has developed as a result of their ingenuity in living under such tutelage within such a limited space. But this has been at the cost of a woman's self being split into two. A woman must continually watch herself. She is almost continually accompanied by her own image of herself. . . . she comes to consider the surveyor and the surveyed within her as the two constituent yet always distinct elements of her identity as a woman. She has to survey everything she is and everything she does because how she appears to others, and ultimately how she appears to men, *is of crucial importance for what is normally thought of as the success of her life.* Her own sense of being in herself is supplanted by a sense of being appreciated as herself by another. One might simplify this by saying: men act; women appear. *Men look at women. Women watch themselves being looked at.* This determines not only most relations between men and women but also the relation of women to themselves. The surveyor of woman in herself is male: the surveyed, female. Thus she turns herself into an object—and most particularly an object of vision: a sight" (John Berger, *Ways of Seeing* [New York: Viking Press, 1972], pp. 46, 47 [my emphasis]). All that is missing here is an explicit recognition that this process embodies what the sexuality of women is about and that it expresses an inequality in social power. In a feminist context, aesthetics, including beauty and imagery, becomes the most political of subjects. See Purple September Staff, "The Normative Status of Heterosexuality," in *Lesbianism and the Women's Movement,* ed. Charlotte Bunch and Nancy Myron (Baltimore: Diana Press, 1975), pp. 79–83, esp. pp. 80–81.

Marxist attempts to deal with sexual objectification have not connected the issue with the politics of aesthetics or with subordination: "She becomes a sexual object only in a relationship, when she allows man to treat her in a certain depersonalizing, degrading way; and vice versa, a woman does not become a sexual subject simply by neglecting her appearance. There is no reason why a women's liberation activist should not try to look pretty and attractive. One of the universal human aspirations of all times was to raise reality to the level of art. . . . Beauty is a value in itself" (Marković [n. 17 above], pp. 165–66). Other attempts come closer, still without achieving the critique, e.g., Power of Women Collective, "What Is a Sex Object?" *Socialist Woman: A Journal of the International Marxist Group* 1, no. 1 (March/April 1974): 7; Dana Densmore, "On the Temptation to Be a Beautiful Object," in *Toward a Sociology of Women,* ed. C. Safilios-Rothschild (Lexington, Mass.: Xerox Publication, 1972); Rita Arditti, "Women as Objects: Science and Sexual Politics," *Science for the People,* vol. 6, no. 5 (September 1974); Charley Shively, "Cosmetics as an Act of Revolution," *Fag Rag* (Boston), reprinted in *Pink Triangles: Radical Perspectives on Gay Liberation,* ed. Pam Mitchell (Boston: Alyson Publication, 1980). Resentment of white beauty standards is prominent in Black feminism. Beauty standards incapable of achievement by any woman seem to fulfill a dual function. They keep women buying products (to the profit of capitalism) and competing for men (to be affirmed by the standard that matters). That is, they make women feel ugly and inadequate so we need men and money to defend against rejection/self-revulsion. Black women are further from being able concretely to achieve the standard that no woman can ever achieve, or it would lose its point.

orgasm;[60] hence, faked orgasms altogether.[61] Women's sexualness, like male prowess, is no less real for being mythic. It is embodied. Commodities do have value, but only because value is a social property arising from the totality of the same social relations which, unconscious of their determination, fetishize it. Women's bodies possess no less real desirability—or, probably, desire. Sartre exemplifies the problem on the epistemological level: "But if I desire a house, or a glass of water, or a woman's body, how could this body, this glass, this piece of property reside in my desire and how can my desire be anything but the consciousness of these objects as desirable?"[62] Indeed. Objectivity is the methodological stance of which objectification is the social process. Sexual objectification is the primary process of the subjection of women. It unites act with word, construction with expression, perception with enforcement, myth with reality. Man fucks woman; subject verb object.

The distinction between objectification and alienation is called into question by this analysis. Objectification in marxist materialism is thought to be the foundation of human freedom, the work process whereby a subject becomes embodied in products and relationships.[63] Alienation is the socially contingent distortion of that process, a reification of products and relations which prevents them from being, and being seen as, dependent on human agency.[64] But from the point of view of the object, objectification *is* alienation. For women, there is no

60. Anne Koedt, "The Myth of the Vaginal Orgasm," in Koedt et al., eds. (n. 46 above), pp. 198–207; TiGrace Atkinson, "Vaginal Orgasm as a Mass Hysterical Survival Response," in *Amazon Odyssey* (n. 46 above), pp. 5–8.

61. Shere Hite, *The Hite Report: A Nationwide Study of Female Sexuality* (New York: Dell Publishing Co., 1976), "Do you ever fake orgasms?" pp. 257–66.

62. Jean-Paul Sartre, *Existential Psychoanalysis,* trans. Hazel E. Barnes (Chicago: Henry Regnery Co., 1973), p. 20. A similar treatment of "desire" occurs in Deleuze and Guattari's description of man as "desiring-machine," of man in relation to the object world: "Not man as the king of creation, but rather as the being who is in intimate contact with the profound life of all forms or all types of beings, who is responsible for even the stars and animal life, and who ceaselessly plugs an organ-machine into an energy-machine, a tree into his body, a breast into his mouth, the sun into his asshole; the eternal custodian of the machines of the universe" (Deleuze and Guattari [n. 1 above], p. 4). Realizing that women, socially, inhabit the object realm transforms this discourse into a quite accurate description of the feminist analysis of women's desirability to man—the breast in his mouth, the energy machine into which he ceaselessly plugs an organ machine. Extending their inquiry into the extent to which this kind of objectification of woman is specific to capitalism (either as a process or in its particular form) does little to redeem the sex blindness (blind to the sex of its standpoint) of this supposedly general theory. Women are not desiring-machines.

63. Peter Berger and Stanley Pullberg, "Reification and the Sociological Critique of Consciousness," *New Left Review,* vol. 35 (January–February 1966); Herbert Marcuse, "The Foundation of Historical Materialism," in *Studies in Critical Philosophy,* trans. Joris De Bres (Boston: Beacon Press, 1972); Karl Klare, "Law-Making as Praxis," *Telos* 12, no. 2 (Summer 1979): 123–35, esp. 131.

64. Istvan Meszaros, *Marx's Theory of Alienation* (London: Merlin Press, 1972); Bertell Ollman, *Alienation: Marx's Conception of Man in Capitalist Society* (London: Cambridge University Press, 1971); Marcuse, *Eros and Civilization* (n. 22 above), pp. 93–94, 101–2.

distinction between objectification and alienation because women have not authored objectifications, we have been them. Women have been the nature, the matter, the acted upon, to be subdued by the acting subject seeking to embody himself in the social world. Reification is not just an illusion to the reified; it is also their reality. The alienated who can only grasp self as other is no different from the object who can only grasp self as thing. To be man's other *is* to be his thing. Similarly, the problem of how the object can know herself as such is the same as how the alienated can know its own alienation. This, in turn, poses the problem of feminism's account of women's consciousness. How can women, as created, "thingified in the head,"[65] complicit in the body, see our condition as such?

In order to account for women's consciousness (much less propagate it) feminism must grasp that male power produces the world before it distorts it. Women's acceptance of their condition does not contradict its fundamental unacceptability if women have little choice but to *become* persons who freely choose women's roles. For this reason, the reality of women's oppression is, finally, neither demonstrable nor refutable empirically. Until this is confronted on the level of method, criticism of what exists can be undercut by pointing to the reality to be criticized. Women's bondage, degradation, damage, complicity, and inferiority—together with the possibility of resistance, movement, or exceptions—will operate as barriers to consciousness rather than as means of access to what women need to become conscious of in order to change.

Male power is real; it is just not what it claims to be, namely, the only reality. Male power is a myth that makes itself true. What it is to raise consciousness is to confront male power in this duality: as total on one side and a delusion on the other. In consciousness raising, women learn they have *learned* that men are everything, women their negation, but that the sexes are equal. The content of the message is revealed true and false at the same time; in fact, each part reflects the other transvalued. If "men are all, women their negation" is taken as social criticism rather than simple description, it becomes clear for the first time that women *are* men's equals, everywhere in chains. Their chains become visible, their inferiority—their inequality—a product of subjection and a mode of its enforcement. Reciprocally, the moment it is seen that this—life as we know it—is not equality, that the sexes are not socially equal, womanhood can no longer be defined in terms of lack of maleness, as negativity. For the first time, the question of what a woman *is* seeks its ground in and of a world understood as neither of its making nor in its image, and finds, within a critical embrace of woman's fractured and alien image, that world women have made and a vision of its wholeness.

65. Rowbotham, *Women's Liberation and the New Politics* (n. 17 above), p. 17.

Feminism has unmasked maleness as a form of power that is both omnipotent and nonexistent, an unreal thing with very real consequences. Zora Neale Hurston captured its two-sidedness: "The town has a basketfull of feelings good and bad about Joe's positions and possessions, but none had the temerity to challenge him. They bowed down to him rather, because he was all of these things, and then again he was all of these things because the town bowed down."[66] If "positions and possessions" and rulership create each other, in relation, the question becomes one of form and inevitability. This challenges feminism to apply its theory of women's standpoint to the regime.[67]

Feminism is the first theory to emerge from those whose interest it affirms. Its method recapitulates as theory the reality it seeks to capture. As marxist method is dialectical materialism, feminist method is consciousness raising: the collective critical reconstitution of the meaning of women's social experience, as women live through it. Marxism and feminism on this level posit a different relation between thought and thing, both in terms of the relationship of the analysis itself to the social life it captures and in terms of the participation of thought in the social life it analyzes. To the extent that materialism is scientific it posits and refers to a reality outside thought which it considers to have an objective—that is, truly nonsocially perspectival—content. Consciousness raising, by contrast, inquires into an intrinsically social situation, into that mixture of thought and materiality which is women's sexuality in the most generic sense. It approaches its world through a process that shares its determination: women's consciousness, not as individual or subjective ideas, but as collective social being. This method stands inside its own determinations in order to uncover them, just as it criticizes them in order to value them on its own terms—in order to *have* its own terms at all. Feminism turns theory itself—the pursuit of a true analysis of social life—into the pursuit of consciousness and turns an analysis of inequality into a critical embrace of its own determinants. The process is transformative as well as perceptive, since thought and thing are inextricable and reciprocally constituting of women's oppression, just as the state as coercion and the state as legitimizing ideology are indistinguishable, and for the same reasons. The pursuit of consciousness becomes a form of political practice. Consciousness raising has revealed gender relations to be a collective fact, no more simply personal than class relations. This implies that class relations may also be personal, no less so for being at the same time collective. The failure of marxism to realize this may connect the

66. Zora Neale Hurston, *Their Eyes Were Watching God* (Urbana: University of Illinois Press, 1978), pp. 79–80.

67. In the second part of this article, "Feminism, Marxism, Method, and the State: Toward Feminist Jurisprudence" (forthcoming in *Signs*), I argue that the state is male in that objectivity is its norm.

failure of workers in advanced capitalist nations to organize in the socialist sense with the failure of left revolutions to liberate women in the feminist sense.

Feminism stands in relation to marxism as marxism does to classical political economy: its final conclusion and ultimate critique. Compared with marxism, the place of thought and things in method and reality are reversed in a seizure of power that penetrates subject with object and theory with practice. In a dual motion, feminism turns marxism inside out and on its head.

To answer an old question—how is value created and distributed?—Marx needed to create an entirely new account of the social world. To answer an equally old question, or to question an equally old reality—what explains the inequality of women to men? or, how does desire become domination? or, what is male power?—feminism revolutionizes politics.

Stanford Law School
Stanford University

Father-Daughter Incest

Judith Herman and Lisa Hirschman

A Feminist Theoretical Perspective

The incest taboo is universal in human culture. Though it varies from one culture to another, it is generally considered by anthropologists to be the foundation of all kinship structures. Lévi-Strauss describes it as the basic social contract; Mead says its purpose is the preservation of the human social order.[1] All cultures, including our own, regard violations of the taboo with horror and dread. Death has not been considered too extreme a punishment in many societies. In our laws, some states punish incest by up to twenty years' imprisonment.[2]

In spite of the strength of the prohibition on incest, sexual relations between family members do occur. Because of the extreme secrecy which surrounds the violation of our most basic sexual taboo, we have little clinical literature and no accurate statistics on the prevalence of incest. This paper attempts to review what is known about the occurrence of incest between parents and children, to discuss common social attitudes which pervade the existing clinical literature, and to offer a theoretical perspective which locates the incest taboo and its violations within the structure of patriarchy.

The authors gratefully acknowledge the contributions of the incest victims themselves and of the therapists who shared their experience with us. For reasons of confidentiality, we cannot thank them by name.

1. Claude Lévi-Strauss, *The Elementary Structures of Kinship* (Boston: Beacon Press, 1969), p. 481; Margaret Mead, "Incest," in *International Encyclopedia of the Social Sciences,* ed. David L. Sills (New York: Crowell, Collier & Macmillan, 1968).

2. Herbert Maisch, *Incest* (London: Andre Deutsch, 1973), p. 69.

The Occurrence of Incest

The Children's Division of the American Humane Association estimates that a minimum of 80,000–100,000 children are sexually molested
each year.[3] In the majority of these cases the offender is well known to
the child, and in about 25 percent of them, a relative. These estimates
are based on New York City police records and the experience of social
workers in a child protection agency. They are, therefore, projections
based on observing poor and disorganized families who lack the resources to preserve secrecy. There is reason to believe, however, that
most incest in fact occurs in intact families and entirely escapes the attention of social agencies. One in sixteen of the 8,000 white, middle-class
women surveyed by Kinsey et al. reported sexual contact with an adult
relative during childhood.[4] In the vast majority of these cases, the incident remained a secret.

A constant finding in all existing surveys is the overwhelming predominance of father-daughter incest. Weinberg, in a study of 200 court
cases in the Chicago area, found 164 cases of father-daughter incest,
compared with two cases of mother-son incest.[5] Maisch, in a study of
court cases in the Federal Republic of Germany, reported that 90 percent of the cases involved fathers and daughters, step-fathers and step-
daughters, or (infrequently) grandfathers and granddaughters.[6] Fathers
and sons accounted for another 5 percent. Incest between mothers and
sons occurred in only 4 percent of the cases. Incest appears to follow the
general pattern of sexual abuse of children, in which 92 percent of the
victims are female, and 97 percent of the offenders are male.[7]

It may be objected that these data are all based on court records and
perhaps reflect only a difference in complaints rather than a difference
in incidence. The Kinsey reports, however, confirm the impression of a
major discrepancy between the childhood sexual contacts of boys and
girls. If, as noted above, more than 6 percent of the female sample
reported sexual approaches by adult relatives, only a small number of
the 12,000 men surveyed reported sexual contact with any adult, relative
or stranger. (Exact figures were not reported.) Among these few, contact
with adult males seemed to be more common than with adult females. As
for mother-son incest, the authors concluded that "heterosexual incest
occurs more frequently in the thinking of clinicians and social workers

3. Vincent De Francis, ed., *Sexual Abuse of Children* (Denver: Children's Division of
the American Humane Association, 1967).

4. Alfred Kinsey, W. B. Pomeroy, C. E. Martin, and P. Gebhard, *Sexual Behavior in the
Human Female* (Philadelphia: Saunders & Co., 1953), pp. 116–22.

5. S. Kirson Weinberg, *Incest Behavior* (New York: Citadel Press, 1955).

6. See n. 2 above.

7. De Francis.

than it does in actual performance."[8] None of the existing literature, to our knowledge, makes any attempt to account for this striking discrepancy between the occurrence of father-daughter and mother-son incest.

Common Attitudes toward Incest in the Professional Literature

Because the subject of incest inspires such strong emotional responses, few authors have even attempted a dispassionate examination of its actual occurrence and effects. Those who have approached the subject have often been unable to avoid defensive reactions such as denial, distancing, or blaming. We undertake this discussion with the full recognition that we ourselves are not immune to these reactions, which may be far more apparent to our readers than to ourselves.

Undoubtedly the most famous and consequential instance of denial of the reality of incest occurs in Freud's 1897 letter to Fliess. In it, Freud reveals the process by which he came to disbelieve the reports of his female patients and develop his concepts of infantile sexuality and the infantile neurosis: "Then there was the astonishing thing that in every case blame was laid on perverse acts by the father, and realization of the unexpected frequency of hysteria, in every case of which the same thing applied, though it was hardly credible that perverted acts against children were so general."[9]

Freud's conclusion that the sexual approaches did not occur in fact was based simply on his unwillingness to believe that incest was such a common event in respectable families. To experience a sexual approach by a parent probably *was* unlikely for a boy: Freud concluded incorrectly that the same was true for girls. Rather than investigate further into the question of fact, Freud's followers chose to continue the presumption of fantasy and made the child's desire and fantasy the focus of psychological inquiry. The adult's desire (and capacity for action) were forgotten. Psychoanalytic investigation, then, while it placed the incest taboo at the center of the child's psychological development, did little to dispel the secrecy surrounding the actual occurrence of incest. As one child psychiatrist commented: "Helene Deutsch and other followers of Freud have, in my opinion, gone too far in the direction of conceptualizing patients' reports of childhood sexual abuse in terms of fantasy. My own experience, both in private practice and with several hundred child victims brought to us . . . [at the Center for Rape Concern] . . . in Philadelphia, has convinced me that analysts too often dismissed as fan-

---

8. Alfred C. Kinsey, W. B. Pomeroy, and Clyde Martin, *Sexual Behavior in the Human Male* (Philadelphia: Saunders & Co., 1948), pp. 167, 558.

9. Freud, *The Origins of Psychoanalysis: Letters to Wilhelm Fliess, Drafts and Notes: 1887–1902* (New York: Basic Books, 1954), p. 215.

tasy what was the real sexual molestation of a child. . . . As a result, the victim was isolated and her trauma compounded."[10]

Even those investigators who have paid attention to cases of actual incest have often shown a tendency to comment or make judgments concerning the guilt or innocence of the participants. An example:

> These children undoubtedly do not deserve completely the cloak of innocence with which they have been endowed by moralists, social reformers, and legislators. The history of the relationship in our cases usually suggests at least some cooperation of the child in the activity, and in some cases the child assumed an active role in initiating the relationship. . . . It is true that the child often rationalized with excuses of fear of physical harm or the entice-ment of gifts, but there were obviously secondary reasons. Even in the cases where physical force may have been applied by the adult, this did not wholly account for the frequent repetition of the prac-tice.
>
> Finally, a most striking feature was that these children were dis-tinguished as unusually charming and attractive in their outward personalities. Thus, it was not remarkable that frequently we con-sidered the possibility that the child might have been the actual seducer, rather than the one innocently seduced.[11]

In addition to denial and blame, much of the existing literature on incest shows evidence of social and emotional distancing between the investigators and their subjects. This sometimes takes the form of an assertion that incestuous behavior is accepted or condoned in some cul-ture other than the investigator's own. Thus, a British study of Irish working-class people reports that father-daughter incest, which oc-curred in 4 percent of an unselected outpatient clinic population, was a "cultural phenomenon" precipitated by social isolation or crowding, and had "no pathological effects."[12] The several investigators who have also reported instances where children, in their judgment, were not harmed by the incest experience do not usually state the criteria on which this judgment is based.[13] Still other investigators seem fearful to commit themselves to an opinion on the question of harm. Thus, for example, although 70 percent of the victims in Maisch's survey showed evidence of disturbed personality development, the author is uncertain about ascribing this to the effects of incest per se.

10. Joseph Peters, "Letter to the Editor," *New York Times Book Review* (November 16, 1975).

11. L. Bender and A. Blau, "The Reaction of Children to Sexual Relations with Adults," *American Journal of Orthopsychiatry* 7 (1937): 500–518.

12. N. Lukianowitz, "Incest," *British Journal of Psychiatry* 120 (1972): 301–13.

13. Yokoguchi, "Children Not Severely Damaged by Incest with a Parent," *Journal of the American Academy of Child Psychiatry* 5 (1966): 111–24; J. B. Weiner, "Father-Daughter Incest," *Psychiatric Quarterly* 36 (1962): 1132–38.

A few investigators, however, have testified to the destructive effects of the incest experience on the development of the child. Sloane and Karpinski, who studied five incestuous families in rural Pennsylvania, conclude: "Indulgence in incest in the post-adolescent period leads to serious repercussions in the girl, even in an environment where the moral standards are relaxed."[14] Kaufman, Peck, and Tagiuri, in a thorough study of eleven victims and their families who were seen at a Boston clinic, report: "Depression and guilt were universal as clinical findings. . . . The underlying craving for an adequate parent . . . dominated the lives of these girls."[15]

Several retrospective studies, including a recent report by Benward and Densen-Gerber, document a strong association between reported incest history and the later development of promiscuity or prostitution.[16] In fact, failure to marry or promiscuity seems to be the only criterion generally accepted in the literature as conclusive evidence that the victim has been harmed.[17] We believe that this finding in itself testifies to the traditional bias which pervades the incest literature.

Our survey of what has been written about incest, then, raises several questions. Why does incest between fathers and daughters occur so much more frequently than incest between mothers and sons? Why, though this finding has been consistently documented in all available sources, has no previous attempt been made to explain it? Why does the incest victim find so little attention or compassion in the literature, while she finds so many authorities who are willing to assert either that the incest did not happen, that it did not harm her, or that she was to blame for it? We believe that a feminist perspective must be invoked in order to address these questions.

Incest and Patriarchy

In a patriarchal culture, such as our own, the incest taboo must have a different meaning for the two sexes and may be observed by men and women for different reasons.

Major theorists in the disciplines of both psychology and anthropology explain the importance of the incest taboo by placing it at the center of an agreement to control warfare among men. It represents the first and most basic peace treaty. An essential element of the agreement is the

14. P. Sloane and E. Karpinski, "Effects of Incest on the Participants," *American Journal of Orthopsychiatry* 12 (1942): 666–73.

15. I. Kaufman, A. Peck, and L. Tagiuri, "The Family Constellation and Overt Incestuous Relations between Father and Daughter," *American Journal of Orthopsychiatry* 24 (1954): 266–79.

16. J. Benward and J. Densen-Gerber, *Incest as a Causative Factor in Anti-social Behavior: An Exploratory Study* (New York: Odyssey Institute, 1975).

17. Weinberg.

concept that women are the possessions of men; the incest taboo represents an agreement as to how women shall be shared. Since virtually all known societies are dominated by men, all versions of the incest taboo are agreements among men regarding sexual access to women. As Mitchell points out, men create rules governing the exchange of women; women do not create rules governing the exchange of men.[18] Because the taboo is created and enforced by men, we argue that it may also be more easily and frequently violated by men.

The point at which the child learns the meaning of the incest taboo is the point of initiation into the social order. Boys and girls, however, learn different versions of the taboo. To paraphrase Freud once again, the boy learns that he may not consummate his sexual desires for his mother because his mother belongs to his father, and his father has the power to inflict the most terrible of punishments on him: to deprive him of his maleness.[19] In compensation, however, the boy learns that when he is a man he will one day possess women of his own.

When this little boy grows up, he will probably marry and may have a daughter. Although custom will eventually oblige him to give away his daughter in marriage to another man (note that mothers do not give away either daughters or sons), the taboo against sexual contact with his daughter will never carry the same force, either psychologically or socially, as the taboo which prohibited incest with his mother. *There is no punishing father to avenge father-daughter incest.*

What the little girl learns is not at all parallel. Her initiation into the patriarchal order begins with the realization that she is not only comparatively powerless as a child, but that she will remain so as a woman. She may acquire power only indirectly, as the favorite of a powerful man. As a child she may not possess her mother *or* her father; when she is an adult, her best hope is to *be* possessed by someone like her father. Thus, according to Freud she has less incentive than the boy to come to a full resolution of the Oedipus complex.[20] Since she has no hope of acquiring the privileges of an adult male, she can neither be rewarded for giving up her incestuous attachments, nor punished for refusing to do so. Chesler states the same conclusion more bluntly: "Women are encouraged to commit incest as a way of life. . . . As opposed to marrying our fathers, we marry men like our fathers . . . men who are older than us, have more money than us, more power than us, are taller than us, are stronger than us . . . our fathers."[21]

18. Juliet Mitchell, *Psychoanalysis and Feminism* (New York: Pantheon Books, 1974).

19. Freud, *Three Essays on the Theory of Sexuality* (New York: Avon Books, 1962).

20. Freud, "Some Psychical Consequences of the Anatomical Distinction between the Sexes" (1925), "Female Sexuality" (1931), and "Femininity" (1933), all reprinted in *Women and Analysis,* ed. Jean Strouse (New York: Viking Press, 1974).

21. Phyllis Chesler, "Rape and Psychotherapy," in *Rape: The First Sourcebook for Women,* ed. Noreen Connell and Cassandra Wilson (New York: New American Library, 1974), p. 76.

A patriarchal society, then, most abhors the idea of incest between mother and son, because this is an affront to the father's prerogatives. Though incest between father and daughter is also forbidden, the prohibition carries considerably less weight and is, therefore, more frequently violated. We believe this understanding of the asymmetrical nature of the incest taboo under patriarchy offers an explanation for the observed difference in the occurrence of mother-son and father-daughter incest.

If, as we propose, the taboo on father-daughter incest is relatively weak in a patriarchal family system, we might expect violations of the taboo to occur most frequently in families characterized by extreme paternal dominance. This is in fact the case. Incest offenders are frequently described as "family tyrants": "These fathers, who are often quite incapable of relating their despotic claim to leadership to their social efforts for the family, tend toward abuses of authority of every conceivable kind, and they not infrequently endeavor to secure their dominant position by socially isolating the members of the family from the world outside. Swedish, American, and French surveys have pointed time and again to the patriarchal position of such fathers, who set up a 'primitive family order.' "[22] Thus the seduction of daughters is an abuse which is inherent in a father-dominated family system; we believe that the greater the degree of male supremacy in any culture, the greater the likelihood of father-daughter incest.

A final speculative point: since, according to this formulation, women neither make nor enforce the incest taboo, why is it that women apparently observe the taboo so scrupulously? We do not know. We suspect that the answer may lie in the historic experience of women both as sexual property and as the primary caretakers of children. Having been frequently obliged to exchange sexual services for protection and care, women are in a position to understand the harmful effects of introducing sex into a relationship where there is a vast inequality of power. And, having throughout history been assigned the primary responsibility for the care of children, women may be in a position to understand more fully the needs of children, the difference between affectionate and erotic contact, and the appropriate limits of parental love.

A Clinical Report

The following is a clinical case study of fifteen victims of father-daughter incest. All the women were clients in psychotherapy who reported their incest experiences to their therapists after the fact. Seven were women whom the authors had personally evaluated or seen in psychotherapy. The remaining eight were clients in treatment with

22. Maisch, p. 140.

other therapists. No systematic case-finding effort was made; the authors simply questioned those practitioners who were best known to us through an informal network of female professionals. Four out of the first ten therapists we questioned reported that at least one of her clients had an incest history. We concluded from this admittedly small sample that a history of incest is frequently encountered in clinical practice.

Our combined group of six therapists (the authors and our four informants) had interviewed close to 1,000 clients in the past five years. In this population, the incidence of reported father-daughter incest was 2–3 percent. We believe this to be a minimum estimate, since in most cases no particular effort was made to elicit the history. Our estimate accords with the data of the Kinsey report,[23] in which 1.5 percent of the women surveyed stated that they had been molested by their fathers.

For the purposes of this study, we defined incest as overt sexual contact such as fondling, petting, masturbation, or intercourse between parent and child. We included only those cases in which there was no doubt in the daughter's mind that explicit and intentionally sexual contact occurred and that secrecy was required. Thus we did not include in our study the many women who reported seductive behaviors such as verbal sharing of sexual secrets, flirting, extreme possessiveness or jealousy, or intense interest in their bodies or their sexual activities on the part of their fathers. We recognize that these cases represent the extreme of a continuum of father-daughter relationships which range from the affectionate through the seductive to the overtly sexual. Information about the incest history was initially gathered from the therapists. Those clients who were willing to discuss their experiences with us in person were then interviewed directly.

The fifteen women who reported that they had been molested during childhood were in other respects quite ordinary women. Nothing obvious distinguished them from the general population of women entering psychotherapy (see table 1). They ranged in age from fifteen to fifty-five. Most were in their early twenties at the time they first requested psychotherapy. They were all white. Four were single, seven married, and four separated or divorced. Half had children. The majority had at least some college education. They worked at common women's jobs: housewife, waitress, factory worker, office worker, prostitute, teacher, nurse. They complained mostly of depression and social isolation. Those who were married or recently separated complained of marital problems. The severity of their complaints seemed to be related to the degree of family disorganization and deprivation in their histories rather than to the incest history per se. Five of the women had been hospitalized at some point in their lives; three were or had been actively suicidal, and two were addicted to drugs or alcohol. Seven women brought up the

23. Kinsey et al. (n. 4 above), p. 121.

Table 1
Characteristics of Incest Victims Entering Therapy

Characteristic	Victims (N)
Age (years):	
15–20	3
21–25	7
26–30	2
30+	3
Marital Status:	
Single	4
Married	7
Separated or divorced	4
Occupation:	
Blue collar	4
White collar	4
Professional	3
Houseworker	1
Student	3
Education:	
High school not completed	4
High school completed	2
1–2 years college	3
College completed	5
Advanced degree	1
Presenting complaints:	
Marital problems	5
Depression	3
Anxiety	3
Social isolation	4
Drug or alcohol abuse	4
Suicide attempt	2

incest history among their initial complaints; the rest revealed it only after having established a relationship with the therapist. In some cases, the history was not disclosed for one, two, or even three years after therapy had begun.

The incest histories were remarkably similar (see table 2). The majority of the victims were oldest or only daughters and were between the ages of six and nine when they were first approached sexually by their fathers or male guardians (nine fathers, three stepfathers, a grandfather, a brother-in-law, and an uncle). The youngest girl was four years old; the oldest fourteen. The sexual contact usually took place repeatedly. In most cases the incestuous relationship lasted three years or more. Physical force was not used, and intercourse was rarely attempted with girls who had not reached puberty; the sexual contact was limited to masturbation and fondling. In three cases, the relationship was terminated when the father attempted intercourse.

> LENORE: I had already started to develop breasts at age nine and had my period when I was eleven. All this time he's still calling

me into bed for "little chats" with him. I basically trusted him although I felt funny about it. Then one time I was twelve or thirteen, he called me into bed and started undressing me. He gave this rationale about preparing me to be with boys. He kept saying I was safe as long as I didn't let them take my pants down. Meantime he was doing the same thing. I split. I knew what he was trying to do, and that it was wrong. That was the end of the overt sexual stuff. Not long after that he found an excuse to beat me.

In all but two of these fifteen cases the sexual relationship between father and daughter remained a secret, and there was no intervention in the family by the courts or child-protection authorities. Previous studies are based on court referrals and therefore give the erroneous impression that incest occurs predominantly in families at the lower end of the socioeconomic scale. This was not the case in the families of our victims. Of these, four fathers were blue-collar workers, two were white-collar workers, six were professionals, and the occupations of three were not known. The fathers' occupations cut across class lines. Several held jobs that required considerable personal competence and commanded social

Table 2

Characteristics of the Incest History

Characteristic	Incidence
Daughter's place in sibship:	
Oldest daughter	9
Only daughter	3
Middle or youngest daughter	1
Unknown	2
Daughter's age at onset of incestuous relationship (years):	
4	1
5	0
6	2
7	3
8	4
9	2
10	0
11	1
12	0
13	0
14	1
Unknown	1
Duration of incestuous relationship (years):	
Single incident	1
1–2	1
3–4	3
5–6	5
7–10	2
Unknown	3

respect: college administrator, policeman, army officer, engineer. Others were skilled workers, foremen, or managers in factories or offices. All the mothers were houseworkers. Five of the fifteen families could certainly be considered disorganized, with histories of poverty, unemployment, frequent moves, alcoholism, violence, abandonment and foster care. Not surprisingly, the women who came from these families were those who complained of the most severe distress. The majority of the families, however, were apparently intact and maintained a façade of respectability.

The Incestuous Family Constellation

Both the apparently intact and the disorganized families shared certain common features in the pattern of family relationships. The most striking was the almost uniform estrangement of the mother and daughter, an estrangement that preceded the occurrence of overt incest. Over half the mothers were partially incapacitated by physical or mental illness or alcoholism and either assumed an invalid role within the home or were periodically absent because of hospitalization. Their oldest daughters were often obliged to take over the household duties. Anne-Marie remembered being hidden from the truant officer by her mother so that she could stay home and take care of the younger children. Her mother had tuberculosis. Claire's mother, who was not ill, went to work to support the family because her father, a severe alcoholic, brought home no money. In her absence, Claire did the housework and cooking and cared for her older brother.

At best, these mothers were seen by their daughters as helpless, frail, downtrodden victims, who were unable to take care of themselves, much less to protect their children.

> ANNE-MARIE: She used to say, "give with one hand and you'll get with the other" but she gave with two hands and always went down. . . . She was nothing but a floor mat. She sold out herself and her self-respect. She was a love slave to my father.
>
> CLAIRE: I always felt sorry for her. She spent her life suffering, suffering, suffering.

Some of the mothers habitually confided in their oldest daughters and unburdened their troubles to them. Theresa felt her mother was "more like a sister." Joan's mother frequently clung to her and told her, "You're the only one who understands me." By contrast, the daughters felt unable to confide in their mothers. In particular, the daughters felt unable to go to their mothers for support or protection once their fathers had begun to make sexual advances to them. Some feared that their mothers would take action to expel the father from the house, but more commonly these daughters expected that their mothers would do nothing; in many cases the mothers tolerated a great deal of abuse themselves, and the daughters had learned not to expect any protection. Five of the women said they suspected that their mothers knew about the incest and tacitly condoned it. Two made attempts to bring up the subject but were put off by their mothers' denial or indifference.

Only two of the fifteen women actually told their mothers. Both had reason to regret it. Paula's mother reacted by committing her to an institution: "She was afraid I would become a lesbian or a whore." Sandra's mother initially took her husband to court. When she realized that a conviction would lead to his imprisonment, she reversed her testimony and publicly called her twelve-year-old daughter a "notorious liar and slut."

The message that these mothers transmitted over and over to their daughters was: your father first, you second. It is dangerous to fight back, for if I lose him I lose everything. For my own survival I must leave you to your own devices. I cannot defend you, and if necessary I will sacrifice you to your father.

At worst, the mother-daughter relations were marked by frank and open hostility. Some of the daughters stated they could remember no tenderness or caring in the relationship.

> MARTHA: She's always picking on me. She's so fuckin' cold.
> PAULA: She's an asshole. I really don't like my mom. I guess I am bitter. She's very selfish. She did a lousy job of bringing me up.

The most severe disruption in the mother-daughter relationship occurred in Rita's case. She remembers receiving severe beatings from her mother, and her father intervening to rescue her. Though the physical attacks were infrequent, Rita recalls her mother as implacably hostile and critical, and her father as by far the more nurturant parent.

Previous studies of incestuous families document the disturbance in the mother-daughter relationship as a constant finding.[24] In a study of eleven girls who were referred by courts to a child guidance center, Kaufman et al. reported that the girls uniformly saw their mothers as cruel, unjust and depriving, while the fathers were seen much more ambivalently: "These girls had long felt abandoned by the mother as a protective adult. This was their basic anxiety. . . . Though the original sexual experience with the father was at a genital level, the meaning of the sexual act was pregenital, and seemed to have the purpose of receiving some sort of parental interest."[25]

In contrast, almost all the victims expressed some warm feelings

24. Maisch.
25. Kaufman et al., p. 270.

toward their fathers. Many described them in much more favorable terms than their mothers. Some examples:

> ANNE-MARIE: A handsome devil.
> THERESA: Good with kids. An honest, decent guy.
> LENORE: He was my confidant.
> RITA: My savior.

Although it may seem odd to have expressed such attitudes toward blatantly authoritarian fathers, there are explanations. These were men whose presentation to the outside world made them liked and often respected members of the community. The daughters responded to their fathers' social status and power and derived satisfaction from being their fathers' favorites. They were "daddy's special girls," and often they were special to no one else. Feelings of pity for the fathers were also common, especially where the fathers had lost social status. The daughters seemed much more willing to forgive their fathers' failings and weaknesses than to forgive their mothers, or themselves.

> SANDRA: He was a sweet, decent man. My mother ruined him. I saw him lying in his bed in the hospital, and I kept thinking why don't they let him die. When he finally did, everyone cried at the funeral but me. I was glad he was dead. He had a miserable life. He had nothing. No one cared, not even me. I didn't help him much.

The daughters not only felt themselves abandoned by their mothers, but seemed to perceive their fathers as likewise deserted, and they felt the same pity for their fathers as they felt for themselves.

The victims rarely expressed anger toward their fathers, even about the incestuous act itself. Two of the three women who did express anger were women who had been repeatedly beaten as well as sexually abused by their fathers. Not surprisingly, they were angrier about the beatings than about the sexual act, which they viewed ambivalently. Most women expressed feelings of fear, disgust, and intense shame about the sexual contact and stated that they endured it because they felt they had no other choice. Several of the women stated that they learned to deal with the sexual approach by "tuning out" or pretending that it was not happening. Later, this response generalized to other relationships. Half of the women acknowledged, however, that they had felt some degree of pleasure in the sexual contact, a feeling which only increased their sense of guilt and confusion.

> KITTY: I was in love with my father. He called me his special girlfriend.

LENORE: The whole issue is very complicated. I was very attracted
to my father, and that just compounded the guilt.
PAULA: I was scared of him, but basically I liked him.

Though these women sometimes expressed a sense of disappointment and even contempt for their fathers, they did not feel as keenly the
sense of betrayal as they felt toward their mothers. Having abandoned
the hope of pleasing their mothers, they seemed relieved to have found
some way of pleasing their fathers and gaining their attention.

Susan Brownmiller, in her study of rape as a paradigm of relations
between men and women, refers briefly to father-daughter incest.
Stressing the coercive aspect of the situation, she calls it "father-rape."[26]
To label it thus is to understate the complexity of the relationship. The
father's sexual approach is clearly an abuse of power and authority, and
the daughter almost always understands it as such. But, unlike rape, it
occurs in the context of a caring relationship. The victim feels overwhelmed by her father's superior power and unable to resist him; she
may feel disgust, loathing, and shame. But at the same time she often
feels that this is the only kind of love she can get, and prefers it to no love
at all. The daughter is not raped, but seduced.

In fact, to describe what occurs as a rape is to minimize the harm to
the child, for what is involved here is not simply an assault, it is a betrayal. A woman who has been raped can cope with the experience in the
same way that she would react to any other intentionally cruel and harmful attack. She is not socially or psychologically dependent upon the
rapist. She is free to hate him. But the daughter who has been molested
is dependent on her father for protection and care. Her mother is not an
ally. She has no recourse. She does not dare express, or even feel, the
depths of her anger at being used. She must comply with her father's
demands or risk losing the parental love that she needs. She is not an
adult. She cannot walk out of the situation (though she may try to run
away). She must endure it, and find in it what compensations she can.

Although the victims reported that they felt helpless and powerless
against their fathers, the incestuous relationship did give them some
semblance of power within the family. Many of the daughters effectively
replaced their mothers and became their fathers' surrogate wives. They
were also deputy mothers to the younger children and were generally
given some authority over them. While they resented being exploited
and robbed of the freedom ordinarily granted to dependent children,
they did gain some feeling of value and importance from the role they
were given. Many girls felt an enormous sense of responsibility for holding the family together. They also knew that, as keepers of the incest
secret, they had an extraordinary power which could be used to destroy
the family. Their sexual contact with their fathers conferred on them a

26. S. Brownmiller, *Against Our Will: Men, Women and Rape* (New York: Simon &
Schuster, 1975), p. 281.

sense of possessing a dangerous, secret power over the lives of others, power which they derived from no other source. In this situation, keeping up appearances and doing whatever was necessary to maintain the integrity of the family became a necessary, expiating act at the same time that it increased the daughters' sense of isolation and shame.

> THERESA: I was mortified. My father and mother had fights so loud that you could hear them yelling all over the neighborhood. I used to think that my father was really yelling at my mother because she wouldn't give him sex. I felt I had to make it up to him.

What is most striking to us about this family constellation, in which the daughter replaces the mother in her traditional role, is the underlying assumption about that role shared apparently by all the family members. Customarily, a mother and wife in our society is one who nurtures and takes care of children and husband. If, for whatever reasons, the mother is unable to fulfill her ordinary functions, it is apparently assumed that some other female must be found to do it. The eldest daughter is a frequent choice. The father does not assume the wife's maternal role when she is incapacitated. He feels that his first right is to continue to receive the services which his wife formerly provided, sometimes including sexual services. He feels only secondarily responsible for giving care to his children. This view of the father's prerogative to be served not only is shared by the fathers and daughters in these families, but is often encouraged by societal attitudes. Fathers who feel abandoned by their wives are not generally expected or taught to assume primary parenting responsibilities. We should not find it surprising, then, that fathers occasionally turn to their daughters for services (domestic and sexual) that they had formerly expected of their wives.

The Victims

The fifteen women who reported their incest experiences were all clients in psychotherapy. That is to say, all had admitted to themselves and at least one other person that they were suffering and needed help. Although we do not know whether they speak for the vast majority of victims, some of their complaints are so similar that we believe that they represent a pattern common to most women who have endured prolonged sexual abuse in childhood at the hands of parents.

One of the most frequent complaints of the victims entering therapy was a sense of being different, and distant, from ordinary people. The sense of isolation and inability to make contact was expressed in many different ways:

> KITTY: I'm dead inside.
> LENORE: I have a problem getting close to people. I back off.
> LOIS: I can't communicate with anyone.

Their therapists described difficulty in forming relationships with them, confirming their assessment of themselves. Therapists frequently made comments like "I don't really know whether I'm in touch with her," or "she's one of the people that's been the hardest for me to figure out." These women complained that most of their relationships were superficial and empty, or else extremely conflictual. They expressed fear that they were unable to love. The sense of an absence of feeling was most marked in sexual relationships, although most women were sexually responsive in the narrow sense of the word; that is, capable of having orgasms.

In some cases, the suppression of feeling was clearly a defense which had been employed in the incestuous relationship in childhood. The distance or isolation of affect seemed originally to be a device set up as protection against the feelings aroused by the molesting father. One woman reported that when she "shut down," did not move or speak, her father would leave her alone. Another remembered that she would tell herself over and over "this isn't really happening" during the sexual episode. Passive resistance and dissociation of feeling seemed to be among the few defenses available in an overwhelming situation. Later, this carried over into relations with others.

The sense of distance and isolation which these women experienced was uniformly painful, and they made repeated, often desperate efforts to overcome it. Frequently, the result was a pattern of many brief unsatisfactory sexual contacts. Those relationships which did become more intense and lasting were fraught with difficulty.

Five of the seven married women complained of marital conflict, either feeling abused by their husbands or indifferent toward them. Those who were single or divorced uniformly complained of problems in their relationships with men. Some expressed negative feelings toward men in general:

> STEPHANIE: When I ride the bus I look at all the men and think, "all they want to do is stick their pricks into little girls."

Most, however, overvalued men and kept searching for a relationship with an idealized protector and sexual teacher who would take care of them and tell them what to do. Half the women had affairs during adolescence with older or married men. In these relationships, the sense of specialness, power, and secrecy of the incestuous relationship was regained. The men were seen as heroes and saviors.

In many cases, these women became intensely involved with men who were cruel, abusive, or neglectful, and tolerated extremes of mistreatment. Anne-Marie remained married for twenty years to a psychotic husband who beat her, terrorized their children, and never supported the family. She felt she could not leave him because he would fall apart without her. "We were his kingdom," she said, "to bully and beat." She eventually sought police protection and separation only after it was clear that her life was in danger. Her masochistic behavior in this relationship was all the more striking, since other areas of her life were relatively intact. She was a warm and generous mother, a valued worker, and an active, respected member of her community. Lois was raped at age nineteen by a stranger whom she married a week later. After this marriage ended in divorce, she began to frequent bars where she would pick up men who beat her repeatedly. She expressed no anger toward these men. Three other women in this group of fifteen were also rape victims. Only one expressed anger toward her attackers; the others felt they "deserved it." Some of the women recognized and commented on their predilection for abusive men. As Sandra put it: "I'm better off with a bum. I can handle that situation."

Why did these women feel they deserved to be beaten, raped, neglected, and used? The answer lies in their image of themselves. It is only through understanding how they perceived themselves that we can make sense of their often highly destructive relations with others. Almost every one of these fifteen women described herself as a "witch," "bitch," or "whore." They saw themselves as socially "branded" or "marked," even when no social exposure of their sexual relations had occurred or was likely to occur. They experienced themselves as powerful and dangerous to men: their self-image had almost a magical quality. Kitty, for instance, called herself a "devil's child," while Sandra compared herself to the twelve-year-old villainess of a popular melodrama, *The Exorcist,* a girl who was possessed by the devil. Some felt they were invested with special seductive prowess and could captivate men simply by looking at them. These daughters seemed almost uniformly to believe that they had seduced their fathers and therefore could seduce any man.

At one level, this sense of malignant power can be understood to have arisen as a defense against the child's feelings of utter helplessness. In addition, however, this self-image had been reinforced by the long-standing conspiratorial relationship with the father, in which the child had been elevated to the mother's position and did indeed have the power to destroy the family by exposing the incestuous secret.

Moreover, most of the victims were aware that they had experienced some pleasure in the incestuous relationship and had joined with their fathers in a shared hatred of their mothers. This led to intense feelings of shame, degradation, and worthlessness. Because they had enjoyed their fathers' attention and their mothers' defeat, these women felt responsible for the incestuous situation. Almost uniformly, they distrusted their own desires and needs and did not feel entitled to care and respect. Any relationship that afforded some kind of pleasure seemed to increase the sense of guilt and shame. These women constantly sought to expiate their guilt and relieve their shame by serving and giving to others and by observing the strictest and most rigorous codes of religion and morality. Any lapse from a rigid code of behavior was felt as confirming evidence of their innate evilness. Some of the women embraced their negative identity with a kind of defiance and pride. As Sandra boasted: "There's *nothing* I haven't done!"

Those women who were mothers themselves seemed to be preoccupied with the fear that they would be bad mothers to their children, as they felt their mothers had been to them. Several sought treatment when they began to be aware of feelings of rage and resentment toward their children, especially their daughters. Any indulgence in pleasure seeking or attention to personal needs reinforced their sense that they were "whores" and unfit mothers. In some, the fear of exposure took the form of a constant worry that the authorities would intervene to take the children away. Other mothers worried that they would not be able to protect their daughters from a repetition of the incest situation. As one victim testified:

> I could a been the biggest bum. My father called me a "big whore" and my mother believed him. I could a got so disgusted that I could a run around with anyone I saw. I met my husband and told him about my father and my child. He stuck by me and we was married. I got to the church and I'm not so shy like I was. It always come back to me that this thing might get on the front pages and people might know about it. I'm getting over it since the time I joined the church.

Her husband testified:

> The wife is nervous and she can't sleep. She gets up yesterday night about two o'clock in the morning and starts fixing the curtains. She works that way till five, then she sleeps like a rock. She's cold to me but she tells me she likes me. She gets cold once in a while and she don't know why herself. She watches me like a hawk with those kids. She don't want me to be loving with them and to be too open about sex. It makes her think of her old man. I got to take it easy with her or she blows up.[27]

In our opinion, the testimony of these victims, and the observations of their therapists, is convincing evidence that the incest experience was harmful to them and left long-lasting scars. Many victims had severely impaired object relations with both men and women. The overvaluation of men led them into conflictual and often intensely masochistic relationships with men. The victims' devaluation of themselves and their mothers impaired development of supportive friendships with women. Many of the victims also had a well-formed negative identity as witch,

27. Weinberg, pp. 151–52.

bitch, or whore. In adult life they continued to make repeated ineffective attempts to expiate their intense feelings of guilt and shame.

Therapy for the Incest Victim and Her Family

Very little is known about how to help the incest victim. If the incestuous secret is discovered while the victim is still living with her parents, the most common social intervention is the destruction of the family. This outcome is usually terrifying even to an exploited child, and most victims will cooperate with their fathers in maintaining secrecy rather than see their fathers jailed or risk being sent away from home.

We know of only one treatment program specifically designed for the rehabilitation of the incestuous family.[28] This program, which operates out of the probation department of the Santa Clara County Court in California, involves all members of the incestuous family in both individual and family therapy and benefits from a close working alliance with Daughters United, a self-help support group for victims. The program directors acknowledge that the coercive power of the court is essential for obtaining the cooperation of the fathers. An early therapeutic goal in this program is a confrontation between the daughter and her mother and father, in which they admit to her that she has been the victim of "poor parenting." This is necessary in order to relieve the daughter from her feeling of responsibility for the incest. Mothers appear to be more willing than fathers to admit this to their daughters.

Though this program offers a promising model for the treatment of the discovered incestuous family, it does not touch the problem of undetected incest. The vast majority of incest victims reach adulthood still bearing their secrets. Some will eventually enter psychotherapy. How can the therapist respond appropriately to their needs?

We believe that the male therapist may have great difficulty in validating the victim's experience and responding empathically to her suffering. Consciously or not, the male therapist will tend to identify with the father's position and therefore will tend to deny or excuse his behavior and project blame onto the victim. Here is an example of a male therapist's judgmental perception of an incest victim:

> This woman had had a great love and respect for her father until puberty when he had made several sexual advances toward her. In analysis she talked at first only of her good feelings toward him because she had blocked out the sexual episodes. When they were finally brought back into consciousness, all the fury returned which she had experienced at the age of thirteen. She felt that her father was an impotent, dirty old man who had taken advantage of

28. H. Giarretto, "Humanistic Treatment of Father-Daughter Incest," in *Child Abuse and Neglect—the Family and the Community,* ed. R. E. Helfer and C. H. Kemp (Cambridge, Mass.: Ballinger Publishing Co., 1976).

her trusting youthful innocence. From some of the details which she related of her relationship to her father, *it was obvious that she was not all that innocent.* [Our italics]²⁹

Not surprisingly, the client in this case became furious with her therapist, and therapy was unsuccessful.

If the male therapist identifies with the aggressor in the incest situation, it is also clear that the female therapist tends to identify with the victim and that this may limit her effectiveness. In a round-table discussion of experiences with incest victims, most of the contributing therapists acknowledged having shied away from a full and detailed exploration of the incestuous relationship. In some cases the therapist blatantly avoided the issue. In these cases, no trust was established in the relationship, and the client quickly discontinued therapy. In effect, the therapists had conveyed to these women that their secrets were indeed too terrible to share, thus reinforcing their already intense sense of isolation and shame.

Two possible explanations arise for the female therapist's flight. Traditional psychoanalytic theory might suggest that the therapist's own incestuous wishes and fantasies are too threatening for her to acknowledge. This might seem to be the most obvious reason for such a powerful countertransference phenomenon. The second reason, though less apparent, may be equally powerful: the female therapist confronting the incest victim reexperiences her own fear of her father and recognizes how easily she could have shared the victim's fate. We suspect that many women have been aware of, and frightened by, seductive behavior on the part of their own fathers. For every family in which incest is consummated there are undoubtedly hundreds with essentially similar, if less extreme, psychological dynamics. Thus the incest victim forces the female therapist to confront her own condition and to reexperience not only her infantile desires but also her (often realistic) childhood fears.

If the therapist overcomes this obstacle, and does not avoid addressing the issue with her client, another trap follows. As one therapist put it during the round-table discussion: "I get angry *for* her. How can she *not* be angry with her father?" Getting angry for a client is a notoriously unsuccessful intervention. Since the victim is more likely to feel rage toward the mother who abandoned her to her fate than toward her father, the therapeutic relationship must provide a place where the victim feels she can safely express her hostile feelings. Rage against the mother must be allowed to surface, for it is only when the client feels she can freely express her full range of feelings without driving the therapist away that she loses her sense of being malignantly "marked."

29. R. Stein, *Incest and Human Love: The Betrayal of the Soul in Psychotherapy* (New York: Third Press, 1973), pp. 45–46.

The feminist therapist may have particular difficulty facing the degree of estrangement between mother and daughter that occurs in these families. Committed as she is to building solidarity among women, she is bound to be distressed by the frequent histories of indifference, hostility, and cruelty in the mother-daughter relationship. She may find herself rushing to the defense of the mother, pointing out that the mother, herself, was a victim, and so on. This may be true, but not helpful. Rather than denying the situation or making excuses for anyone, the therapist must face the challenge that the incestuous family presents to all of us: How can we overcome the deep estrangement between mothers and daughters that frequently exists in our society, and how can we better provide for the security of both?

Beyond Therapy

For both social and psychological reasons, therapy alone seems to be an insufficient response to the situation of the incest victim. Because of its confidential nature, the therapy relationship does not lend itself to a full resolution of the issue of secrecy. The woman who feels herself to be the guardian of a terrible, almost magical secret may find considerable relief from her shame after sharing the secret with another person. However, the shared secrecy then recreates a situation similar to the original incestuous relationship. Instead of the victim alone against the world, there is the special dyad of the victim and her confidant. This, in fact, was a difficult issue for all the participants in our study, since the victims once again were the subject of special interest because of their sexual history.

The women's liberation movement has demonstrated repeatedly to the mental health profession that consciousness raising has often been more beneficial and empowering to women than psychotherapy. In particular, the public revelation of the many and ancient sexual secrets of women (orgasm, rape, abortion) may have contributed far more toward the liberation of women than the attempt to heal individual wounds through a restorative therapeutic relationship.

The same should be true for incest. The victims who feel like bitches, whores, and witches might feel greatly relieved if they felt less lonely, if their identities as the special guardians of a dreadful secret could be shed. Incest will begin to lose its devastating magic power when women begin to speak out about it publicly and realize how common it is.

We know that most cases do not come to the attention of therapists, and those that do, come years after the fact. Thus, as a social problem incest is clearly not amenable to a purely psychotherapeutic approach. Prevention, rather than treatment, seems to be indicated. On the basis of our study and the testimony of these victims, we favor all measures which strengthen and support the mother's role within the family, for it is clear that these daughters feel prey to their fathers' abuse when their mothers are too ill, weak, or downtrodden to protect them. We favor the strengthening of protective services for women and children, including adequate and dignified financial support for mothers, irrespective of their marital status; free, public, round-the-clock child care, and refuge facilities for women in crisis. We favor the vigorous enforcement (by female officials) of laws prohibiting the sexual abuse of children. Offenders should be isolated and reeducated. We see efforts to reintegrate fathers into the world of children as a positive development, but only on the condition that they learn more appropriate parental behavior. A seductive father is not much of an improvement over an abandoning or distant one.

As both Shulamith Firestone and Florence Rush have pointed out, the liberation of children is inseparable from our own.[30] In particular, as long as daughters are subject to seduction in childhood, no adult woman is free. Like prostitution and rape, we believe father-daughter incest will disappear only when male supremacy is ended.

Cambridgeport Problem Center (Hirschman)

Somerville Women's Mental Health Collective (Herman)

30. Shulamith Firestone, *The Dialectic of Sex: The Case for Feminist Revolution* (New York: Bantam Books, 1970); Florence Rush, "The Sexual Abuse of Children: A Feminist Point of View," in Connell and Wilson.

The Laugh of the Medusa

Hélène Cixous

Translated by Keith Cohen and Paula Cohen

I shall speak about women's writing: about *what it will do*. Woman must write her self: must write about women and bring women to writing, from which they have been driven away as violently as from their bodies—for the same reasons, by the same law, with the same fatal goal. Woman must put herself into the text—as into the world and into history—by her own movement.

The future must no longer be determined by the past. I do not deny that the effects of the past are still with us. But I refuse to strengthen them by repeating them, to confer upon them an irremovability the equivalent of destiny, to confuse the biological and the cultural. Anticipation is imperative.

Since these reflections are taking shape in an area just on the point of being discovered, they necessarily bear the mark of our time—a time during which the new breaks away from the old, and, more precisely, the (feminine) new from the old (*la nouvelle de l'ancien*). Thus, as there are no grounds for establishing a discourse, but rather an arid millennial ground to break, what I say has at least two sides and two aims: to break up, to destroy; and to foresee the unforeseeable, to project.

I write this as a woman, toward women. When I say "woman," I'm speaking of woman in her inevitable struggle against conventional man; and of a universal woman subject who must bring women to their senses

This is a revised version of "Le Rire de la Méduse," which appeared in *L'Arc* (1975), pp. 39–54.

and to their meaning in history. But first it must be said that in spite of the enormity of the repression that has kept them in the "dark"—that dark which people have been trying to make them accept as their attribute—there is, at this time, no general woman, no one typical woman. What they have *in common* I will say. But what strikes me is the infinite richness of their individual constitutions: you can't talk about *a* female sexuality, uniform, homogeneous, classifiable into codes—any more than you can talk about one unconscious resembling another. Women's imaginary is inexhaustible, like music, painting, writing: their stream of phantasms is incredible.

I have been amazed more than once by a description a woman gave me of a world all her own which she had been secretly haunting since early childhood. A world of searching, the elaboration of a knowledge, on the basis of a systematic experimentation with the bodily functions, a passionate and precise interrogation of her erotogeneity. This practice, extraordinarily rich and inventive, in particular as concerns masturbation, is prolonged or accompanied by a production of forms, a veritable aesthetic activity, each stage of rapture inscribing a resonant vision, a composition, something beautiful. Beauty will no longer be forbidden.

I wished that that woman would write and proclaim this unique empire so that other women, other unacknowledged sovereigns, might exclaim: I, too, overflow; my desires have invented new desires, my body knows unheard-of songs. Time and again I, too, have felt so full of luminous torrents that I could burst—burst with forms much more beautiful than those which are put up in frames and sold for a stinking fortune. And I, too, said nothing, showed nothing; I didn't open my mouth, I didn't repaint my half of the world. I was ashamed. I was afraid, and I swallowed my shame and my fear. I said to myself: You are mad! What's the meaning of these waves, these floods, these outbursts? Where is the ebullient, infinite woman who, immersed as she was in her naiveté, kept in the dark about herself, led into self-disdain by the great arm of parental-conjugal phallocentrism, hasn't been ashamed of her strength? Who, surprised and horrified by the fantastic tumult of her drives (for she was made to believe that a well-adjusted normal woman has a . . . divine composure), hasn't accused herself of being a monster? Who, feeling a funny desire stirring inside her (to sing, to write, to dare to speak, in short, to bring out something new), hasn't thought she was sick? Well, her shameful sickness is that she resists death, that she makes trouble.

And why don't you write? Write! Writing is for you, you are for you; your body is yours, take it. I know why you haven't written. (And why I didn't write before the age of twenty-seven.) Because writing is at once too high, too great for you, it's reserved for the great—that is, for "great men"; and it's "silly." Besides, you've written a little, but in secret. And it wasn't good, because it was in secret, and because you punished yourself for writing, because you didn't go all the way; or because you wrote, irresistibly, as when we would masturbate in secret, not to go further, but to attenuate the tension a bit, just enough to take the edge off. And then as soon as we come, we go and make ourselves feel guilty—so as to be forgiven; or to forget, to bury it until the next time.

Write, let no one hold you back, let nothing stop you: not man; not the imbecilic capitalist machinery, in which publishing houses are the crafty, obsequious relayers of imperatives handed down by an economy that works against us and off our backs; and not *yourself*. Smug-faced readers, managing editors, and big bosses don't like the true texts of women—female-sexed texts. That kind scares them.

I write woman: woman must write woman. And man, man. So only an oblique consideration will be found here of man; it's up to him to say where his masculinity and femininity are at: this will concern us once men have opened their eyes and seen themselves clearly.[1]

Now women return from afar, from always: from "without," from the heath where witches are kept alive; from below, from beyond "culture"; from their childhood which men have been trying desperately to make them forget, condemning it to "eternal rest." The little girls and their "ill-mannered" bodies immured, well-preserved, intact unto themselves, in the mirror. Frigidified. But are they ever seething underneath! What an effort it takes—there's no end to it—for the sex cops to bar their threatening return. Such a display of forces on both sides that the struggle has for centuries been immobilized in the trembling equilibrium of a deadlock.

Here they are, returning, arriving over and again, because the unconscious is impregnable. They have wandered around in circles, confined to the narrow room in which they've been given a deadly brainwashing. You can incarcerate them, slow them down, get away with the old Apartheid routine, but for a time only. As soon as they begin to speak, at the same time as they're taught their name, they can be taught that their territory is black: because you are Africa, you are black. Your

---

1. Men still have everything to say about their sexuality, and everything to write. For what they have said so far, for the most part, stems from the opposition activity/passivity, from the power relation between a fantasized obligatory virility meant to invade, to colonize, and the consequential phantasm of woman as a "dark continent" to penetrate and to "pacify." (We know what "pacify" means in terms of scotomizing the other and misrecognizing the self.) Conquering her, they've made haste to depart from her borders, to get out of sight, out of body. The way man has of getting out of himself and into her whom he takes not for the other but for his own, deprives him, he knows, of his own bodily territory. One can understand how man, confusing himself with his penis and rushing in for the attack, might feel resentment and fear of being "taken" by the woman, of being lost in her, absorbed, or alone.

continent is dark. Dark is dangerous. You can't see anything in the dark, you're afraid. Don't move, you might fall. Most of all, don't go into the forest. And so we have internalized this horror of the dark.

Men have committed the greatest crime against women. Insidiously, violently, they have led them to hate women, to be their own enemies, to mobilize their immense strength against themselves, to be the executants of their virile needs. They have made for women an antinarcissism! A narcissism which loves itself only to be loved for what women haven't got! They have constructed the infamous logic of antilove.

We the precocious, we the repressed of culture, our lovely mouths gagged with pollen, our wind knocked out of us, we the labyrinths, the ladders, the trampled spaces, the bevies—we are black and we are beautiful.

We're stormy, and that which is ours breaks loose from us without our fearing any debilitation. Our glances, our smiles, are spent; laughs exude from all our mouths; our blood flows and we extend ourselves without ever reaching an end; we never hold back our thoughts, our signs, our writing; and we're not afraid of lacking.

What happiness for us who are omitted, brushed aside at the scene of inheritances; we inspire ourselves and we expire without running out of breath, we are everywhere!

From now on, who, if we say so, can say no to us? We've come back from always.

It is time to liberate the New Woman from the Old by coming to know her—by loving her for getting by, for getting beyond the Old without delay, by going out ahead of what the New Woman will be, as an arrow quits the bow with a movement that gathers and separates the vibrations musically, in order to be more than her self.

I say that we must, for, with a few rare exceptions, there has not yet been any writing that inscribes femininity; exceptions so rare, in fact, that, after plowing through literature across languages, cultures, and ages,[2] one can only be startled at this vain scouting mission. It is well known that the number of women writers (while having increased very slightly from the nineteenth century on) has always been ridiculously small. This is a useless and deceptive fact unless from their species of female writers we do not first deduct the immense majority whose workmanship is in no way different from male writing, and which either obscures women or reproduces the classic representations of women (as sensitive—intuitive—dreamy, etc.)[3]

2. I am speaking here only of the place "reserved" for women by the Western world.

3. Which works, then, might be called feminine? I'll just point out some examples: one would have to give them full readings to bring out what is pervasively feminine in their significance. Which I shall do elsewhere. In France (have you noted our infinite poverty in this field?—the Anglo-Saxon countries have shown resources of distinctly greater consequence), leafing through what's come out of the twentieth century—and it's not much—the

Let me insert here a parenthetical remark. I mean it when I speak of male writing. I maintain unequivocally that there is such a thing as *marked* writing; that, until now, far more extensively and repressively than is ever suspected or admitted, writing has been run by a libidinal and cultural—hence political, typically masculine—economy; that this is a locus where the repression of women has been perpetuated, over and over, more or less consciously, and in a manner that's frightening since it's often hidden or adorned with the mystifying charms of fiction; that this locus has grossly exaggerated all the signs of sexual opposition (and not sexual difference), where woman has never *her* turn to speak—this being all the more serious and unpardonable in that writing is precisely *the very possibility of change,* the space that can serve as a springboard for subversive thought, the precursory movement of a transformation of social and cultural structures.

Nearly the entire history of writing is confounded with the history of reason, of which it is at once the effect, the support, and one of the privileged alibis. It has been one with the phallocentric tradition. It is indeed that same self-admiring, self-stimulating, self-congratulatory phallocentrism.

With some exceptions, for there have been failures—and if it weren't for them, I wouldn't be writing (I-woman, escapee)—in that enormous machine that has been operating and turning out its "truth" for centuries. There have been poets who would go to any lengths to slip something by at odds with tradition—men capable of loving love and hence capable of loving others and of wanting them, of imagining the woman who would hold out against oppression and constitute herself as a superb, equal, hence "impossible" subject, untenable in a real social framework. Such a woman the poet could desire only by breaking the codes that negate her. Her appearance would necessarily bring on, if not revolution—for the bastion was supposed to be immutable—at least harrowing explosions. At times it is in the fissure caused by an earthquake, through that radical mutation of things brought on by a material upheaval when every structure is for a moment thrown off balance and an ephemeral wildness sweeps order away, that the poet slips something by, for a brief span, of woman. Thus did Kleist expend himself in his yearning for the existence of sister-lovers, maternal daughters, mother-sisters, who never hung their heads in shame. Once the palace of magistrates is restored, it's time to pay: immediate bloody death to the uncontrollable elements.

But only the poets—not the novelists, allies of representationalism. Because poetry involves gaining strength through the unconscious and

---

only inscriptions of femininity that I have seen were by Colette, Marguerite Duras, . . . and Jean Genêt.

because the unconscious, that other limitless country, is the place where the repressed manage to survive: women, or as Hoffmann would say, fairies.

She must write her self, because this is the invention of a *new insurgent* writing which, when the moment of her liberation has come, will allow her to carry out the indispensable ruptures and transformations in her history, first at two levels that cannot be separated.

a) Individually. By writing her self, woman will return to the body which has been more than confiscated from her, which has been turned into the uncanny stranger on display—the ailing or dead figure, which so often turns out to be the nasty companion, the cause and location of inhibitions. Censor the body and you censor breath and speech at the same time.

Write your self. Your body must be heard. Only then will the immense resources of the unconscious spring forth. Our naphtha will spread, throughout the world, without dollars—black or gold —nonassessed values that will change the rules of the old game.

To write. An act which will not only "realize" the decensored relation of woman to her sexuality, to her womanly being, giving her access to her native strength; it will give her back her goods, her pleasures, her organs, her immense bodily territories which have been kept under seal; it will tear her away from the superegoized structure in which she has always occupied the place reserved for the guilty (guilty of everything, guilty at every turn: for having desires, for not having any; for being frigid, for being "too hot"; for not being both at once; for being too motherly and not enough; for having children and for not having any; for nursing and for not nursing . . .)—tear her away by means of this research, this job of analysis and illumination, this emancipation of the marvelous text of her self that she must urgently learn to speak. A woman without a body, dumb, blind, can't possibly be a good fighter. She is reduced to being the servant of the militant male, his shadow. We must kill the false woman who is preventing the live one from breathing. Inscribe the breath of the whole woman.

b) An act that will also be marked by woman's *seizing* the occasion to *speak*, hence her shattering entry into history, which has always been based *on her suppression*. To write and thus to forge for herself the antilogos weapon. To become *at will* the taker and initiator, for her own right, in every symbolic system, in every political process.

It is time for women to start scoring their feats in written and oral language.

Every woman has known the torment of getting up to speak. Her heart racing, at times entirely lost for words, ground and language slipping away—that's how daring a feat, how great a transgression it is for a woman to speak—even just open her mouth—in public. A double distress, for even if she transgresses, her words fall almost always upon the deaf male ear, which hears in language only that which speaks in the masculine.

It is by writing, from and toward women, and by taking up the challenge of speech which has been governed by the phallus, that women will confirm women in a place other than that which is reserved in and by the symbolic, that is, in a place other than silence. Women should break out of the snare of silence. They shouldn't be conned into accepting a domain which is the margin or the harem.

Listen to a woman speak at a public gathering (if she hasn't painfully lost her wind). She doesn't "speak," she throws her trembling body forward; she lets go of herself, she flies; all of her passes into her voice, and it's with her body that she vitally supports the "logic" of her speech. Her flesh speaks true. She lays herself bare. In fact, she physically materializes what she's thinking; she signifies it with her body. In a certain way she *inscribes* what she's saying, because she doesn't deny her drives the intractable and impassioned part they have in speaking. Her speech, even when "theoretical" or political, is never simple or linear or "objectified," generalized: she draws her story into history.

There is not that scission, that division made by the common man between the logic of oral speech and the logic of the text, bound as he is by his antiquated relation—servile, calculating—to mastery. From which proceeds the niggardly lip service which engages only the tiniest part of the body, plus the mask.

In women's speech, as in their writing, that element which never stops resonating, which, once we've been permeated by it, profoundly and imperceptibly touched by it, retains the power of moving us—that element is the song: first music from the first voice of love which is alive in every woman. Why this privileged relationship with the voice? Because no woman stockpiles as many defenses for countering the drives as does a man. You don't build walls around yourself, you don't forego pleasure as "wisely" as he. Even if phallic mystification has generally contaminated good relationships, a woman is never far from "mother" (I mean outside her role functions: the "mother" as nonname and as source of goods). There is always within her at least a little of that good mother's milk. She writes in white ink.

Woman for women.—There always remains in woman that force which produces/is produced by the other—in particular, the other woman. *In* her, matrix, cradler; herself giver as her mother and child; she is her own sister-daughter. You might object, "What about she who is the hysterical offspring of a bad mother?" Everything will be changed once woman gives woman to the other woman. There is hidden and always ready in woman the source; the locus for the other. The mother, too, is a metaphor. It is necessary and sufficient that the best of herself be given to woman by another woman for her to be able to love herself and return in love the body that was "born" to her. Touch me, caress me, you the living no-name, give me my self as myself. The relation to the "mother," in terms of intense pleasure and violence, is curtailed no more than the relation to childhood (the child that she was, that she is, that she makes, remakes, undoes, there at the point where, the same, she others herself). Text: my body—shot through with streams of song; I don't mean the overbearing, clutchy "mother" but, rather, what touches you, the equivoice that affects you, fills your breast with an urge to come to language and launches your force; the rhythm that laughs you; the intimate recipient who makes all metaphors possible and desirable; body (body? bodies?), no more describable than god, the soul, or the Other; that part of you that leaves a space between yourself and urges you to inscribe in language your woman's style. In women there is always more or less of the mother who makes everything all right, who nourishes, and who stands up against separation; a force that will not be cut off but will knock the wind out of the codes. We will rethink womankind beginning with every form and every period of her body. The Americans remind us, "We are all Lesbians"; that is, don't denigrate woman, don't make of her what men have made of you.

Because the "economy" of her drives is prodigious, she cannot fail, in seizing the occasion to speak, to transform directly and indirectly *all* systems of exchange based on masculine thrift. Her libido will produce far more radical effects of political and social change than some might like to think.

Because she arrives, vibrant, over and again, we are at the beginning of a new history, or rather of a process of becoming in which several histories intersect with one another. As subject for history, woman always occurs simultaneously in several places. Woman un-thinks[4] the unifying, regulating history that homogenizes and channels forces, herding contradictions into a single battlefield. In woman, personal history blends together with the history of all women, as well as national and world history. As a militant, she is an integral part of all liberations. She must be farsighted, not limited to a blow-by-blow interaction. She foresees that her liberation will do more than modify power relations or toss the ball over to the other camp; she will bring about a mutation in human relations, in thought, in all praxis: hers is not simply a class struggle, which she carries forward into a much vaster movement. Not that in order to be a woman-in-struggle(s) you have to leave the class struggle or repudiate it; but you have to split it open, spread it out, push it forward, fill it with the fundamental struggle so as to prevent the class struggle, or any other struggle for the liberation of a class or people, from operating as a form of repression, pretext for postponing the inevitable, the staggering alteration in power relations and in the pro-

---

4. "*Dé-pense*," a neologism formed on the verb *penser*, hence "unthinks," but also "spends" (from *dépenser*) (translator's note).

duction of individualities. This alteration is already upon us—in the United States, for example, where millions of night crawlers are in the process of undermining the family and disintegrating the whole of American sociality.

The new history is coming; it's not a dream, though it does extend beyond men's imagination, and for good reason. It's going to deprive them of their conceptual orthopedics, beginning with the destruction of their enticement machine.

It is impossible to *define* a feminine practice of writing, and this is an impossibility that will remain, for this practice can never be theorized, enclosed, coded—which doesn't mean that it doesn't exist. But it will always surpass the discourse that regulates the phallocentric system; it does and will take place in areas other than those subordinated to philosophico-theoretical domination. It will be conceived of only by subjects who are breakers of automatisms, by peripheral figures that no authority can ever subjugate.

Hence the necessity to affirm the flourishes of this writing, to give form to its movement, its near and distant byways. Bear in mind to begin with (1) that sexual opposition, which has always worked for man's profit to the point of reducing writing, too, to his laws, is only a historico-cultural limit. There is, there will be more and more rapidly pervasive now, a fiction that produces irreducible effects of femininity. (2) That it is through ignorance that most readers, critics, and writers of both sexes hesitate to admit or deny outright the possibility or the pertinence of a distinction between feminine and masculine writing. It will usually be said, thus disposing of sexual difference: either that all writing, to the extent that it materializes, is feminine; or, inversely—but it comes to the same thing—that the act of writing is equivalent to masculine masturbation (and so the woman who writes cuts herself out a paper penis); or that writing is bisexual, hence neuter, which again does away with differentiation. To admit that writing is precisely working (in) the in-between, inspecting the process of the same and of the other without which nothing can live, undoing the work of death—to admit this is first to want the two, as well as both, the ensemble of the one and the other, not fixed in sequences of struggle and expulsion or some other form of death but infinitely dynamized by an incessant process of exchange from one subject to another. A process of different subjects knowing one another and beginning one another anew only from the living boundaries of the other: a multiple and inexhaustible course with millions of encounters and transformations of the same into the other and into the in-between, from which woman takes her forms (and man, in his turn; but that's his other history).

In saying "bisexual, hence neuter," I am referring to the classic conception of bisexuality, which, squashed under the emblem of castration fear and along with the fantasy of a "total" being (though composed of two halves), would do away with the difference experienced as an operation incurring loss, as the mark of dreaded sectility.

To this self-effacing, merger-type bisexuality, which would conjure away castration (the writer who puts up his sign: "bisexual written here, come and see," when the odds are good that it's neither one nor the other), I oppose the *other bisexuality* on which every subject not enclosed in the false theater of phallocentric representationalism has founded his/her erotic universe. Bisexuality: that is, each one's location in self (*répérage en soi*) of the presence—variously manifest and insistent according to each person, male or female—of both sexes, nonexclusion either of the difference or of one sex, and, from this "self-permission," multiplication of the effects of the inscription of desire, over all parts of my body and the other body.

Now it happens that at present, for historico-cultural reasons, it is women who are opening up to and benefiting from this vatic bisexuality which doesn't annul differences but stirs them up, pursues them, increases their number. In a certain way, "woman is bisexual"; man—it's a secret to no one—being poised to keep glorious phallic monosexuality in view. By virtue of affirming the primacy of the phallus and of bringing it into play, phallocratic ideology has claimed more than one victim. As a woman, I've been clouded over by the great shadow of the scepter and been told: idolize it, that which you cannot brandish. But at the same time, man has been handed that grotesque and scarcely enviable destiny (just imagine) of being reduced to a single idol with clay balls. And consumed, as Freud and his followers note, by a fear of being a woman! For, if psychoanalysis was constituted from woman, to repress femininity (and not so successful a repression at that—men have made it clear), its account of masculine sexuality is now hardly refutable; as with all the "human" sciences, it reproduces the masculine view, of which it is one of the effects.

Here we encounter the inevitable man-with-rock, standing erect in his old Freudian realm, in the way that, to take the figure back to the point where linguistics is conceptualizing it "anew," Lacan preserves it in the sanctuary of the phallos (ϕ) "sheltered" from *castration's lack*! Their "symbolic" exists, it holds power—we, the sowers of disorder, know it only too well. But we are in no way obliged to deposit our lives in their banks of lack, to consider the constitution of the subject in terms of a drama manglingly restaged, to reinstate again and again the religion of the father. Because we don't want that. We don't fawn around the supreme hole. We have no womanly reason to pledge allegiance to the negative. The feminine (as the poets suspected) affirms: ". . . And yes," says Molly, carrying *Ulysses* off beyond any book and toward the new writing; "I said yes, I will Yes."

The Dark Continent is neither dark nor unexplorable. —It is still unexplored only because we've been made to believe that it was too dark to be explorable. And because they want to make us believe that what interests us is the white continent, with its monuments to Lack. And we believed. They riveted us between two horrifying myths: between the Medusa and the abyss. That would be enough to set half the world laughing, except that it's still going on. For the phallologocentric sublation[5] is with us, and it's militant, regenerating the old patterns, anchored in the dogma of castration. They haven't changed a thing: they've theorized their desire for reality! Let the priests tremble, we're going to show them our sexts!

Too bad for them if they fall apart upon discovering that women aren't men, or that the mother doesn't have one. But isn't this fear convenient for them? Wouldn't the worst be, isn't the worst, in truth, that women aren't castrated, that they have only to stop listening to the Sirens (for the Sirens were men) for history to change its meaning? You only have to look at the Medusa straight on to see her. And she's not deadly. She's beautiful and she's laughing.

Men say that there are two unrepresentable things: death and the feminine sex. That's because they need femininity to be associated with death; it's the jitters that gives them a hard-on! for themselves! They need to be afraid of us. Look at the trembling Perseuses moving backward toward us, clad in apotropes. What lovely backs! Not another minute to lose. Let's get out of here.

Let's hurry: the continent is not impenetrably dark. I've been there often. I was overjoyed one day to run into Jean Genêt. It was in *Pompes funèbres*.[6] He had come there led by his Jean. There are some men (all too few) who aren't afraid of femininity.

Almost everything is yet to be written by women about femininity: about their sexuality, that is, its infinite and mobile complexity, about their eroticization, sudden turn-ons of a certain miniscule-immense area of their bodies; not about destiny, but about the adventure of such and such a drive, about trips, crossings, trudges, abrupt and gradual awakenings, discoveries of a zone at one time timorous and soon to be forthright. A woman's body, with its thousand and one thresholds of ardor—once, by smashing yokes and censors, she lets it articulate the profusion of meanings that run through it in every direction—will make the old single-grooved mother tongue reverberate with more than one language.

We've been turned away from our bodies, shamefully taught to ignore them, to strike them with that stupid sexual modesty; we've been made victims of the old fool's game: each one will love the other sex. I'll give you your body and you'll give me mine. But who are the men who give women the body that women blindly yield to them? Why so few

---

5. Standard English term for the Hegelian *Aufhebung,* the French *la relève.*
6. Jean Genêt, *Pompes funèbres* (Paris, 1948), p. 185.

texts? Because so few women have as yet won back their body. Women must write through their bodies, they must invent the impregnable language that will wreck partitions, classes, and rhetorics, regulations and codes, they must submerge, cut through, get beyond the ultimate reserve-discourse, including the one that laughs at the very idea of pronouncing the word "silence," the one that, aiming for the impossible, stops short before the word "impossible" and writes it as "the end."

Such is the strength of women that, sweeping away syntax, breaking that famous thread (just a tiny little thread, they say) which acts for men as a surrogate umbilical cord, assuring them—otherwise they couldn't come—that the old lady is always right behind them, watching them make phallus, women will go right up to the impossible.

When the "repressed" of their culture and their society returns, it's an explosive, *utterly* destructive, staggering return, with a force never yet unleashed and equal to the most forbidding of suppressions. For when the Phallic period comes to an end, women will have been either annihilated or borne up to the highest and most violent incandescence. Muffled throughout their history, they have lived in dreams, in bodies (though muted), in silences, in aphonic revolts.

And with such force in their fragility; a fragility, a vulnerability, equal to their incomparable intensity. Fortunately, they haven't sublimated; they've saved their skin, their energy. They haven't worked at liquidating the impasse of lives without futures. They have furiously inhabited these sumptuous bodies: admirable hysterics who made Freud succumb to many voluptuous moments impossible to confess, bombarding his Mosaic statue with their carnal and passionate body words, haunting him with their inaudible and thundering denunciations, dazzling, more than naked underneath the seven veils of modesty. Those who, with a single word of the body, have inscribed the vertiginous immensity of a history which is sprung like an arrow from the whole history of men and from biblico-capitalist society, are the women, the supplicants of yesterday, who come as forebears of the new women, after whom no intersubjective relation will ever be the same. You, Dora, you the indomitable, the poetic body, you are the true "mistress" of the Signifier. Before long your efficacity will be seen at work when your speech is no longer suppressed, its point turned in against your breast, but written out over against the other.

In body.—More so than men who are coaxed toward social success, toward sublimation, women are body. More body, hence more writing. For a long time it has been in body that women have responded to persecution, to the familial-conjugal enterprise of domestication, to the repeated attempts at castrating them. Those who have turned their tongues 10,000 times seven times before not speaking are either dead

from it or more familiar with their tongues and their mouths than anyone else. Now, I-woman am going to blow up the Law: an explosion
henceforth possible and ineluctable; let it be done, right now, *in*
language.

Let us not be trapped by an analysis still encumbered with the old
automatisms. It's not to be feared that language conceals an invincible
adversary, because it's the language of men and their grammar. We
mustn't leave them a single place that's any more theirs alone than we
are.

If woman has always functioned "within" the discourse of man, a
signifier that has always referred back to the opposite signifier which
annihilates its specific energy and diminishes or stifles its very different
sounds, it is time for her to dislocate this "within," to explode it, turn it
around, and seize it; to make it hers, containing it, taking it in her own
mouth, biting that tongue with her very own teeth to invent for herself a
language to get inside of. And you'll see with what ease she will spring
forth from that "within"—the "within" where once she so drowsily
crouched—to overflow at the lips she will cover the foam.

Nor is the point to appropriate their instruments, their concepts,
their places, or to begrudge them their position of mastery. Just because
there's a risk of identification doesn't mean that we'll succumb. Let's
leave it to the worriers, to masculine anxiety and its obsession with how
to dominate the way things work—knowing "how it works" in order to
"make it work." For us the point is not to take possession in order to
internalize or manipulate, but rather to dash through and to "fly."[7]

Flying is woman's gesture—flying in language and making it fly. We
have all learned the art of flying and its numerous techniques; for centuries we've been able to possess anything only by flying; we've lived in
flight, stealing away, finding, when desired, narrow passageways, hidden
crossovers. It's no accident that *voler* has a double meaning, that it plays
on each of them and thus throws off the agents of sense. It's no accident:
women take after birds and robbers just as robbers take after women
and birds. They (*illes*)[8] go by, fly the coop, take pleasure in jumbling the
order of space, in disorienting it, in changing around the furniture,
dislocating things and values, breaking them all up, emptying structures,
and turning propriety upside down.

What woman hasn't flown/stolen? Who hasn't felt, dreamt, per-,
formed the gesture that jams sociality? Who hasn't crumbled, held up to
ridicule, the bar of separation? Who hasn't inscribed with her body the
differential, punctured the system of couples and opposition? Who, by

7. Also, "to steal." Both meanings of the verb *voler* are played on, as the text itself
explains in the following paragraph (translator's note).

8. *Illes* is a fusion of the masculine pronoun *ils*, which refers back to birds and
robbers, with the feminine pronoun *elles*, which refers to women (translator's note).

some act of transgression, hasn't overthrown successiveness, connection, the wall of circumfusion?

A feminine text cannot fail to be more than subversive. It is volcanic; as it is written it brings about an upheaval of the old property crust, carrier of masculine investments; there's no other way. There's no room for her if she's not a he. If she's a her-she, it's in order to smash everything, to shatter the framework of institutions, to blow up the law, to break up the "truth" with laughter.

For once she blazes *her* trail in the symbolic, she cannot fail to make of it the chaosmos of the "personal"—in her pronouns, her nouns, and her clique of referents. And for good reason. There will have been the long history of gynocide. This is known by the colonized peoples of yesterday, the workers, the nations, the species off whose backs the history of men has made its gold; those who have known the ignominy of persecution derive from it an obstinate future desire for grandeur; those who are locked up know better than their jailers the taste of free air. Thanks to their history, women today know (how to do and want) what men will be able to conceive of only much later. I say woman overturns the "personal," for if, by means of laws, lies, blackmail, and marriage, her right to herself has been extorted at the same time as her name, she has been able, through the very movement of mortal alienation, to see more closely the inanity of "propriety," the reductive stinginess of the masculine-conjugal subjective economy, which she doubly resists. On the one hand she has constituted herself necessarily as that "person" capable of losing a part of herself without losing her integrity. But secretly, silently, deep down inside, she grows and multiplies, for, on the other hand, she knows far more about living and about the relation between the economy of the drives and the management of the ego than any man. Unlike man, who holds so dearly to his title and his titles, his pouches of value, his cap, crown, and everything connected with his head, woman couldn't care less about the fear of decapitation (or castration), adventuring, without the masculine temerity, into anonymity, which she can merge with without annihilating herself: because she's a giver.

I shall have a great deal to say about the whole deceptive problematic of the gift. Woman is obviously not that woman Nietzsche dreamed of who gives only in order to.[9] Who could ever think of the gift as a gift-that-takes? Who else but man, precisely the one who would like to take everything?

9. Reread Derrida's text, "Le Style de la femme," in *Nietzsche aujourd'hui* (Paris: Union Générale d'Editions, Coll. 10/18), where the philosopher can be seen operating an *Aufhebung* of all philosophy in its systematic reducing of woman to the place of seduction: she appears as the one who is taken for; the bait in person, all veils unfurled, the one who doesn't give but who gives only in order to (take).

If there is a "propriety of woman," it is paradoxically her capacity to depropriate unselfishly: body without end, without appendage, without principal "parts." If she is a whole, it's a whole composed of parts that are wholes, not simple partial objects but a moving, limitlessly changing ensemble, a cosmos tirelessly traversed by Eros, an immense astral space not organized around any one sun that's any more of a star than the others.

This doesn't mean that she's an undifferentiated magma, but that she doesn't lord it over her body or her desire. Though masculine sexuality gravitates around the penis, engendering that centralized body (in political anatomy) under the dictatorship of its parts, woman does not bring about the same regionalization which serves the couple head/genitals and which is inscribed only within boundaries. Her libido is cosmic, just as her unconscious is worldwide. Her writing can only keep going, without ever inscribing or discerning contours, daring to make these vertiginous crossings of the other(s) ephemeral and passionate sojourns in him, her, them, whom she inhabits long enough to look at from the point closest to their unconscious from the moment they awaken, to love them at the point closest to their drives; and then further, impregnated through and through with these brief, identificatory embraces, she goes and passes into infinity. She alone dares and wishes to know from within, where she, the outcast, has never ceased to hear the resonance of fore-language. She lets the other language speak—the language of 1,000 tongues which knows neither enclosure nor death. To life she refuses nothing. Her language does not contain, it carries; it does not hold back, it makes possible. When id is ambiguously uttered—the wonder of being several—she doesn't defend herself against these unknown women whom she's surprised at becoming, but derives pleasure from this gift of alterability. I am spacious, singing flesh, on which is grafted no one knows which I, more or less human, but alive because of transformation.

Write! and your self-seeking text will know itself better than flesh and blood, rising, insurrectionary dough kneading itself, with sonorous, perfumed ingredients, a lively combination of flying colors, leaves, and rivers plunging into the sea we feed. "Ah, there's her sea," he will say as he holds out to me a basin full of water from the little phallic mother from whom he's inseparable. But look, our seas are what we make of them, full of fish or not, opaque or transparent, red or black, high or smooth, narrow or bankless; and we are ourselves sea, sand, coral, seaweed, beaches, tides, swimmers, children, waves. . . . More or less wavily sea, earth, sky—what matter would rebuff us? We know how to speak them all.

Heterogeneous, yes. For her joyous benefit she is erogenous; she is the erotogeneity of the heterogeneous: airborne swimmer, in flight, she does not cling to herself; she is dispersible, prodigious, stunning, desirous and capable of others, of the other woman that she will be, of the other woman she isn't, of him, of you.

Woman be unafraid of any other place, of any same, or any other. My eyes, my tongue, my ears, my nose, my skin, my mouth, my body-for-(the)-other—not that I long for it in order to fill up a hole, to provide against some defect of mine, or because, as fate would have it, I'm spurred on by feminine "jealousy"; not because I've been dragged into the whole chain of substitutions that brings that which is substituted back to its ultimate object. That sort of thing you would expect to come straight out of "Tom Thumb," out of the *Penisneid* whispered to us by old grandmother ogresses, servants to their father-sons. If they believe, in order to muster up some self-importance, if they really need to believe that we're dying of desire, that we are this hole fringed with desire for their penis—that's their immemorial business. Undeniably (we verify it at our own expense—but also to our amusement), it's their business to let us know they're getting a hard-on, so that we'll assure them (we the maternal mistresses of their little pocket signifier) that they still can, that it's still there—that men structure themselves only by being fitted with a feather. In the child it's not the penis that the woman desires, it's not that famous bit of skin around which every man gravitates. Pregnancy cannot be traced back, except within the historical limits of the ancients, to some form of fate, to those mechanical substitutions brought about by the unconscious of some eternal "jealous woman"; not to penis envies; and not to narcissism or to some sort of homosexuality linked to the ever-present mother! Begetting a child doesn't mean that the woman or the man must fall ineluctably into patterns or must recharge the circuit of reproduction. If there's a risk there's not an inevitable trap: may women be spared the pressure, under the guise of consciousness-raising, of a supplement of interdictions. Either you want a kid or you don't—*that's your business.* Let nobody threaten you; in satisfying your desire, let not the fear of becoming the accomplice to a sociality succeed the old-time fear of being "taken." And man, are you still going to bank on everyone's blindness and passivity, afraid lest the child make a father and, consequently, that in having a kid the woman land herself more than one bad deal by engendering all at once child—mother—father—family? No; it's up to you to break the old circuits. It will be up to man and woman to render obsolete the former relationship and all its consequences, to consider the launching of a brand-new subject, alive, with defamilialization. Let us demater-paternalize rather than deny woman, in an effort to avoid the co-optation of procreation, a thrilling era of the body. Let us defetishize. Let's get away from the dialectic which has it that the only good father is a dead one, or that the child is the death of his parents. The child is the other, but the other without violence, bypassing loss, struggle. We're fed up with the reuniting of bonds forever to be severed, with the litany of castration that's handed down and genealogized. We won't advance backward anymore; we're not going to repress something so simple as the desire for life. Oral drive, anal drive, vocal drive—all these drives are our strengths, and among them is the gestation drive —just like the desire to write: a desire to live self from within, a desire for the swollen belly, for language, for blood. We are not going to refuse, if it should happen to strike our fancy, the unsurpassed pleasures of pregnancy which have actually been always exaggerated or conjured away—or cursed—in the classic texts. For if there's one thing that's been repressed here's just the place to find it: in the taboo of the pregnant woman. This says a lot about the power she seems invested with at the time, because it has always been suspected, that, when pregnant, the woman not only doubles her market value, but—what's more important—takes on intrinsic value as a woman in her own eyes and, undeniably, acquires body and sex.

There are thousands of ways of living one's pregnancy; to have or not to have with that still invisible other a relationship of another intensity. And if you don't have that particular yearning, it doesn't mean that you're in any way lacking. Each body distributes in its own special way, without model or norm, the nonfinite and changing totality of its desires. Decide for yourself on your position in the arena of contradictions, where pleasure and reality embrace. Bring the other to life. Women know how to live detachment; giving birth is neither losing nor increasing. It's adding to life an other. Am I dreaming? Am I mis-recognizing? You, the defenders of "theory," the sacrosanct yes-men of Concept, enthroners of the phallus (but not of the penis):

Once more you'll say that all this smacks of "idealism," or what's worse, you'll splutter that I'm a "mystic."

And what about the libido? Haven't I read the "Signification of the Phallus"? And what about separation, what about that bit of self for which, to be born, you undergo an ablation—an ablation, so they say, to be forever commemorated by your desire?

Besides, isn't it evident that the penis gets around in my texts, that I give it a place and appeal? Of course I do. I want all. I want all of me with all of him. Why should I deprive myself of a part of us? I want all of us. Woman of course has a desire for a "loving desire" and not a jealous one. But not because she is gelded; not because she's deprived and needs to be filled out, like some wounded person who wants to console herself or seek vengeance: I don't want a penis to decorate my body with. But I do desire the other for the other, whole and entire, male or female; because living means wanting everything that is, everything that lives, and wanting it alive. Castration? Let others toy with it. What's a desire originating from a lack? A pretty meager desire.

The woman who still allows herself to be threatened by the big dick, who's still impressed by the commotion of the phallic stance, who still leads a loyal master to the beat of the drum: that's the woman of yesterday. They still exist, easy and numerous victims of the oldest of farces: either they're cast in the original silent version in which, as titanesses lying under the mountains they make with their quivering, they never see erected that theoretic monument to the golden phallus looming, in the old manner, over their bodies. Or, coming today out of their *infans* period and into the second, "enlightened" version of their virtuous debasement, they see themselves suddenly assaulted by the builders of the analytic empire and, as soon as they've begun to formulate the new desire, naked, nameless, so happy at making an appearance, they're taken in their bath by the new old men, and then, whoops! Luring them with flashy signifiers, the demon of interpretation—oblique, decked out in modernity—sells them the same old handcuffs, baubles, and chains. Which castration do you prefer? Whose degrading do you like better, the father's or the mother's? Oh, what pwetty eyes, you pwetty little girl. Here, buy my glasses and you'll see the Truth-Me-Myself tell you everything you should know. Put them on your nose and take a fetishist's look (you are me, the other analyst—that's what I'm telling you) at your body and the body of the other. You see? No? Wait, you'll have everything explained to you, and you'll know at last which sort of neurosis you're related to. Hold still, we're going to do your portrait, so that you can begin looking like it right away.

Yes, the naives to the first and second degree are still legion. If the New Women, arriving now, dare to create outside the theoretical, they're called in by the cops of the signifier, fingerprinted, remonstrated, and brought into the line of order that they are supposed to know; assigned by force of trickery to a precise place in the chain that's always formed for the benefit of a privileged signifier. We are pieced back to the string which leads back, if not to the Name-of-the-Father, then, for a new twist, to the place of the phallic-mother.

Beware, my friend, of the signifier that would take you back to the authority of a signified! Beware of diagnoses that would reduce your generative powers. "Common" nouns are also proper nouns that disparage your singularity by classifying it into species. Break out of the circles; don't remain within the psychoanalytic closure. Take a look around, then cut through!

And if we are legion, it's because the war of liberation has only made as yet a tiny breakthrough. But women are thronging to it. I've seen them, those who will be neither dupe nor domestic, those who will not fear the risk of being a woman; will not fear any risk, any desire, any space still unexplored in themselves, among themselves and others or anywhere else. They do not fetishize, they do not deny, they do not hate. They observe, they approach, they try to see the other woman, the child, the lover—not to strengthen their own narcissism or verify the solidity or weakness of the master, but to make love better, to invent

Other love.—In the beginning are our differences. The new love dares for the other, wants the other, makes dizzying, precipitous flights between knowledge and invention. The woman arriving over and over again does not stand still; she's everywhere, she exchanges, she is the desire-that-gives. (Not enclosed in the paradox of the gift that takes nor under the illusion of unitary fusion. We're past that.) She comes in, comes-in-between herself me and you, between the other me where one is always infinitely more than one and more than me, without the fear of ever reaching a limit; she thrills in our becoming. And we'll keep on becoming! She cuts through defensive loves, motherages, and devourations: beyond selfish narcissism, in the moving, open, transitional space, she runs her risks. Beyond the struggle-to-the-death that's been removed to the bed, beyond the love-battle that claims to represent exchange, she scorns at an Eros dynamic that would be fed by hatred. Hatred: a heritage, again, a remainder, a duping subservience to the phallus. To love, to watch-think-seek the other in the other, to despecularize, to unhoard. Does this seem difficult? It's not impossible, and this is what nourishes life—a love that has no commerce with the apprehensive desire that provides against the lack and stultifies the strange; a love that rejoices in the exchange that multiplies. Wherever history still unfolds as the history of death, she does not tread. Opposition, hierarchizing exchange, the struggle for mastery which can end only in at least one death (one master—one slave, or two nonmasters ≠ two dead)—all that comes from a period in time governed by phallocentric values. The fact that this period extends into the present doesn't prevent woman from starting the history of life somewhere else. Elsewhere, she gives. She doesn't "know" what she's giving, she doesn't measure it; she gives, though, neither a counterfeit impression nor something she hasn't got. She gives more, with no assurance that she'll get back even some unexpected profit from what she puts out. She gives that there may be life, thought, transformation. This is an "economy" that can no longer be put in economic terms. Wherever she loves, all the old concepts of management are left behind. At the end of a more or less conscious computation, she finds not her sum but her differences. I am for you what you want me to be at the moment you look at me in a way you've never seen me before: at every instant. When I write, it's everything that we don't know we can be that is written out of me, without exclusions, without stipulation, and everything we will be calls us to the unflagging, intoxicating, unappeasable search for love. In one another we will never be lacking.

University of Paris VIII—Vincennes